HUDSON VA Y & THE CATSKILLS

NIKKI GOTH ITOI

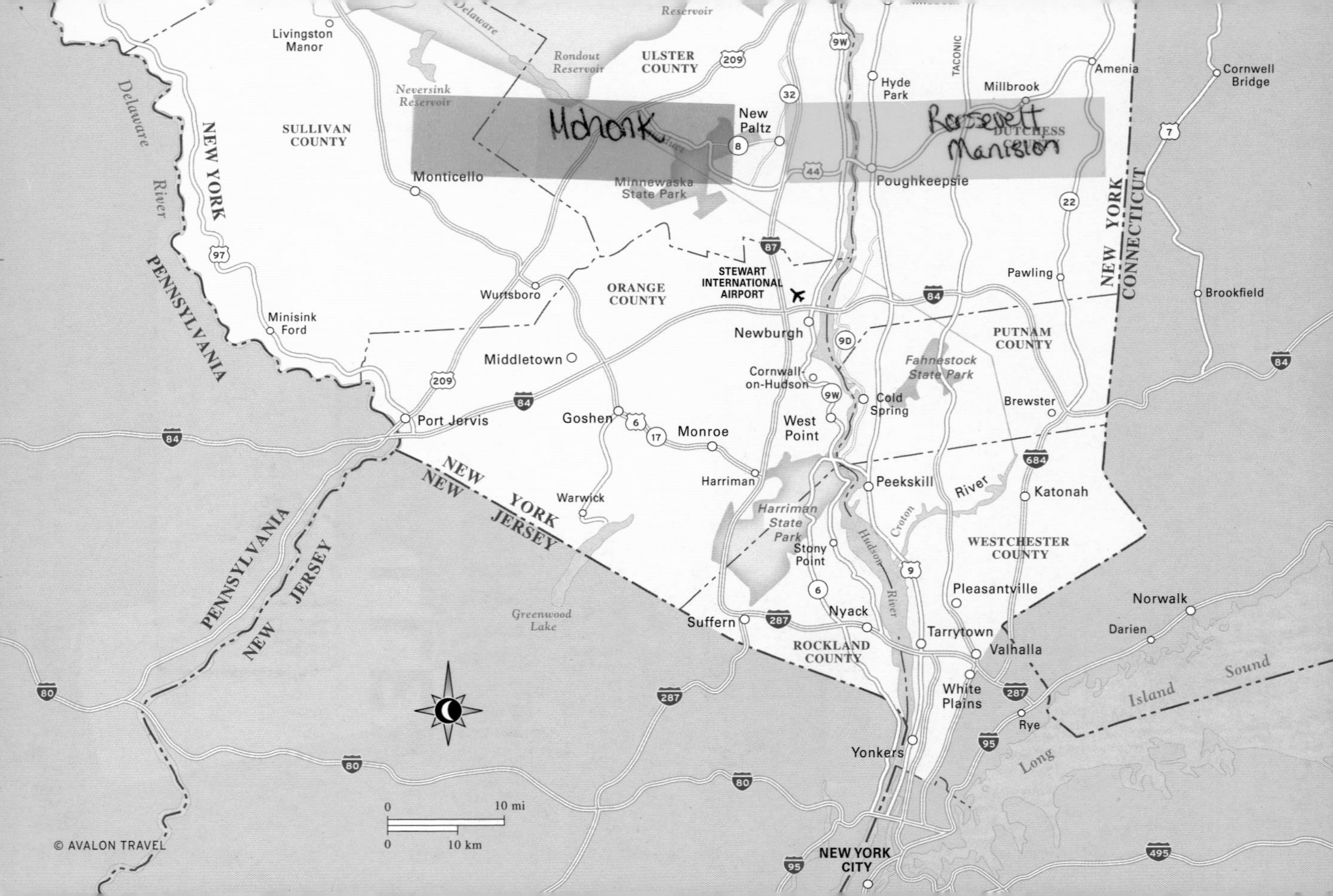

Livingston Manor
Delaware River
NEW YORK
PENNSYLVANIA
NEW JERSEY
SULLIVAN COUNTY
Neversink Reservoir
Rondout Reservoir
ULSTER COUNTY
Monticello
Minnewaska State Park
New Paltz
Hyde Park
TACONIC
Millbrook
Amenia
Cornwell Bridge
DUTCHESS COUNTY
Poughkeepsie
Minisink Ford
Wurtsboro
ORANGE COUNTY
STEWART INTERNATIONAL AIRPORT
Pawling
Brookfield
Newburgh
PUTNAM COUNTY
NEW YORK
CONNECTICUT
Middletown
Cornwall-on-Hudson
Fahnestock State Park
Cold Spring
Port Jervis
Goshen
Monroe
West Point
Brewster
Harriman
Peekskill
Katonah
Croton River
Warwick
Harriman State Park
Stony Point
WESTCHESTER COUNTY
Hudson River
Pleasantville
Greenwood Lake
Suffern
Nyack
Tarrytown
Norwalk
Darien
ROCKLAND COUNTY
Valhalla
White Plains
Rye
Long Island Sound
Yonkers
NEW YORK CITY
0 10 mi
0 10 km
© AVALON TRAVEL

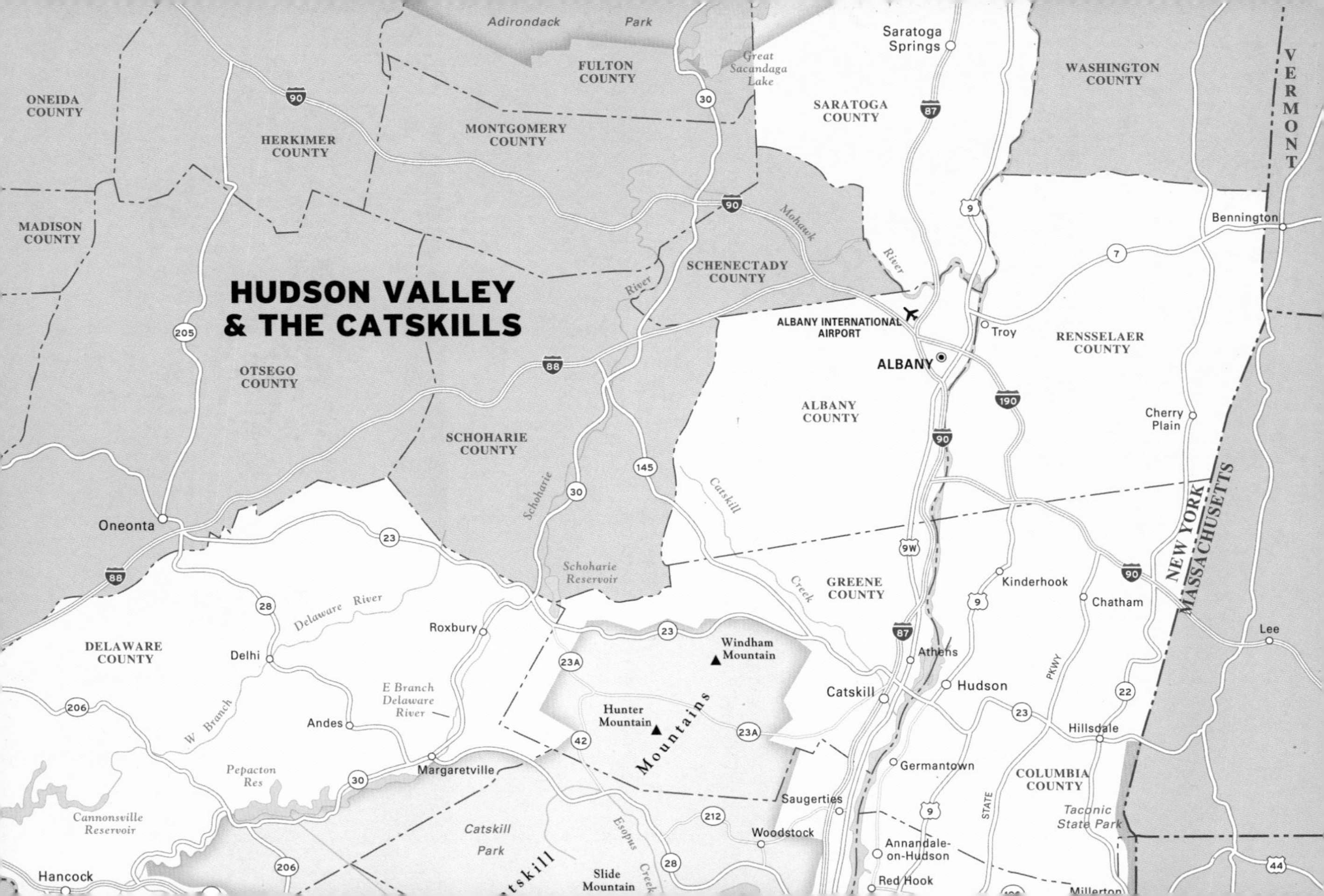
HUDSON VALLEY
& THE CATSKILLS
ONEIDA COUNTY
MADISON COUNTY
HERKIMER COUNTY
MONTGOMERY COUNTY
FULTON COUNTY
Adirondack Park
Great Sacandaga Lake
SARATOGA COUNTY
Saratoga Springs
WASHINGTON COUNTY
VERMONT
OTSEGO COUNTY
SCHOHARIE COUNTY
SCHENECTADY COUNTY
Mohawk River
ALBANY INTERNATIONAL AIRPORT
ALBANY
Troy
RENSSELAER COUNTY
Bennington
ALBANY COUNTY
Cherry Plain
Oneonta
Schoharie
Schoharie Reservoir
Catskill Creek
GREENE COUNTY
Kinderhook
Chatham
NEW YORK
MASSACHUSETTS
Lee
DELAWARE COUNTY
Delhi
Delaware River
Roxbury
Windham Mountain
Hunter Mountain
Mountains
E Branch Delaware River
W Branch
Andes
Margaretville
Pepacton Res
Cannonsville Reservoir
Catskill Park
Catskill
Athens
Hudson
PKWY
STATE
Hillsdale
Germantown
COLUMBIA COUNTY
Saugerties
Woodstock
Esopus Creek
Slide Mountain
Annandale-on-Hudson
Red Hook
Taconic State Park
Millerton
Hancock

Contents

DISCOVER

Hudson Valley & the Catskills

Nostalgic for the simplicity of rural life, today's travelers and weekend warriors crave the small-town experience with a modern flair. They are finding it, increasingly, in the Hudson River Valley.

The towns of Beacon, Catskill, Hudson, and Kingston have reinvented themselves. Antiques hot spots are emerging around Saugerties and Millerton, and the valley's farms are going organic. It's enough to make you pack your bags and head for the hills.

But it's not the first time the region has come *en vogue*. For nearly four centuries, travelers have ventured up the Hudson River in search of opportunity, inspiration, and a breath of fresh air. It is here that Washington Irving wrote "The Legend of Sleepy Hollow" and Thomas Cole created the landscape paintings that marked the dawn of the romantic era.

Old-world roots, ecological diversity, and an ever-changing economy give the Hudson River Valley the depth and complexity of an aged red wine. Measured by numbers, the river itself is unexceptional—only 315 miles long, 3.5 miles across at its widest point, and 216 feet at its deepest. Carved by a glacier 75 million years ago, the river originates from Lake Tear of the Clouds in the rugged

Clockwise from top left: Walkway Over the Hudson State Historic Park; scarecrow in Windham; Fix Brothers Fruit Farm in Columbia County; pumpkins for sale at a Columbia County orchard; Sawkill farm, Dutchess County; a meadow at the base of the Catskill High Peaks, Green County.

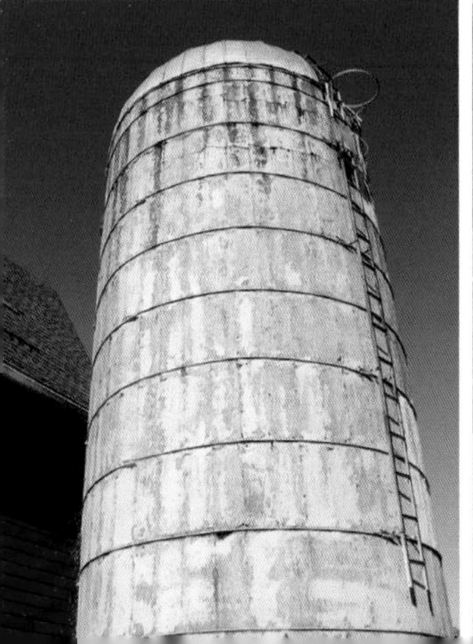

Adirondack Mountains and becomes navigable at Troy, north of Albany. From the Federal Dam at Troy all the way to New York Harbor, the Hudson is a 150-mile-long estuary that ebbs and floods with ocean tides, mixing saltwater with fresh as far up as Kingston in Ulster County. The Algonquins called it "Muhheakantuck," meaning "the river that flows both ways," or, "great waters constantly in motion."

The constant mixing supports the largest single wildlife resource in New York State. Deciduous trees, rocky bluffs, and gentle foothills line both shores. Mallard ducks paddle across narrow inlets, while fishing boats troll for striped bass. Beyond the river's edge, narrow country lanes lead to historic parks, working fruit and dairy farms, and mountains that stretch 4,000 feet into the sky. From distilleries to farm stays, the valley continues to adapt to changing traveler interests.

At its heart, the Hudson River Valley is a place of contrasts—where dairy farmers mingle with concrete factory workers, where hunters share the forest with conservationists, and where the cosmopolitan meets small-town America. Along this historic river, the familiar still has the power to surprise.

Clockwise from top left: the Mohonk Mountain House overlooking Lake Mohonk in New Platz; Minnewaska State Park in Ulster County; centuries-old stonework along Huguenot Street in New Platz; the *USS Slater* museum

Planning Your Trip

Where to Go

Lower Hudson Valley

The Hudson River Valley stretches north from New York City and the New Jersey border, leading to many densely populated bedroom communities of **Westchester and Rockland Counties.** The area is not a destination in itself, but several attractive mansions and gardens are worth a stop. The best of the bunch is **Kykuit,** the former Rockefeller family residence near **Tarrytown.** The food and entertainment are on par with what you'll find in Manhattan.

The Hudson Highlands

The Hudson Highlands encompass **Orange and Putnam Counties** along the most dramatic-looking stretch of the river. A solid granite mountain range called the **Appalachian Plateau** crosses the Hudson here, and the river has carved a narrow and deep path through the range. A dreamy mist often clings to the peaks of **Storm King Mountain** and **Breakneck Ridge** on opposite shores. It's an easy daytrip from New York City to browse the antiques shops along **Main Street** in **Cold Spring,** or visit the **West Point** campus for a military history refresher.

Mid-Hudson Valley and the Southern Catskills

Part commuter district, part bucolic getaway, the middle section of the valley starts to resemble a traveler's destination. The **Shawangunk Mountains** of **Ulster County** and the riverside mansions of **Dutchess County** define the landscape. Rolling hills and farm fields intersperse with lakes, streams, and forests. The towns of **New Paltz, Saugerties,** and **Woodstock** make a convenient base for exploration. **Dia:Beacon** exhibits artwork from the 1960s to the present, and the **Culinary Institute of America** trains first-rate chefs.

Western Catskills to the Delaware River

Wellness resorts and farm stays have replaced yesterday's summer boarding houses in the Western Catskills region. Many visitors head here to try an off-the-grid existence. Small communities include young farmers, artists, and second-home owners. Historic covered bridges span the **Willowemoc Creek** and **Beaverkill Rivers,** while hundreds of lakes and streams create a playground for anglers and bird-watchers. Spend an hour inside the **Catskill Fly Fishing Center and Museum,** even if you're not the fishing type.

Upper Hudson Valley and the Northern Catskills

The **Catskill and Berkshire Mountains** frame the upper section of the Hudson River Valley in **Greene and Columbia Counties.** Adventure-seekers come here to hike and ski, but there are pockets of culture too, in the towns of Hudson and Catskill. **Leaf peeping** is arguably the best in this forested region. The topography of the Catskills inspired the first generation of the Hudson River School of painters. The Livingston family home at **Clermont** and the Persian-style **Olana,** which belonged to painter Frederic Church, are worth a visit.

The Capital-Saratoga Region

The Capital-Saratoga region marks the end of the navigable Hudson River and the gateway to the rugged **Adirondack wilderness.** Business travel brings most people to Albany, while horseracing or healing waters might lead one

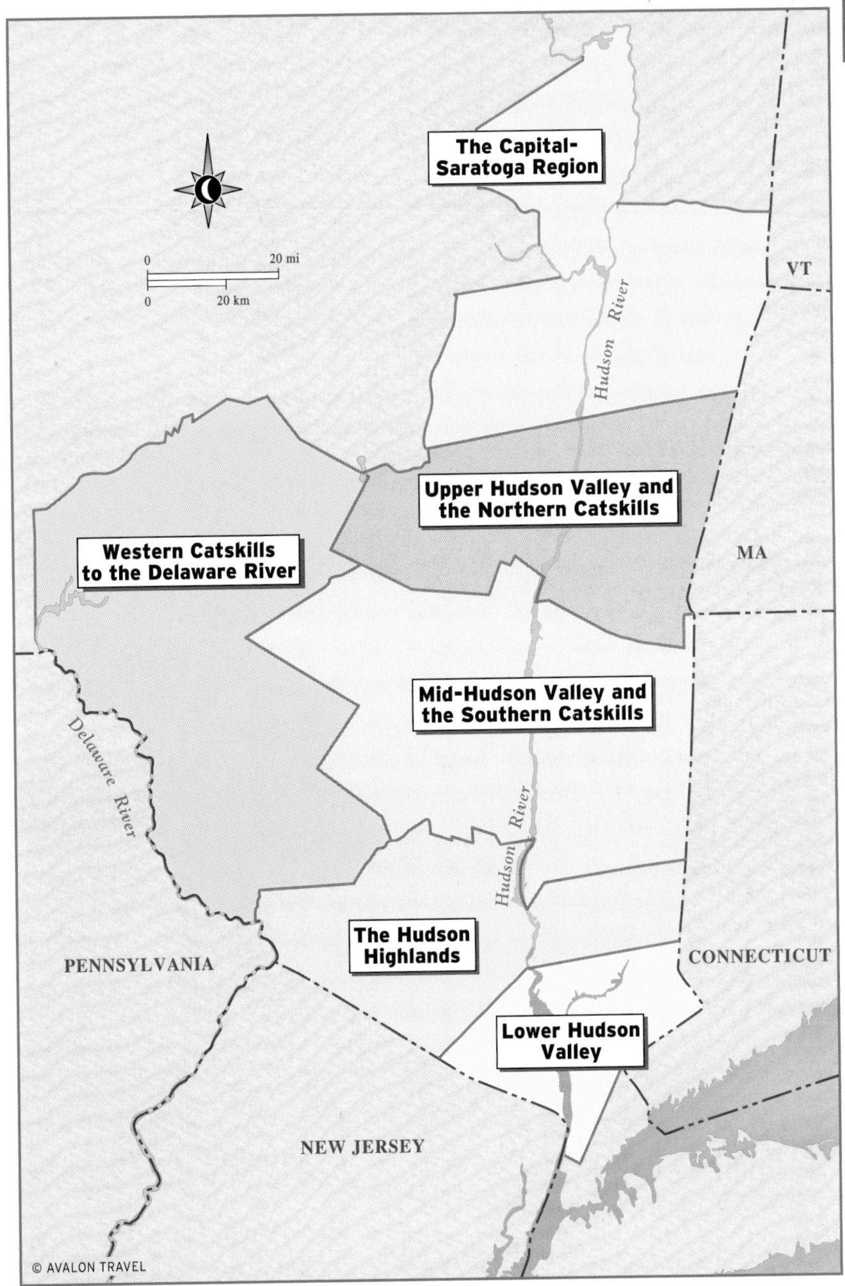
The Capital-Saratoga Region
0
20 mi
0
20 km
VT
Hudson River
Upper Hudson Valley and the Northern Catskills
Western Catskills to the Delaware River
MA
Mid-Hudson Valley and the Southern Catskills
Delaware River
Hudson River
The Hudson Highlands
PENNSYLVANIA
CONNECTICUT
Lower Hudson Valley
NEW JERSEY
© AVALON TRAVEL

farther north to **Saratoga Springs.** While in the state capital, see some modern art, learn about the colonial history, and taste the local bounty. Across the river, **Rensselaer County** consists of industrial Troy, a top-notch engineering school, and many small rural towns.

When to Go

The best times to visit the Lower Hudson Valley are **late spring** to **early summer,** and **early to mid-fall.** July and August tend to be hot and muggy, especially close to New York City.

Fall Foliage

The fall foliage season begins in **mid-September** and can last until **late October,** depending on the weather. A heavy rain or snow will end the season early. Most years, the colors are best around **Columbus Day weekend** in mid-October. The prime leaf-peeping window varies by as much as a week or two from the lower to upper parts of the valley.

Winter Travel

Winter storms can make a mess of the valley **October-April. November** can be especially cold, damp, and dreary. Snow typically begins to fall in **December,** with a cold snap of below-zero temperatures often occurring in **January.** Winter conditions last through **February,** when the maple-sugaring season begins.

Before You Go

Many small-town sights, restaurants, and accommodations have **variable hours** in the off-season, and it's a good idea to call ahead to confirm hours of operation. **Reservations** are essential during the fall foliage season and when major festivals, car shows, or county fairs are in town.

For outdoor adventures, **pack layers,** as temperatures can change rapidly with elevation and proximity to the river. Field guides, sports equipment, rain gear, sunscreen, and insect repellent will also come in handy.

Transportation

Some of the most spectacular river views are only accessible by **train,** but for travelers who want to explore the area's hidden gems, a **car** affords more flexibility and spontaneity.

Motorists have many options, from winding country roads to open interstates. **Route 9** and its many permutations (9D, 9G, 9H, 9J) hug the eastern shoreline, except for Route 9W, which runs parallel on the Hudson's west side. The speediest way to get from the wilderness to the sea is the **New York State Thruway (I-87),** a multilane toll road that connects New York City to Albany.

Day Trips from New York City

Tarrytown and the Rockefeller Estate

Plan ahead for this trip by prebooking your preferred Kykuit tour online. Start your day at Grand Central Station and catch an early morning train on the Hudson Line north to **Tarrytown.**

Walk up **Main Street** and grab a cup of coffee at Coffee Labs. Take a cab or shuttle to the Kykuit Visitor Center in neighboring **Sleepy Hollow.** Check in for your tour of the **Rockefeller Estate** at Pocantico Hills.

After the tour, head to **Stone Barns** to see a working, sustainable farm in action. The next stop is **Sunnyside,** Washington Irving's romantic-era estate on the border between Tarrytown and Irvington. After the house tour, browse the museum shop and pick up one of Irving's books for the train ride home.

Boscobel and Cold Spring Village

If you want to browse antiques shops, tour a neoclassical mansion, or paddle around the river, stay on the train until it arrives at Cold Spring Station in **Putnam County.** Exit the station and stop at the visitors booth on Main Street to pick up a map and inquire about the shuttle to Boscobel, the site of the annual **Hudson Valley Shakespeare Festival.**

Grab a freshly baked scone at the Foundry Café just up the street, then walk down to the riverside gazebo to take in the view of **West Point** and the surrounding cliffs across the river.

Hop on the shuttle to Boscobel and admire the apple trees, river views, and collections of silver, china, and glassware inside. Later, head down to the river's edge to explore the **Constitution Marsh Center & Sanctuary,** run by the National Audubon Society.

Catch the shuttle back to **Cold Spring Village** to browse the antiques shops along Main Street. Stay for dinner at Cathryn's Tuscan Grill or the Cold Spring Depot, or walk a few blocks north along **Fair Street** to enjoy views

antiques shopping in the Hudson River Valley

of the Hudson at Riverview. When the sun has set, it's time to catch the return train south to Grand Central.

Dia:Beacon

River views and the innovative restoration of an old factory make for an enjoyable day of modern art at this **Dutchess County** museum. An added plus is the location within walking distance of the Beacon Metro-North train station. Catch an early morning train from Grand Central to Beacon and allow a few hours to explore the galleries. Plan ahead to time your visit with a museum event, such as a gallery talk or film screening. A café on-site serves light breakfast and lunch fare, or you can walk or take a cab over to **Main Street** for a more substantial lunch and more art galleries.

Outdoor Adventures

Fresh air and challenging terrain for a wide range of sports are two primary factors that draw visitors to the more remote parts of the Hudson River Valley. Whether you choose to hike, bike, or ski, you'll have plenty of choices for a memorable outdoor adventure.

Hiking

Some 200 miles of trails traverse the Catskill Forest Preserve. High above the Hudson River Valley are **Kaaterskill Falls** and the **Escarpment Trail,** a magical wilderness setting where the Hudson River School of painters found inspiration and the Catskill Mountain House entertained prominent guests. The rugged 23-mile trail connects the towns of Haines Falls and Windham, changing 10,000 feet in elevation along the way. The highest peak along the trail is 3,940-foot **Blackhead Mountain.** Allow two days for a challenging overnight hike, or three days for side trips at either end of the hike.

Near New Paltz in Ulster County, **Minnewaska State Park Preserve** has rare dwarf pines and peregrine falcons to see, plus gorgeous vistas at every bend in the trail.

Swimming and Boating

The Hudson and its tributaries lure water sports enthusiasts for fishing, sailing, tubing, kayaking, and more. Tubing on the **Esopus** in Ulster County is especially popular in summer. Sailing school is an option out of Kingston. **Greenwood Lake** in Orange County, **Lake Taghkanic** in Columbia County, and several lakes near Saratoga Springs have beaches for swimming and facilities for boats.

Kayakers can paddle lakes, ponds, creeks, and of course the Hudson River in Dutchess County. Several shops in the region rent gear and offer guided trips.

Cycling

Cyclists enjoy endless miles of rolling hills on quiet country roads, and several counties have converted long stretches of abandoned train tracks into paths for walking, jogging, or biking. **Piermont** and **New Paltz** are popular cycling towns, and many local clubs plan group rides on summer weekends. You might tour one county at a time, or attempt the 180-mile multiday ride from New York City to Albany. Include as many bridge crossings as possible, and allow time to take in some of the sights along the way. Several companies offer guided bike tours of the area; an amateur bike race is another way to discover many of the back roads.

Skiing

Falling temperatures mean one thing to winter sports enthusiasts: the possibility of powder. Ski resorts in the Catskills and Adirondacks start making snow as soon as it will freeze, and then hope for a little help from Mother Nature as the season progresses. Whether you prefer the thrill of downhill or the serenity of the open trail, the

Grand Estates

A handful of majestic estates line the Hudson River, representing several centuries of architectural and cultural trends including American Renaissance, Georgian, Federal, Romantic, Greek Revival, and Gothic Revival. Many have been turned into interpretive museums that are open to the public. Here are some of the most popular mansions to visit:

- **Kykuit:** The sprawling hilltop estate of the Rockefeller family is a must-see in the Lower Hudson River Valley. The three-hour Grand Tour is well worth the time investment.
- **Union Church of Pocantico Hills:** After a Kykuit tour, stop here to admire stained glass windows designed by Henri Matisse and Marc Chagall for the Rockefeller family.
- **Sunnyside:** The Romantic-style home of Washington Irving, America's first man of letters, is a whimsical place right on the river's edge just south of Tarrytown in Westchester County.
- **Lyndhurst:** Financier Jay Gould's former residence, also near Tarrytown, is considered the finest example of Gothic Revival style in the United States.
- **Boscobel House and Gardens:** This restored neoclassical mansion near Cold Spring is the home of the Hudson Valley Shakespeare Festival.
- **Home of Franklin D. Roosevelt National Historic Site:** FDR's presidential library and museum are just up the road from the Culinary Institute of America in Hyde Park.
- **Vanderbilt Estate:** Fifty rooms range from Renaissance to Rococo, and the lawn is a great place for a summer picnic in the Mid-Hudson River Valley.
- **Montgomery Place:** Built in the Federal style, this riverside estate presents scenic views of the Catskill Mountains.
- **Clermont State Historic Site:** The Georgian-style estate of Robert Livingston Jr. reflects the influence of seven generations of the prominent Livingston family.
- **Olana State Historic Site:** Romantic landscape painter Frederic Church designed his Persian-style home after a trip to the Middle East.

Vanderbilt Estate

greater Hudson River Valley has much to offer December-March.

For downhill thrills, head to **Windham, Hunter,** or **Belleayre** in the northern Catskill Mountains, where snow guns cover nearly 100 percent of the terrain. For more solitude on Nordic trails, choose the Capital-Saratoga region: **John Boyd Thacher State Park** near Albany and **Lapland Lake** near Saratoga Springs are good bets.

Revolutionary War Route

The outcome of the nine-year struggle for independence from the British hinged largely on who controlled the Hudson River. From the boycott of British tea to the turning point at Saratoga, many of the war's pivotal events took place in the surrounding valley. Today, a number of interpretive museums and historic sites preserve and commemorate various events and decisions that took place in those long years between 1774 and 1783.

The following itinerary identifies major Revolutionary War sights along the river, from south to north. Other options are to follow the Henry Knox Cannon Trail through Saratoga Springs, Albany, and Columbia County; or to trace the Washington-Rochambeau Revolutionary Route, through the Lower Hudson Valley.

Day 1

This tour begins at the former home of loyalist Frederick Philipse III, who was arrested by General George Washington in 1776, after signing the Declaration of Independence. Both the family residence, **Philipse Manor Hall** in **Yonkers,** and the **Philipsburg Manor** in **Sleepy Hollow** were confiscated by the state and later preserved as museums. Situated in the neutral zone, **Van Cortlandt Manor** hosted loyalists and patriots alike during the war.

An American victory at **Stony Point Battlefield** in 1779 boosted morale and severely damaged British forces. To reach this state historic site, cross the Hudson at the Bear Mountain Bridge and head south into Rockland County.

Retrace your steps north to the **United States Military Academy** at **West Point,** a training ground for army officers since 1802. The academy sits on the bluffs overlooking the narrow stretch of the river that was chained to keep the British out. You can begin your tour with a walk through the museum (outside the gate), which includes Washington's pistols among its exhibits. Next, book a bus or river tour at the visitors center and have lunch at the stately Thayer Hotel just inside the campus gate. Add half a day for a visit to **Constitution Island.**

Day 2

The first Purple Heart was issued at the Hasbrouck family farmhouse, where George Washington stayed for 16 months at the end of the war. **Washington's Headquarters** in **Newburgh** became the first national historic site in the United States. His army camped at New Windsor Cantonment in Vails Gate, now also the site of the **National Purple Heart Hall of Honor.**

In the afternoon, visit the **Mount Gulian Historic Site** outside of Beacon, an 18th-century Dutch stone barn that once belonged to the Verplanck family and served as headquarters for Revolutionary War General Friedrich Wilhelm Augustus von Steuben.

In keeping with the historic theme, join the likes of George Washington, Philip Schuyler, Benedict Arnold, and Alexander Hamilton in spending the night at the **1766 Beekman Arms** in Rhinebeck, where local townspeople gathered inside for safety while the British burned Kingston to the ground across the Hudson.

Day 3

Today begins with a drive across the river to visit **Kingston,** a colonial city that the British burned to the ground. They landed at Rondout Battlefield, where periodic reenactments now take place. In Kingston's Stockade District, the **Senate House** hosted the first Senate of New York State in 1777.

Cross the river on the Kingston-Rhinecliff Bridge and make your way north to **Clermont,** colonial estate of the Livingston family. The British torched it in 1777, but the family promptly rebuilt the home during the war.

Cycling the Hudson Valley

In a six-day tour, riding 35-45 miles per day, you can cover the length of the Hudson River Valley, hitting key sights, vistas, and attractions on both sides of the river. Total distance is approximately 200 miles. This suggested itinerary starts in the town of Hudson, in the Upper Hudson River Valley. Use your arrival day to get oriented, stock up on supplies, and check out your gear. Steiner's Sports on Warren Street can see to all your last-minute needs. If you have extra time, take a warm-up ride over to Olana (12 miles) to tour Frederic Church's historic estate. Book accommodations in or near the towns of Hudson, Kingston, Hyde Park, Garrison, and Nyack.

DAY 1: HUDSON TO KINGSTON

Get an early start for the first ride of the week, which starts in Hudson (Columbia County) and finishes in Kingston (Ulster County). Along the way, stop to visit **Montgomery Place** and refuel in Rhinebeck. Cross the river at the Kingston-Rhinecliff Bridge. When you reach downtown Kingston, walk through the **Stockade District,** check in to your hotel, and then look to the **Rondout Creek** area for dinner.

DAY 2: KINGSTON TO HYDE PARK

Ride along part of the **Wallkill Valley Rail Trail** and through the college town of **New Paltz.** Be sure to see the historical homes along **Huguenot Street** and stop at a **winery** or two. End the day by crossing the river on the **Walkway Over the Hudson** and looping back north to Hyde Park.

DAY 3: HYDE PARK REST DAY

Take a day off to visit FDR's home and library, the **Vanderbilt Estate,** and the **Culinary Institute of America.** Or add an optional loop through the countryside and wineries of **eastern Dutchess County** instead.

DAY 4: HYDE PARK TO GARRISON

Fuel up for an action-packed ride through **Poughkeepsie, Beacon,** and **Cold Spring.** Optional side trips include the **Dia:Beacon modern art museum** and a **paddle on the river** from a launch near Cold Spring. Finish the day in **Garrison** (Putnam County).

DAY 5: GARRISON TO NYACK

Ride across the **Bear Mountain Bridge** and head south over **Storm King Mountain** to **West Point.** Take a tour of the **military academy,** and have lunch at the **Thayer Hotel.** For more mileage, add an optional route through **Bear Mountain State Park.** Or get off the bike for a few hours to hike along a section of the **Appalachian Trail.** Overnight in Nyack or Piermont.

DAY 6: NYACK TO NEW YORK CITY

Finish the ride along the Hudson with a ride under the **cliffs of the Palisades** and end at the **George Washington Bridge.** Alternatively, cross the river at Nyack to explore **Tarrytown** and the **Rockefeller Estate.** From Tarrytown, you can catch Amtrak back to Hudson, or plot a new cycling route for the return trip, with stops in Peekskill, Red Hook, and Catskill, for example.

Day 4

Start the day with a drive across the **Rip Van Winkle Bridge** and continue north along Route 9W to the **Bronck Museum,** where New Yorkers signed the Coxsackie Declaration of Independence in 1775. From there, it's about 25 miles north to **Albany** and the **Schuyler Mansion,** home of Major General Philip Schuyler and the place where British General Burgoyne was imprisoned after his defeat at Saratoga.

Complete the trip at the **Saratoga National Historical Park,** which commemorates the Battle of Saratoga. Here, you can follow a 10-stop auto tour that interprets the battle.

Fun for Foodies

Many Hudson River Valley chefs were among the pioneers of the locavore trend. A love of fresh food prepared with a creative flair is a prerequisite for enjoying all that the Hudson River Valley has to offer.

COOKING CLASSES

The main campus of the nation's premier culinary college sits on 80 acres overlooking the river at Hyde Park. The **Culinary Institute of America** runs five restaurants, a bookstore, and courses for cooking professionals and enthusiasts. For serious training, enthusiasts can enroll in one of the CIA's Boot Camp programs.

FRESH PRODUCE

Every county in the region has its share of apple orchards, berry patches, organic farms, and cornfields. Flavors differ from one hillside to the next, in what farmers call micro-terroirs. Farmers markets and farm stands bring the local harvest to a central location each week, building a sense of community in the process.

Fernlike fiddleheads appear on many menus in the early spring. For those who like to forage for their food, spring rains bring wild mushrooms, including morels and chanterelles. In summer, the local garlic harvest begins in **Saugerties,** and farm stands overflow with fresh-picked corn, tomatoes, peppers, eggplant, and other vegetables. Strawberries and cherries ripen through June and July, and blueberries last July-September. You can pick apples July-November, and pumpkin patches do a steady business in September and October.

GOURMET RESTAURANTS

You'll find mind-blowing cuisine all across the Hudson River Valley. The towns of **Hudson, Rhinebeck, Albany,** and **Saratoga Springs** are places you might travel just to eat. Plan well ahead to dine at the best of the best: **Blue Hill at Stone Barns** in Westchester, **American Bounty Restaurant** on the CIA campus, **Valley Restaurant at the Garrison,** and **Stone & Thistle Farm** are travel destinations on their own, and advance reservations are a must.

WINERIES AND DISTILLERIES

Hudson River Valley grape growers introduced French-American hybrid grapes in the 1970s to please an increasingly sophisticated consumer base. The switch put the region on the New York State wine map, producing award-winning Italian-style whites, as well as pinot noirs and cabernet francs. The **Dutchess Wine Trail** includes **Alison Wines, Clinton Vineyards,** and **Millbrook Vineyards & Winery** and covers miles of pretty countryside. Meanwhile, the wineries themselves produce some of the highest-quality labels in New York State.

On the other side of the Hudson, the **Shawangunk Wine Trail** is a 30-mile loop connecting nine family-owned wineries. The trail runs along back roads between the New York State Thruway, I-84, and Route 17 between New Paltz in Ulster County and Warwick in Orange County. Some of the most popular stops include **Applewood Winery** and the **Warwick Valley Winery & Distillery.**

Passage of the New York State Farm Distillery bill in 2008 opened the door to a wave of micro-distilleries across the valley, with new tasting rooms in Albany, Gardiner, Roxbury, Ancram, and Warwick. Local grains and fruits are used to make high-end whiskey and bourbon, and creative spirits such as apple brandy and other fruit liquors.

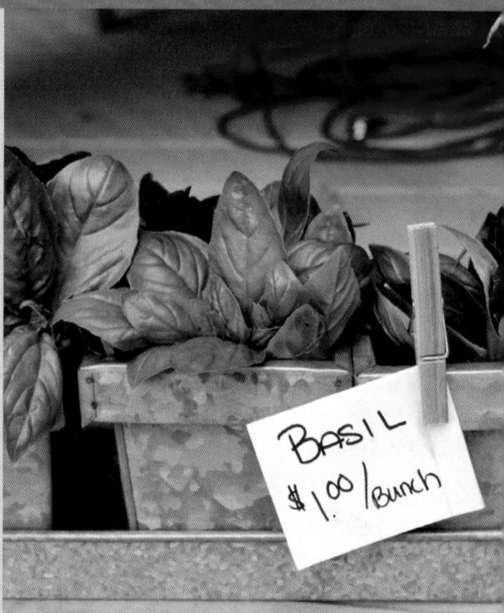

fresh-picked basil for sale

Contemporary Art, Indoors and Out

The arts scene is alive and well in the Hudson River Valley. Artists-in-residence can arrange long-term retreats, while the public gets to experience the results of their creativity. Several premier museums, galleries, and outdoor sculpture parks can anchor a multiday tour of the region. This tour starts in the Capital District and makes its way to the Lower Hudson Valley.

Day 1

Start this itinerary in Albany and head north to the college town of Saratoga Springs, where the **Tang Teaching Museum and Art Gallery** serves as an integral part of the curriculum for Skidmore College students. Rotating multimedia exhibits combine objects like Hudson River School landscapes or Shaker furniture with new works of international contemporary art. Spend the rest of the day enjoying a leisurely lunch on Broadway, or get outside to tour Saratoga Spa State Park. Spend the night at the **Saratoga Arms,** or head back to accommodations in Albany.

Day 2

Walk the Empire State Plaza in downtown Albany to see the **New York State Art Collection.** A legacy of former Governor Nelson A. Rockefeller, the sculptures are considered one of the most important collections of modern art found anywhere in the United States. Stay at **Morgan State House** or the **State Street Mansion Bed & Breakfast** for the evening. Head to **Angelo's 677 Prime** for a steak dinner or catch a show in the theater district.

Day 3

In the morning, pack the car and head east to the town of Ghent and **The Fields Sculpture Park** at the Omi International Arts Center, which features works by Richard Nonas and Stanley Whitney, among other contemporary artists. Have lunch at the museum café, then continue the journey south to the river town of **Hudson,** a revived artist's mecca. Walk the length of Warren Street, noting the mix of old and new. Stay over at **The Barlow hotel** and plan dinner at **Fish & Game,** or catch a show at **Club Helsinki** dinner theater if anyone is performing that night.

Day 4

Start the day with a hot cup of tea at **Verdigris Tea & Chocolate Bar,** and point the GPS to the south. Your destination is **Dia:Beacon** to view the Richard Serra installations and other modern works in a converted factory along the river. Head to Main Street, Beacon after the museum tour for lunch on the patio at **The Roundhouse at Beacon Falls.** Alternatively, skip Dia:Beacon and walk the grounds of the **Storm King Art Center,** an outdoor sculpture garden on the other side of the river. For dinner, try **MacArthur's Riverview Restaurant** at West Point or **Valley Restaurant at the Garrison.**

Fall Foliage Tours

ON FOOT

The hardwood forests of the **Catskill** and **Shawangunk** ranges explode in shades of red, orange, and yellow each autumn.

Catskills Hike

One of the most difficult but rewarding fall hikes is a triple-summit over the Catskill High Peaks of **Thomas Cole, Black Dome,** and **Blackhead peaks.** Windham or Hunter make equidistant launching points for the day. You'll need two vehicles to complete this one-way hike. Park the pickup vehicle at the eastern end of Big Hollow Road, off Maplecrest Road/County Route 40 in the town of **Jewett.** Then drive to the eastern end of Barnum Road, also off Maplecrest Road/County Route 40, to begin the hike (6.1 miles one-way) on an old logging road. A mixed hardwood forest of oak, maple, and beech trees puts on the initial display.

Shawangunks Hike

Fall colors are all the more striking against a pair of sparkling lakes in the **Minnewaska State Park Preserve.** For a moderate day hike on a network of carriage trails, park at the Wildmere lot off Route 44 and follow the red trail markers as you pass **Lake Minnewaska.** Pick up the Castle Point Carriageway (blue markers) on the west side of the lake. Enjoy the views of Gertrude's Nose from the trailside gazebo. After the hike, drive to **High Falls** for a casual dinner at The Eggs Nest.

BY CAR

Taconic State Parkway

This tree-lined road offers changing scenery around every bend, with occasional vistas across the surrounding valley. The stretch from Route 55 north to Chatham is beautiful in the fall and takes about an hour to drive. Along the way, **Clinton Vineyards** and **Millbrook Vineyards & Winery** make easy side trips.

Route 9W

Hugging the river's western shoreline, Route 9W passes through long stretches of hardwood forest between Newburgh and Coxsackie. Begin the day's drive at the **Bear Mountain Bridge** and make your way north, stopping for lunch and antiques shopping in **Saugerties.** Allow about three hours of driving time to reach downtown **Albany.**

Route 23/23A

This is a good route for an early-season tour, as the elevation means color will peak a bit sooner than lower in the valley. Begin the drive in the village of **Catskill,** after grabbing a cup of coffee at Retriever Roasters on Main Street. Follow Route 9W south to pick up Route 23A west. At **Palenville,** you'll begin to climb. Look for a trailhead on the right for **Kaaterskill Falls** if you want to hike; otherwise, continue the winding road uphill to **Tannersville,** where you can tour the **Mountain Top Arboretum.** Grab lunch at Hunter Village or wait until Windham; then complete the loop by following Route 23 down the mountain and back to the village of Catskill. Total distance is about 80 miles.

Route 44

Pick up Route 44 from the Taconic State Parkway heading east and follow it through Millbrook, taking the **Millbrook Vineyards & Winery** detour if time permits. Browse the boutiques in Millbrook, or continue east through Amenia to Millerton. In **Millerton,** park near the Harney & Sons tea company and walk part of the **Harlem Valley Rail Trail.** Afterward, warm up with a cup of tea at the Harney & Sons Tea Tasting Room. Total driving time will be about an hour from the Taconic State Parkway to the state line. Retrace your steps at day's end to have dinner at Millbrook's Café Les Baux.

Hawk's Nest

This drive begins in western Orange County, near the **Delaware River.** Exit I-84 at Port Jervis and pick up **Route 97 north.** It's about a two-hour scenic drive along the Delaware, past Minisink Battleground and Narrowsburg to Hancock, where you'll pick up Route 17 heading back east and south. Stop for lunch in **Narrowsburg** at Lander's River Café overlooking the river. When you reach Roscoe and Livingston Manor on Route 17, consider a visit to the **Catskill Fly Fishing Center and Museum** on your way through Livingston Manor, then finish the day with dinner at Ianine's inside the DeBruce Country Inn along the **Willowemoc Creek.**

AERIAL VIEWS

Skydiving in the Hudson River Valley is the best around, and what better time to attempt a jump than during the leaf-peeping season? Contact **Skydive the Ranch** in the Mid-Hudson for your aerial adventures.

Lower Hudson Valley

Look for ★ to find recommended sights, activities, dining, and lodging.

Highlights

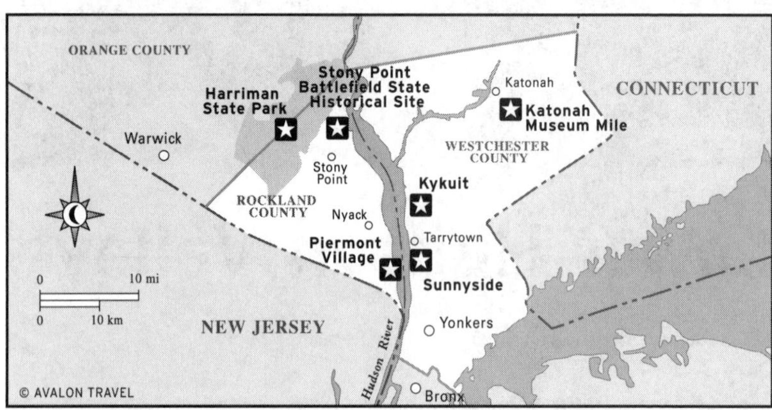

★ **Sunnyside:** The Romantic-era home of author Washington Irving is set amid rolling hills, a babbling brook, and the purple and white flowers of wisteria that climb all the way up to the gabled roof (page 29).

★ **Kykuit:** John D. Rockefeller built a six-story, 40-room mansion in the Pocantico Hills near Tarrytown, with breathtaking views of the Hudson River and the Palisades (page 31).

★ **Katonah Museum Mile:** Katonah is home to three first-rate museums, all located within a mile of each other: the Caramoor Center for Music and the Arts, the Katonah Museum of Art, and the John Jay Homestead (page 37).

★ **Piermont Village:** Three miles south of the Tappan Zee Bridge, on a steep hillside between Route 9W and the riverbank, is the upscale village of Piermont, a haven for cyclists, foodies, and creative types (page 49).

★ **Stony Point Battlefield State Historical Site:** Located on Haverstraw Bay is the site of a small but important victory in the American Revolution, with a riverside park and museum that includes the oldest lighthouse on the Hudson (page 52).

★ **Harriman State Park:** The first section of the Appalachian Trail was cleared here in 1923; today, hikers can access several lakes, plus 200 miles of trails, inside the park (page 53).

The Hudson River Valley's most populous counties are closest to New York City, with a complex maze of highways, bridges, trains, and buses to shuttle residents in and out of the five boroughs every day. Although no longer the rural destination it once was, the Lower Hudson Valley is packed with historic mansions and restored gardens at every bend in the road. John Jay, Frederick Philipse, the Vanderbilts, and the Harrimans all left their mark, but the grandest estate of all was the sprawling Rockefeller residence at Pocantico Hills near Tarrytown. As a legacy of these large estates, Westchester and Rockland Counties were able to preserve wilderness areas that rival many upstate parks and preserves, even as they struggled to cope with rapid industrial and housing development. More than a dozen gardens are open to the public and easily accessible in a day trip from New York City.

Both counties support diverse populations that represent the very highest and lowest income brackets, as well as many different nations and cultures. Local restaurants prepare menus you only expect to find domestically in New York City or San Francisco, including specialties from Brazil, China, India, and Japan, as well as Italy, Spain, and France. And unlike in other parts of the Hudson River Valley, night owls who visit the Lower Hudson have many choices for evening entertainment, from the Westchester Broadway Theatre in Elmsford to the Performing Arts Center in Purchase and the Caramoor Center for Music and the Arts in Katonah.

The Tappan Zee Bridge connects the two counties at the widest part of the Hudson River, while the Bear Mountain Bridge spans the river at Westchester's northern border.

PLANNING YOUR TIME

Whether you want to add an easy day trip to a longer New York City stay or find a new stopover on your way to a regular weekend getaway farther north, Westchester and Rockland Counties offer many choices for historic tours, outdoor entertainment, and

Previous: Washington Irving's Sunnyside estate; Philipsburg Manor in Sleepy Hollow. **Above:** Union Church of Pocantico Hills.

Lower Hudson Valley

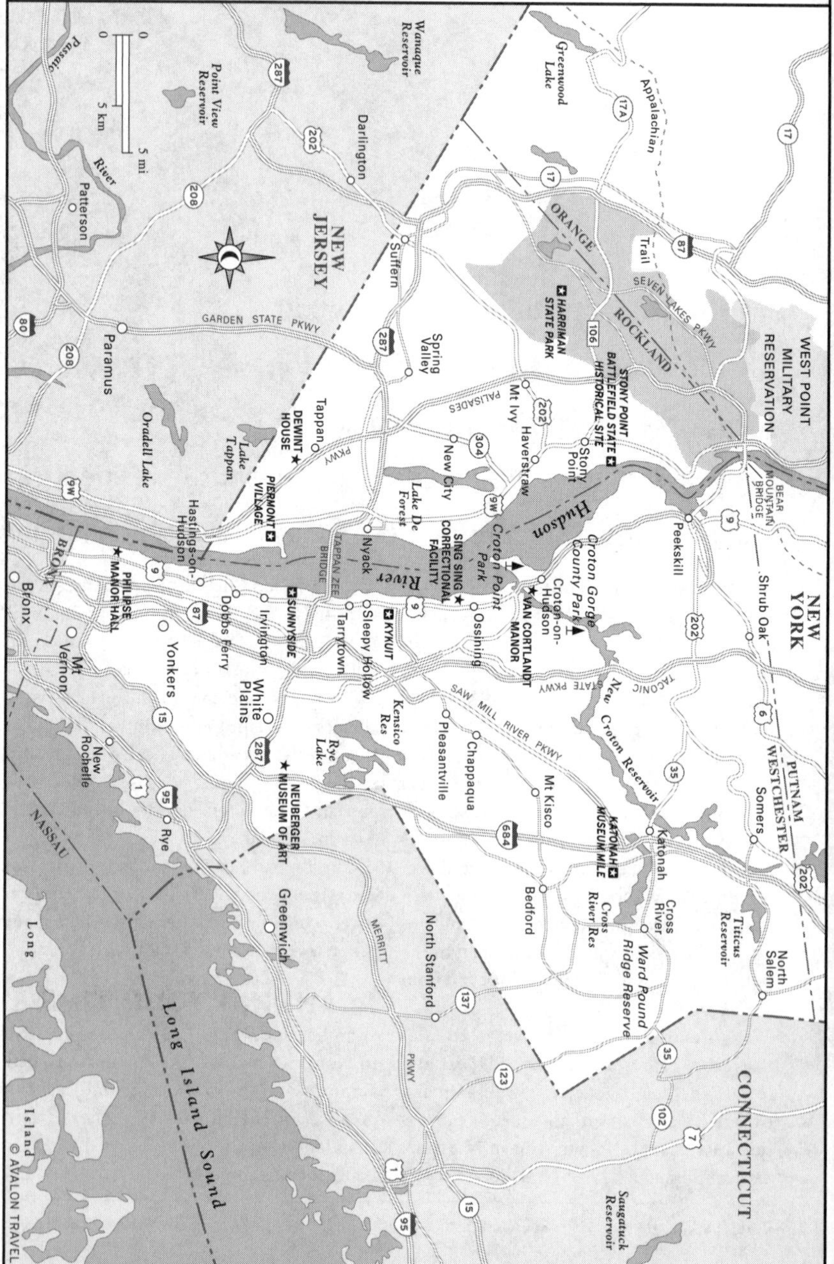

fine-dining experiences. And the well-developed New York and New Jersey transit systems make it easy to leave the car behind.

If you have one day to explore the area, head to the gardens of the former Rockefeller Estate at Kykuit, in Sleepy Hollow, and choose a restaurant for dinner in Tarrytown. Alternatively, plan to tackle a section of the 26-mile Old Croton Aqueduct by foot, bike, or horseback.

In Rockland County, head to the Piermont area for the perfect mix of entertainment, food, and outdoor recreation. Then drive north on Route 9W to visit a series of Revolutionary War sites and scenic river overlooks. Or forget the history lesson and get away from it all with a backcountry hike in Harriman State Park.

Longer itineraries allow you to visit multiple historic homes, such as Jay Gould's Lyndhurst and Washington Irving's Sunnyside, or to contemplate the works of art in one of several well-funded museums. Add half a day to sample the wild mushrooms at the Nyack Farmers Market or attend a White Plains Antique Show. Add another day to tour the gardens in Somers and Purchase. When planning an overnight visit, beware that choices in accommodations will be limited primarily to business hotels. If quaint and memorable lodging is a priority, consider visiting the Lower Hudson on a day trip from New York City or when passing through to parts north.

Westchester County

Bordering the Bronx, the southern edge of Westchester County is just 15 minutes from Manhattan by train. The county boasts the largest population and the highest population density in the Hudson River Valley—and a surprising blend of wealthy suburbs, ample green space, and historic sites. Yonkers, Mount Vernon, New Rochelle, Rye, and White Plains are the largest cities, and White Plains is the county seat.

The New York Assembly established Westchester County in 1683, and the first English settlements popped up in the eastern part of the county at Rye, Mamaroneck, Eastchester, and Bedford. The manor of Frederick Philipse, deeded through a royal grant, covered more than 52,000 acres between Yonkers and Tarrytown. Roads, taverns, and ferries were built in the 18th century, and by the end of the century, Westchester had become the wealthiest and most populous county in New York.

The American Revolution took its toll, however, through the battles of Pelham and White Plains. Westchester found itself stuck between the American headquarters, near Peekskill, and the British, in New York City. It took decades for local communities to rebound from the expense and disruption of war.

Westchester County became a commuter base as early as the 19th century, when rail travel made it possible to reach New York City in just a few hours. As transportation evolved from steamboat to rail to car, Westchester grew at a frenzied pace. Its river towns began to produce medicines, cars, beer, sugar, and elevators, among other goods. Expansion of the New York City watershed created more jobs and further accelerated growth. Today's population is more than 949,000 and counting, and along with the crowds came upscale shopping, first-rate cultural attractions, and reputable international cuisine.

ALONG THE RIVER: ROUTE 9

Yonkers

Start a tour of Westchester's river towns from the West Side Highway in Manhattan and follow Route 9A north to Yonkers. This diverse city of approximately 200,000 people is

Three Perfect Days in Westchester County

So many sights, so little time. Can you fit it all in during one long weekend? With Tarrytown as a home base, this ambitious plan offers a good mix of art, history, and culture.

DAY 1

Arrive via Westchester County Airport or any New York City airport and transfer to the Tarrytown area via rental car or take the Metro-North Hudson Line to Tarrytown.

Book a tour of Kykuit, the Rockefeller Estate, in advance, for your first morning; then head to Tarrytown for lunch. In the afternoon, tour Lyndhurst, Jay Gould's Gothic Revival mansion. Check in to a Tarrytown hotel and enjoy an evening of dinner and entertainment at the Westchester Broadway Theatre in Elmsford.

DAY 2

Tour the Caramoor Center for Music and the Arts and walk downtown Katonah. Have lunch in White Plains before shopping at The Westchester mall. Drive through the PepsiCo Sculpture Garden or visit the Neuberger Museum of Art in Purchase. Reserve a table months in advance at Blue Hill at Stone Barns for dinner.

DAY 3

Tour Washington Irving's Romantic estate, Sunnyside, then grab lunch at Sushi Mike's in Dobbs Ferry. Visit the Hudson River Museum in Yonkers as a last stop before your departure.

a major transportation hub and is the fourth-largest city in New York State. Its name derives from *jonkheer,* the Dutch word for "young nobleman," in reference to Dutchman Adriaen van der Donck, who built a sawmill where the tiny Nepperhan River (later renamed the Saw Mill River) empties into the Hudson. Four miles of frontage on the eastern bank of the Hudson offer beautiful views of the Palisades in New Jersey and Rockland County.

Legendary jazz singer Ella Fitzgerald was raised in Yonkers, and a statue of her greets passengers arriving at the train station. Nearby, where Main Street meets the river, is the hundred-year-old **Yonkers Recreational Pier,** newly renovated to hold community events and festivals.

Two notable museums are within walking distance of the train station. Two blocks east on Warburton Avenue is **Philipse Manor Hall** (29 Warburton Ave. at Dock St., 914/965-4027, www.philipsemanorfriends.blogspot.com, 9am-5pm Mon.-Sat., hourly tours 10am-4pm Thurs.-Sat. Apr.-Oct. and 10am-3pm Nov.-Mar., adults $5, seniors and students $3, under 12 free, on-site parking free). This Georgian mansion housed three generations of the Philipse family until loyalist Frederick Philipse III was arrested in 1776 and forced to flee to England. The building dates to 1682, and exhibits inside trace the history of Yonkers.

Also on Warburton Avenue, the **Hudson River Museum** (511 Warburton Ave., 914/963-4550, www.hrm.org, noon-5pm Wed.-Sun., adults $6, youth $3, seniors and students with ID $4, members free) was founded in 1919 with a focus on Hudson River art, history, and science. Exhibits include landscape paintings from the Hudson River School of painters, historic photographs, sculpture, and prints. After browsing the collection of 19th- and 20th-century art, enjoy river views from the museum café. Then learn about the natural history of the Hudson and the summer night sky inside the Andrus Planetarium.

Inside the Glenview Mansion, which is also

part of the museum, six rooms are furnished in turn-of-the-20th-century style. The sitting room holds one of the highlights of a house tour: a delicately carved and inlaid sunflower pattern in the woodwork, representative of the rare American Eastlake interior style. In addition to these varied exhibits, the museum hosts an annual jazz series each summer.

Three River Towns: Hastings-on-Hudson, Dobbs Ferry, and Irvington

If you have only one day to spend on the **Old Croton Aqueduct** (15 Walnut St., Dobbs Ferry, 914/693-5259, www.nysparks.com), choose the section that connects the three river towns above Yonkers: Hastings-on-Hudson, Dobbs Ferry, and Irvington. Artists and commuters have made these towns their home, and the route leads to one delight after another—from historical homes and shady lanes to local parks and river views, with the Palisades always looming in the distance. Farmers markets, bookstores, antiques stores, and other shops provide good diversions from the trail. The Ossining aqueduct tunnel is open June-October by reservation only; the rest of the park is open sunrise-sunset year-round.

The most famous resident of Hastings-on-Hudson began his career as an architect and later became a painter associated with the first generation of the Hudson River School. Like his fellow Romantic artists, Jasper Francis Cropsey (1823-1900) depicted the Hudson River, Catskill Mountain House, and Lake George, as well as other natural wonders in the northeast, in a series of colorful and fantastical landscapes. The **Newington Cropsey Gallery** (25 Cropsey Ln., Hastings-on-Hudson, 914/478-7990, www.newingtoncropsey.com, permanent collection and gallery tours by appointment only, gallery closed Jan. and Aug.), located near the train station, contains an exhaustive collection of Cropsey's works, including oil paintings, watercolors, drawings, and architectural renderings. A guided tour of the gallery takes about 45 minutes. Also in town, the yellow 1835 **Cropsey Homestead** (49 Washington Ave., Hastings-on-Hudson, 914/478-7990, www.newingtoncropsey.com, tours available by appointment 10am-1pm Mon.-Fri., closed Jan. and Aug.), called Ever Rest, has been furnished and decorated to reflect 19th-century sensibility. The separate art studio dates to 1885, and many of Cropsey's sketches and studies are on display inside the home and studio.

During the same time period, a 19th-century photographer and astronomer named John William Draper (1811-1882), who took some of the earliest pictures of the moon, built a federal-style farmhouse on 20 acres in Hastings. His two sons later built a famous observatory that hosted the likes of Thomas Edison and Samuel Morse. Today, the **Draper Observatory Cottage** (41 Washington Ave., Hastings-on-Hudson, 914/478-2249, www.hastingshistorical.org, 10am-2pm Mon. and Thurs.) holds the Hastings-on-Hudson Historical Society, with an archive of books, maps, paintings, and other town memorabilia. After browsing the museums, enjoy a picnic and the riverside views at MacEachron Waterfront Park, next to the train station.

Much of the 2002 movie *Unfaithful*, starring Diane Lane and Richard Gere, was filmed in neighboring Dobbs Ferry, a town that locals affectionately call the Sausalito of the east, referring to its setting on a hillside overlooking the Hudson River. Settled by Irish, Italian, and other European immigrants during the Industrial Revolution, this town of 10,000 residents was named for a ferry service that operated in the 1700s. Journalist and railroad financier Henry Villard (1835-1900) joined the well-to-do here in 1879. Many of the original homes feature long-lasting Vermont slate roofs. A handful of art galleries are located along Main Street and Broadway.

Irvington takes its name from Washington Irving, but the town is better known as the home of the first African American millionaire and philanthropist,

Old Croton Aqueduct State Historic Park

air vents along the Old Croton Aqueduct

Yonkers is the southern terminus for the most unique outdoor space in all of Westchester County: the Old Croton Aqueduct State Historic Park. In the early 19th century, a thirsty New York City, plagued by fire and illness, turned to abundant upstate resources for a clean and ready supply of water. The Croton River delivered, and the city has feuded with rural upstate towns over rights to water ever since.

Engineers diverted the river through a 26.2-mile aqueduct to the Bronx. They built a stone tunnel 8.5 feet tall by 7.5 feet wide that sloped just enough to use the force of gravity. They then laid the length of it with brick, adding a stone shaft at every mile for ventilation. Completed in 1842 at a cost of $12 million, the Old Croton Aqueduct served the growing city well until the turn of the next century. When New York needed more, a replacement in 1905 tripled its capacity.

The oldest aqueduct in the New York City watershed is now a National Historic Landmark and a long corridor of a state park. It's also just the perfect length, surface, and terrain to prepare for a marathon. In fact, joggers hit the trail at dawn most days of the year. Historic mansions, riverside villages, and Hudson River views distract them from the work at hand, while the stone markers at every mile ensure they stay on pace.

You don't have to be an endurance athlete to appreciate the trail: Cyclists, walkers, cross-country skiers, and horseback riders of all levels enjoy the path and its ever-changing scenery. Access is convenient to most of the train stations along the Metro-North Hudson Line, including Hastings-on-Hudson, Dobbs Ferry, Irvington, and Greystone in Yonkers. Parking is available at the train stations and also at the Ossining Heritage Area Visitor Center. The community organization **Friends of the Old Croton Aqueduct** (www.aqueduct.org) publishes a detailed color map of the trail for $5.75.

Madam C. J. Walker (1867-1919), who made her fortune selling hair and beauty products. Walker commissioned Vertner Woodson Tandy, considered the first licensed black architect in New York State, to build her dream home on Broadway in 1917. The resulting Italianate structure, called Villa Lewaro, featured river views from the dining room and hosted many black leaders of the time, from Langston Hughes to W. E. B. Du Bois. Villa Lewaro is privately owned today by Helena and Harold Doley.

Tarrytown and Sleepy Hollow

Soon after he moved to the neighboring hamlet of Sleepy Hollow, John D. Rockefeller reportedly tried to purchase and shut down Tarrytown's only tavern. It was a rare instance in which the Puritan business mogul was unable to impose his will on those around him, and Tarrytown remained a lively center for commerce and the arts.

In September 1780, three Tarrytown militiamen captured Benedict Arnold's partner in treason, British Major John André, and found in his boot copies of George Washington's plans for fortifying West Point. André was tried, convicted, and hung across the river in Nyack. A sign in Patriot's Park commemorates the arrest.

Today, a stroll along Main Street, with its coffeehouses and antiques shops, is the perfect

Tarrytown

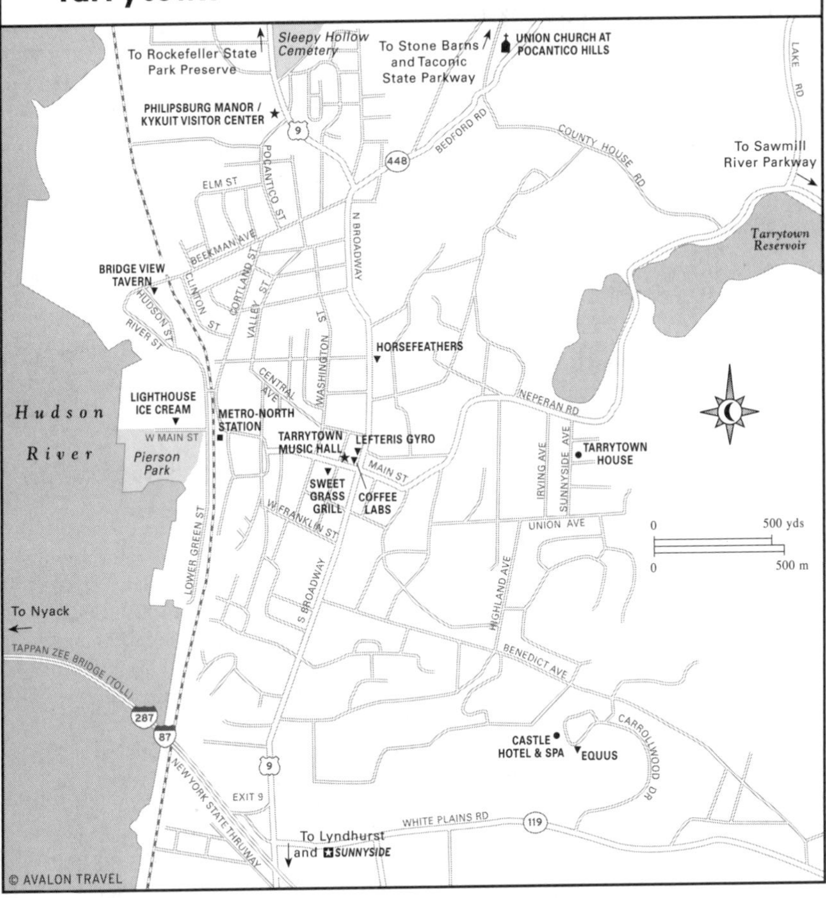

interlude between tours of the surrounding homes and gardens, and it is a convenient stop for nourishment while exploring the Old Croton Aqueduct. At the river's edge, **Pierson Park** (238 W. Main St., Tarrytown) has picnic tables, tennis courts, and a play structure for kids. This is a good place to park and pick up the mile-long Tarrytown-Sleepy Hollow section of the **Westchester RiverWalk.** For motorists, Route 9 turns into Broadway as you approach the center of town. Follow Main Street toward the river to find a public parking lot.

★ Sunnyside

A few miles south, **Sunnyside** (W. Sunnyside Lane, Tarrytown, 914/631-8200, www.hudsonvalley.org, admission by timed tours only 10:30am-3:30pm Wed.-Sun. early May-early Nov., adults $12, seniors $10, children $6, under 3 free), the Romantic-era home of celebrated author Washington Irving, known as America's first man of letters, comes right out of the pages of a children's storybook. Set among rolling hills, a babbling brook, and the purple and white flowers of wisteria that climb all the way up to the gabled roof, Sunnyside

America's First Man of Letters: Washington Irving

Washington Irving was an author, historian, and diplomat who pursued a full-time career in writing and was the first American to do so. He wrote essays, biographies, short stories, and novels to great acclaim in the United States as well as Europe. He also served as the U.S. minister to Spain from 1842 to 1846. His writing paved the way for future writers, including Nathaniel Hawthorne, Herman Melville, Henry Wadsworth Longfellow, and Edgar Allan Poe.

He wrote a multivolume biography of George Washington, as well as *A History of New York,* which is credited with giving rise to the modern American Christmas. Among his best-known works are two short stories, still read today: "Rip Van Winkle," and "The Legend of Sleepy Hollow," in which a schoolmaster named Ichabod Crane encounters the Headless Horseman in a fictitious Dutch settlement named Tarry Town. Attend Legend Weekend at Philipsburg Manor for a reenactment of the story as a precursor to Halloween.

For more on Irving's life and influence over American arts, read ***The Original Knickerbocker: The Life of Washington Irving,*** by Andrew Burstein.

captures the imagination in much the same way that Irving's tales "Rip Van Winkle" and "The Legend of Sleepy Hollow" did.

After a life of international travel and diplomacy, Irving found this peaceful retreat near Tarrytown, a place he remembered well from his childhood. Irving purchased the future site of Sunnyside in 1835 and settled here a year later. After a brief stint as minister to Spain, he returned to Sunnyside to live until his death in 1859. John D. Rockefeller acquired the property in 1945 and opened it to the public two years later.

In Sunnyside, Irving happily mixed and matched architectural styles, according to the Romantic philosophy: Stepped gables and weather vanes reflect the writer's Dutch heritage, while steeply pitched rooflines, irregular window sizes, and a facade of cut stone were borrowed from the Scottish home of Sir Walter Scott, a contemporary of Irving's. Later, Irving added a Spanish-style tower to remind him of the time he had spent living in Spain. The surrounding gardens and grounds were as important to the writer as the design of his home. In a letter sent in 1846, Irving wrote, "I understand my cottage is nearly buried alive among trees I set out, and overrun with roses and honeysuckles and ivy from Melrose Abbey, and my nieces implore me to come back and save them from being buried alive in foliage."

Today, guides in Victorian-era costumes welcome visitors into the enchanted home to experience a day in the life of the writer. A pair of Gothic Revival-style benches line the entrance to the home. Among the furnishings on display are Irving's desk and many of his books. In the kitchen, visitors can admire the cast-iron wood-burning stove and cast-iron pedestal sink, which featured both hot and cold running water, modern conveniences during Irving's time.

Nationally known and loved in his own lifetime, Irving wrote far more than the stories we remember today: Among his last works was an exhaustive biography of his namesake, George Washington. Visitors can tour the inside, walk the grounds, and picnic under the trees. Tours begin with a short film, and visitor services include a café and museum shop stocked with books by and about Irving as well as some of his contemporaries.

Lyndhurst

The Old Croton Aqueduct trail connects Sunnyside to the adjacent **Lyndhurst** property, the former residence of financier Jay Gould (635 S. Broadway, Tarrytown, 914/631-4481, www.hudsonvalley.org, 10am-4pm

Fri.-Sun. and Mon. holidays May-Nov., noon-4pm Mon. June-Sept., adults $12, seniors $11, children 6-16 with paying adult $6, under 6 free). Designed in 1838 by renowned architect Alexander Jackson Davis, the mansion, with its asymmetrical lines, reflects the Gothic Revival style. Gould was third to own the home, after New York City Mayor William Paulding and businessman George Merritt.

The carefully planned gardens on 67 acres are as striking as the ornate rooms inside. Also on the premises, Gould built the largest private conservatory in his day, while his daughter, Helen Gould Shepard, later designed the circular rose garden that still blooms today.

Philipsburg Manor

A tour of the white, three-story **Philipsburg Manor** (381 N. Broadway/Rte. 9, Sleepy Hollow, 914/631-8200, www.hudsonvalley.org, admission by timed tours only 10am-3pm daily, May-Nov., adults $12, seniors $10, children 3-17 $6, under 3 free), at Upper Mills, is an interactive production, with theatrical guides dressed in colonial garb. It is also a sobering experience, designed to give visitors an appreciation for the manual labor required to run an international trading company in the 19th century. The Philipse family was one of the earliest and largest slaveholders in the northeast, and today's museum exhibits address the African American experience on the farm. The tour begins in the basement kitchen and former slave quarters, and then progresses through the house with a narrative that brings the enslaved perspective to life.

Philipsburg Manor is also the departure point for all tours to the Rockefeller Estate, Kykuit. A small café sells basic breakfast fare, snacks, and panini; the adjoining gift shop stocks a variety of relevant books and souvenirs. Across Route 9 from Philipsburg Manor is the **Sleepy Hollow Cemetery,** with the gravesites of Washington Irving, William Cullen Bryant, Andrew Carnegie, Walter Chrysler, William Rockefeller, and others. The property runs for several miles along Route 9, surrounding the **Old Dutch Church** and its historic burial ground.

★ Kykuit

Land prices were at a historic low in 1893 when John D. Rockefeller bought his first 400 acres in the **Pocantico Hills** (po-CAN-tee-co, meaning "water rushing over rocks") north of Tarrytown. Stunning views of the Hudson River and surrounding hills and mountains drew the oil magnate to an area

Jack-o'-lanterns decorate Philipsburg Manor for Halloween.

he described as "a place where fine views invest the soul and where we can live simply and quietly." The family's country estate expanded to 1,600 acres by the turn of the 20th century and 3,000 at its peak. Today, it remains an extraordinary place where visitors can absorb some history, admire a modern art collection, learn about local flora, and reflect on a bygone era.

Rockefeller built 75 homes and 70 miles of roads, all strategically placed to show off the surrounding views. He designed much of the landscape himself, and except for a central private area, he insisted that the grounds be kept open to the public, as long as visitors abided by his rules: no cars, no drinking, and no smoking. As the estate grew, Rockefeller paid handsomely to relocate a small college, a neighborhood of homes, and even a stretch of the New York Central Railroad to the outskirts of his property. A small farm supplied food for the family, and golf became Rockefeller's preferred pastime at Pocantico. He designed a 12-hole course and played year-round, rain or shine.

For the first decade, Rockefeller lived in and remodeled the modest home that had come with the property. When that residence burned down in 1902, the family built a hilltop mansion two miles from the Hudson called Kykuit (pronounced KYE-cut), which means "lookout." It was designed to maximize sunlight in winter. Conceived as an English country house, the structure evolved into a six-story, 40-room ordeal in the American Renaissance style. It was completed in 1913.

Rockefeller's son, Junior, commissioned the estate's garden design to architect William Welles Bosworth, who crafted one of the finest surviving examples of beaux arts gardens found anywhere in the United States. Among the unusual flora are a split-leaf maple and weeping cherry trees. Wisteria blooms in May. A hedge is trimmed to mirror the profile of Hook Mountain in the distance. A table and stools in the form of mushrooms are set back in an overhang. Made of rough-cut stone, the Grotto features a Guastavino tile ceiling and Moravian tile floor. In a characteristic installation, Junior's son, Nelson Rockefeller, added the yellow and green *Futuristic Flowers* by Italian artist Giacomo Balla.

In fact, it was Nelson Rockefeller who first added a sense of fun to the estate, introducing modern art, a card table, and a bowling alley. His collection of modern art is a highlight of any Kykuit tour. A dozen tapestries by

Kykuit, the Rockefeller family estate

Pablo Picasso are hung in lower-level galleries, and sculpture works by Alexander Calder and other 20th-century artists complement the formal Italian-inspired gardens and challenge golfers on the putting green. *The Bathers,* a series of six figures Picasso originally made of driftwood, were cast into bronze and set against a background of white pine near the brook garden and adjacent to the former tennis court. Having a bit of fun with the placement of the installation, Nelson Rockefeller decided to elevate the diver onto a platform.

Five different walking tours—led by knowledgeable guides who cover art, plants, and architecture, as well as the family history—allow visitors to tailor their experience to the areas of the estate that interest them most. The two-hour house and inner gardens tour is oriented toward first-timers. A three-hour Grand Tour includes more of the sculpture and gardens, as well as a tour of the second floor of the home. The first group of the day gets the best view of the river from inside the house; later in the day, other groups a few minutes ahead tend to block the views. Book online at www.hudsonvalley.org (Pocantico Hills, Tarrytown, 914/631-8200, www.hudsonvalley.org, 9am-3:15pm Mon. and Wed.-Fri., 9am-4pm Sat.-Sun. May 7-Nov. 6, adults $23-40).

The only access to **Kykuit** (200 Lake Rd./Rte. 448, www.hudsonvalley.org) is via shuttle bus from the visitors center at Philipsburg Manor. The adjoining **Rockefeller State Park Preserve** (Rte. 117, 1 mile east of Rte. 9, Tarrytown, 914/333-0102, www.friendsrock.org, 7am-sunset daily, $6 parking fee) is open year-round for hiking, fishing, horseback riding, and cross-country skiing.

Route 442 out of Sleepy Hollow leads to Bedford and the **Union Church of Pocantico Hills** (Rte. 448/Bedford Rd., Sleepy Hollow, 914/631-2069, www.hudsonvalley.org, 11am-5pm Wed.-Fri. and Mon., 10am-5pm Sat., 2pm-5pm Sun. Apr.-Oct., 11am-4pm Wed.-Fri. and Mon., 10am-4pm Sat., 2pm-4pm Sun. Nov.-Dec., admission $7). Take the Eastview exit from the Saw Mill River Parkway. This church features stained glass windows designed by Henri Matisse and Marc Chagall to serve as Rockefeller family memorials. Just days before Matisse died, he completed the design for a rose window honoring Abby Aldrich Rockefeller, the founder of the Museum of Modern Art in New York City. The series of one large and eight small windows, completed in 1965, are the only church windows Chagall ever created.

Picasso tapestries in an underground gallery at Kykuit

Stone Barns Center for Food and Agriculture

Just up the road from the Union Church, families, foodies, and backyard gardeners flock to Stone Barns, a nonprofit, four-season farm and educational center that is committed to changing the future of our food system. Set on 80 acres of rolling hills adjoining the Rockefeller State Park Preserve, the center trains young farmers to grow produce and livestock sustainably and educates children and the public about healthy food choices. In the process, it has redefined what it means to eat local and connected the surrounding community to the land. Visitors to **Stone Barns** (630 Bedford Hills Rd., 914/366-6200, www.stonebarnscenter.org, 10am-5pm Wed.-Sun.) can tour the vegetable gardens, collect eggs, observe the beehives, participate in scavenger hunts, visit the livestock, watch chickens take a dust bath, and help farmers shear sheep in spring. There are classes in beekeeping, soil fertility, farm-to-table cooking, and more. Guest speakers have included Michael Pollan, Bill McKibben, and Amanda Hesser of the *New York Times.* The summer farm camp program is popular for kids.

A 90-minute **Insider's Tour** takes place at 11am Friday and 2:30pm on Saturday and Sunday (adults $22, youth $17). Stone Barns also runs a market with fresh vegetables in season, plants, flowers, meats, eggs, and honey (1pm-4pm Fri.-Sun. May-Nov. and once monthly during the winter). Save time for lunch at the casual **Blue Hill Café** (914/366-9600, 10:30am-4:30pm Wed.-Sun., $5-10) or plan ahead for a gourmet dinner inside the farm's outstanding partner restaurant, Blue Hill at Stone Barns. A gift shop on the premises sells farm-themed goodies such as beeswax candles, gardening gifts, and books about growing green. A taxi from the Tarrytown train station to Stone Barns costs about $10.

stained-glass window designed by Marc Chagall at Union Church of Pocantico Hills

Ossining and Croton-on-Hudson

Continuing north along Route 9, Ossining is best known as the location of **Sing Sing Correctional Facility,** which you can see from a small riverfront park near the train station. Ossining's Main Street is busy and attractive in a no-nonsense sort of way, though a Bikram yoga studio suggests the town may be shedding its working-class image. The Old Croton Aqueduct runs straight though the middle of town. And just beyond, **Teatown Lake Reservation** (1600 Spring Valley Rd., Ossining, 914/762-2912, www.teatown.org, trails open year-round dawn to dusk, free admission and parking) is a nature preserve with 14 miles of secluded trails and environmental exhibits. The nature center there is open 9am-5pm Tuesday-Sunday.

The next river town, Croton-on-Hudson, is a major point of transfer for rail commuters coming to and from the northern counties. Croton also boasts the third-largest reservoir in the New York City Watershed. By the turn of the 20th century, New York City needed more water than the original aqueduct could provide, and work began anew. Irish, German, and Italian immigrants labored hard to build the dam that created the **New Croton Reservoir.** It measures nine miles long—touching the towns of Cortlandt, Yorktown, Somers, Bedford, and New Castle—and holds 19 billion gallons at full capacity. The dam is located on Route 19, off Route 9A north of the village of Croton.

At the junction of the Croton and Hudson Rivers and within walking distance of the Croton-on-Hudson train station, the fieldstone **Van Cortlandt Manor** (S. Riverside Ave., Croton-on-Hudson, 914/631-8200, www.hudsonvalley.org, admission by timed tours only 10:30am-3pm Sat.-Sun. July-Aug., adults $12, seniors $10, children $6, under 3 free) hides behind a row of hardwood trees. As the Dutch-style home of a prominent colonial family, the museum contains many original Georgian and Federal period furnishings. On the grounds outside, caretakers plant seasonal heirloom vegetable and herb gardens.

Croton Point Park (Croton Point Ave., Croton-on-Hudson, 8am-dusk daily) occupies a 508-acre peninsula on the Hudson River just outside of town and hosts the annual Clearwater Festival, as well as the Toughman triathlon (www.toughmantri.com). Camping, hiking, and swimming/sunbathing are all possible here, and there is a small nature center at the top of the hill.

Follow Grand Street/Rural Route 129 east out of town for a couple of miles to get to **Croton Gorge County Park** (RR 129, Cortlandt Manor, 914/827-9568) at the base of the New Croton Dam. This 97-acre park has a long grassy lawn, picnic tables, restrooms, and views of the falls. Fishing and cross-country skiing are also permitted. Follow a dirt road by foot or bike to reach the road at the top of the dam. From there, you can follow the Old Croton Aqueduct trail through the woods. The trail has several road crossings between Croton-on-Hudson and Ossining, so watch for traffic.

Peekskill

At the northern edge of Westchester County and just below the Hudson Highlands lies the city of Peekskill, yet another strategic location during the American Revolution. It later became a large manufacturing center and busy river port. After some tough years of decline, Peekskill is quietly attracting artists and small businesses again. Its **Flat Iron Gallery** (105 S. Division St., 914/734-1894, www.flatiron.qpg.com, noon-6pm Thurs.-Sun.) specializes in contemporary fine art and handcrafted jewelry. This is a good place to look for Hudson River landscapes. In June, you can tour local artist studios in the downtown area. Guided and self-guided tours are available. Contact **Peekskill Open Studios** (914/737-1646, www.peekskillartists.org).

Peekskill's **Riverfront Green** is a suitable place to launch a kayak for a paddle around Peekskill Bay. The 1,600-acre **Blue Mountain Reservation** (Welcher Ave., Peekskill, 914/862-5275, parks.westchestergov.com, 8am-dusk daily year-round, parking $10) has 20 miles of bike trails signed for beginner, intermediate, and advanced riders, as well as hiking and picnic grounds. Exit Route 9 at Welcher Avenue and head east to the park entrance.

CENTRAL WESTCHESTER COUNTY

Several old highways traverse the length of central Westchester County, following smaller rivers that empty into the Hudson: The Saw Mill River Parkway connects Manhattan's Upper West Side to the Taconic State Parkway in Mount Pleasant; the Bronx River Parkway connects Mount Vernon to the Taconic at I-287; and the Hutchinson River Parkway runs from Pelham Manor to I-684. In the center of all the traffic is White Plains, a land of corporate headquarters, chain hotels, shopping gallerias, and business conference centers.

Named for the fog that hung over its wetlands when the first settlers arrived, White Plains has secured its place in history: It was the site of a major Revolutionary War battle, and George Washington set up a command from the 1720 **Jacob Purdy House** (60 Park Ave., White Plains, 914/328-1776, www.westchestertourism.com, by appointment only). Unless you seek upscale stores outside of New York City, however, you'll find few sights that require a special trip.

Purchase

East of White Plains, near the Westchester County Airport, is an outstanding modern art museum, the **Neuberger Museum of Art** (735 Anderson Hill Rd., Purchase, 914/251-6100, www.neuberger.org, noon-5pm Tues.-Sun., adults $5, seniors and students $3, children under 12 free, free admission on the first Sat. of the month). In 1969, Purchase College, part of the State University of New York, received a generous donation of 20th-century American art. Roy R. Neuberger enabled the college to begin a collection that now features contemporary and African art, as well as its initial base of modern masterpieces. The permanent collection at the Neuberger Museum of Art includes works by Edward Hopper, Georgia O'Keeffe, Jackson Pollock, and Mark Rothko. Occasional solo exhibitions feature artists who have had a significant impact on the contemporary art world but have not yet been recognized for their contributions. Take Exit 28 from the Hutchinson River Parkway.

While you're in the area, don't miss the chance to tour the **Donald M. Kendall Sculpture Gardens at PepsiCo Headquarters** (700 Anderson Hill Rd., Purchase, 914/253-2000). The company has placed 45 sculptures by 20th-century artists including Rodin on 168 landscaped acres. You can walk or drive the grounds free of charge. Allow about 90 minutes for a complete tour. Simply tell the attendant at the entry booth that you are there to view the gardens. At last check, the gardens were closed until 2015 for construction.

Pleasantville

In a quiet town off the Saw Mill River Parkway, Frank Lloyd Wright introduced the carport and radiant heat as key elements of his Usonian vision for the American residential neighborhood. Isolated examples of the functional suburban style are scattered across New York; however, the only full-scale cooperative that Wright developed is found in Pleasantville, north of where the Taconic State and Saw Mill River Parkways meet.

Pleasantville's **Usonia** was designed with 47 homes on about 100 acres of thickly wooded property. Wright used light, glass, and open designs to blur the lines between inside and out. Two of the homes are relatively easy to find today, but visitors must look from a distance because both are private residences. Look for the Reisley House, at 44 Usonia Road. Exit I-684 at Route 120, then turn left onto Bear Ridge Road, and left again onto Usonia Road. The circular Friedman House is located around the corner, at 11 Orchard Brook Drive.

Chappaqua

For much of his 30-year tenure as founding editor of the *New York Tribune,* journalist Horace Greeley (1811-1872) owned a country home in Chappaqua. Today, the town is better known for high-profile residents Bill and Hillary Clinton.

A contemporary of Abraham Lincoln, Greeley was an influential writer and political figure who campaigned against slavery, hired Karl Marx as a European columnist, and ran for president against Ulysses S. Grant. To learn more about Greeley's life and works, visit the **New Castle Historical Society** (100 King St., 914/238-4666, www.newcastlehs.org, 1pm-4pm Tues.-Thurs. and Sat., and other times by appointment, donations encouraged), or pick up a copy of his autobiography, *Recollections of a Busy Life,* available in paperback from University Press of the Pacific.

Katonah

New York City's need for water left an indelible mark on the hamlet of Katonah. When city officials flooded the Cross River in the 1890s to add new capacity to the Croton Watershed System, they threatened to swallow the homes that had stood on its bank since the first

Europeans arrived. A group of resolute townspeople pooled their resources and moved dozens of buildings to the opposite shore. They planned a simple grid, and the new town thrived as a place of commerce and leisure. As a result, present-day Katonah blends a Victorian look and feel with a modern sensibility. More than 30 Victorian-era buildings make up the Katonah Historic District on Bedford Road, between Edgemont Road and the Terrace. Near the Bedford Village Green at the junction of Routes 22 and 172 are the 1878 courthouse, schoolhouse, general store, post office, and old burying ground.

On Route 35, **Lasdon Park and Arboretum** (914/864-7268, www.lasdonpark.org, 8am-4pm daily) is the largest publically owned arboretum in the county, with 234 acres of woods, meadows, and gardens. It hosts a summer concert series, annual plant sale, and twice-yearly antiques shows.

★ Katonah Museum Mile

This community of 4,600 people supports a remarkable group of cultural institutions, three of which make up the town's Museum Mile, along Route 22. The **Caramoor Center for Music and the Arts** (149 Girdle Ridge Rd., Katonah, 914/232-5035, www.caramoor.org, box office hours 10am-6pm Mon.-Sat., 10am-4pm Sun.) began as the summer home of Walter and Lucie Rosen, both passionate musicians and patrons of the arts. The Rosens purchased the estate in 1928, and they had exquisite taste in furniture, tapestries, china, and jewels—many of which are on display in the 20 rooms that are open to the public today. They invited musicians to perform in the old-world setting of a Spanish courtyard, and over the years, their private concerts evolved into an annual summer festival. Stroll the gardens on a sunny day ($8 per person) for a glimpse of the estate. The Sense Circle is an especially peaceful place to collect your thoughts. But to really experience the place, you must attend a performance. Recent concerts have focused on Irish Music with a Global Twist, American Roots, and Mahler's Vienna.

North of Caramoor on Route 22, the **Katonah Museum of Art** (Rte. 22 at Jay St., Katonah, 914/232-9555, www.katonahmuseum.org, 10am-5pm Tues.-Sat., noon-5pm Sun., adults $10, seniors and students $5, children under 12 free) produces small, high-quality shows that often pair a well-known artist with an emerging local one. In this way, the museum draws a large following while giving exposure to newer works. Exhibits change

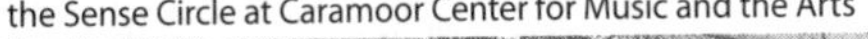

the Sense Circle at Caramoor Center for Music and the Arts

frequently. Summer of 2014 featured an exhibition called *Iceland: Artists Respond to Place,* the first exhibit in the United States to explore the complex relationship of Icelandic artists to their island geography. Don't overlook the sculpture garden outside.

Katonah's third museum is a good place to dive into the early history of the nascent U.S. government. At the conclusion of a distinguished career, diplomat and negotiator John Jay retired to his family's farm in Katonah. A descendant of the Van Cortlandt family, Jay had worked with the Founding Fathers to ensure the future of the new republic. After Jay held a succession of international posts, George Washington appointed him first chief justice of the U.S. Supreme Court. His former residence is now the **John Jay Homestead State Historic Site** (400 Jay St./Rte. 22, Katonah, 914/232-5651, www.johnjayhomestead.org, 8am-6pm daily, adults $7, students and seniors $5, under 12 free), located on Route 22 between Katonah and Bedford Village. Shaded by three linden trees, the main home remains much as it was in Jay's time. Outside, you can view the formal gardens and walk the steep Beech Allee to imagine how it felt to arrive at the estate by carriage. On Saturdays June-October, local farmers bring their harvest to the homestead for a farmers market that's open 9am-1pm.

Katonah is at the junction of the Saw Mill River Parkway and I-684, or Exit 6 off I-684.

Cross River

Westchester County's largest park has been a wildlife sanctuary since 1924. Located east of Katonah at the junction of Routes 35 and 121, **Ward Pound Ridge Reservation** (Rtes. 35 & 121, Cross River, 914/864-7317, parks.westchestergov.com, 8am-dusk daily, admission $10) encompasses 4,700 acres of wildflowers, hiking trails, campsites, and picnic grounds, plus an interpretive **Trailside Museum and Wildlife Center** with Native American exhibits. Its Gallery in the Park offers four rotating exhibitions per year (9am-5pm daily).

Somers

IBM and PepsiCo draw business travelers to the suburban town of Somers, but a couple of unusual sights are worth a peek if you happen to pass through. Apply the concept of heirloom vegetables to fauna, and you've got **Muscoot Farm** (Rte. 100, 914/864-7282, www.muscootfarm.org, 10am-4pm daily, fees vary depending on event). Its rare farm-animal breeds and vintage-equipment exhibits on 777 acres portray the life of the American farmer in the early 20th century. In something of a cross between a petting zoo and a museum, the farm raises pigs, horses, sheep, and ducks. It is also a good place to look for wild butterflies. From Exit 6 on I-684, follow Route 35 west to Route 100. The entrance is a mile down the road, on the right.

Also in Somers is the eclectic **Museum of the Early American Circus** (Rtes. 100 & 202, 914/277-4977, www.somershistoricalsoc.org, 2pm-4pm Thurs., admission by donation), one of a couple dozen museums in the country dedicated to the history of this all-American pastime. Several of the town's residents—including one Hachaliah Bailey, of Barnum & Bailey fame—were instrumental in developing the circus as we know it today. They imported some of the first exotic animals and built the first circus tent. The Somers Historical Society has documented these activities in a three-room museum on the third floor of the old Elephant Hotel.

North Salem

Michael Bloomberg and David Letterman are among the well-to-do who vacation in rural North Salem, across the interstate from Somers and close to the Connecticut border. The **Hammond Museum and Japanese Stroll Garden** (28 Deveau Rd., 914/669-5033, www.hammondmuseum.org, noon-4pm Wed.-Sat., adults $5, seniors $4, under 12 free) blends Eastern and Western aesthetics to create an enchanting outdoor experience. Water lilies, a reflecting pool, and the red maple terrace take visitors back to sixth-century Japan. And a delightful combination

Gardens of Westchester County

Westchester County boasts some of the largest and most elaborate outdoor gardens in the Hudson River Valley. Here is a sampling of the very best:

- Caramoor Center for Music and the Arts, Katonah: Stroll through the Sunken Garden, Butterfly Garden, Iris & Peony Garden, Sense Circle, and Tapestry Hedge on this 90-acre property dedicated to the arts.
- Donald M. Kendall Sculpture Gardens at PepsiCo Headquarters, Purchase: Drive or walk the grounds to see 45 sculptures on 168 acres.
- Hammond Museum and Japanese Stroll Garden, North Salem: Think of Japan as you walk among water lilies, a reflecting pool, and the red maple terrace.
- John Jay Homestead State Historic Site, Katonah: Formal gardens designed in the 19th century are set around a sundial and fountain. Several more flower gardens surround the historic home.
- Kykuit, The Rockefeller Estate, Sleepy Hollow: With so many gardens, there is a tour dedicated to plants and sculpture. Learn about classic garden design while viewing contemporary sculptures in a stunning hilltop setting.
- Luquer-Marble Memorial Wildflower Garden, Ward Pound Ridge Reservation, Cross River: Behind the Trailside Nature Museum in Westchester's largest park, a small wildflower garden honors two conservationists who were instrumental in securing funding for the museum. Best visited in April and May when spring flowers bloom.
- Lyndhurst Rose Garden and Fern Garden, Tarrytown: View 500 roses on a historic 19th-century estate.
- Van Cortlandt Manor, Croton-on-Hudson: Heirloom veggies and herbs grow outside one of the Hudson River Valley's preserved river mansions.
- Wildflower Island at Teatown Lake Reservation, Ossining: Take a guided tour of a two-acre sanctuary for 230 native and endangered species of wildflowers.

of rock, sand, waterfalls, and evergreens stimulates the senses. Inside the Hammond Museum is a collection of Mandarin fans, as well as several hundred portraits taken by music and theater critic Carl Van Vechten. A miniature replica of Mount Fuji is also in the works. The museum has a café open noon-3pm Wednesday-Saturday.

SPORTS AND RECREATION

Winter Sports

Despite its population density, Westchester maintains 17,000 acres of public parks for recreation throughout the year. Many of them are ideal for cross-country skiing after heavy winter storms. Take a loop around the lake on three miles of trails at **Cranberry Lake Preserve** (Old Orchard St., White Plains, 914/428-1005, parks.westchestergov.com, open dawn-dusk daily). Some sections of the gently graded **Old Croton Aqueduct** are also skiable. Try Croton Dam Plaza in Croton or North Tarrytown, near Rockefeller State Park Preserve.

Hiking

Westchester wilderness lends itself more to a walk in the woods than a backcountry experience. But several large green spaces make it possible to get well away from the bustle of everyday suburban life. Many of Westchester's parks are open to residents only and require the purchase of a county park pass (parks.westchestergov.com, $60 for one year). Both **Tibbetts Brook Park** (Midland Ave.,

Yonkers, 914/231-2865, 8am-dusk daily) and **Sprain Ridge Park** (Jackson Ave., Yonkers, 914/231-3450, 8am-dusk daily, Westchester County Park Pass required) have trails for hiking and biking.

Cycling

Westchester County maintains a network of trailways for cyclists—paths that are mostly paved and closed to motorists. The **South County Trailway** is a 14.1-mile path that runs north to south in the southern part of the county. Pick up the northern end by the Eastview park-and-ride at Route 100C. The **North County Trailway** starts at the same park-and-ride and runs north for 22 miles, connecting to the Putnam Trailway. There is a relatively steep climb up from the Croton Reservoir. The **Bronx River Parkway** also closes to traffic for Bicycle Sundays, May-September, 10am-2pm.

The **Westchester Cycle Club** (www.westchestercycleclub.org) hosts the annual Golden Apple Tour in September. Routes of varying distances traverse the countryside in Westchester and Putnam Counties.

Blue Mountain Reservation (Welcher Ave., Peekskill, 914/862-5275, 8am-dusk daily year-round, parking $10) has 20 miles of bike trails designated for riders of all levels.

Run by a pro-level mountain biker, **Trail Masters Touring** (914/325-5916, www.trailmasterstouring.com) offers tours and clinics for riders of all levels. Owner and instructor Tom Oakes offers bike rentals for $40 per day as well as guided tours. He is a Certified Mountain Bike Instructor who is active in local trail building and maintenance, and offers frequent free skills clinics. One of the most popular and scenic rides for visitors begins in Croton Gorge Park and follows the Old Croton Aqueduct through the towns of Croton-on-Hudson and Ossining. Tom can also meet guests at the train station with bikes. **Endless Trail Bikeworx** (56 Main St., Dobbs Ferry, 914/674-8567, www.endlesstrailbw.com, 11am-6pm Tues.-Fri., 10am-5pm Sat., noon-5pm Sun.) is a short walk from the Dobbs Ferry Metro-North train station and rents bikes by the day. Ticket/rental packages are available through **Metro-North getaways program** (http://web.mta.info/mnr/html/getaways.htm).

Golf

New York City executives support some 50 public and private golf courses across the county. The newest course is the **Hudson Hills Golf Course** (400 Croton Dam Rd., Ossining, 914/864-3000, www.hudsonhillsgolf.com, weekends $85, weekdays $65, reduced rates with parks pass). Architect Mark Mungeam, who led the overhaul of Chicago's Olympia Fields Country Club for the 2003 U.S. Open, designed the course. You'll have to fight the city crowd for tee times.

The **Centennial Golf Club** (185 John Simpson Rd., Carmel, 845/225-5700, www.centennialgolf.com, Fri.-Sun. and holidays $135, Mon.-Thurs. $100) offers a golf-cart GPS system as a convenience to players. The Larry Nelson 7,100-yard course enforces a pace-of-play policy, so if you fall behind, you may be gently reminded to keep the game moving. Greens are fast but roll true. First-rate service compensates for the steep fees.

Dunwoodie Golf Course (Wasylenko Lane, Yonkers, 914/231-3490, golf.westchestergov.com, weekends $45, weekdays $41, prices do not include cart, reduced rates with county park pass) is county-owned, and some patrons say it shows in the greens. The short 5,815-yard, par 70 course offers plenty of challenges, with elevation changes and a deep rough.

All 18 tees were renovated and expanded a few years ago at **Maple Moor Golf Course** (1128 North St., White Plains, 914/995-9200, golf.westchestergov.com, weekends $45, weekdays $41, prices do not include cart, reduced rates with county park pass), also county-run. Some greens are slow on this 6,226-yard, par 71 course, but there's enough action to keep it interesting. Don't let the highway noise on the front nine distract you.

Swimming and Boating

Kayak Hudson (Five Islands Park, New Rochelle, 914/682-5135, www.kayakhudson.com, 6am-6:30pm Mon.-Wed., 6am-10pm Thurs., 6am-11pm Fri.) takes paddlers on guided trips along the Hudson River and Long Island Sound.

Fishing and Hunting

Freshwater fishing in Westchester revolves around the reservoir system. With a New York Watershed permit, you can catch large bass and the occasional trout. Rent a canoe to open up the possibilities. **Mohansic Lake** (201 Hawley Rd., North Salem, 914/864-7310) is a zoo on summer weekends, but it is known to have aggressive bass and large crappie. **Kensico Reservoir,** three miles north of White Plains, has rainbow, brown, and lake trout up to about 15 or 20 pounds.

ACCOMMODATIONS

Westchester has mastered the science of the business conference hotel. Although there are a few exceptions, for more choice in charming accommodations, you're better off heading north to Putnam County, or south to New York City.

$100-150

Inn on the Hudson (634 Main St., Peekskill, 914/739-1500, www.innonthehudson.com, $115) is an upgraded motor lodge with river views, a swimming pool, and 53 basic rooms that make for a good value.

$150-200

Close to Van Cortlandt Manor and two blocks from the village of Croton-on-Hudson, the **Alexander Hamilton House** (49 Van Wyck St., Croton-on-Hudson, 914/271-6737, www.alexanderhamiltonhouse.com, $142-299) is a Victorian affair, complete with a white picket fence. Eight rooms and suites have private baths, air-conditioning, and high-speed Internet; some have fireplaces and soaking tubs too. There is a two-night minimum on weekends.

Crabtree's Kittle House (11 Kittle Rd., Chappaqua, 914/666-8044, www.kittlehouse.com, $147-167) is first and foremost an outstanding restaurant, but its 12 moderately priced rooms are an added convenience if you plan to sample more than a taste from its enormous wine cellar. Rooms are decorated simply in pastels and floral linens, and with white trim and dark wood furniture.

With 300 rooms set on 30 acres, the **Renaissance Westchester Hotel** (80 West Red Oak Ln., White Plains, 914/694-5400, www.marriott.com, $119-220) is a comfortable Marriott property that primarily hosts business travelers.

Over $200

One of the priciest places to stay in the Hudson River Valley is the **Castle Hotel & Spa** (400 Benedict Ave., Tarrytown, 914/631-1980, www.castleonthehudson.com, $350-730). Built by the son of a Civil War general on a hilltop outside of Tarrytown, this ultra-luxurious inn features a 75-foot tower that is the highest point in Westchester County. Its rooms feature high ceilings and plenty of natural light. Elegant drapery and furnishings create a decidedly old-world atmosphere. Dinner at the Equus restaurant on-site will be an experience to remember, if only for the views and the bill.

Tarrytown House (49 E. Sunnyside Ln., Tarrytown, 800/553-8118, www.tarrytownhouseestate.com, $229-359) is a full-service conference center set on 26 acres in two 19th-century mansions. More than 200 rooms and suites are designed to accommodate business travelers but also make for a pleasant weekend getaway. The 10 Georgian-era rooms in the King Mansion have the most character.

FOOD

Restaurants are plentiful and diverse in Westchester, serving cuisines from Indian to Southwest. French and Italian themes are most common, and the county offers a number of casual cafés and local farm stands. That said, there are a lot of expense-account traps

A New Food Revolution

A beekeeper tends to the hives at Stone Barns Center.

We are experiencing the beginnings of a global food revolution, and public awareness of the problems with mass-produced food is growing every day. Many of the Hudson River Valley's small farms are playing a vital role in changing the way we think about what we eat. At the **Stone Barns Center for Food and Agriculture,** young farmers are learning the value of resilient, restorative farming techniques and children are forming vital connections to the sources of their food. Combine a historic setting near the Rockefeller Estate with cutting-edge research, and you get 200 varieties of fruits and vegetables on 6.5 acres of cultivated fields. There are no pesticides, herbicides, or chemical additives here. Composting is a full-time job for the center's soil nutrient manager. From heirloom beans to heritage turkeys and Berkshire pigs, the center is helping to make the farm-to-table mantra a way of life for everyone. In 2014, Stone Barns hosted the first New York Times Food for Tomorrow conference, a gathering of some of the most influential people working on food issues today.

to avoid—unless, of course, you're on an expense account.

Along the River: Route 9

★ **Juniper** (575 Warburton Ave., Hastings-on-Hudson, www.juniperhastings.com, 11am-3pm and 5:30pm-9pm Wed.-Fri., 10am-3pm and 5:30pm-9pm Sat., 10am-3pm Sun.) is a find for creative dishes from real food that's grown nearby. The theme is French-New American, which means you might start with a kale apple salad or fried duck egg, then move on to the grilled hanger steak or squid ink tagliatelle. The restaurant can accommodate gluten-free and vegetarian diets, but you have to bring your own bottle of wine. Children are welcome too.

For outdoor dining on a warm summer eve, consider **Harvest on Hudson** (1 River St., Hastings-on-Hudson, 914/478-2800, www.harvest2000.com, dinner daily and lunch Mon.-Fri.). Set in an inviting Tuscan farmhouse, the restaurant serves standard Italian fare that gets mixed reviews from patrons. The dramatic river views are the reason to dine here.

Tarrytown's Main Street has a full menu of choices for casual and fine dining. The "Labs" in ★ **Coffee Labs** (7 Main St., Tarrytown, 914/332-1479, www.coffeelabs.

com, 6:30am-6:30pm Mon.-Tues., 6:30am-8pm Wed.-Thurs., 6:30am-10:30pm Fri., 8am-10:30pm Sat., 8am-7pm Sun., drinks $2-5) refer to Labrador retrievers, which the owners evidently adore. With a 10-year track record, this roaster and café is serious about sustainability. Among a long list of green decisions, the company sends all of its coffee grounds to the Stone Barns compost program. Stop in for a cup of fair trade brew or choose from a great selection of loose-leaf teas.

Lefteris Gyro (1 N. Broadway, Tarrytown, 914/524-9687, www.lefterisgyro.com, 11am-10pm daily, $5-16) packs in the crowds at the corner of Main and Broadway. Neighboring shop owners use this busy Greek restaurant as a barometer for the business level on any given day. Sit outside and enjoy platters of Greek specialties—souvlaki, gyros, or salads—served with warm pita bread. Service is quick and the food is reliably good.

Locavores head to ★ **Sweet Grass Grill** (24 Main St., Tarrytown, 914/631-0000, www.sweetgrassgrill.com, 11:30am-4pm Mon.-Fri., 5pm-9pm Sun.-Thurs., 5pm-10pm Fri.-Sat., 10am-3:30pm Sat.-Sun., $17-24) for seasonal soups, salads, and entrées. In summer, you might start with a chilled golden beet soup and move on to the littleneck clams or grilled arctic char. In winter, go for the roast chicken. Small plates and sides include spinach risotto, couscous quinoa salad, and sweet potato fries. This restaurant sources its food from the nearby Stone Barns Center, as well as other local farms. The menu changes frequently.

Also centrally located, **Horsefeathers** (94 N. Broadway, Tarrytown, 914/631-6606, www.horsefeathersny.com, 11:30am-9pm Sun.-Wed., 11:30am-10pm Thurs.-Sat., $10-40) is known for its literary decor and a tome of a menu, which is arranged by chapters and includes 100 types of beer. Burgers and pub fare prevail. Across from the Tarrytown Hilton Inn, **Eldorado Diner** (460 S. Broadway, Tarrytown, 914/332-5838, www.eldoradodiners.com, $5-21) is a classic diner that's open around the clock. The menu includes burgers, fries, spaghetti with meatballs, and the like. Breakfast is served all day or night.

On a hilltop outside of town, **Equus** (400 Benedict Ave., Tarrytown, 914/631-3646, www.castleonthehudson.com) may be the place to celebrate a special occasion. Part of the Castle Hotel & Spa at Tarrytown, the restaurant offers an outstanding, if pricey, wine list and a seasonal prix fixe menu consisting of four courses. Breakfast is served 8am-10am daily, lunch noon-2pm Mon.-Sat., and dinner 6pm-9:30pm daily. Sunday brunch (11:30am-2:30pm) and high tea are good alternatives to a full lunch or dinner.

★ **Blue Hill at Stone Barns** (630 Bedford Rd., Pocantico Hills, 914/366-9600, www.bluehillfarm.com, 5pm-10pm Wed.-Sat., 1pm-10pm Sun., $148-208) is a once-in-a-lifetime kind of place that takes the concept of farm-to-table to new heights, night after night. Chef Dan Barber has reinvented what it means to eat local and seasonal. He recently wrote The Third Plate, a perspective on the future of food. There are no menus, as the available harvest changes daily. In a nine-course tasting menu during the summer, you might try a "tortilla" made of kohlrabi, a single perfect cherry tomato, quail eggs served over house-made tagliatelle, and a single lamb chop. Each course can be paired with a glass of wine or a nonalcoholic infusion—and the latter are actually more memorable. The presentation is exquisite, start to finish. This dining experience takes a minimum of three hours. Prepare to be amazed.

For a more casual meal at Stone Barns Center, grab a wooden tray and settle at an outdoor table at the ★ **Blue Hill Café.** Espresso, iced tea, and Ronnybrook yogurt drinks will quench your thirst, while creative salads made of the freshest ingredients and homemade baked goods take the edge off your appetite. This may be the only café in the entire Hudson River Valley to offer sea salt at its condiment counter. You can also bring a taste of Stone Barns home by purchasing the café's own spices, oils, and vinegars.

At **Zeph's** (638 Central Ave., Peekskill,

914/736-2159, www.zephsrestaurant.com, open at 5:30pm Thurs.-Sun., closing hours vary, $23-32), Victoria Zeph prepares a creative menu that reflects an ever-changing variety of international influences, from French and Chinese to Moroccan, Caribbean, and Thai. The setting is a converted gristmill outside downtown Peekskill. Another Peekskill find for local food and beer is **Birdsall House** (970 Main St., Peekskill, 914/930-1880, www.birdsallhouse.net, dinner $18-26). All of the pork, beef, chicken, rabbit, and duck that appear on the menu come from nearby Hemlock Hill Farm in Cortlandt Manor, and many of the beers on the restaurant's drink menu are from New York breweries. Munch on Cajun-spiced popcorn or smoky almonds while you down a drink or two. Then sample the house-made charcuterie, or go all out for the buttermilk fried chicken and biscuits.

Located on the Riverfront, **Peekskill Brewery** (47-53 S. Water St., Peekskill, 914/734-2337, www.peekskillbrewery.com, noon-10pm Mon.-Thurs., noon-11pm Fri.-Sat., noon-9pm Sun., mains $14-22) operates a taproom on its first floor that stays open late and features a number of house beers. The second floor is home to a pub that is open for lunch and dinner daily as well as a Sunday brunch featuring oysters, poutine, and pierogi. Reservations are recommended for pub dining.

In Sleepy Hollow, **Bridge View Tavern** (226 Beekman Ave., Sleepy Hollow, 914/332-0078, www.bridgeviewtavern.com, $12-24) serves a popular pulled pork dish and has a menu dedicated to a variety of stuffed hot dogs. Shrimp cake sliders are a tasty way to begin the meal. Try the BVT Bloody Mary or sucker punch to drink, or choose from 18 draught beers. There is a large parking lot across the street and a few tables outside with views of the Tappan Zee Bridge. Live music plays on Thursdays and Saturdays starting at 10pm.

Sushi Mike's (142 Main St., Dobbs Ferry, 914/591-0054, www.sushimikes.com, lunch noon-3pm Mon.-Fri., 4:30pm-10pm Mon.-Thurs., 4:30pm-11pm Fri., noon-11pm Sat., 3pm-10pm Sun., $14-27) is a small Japanese restaurant on the corner of Main and Cedar in Dobbs Ferry. It's usually packed with locals. Order from a menu of creative rolls, or go for one of the hot dishes, such as gyoza, teriyaki, or a soba noodle stir-fry. A block away, **Sam's Italian Restaurant** (128 Main St. at Oak St., Dobbs Ferry, 914/693-2008, www.samsofdobbsferry.com, 11am-10pm Mon.-Sat., 1pm-10pm Sun., $15-25) is a longtime eatery that has managed to keep up with the times. Enjoy pizzas, pasta dishes, and friendly service.

Near the Tarrytown Train Station and RiverWalk path, ★ **Lighthouse Ice Cream** (127 W. Main St., at the Tarrytown Harbor, 914/502-0339, www.lighthouseicecreamkompany.com) is the place for a treat on a summer afternoon. Order an ice cream, gelato, sorbet, or coffee drink. Everything is made on-site from locally sourced ingredients including organic dairy from Battenkill Valley Creamery.

Croton-on-Hudson has several unique dining experiences. **Mex-to-go** (345 S. Riverside Ave., Croton-on-Hudson, 914/271-8646, www.mextogo-croton.com, daily 11am-10pm) makes tortas, burritos, tacos, and other Mexican staples, with reasonably priced lunch specials. **Umami Café** (325 S. Riverside Ave., 914/271-5555, www.umamicafe.com, 5pm-9:30pm Sun.-Thurs., 5pm-10pm Fri.-Sat., $13-20) does creative appetizers and small plates best: tuna tacos, lobster rolls, Peking duck quesadilla, and truffled mac 'n cheese, for example. For ice cream, head to the **Blue Pig** (121 Maple St., Croton-on-Hudson, 914/271-3850, www.thebluepigicecream.com, 11am-8pm Tues.-Thurs., 11am-9:30pm Fri.-Sat., noon-8pm Sun.). Its homemade, locally sourced flavors and soft-serve sorbet are the talk of the town.

Central Westchester County

Coromandel (30 Division St., New Rochelle, 914/235-8390, www.coromandelcuisine.com, noon-2:30pm Mon.-Fri., noon-3pm Sat.-Sun., 5pm-10pm Sun.-Thurs., 5pm-10:30pm

Fri.-Sat., $14-23) ranks among Westchester's best for Indian-inspired fare.

Iron Horse Grill (20 Wheeler Ave., Pleasantville, 914/741-0717, www.ironhorse-pleasantville.com, from 5pm Tues.-Sat., $26-32) serves contemporary American dishes including breast of pheasant and tenderloin of venison. The 60-seat restaurant occupies a converted train station.

A stroll along Katonah's main thoroughfare reveals another handful of tempting places to grab a bite. **Blue Dolphin Ristorante** (175 Katonah Ave., Katonah, 914/232-4791, www.thebluedolphinny.com, lunch 11am-3pm Mon.-Fri., 11:30am-3:30pm Sat., dinner 5pm-9:30pm Mon.-Thurs., 5pm-10pm Fri.-Sat., $14-21) prepares fresh daily seafood specials, and other Italian specialties. Expect to wait for a table on weekends. Across from the train station, **Willy Nick's Café** (17 Katonah Ave., Katonah, 914/232-8030, www.willynicks.com, open at 11:30am daily, $15-32) does comfort food with a twist: lobster mac 'n cheese, baked brie with amaretto glazed fruit, or mussels 'n fries, for example. Across from the train station, **NoKa Joe's** (25 Katonah Ave., Katonah, 914/232-7278, www.nokajoes.com) pours fair trade and organic coffee and espresso drinks for Metro-North commuters, with an inviting bookshop upstairs. Half a block from the train station, **Pizza Station** (27 Parkway Ave., 914/232-6000, www.pizzastationny.com, 9am-10pm daily, $10-17) handles the weekday lunch rush with ease. Order by the slice or wait for a whole pie. This restaurant has a second location in Chappequa (88 South Greeley Ave., 914/238-1400).

★ **Crabtree's Kittle House** (11 Kittle Rd., Chappaqua, 914/666-8044, www.kittlehouse.com, lunch noon-2:30pm Mon.-Fri., brunch noon-2:30pm Sun., dinner from 5:30pm Mon.-Sat. and from 3pm Sun., $24-29) has an unparalleled selection of wines, with more than 50,000 bottles in its cellar. Order a special bottle in advance to have it brought up to temperature or let sediment settle out. A creative American menu leads to some fabulous wine and food pairings. Try a half-bottle of condrieu with the scallop appetizer.

Power business lunches take place at **Mulino's** (99 Court St., White Plains, 914/761-1818, www.mulinosny.com, 11:30am-10:30pm Mon.-Fri., 5pm-11pm Sat., $25-30), known more for its free starter plates than for the northern Italian entrées. **Little Spot** (854 N. Broadway, White Plains, 914/761-1334, $5) is a roadside find, serving split chili dogs and milkshakes to rave reviews.

Fresh fish and reasonable prices bring in the crowds at **Eastchester Fish Gourmet** (837 White Plains Rd., Scarsdale, 914/725-3450, www.eastchesterfish.com, lunch 11:30am-2:30pm Thurs. and Fri. only, dinner at 5pm daily, $12-36). Expect a wait unless you show up early.

ENTERTAINMENT AND EVENTS

Performing Arts

Built by music lovers for music lovers, the **Caramoor Center for Music and the Arts** (149 Girdle Ridge Rd., Katonah, 914/232-1252, www.caramoor.org) features classical and jazz performances in two theaters. The **Performing Arts Center** (735 Anderson Hill Rd., Purchase, 914/251-6200, www.artscenter.org, noon-6pm Tue.-Fri.) holds 600 jazz, cabaret, and classical music events annually. You can catch Tony Bennett on a summer weekend or a performance of *The Wizard of Oz* with the kids.

Another popular evening venue is Elmsford's **Westchester Broadway Theatre** (1 Broadway Plaza, Elmsford, 914/592-2222, www.broadwaytheatre.com, $54-80), a dinner theater that produces musicals, comedy, and children's shows. Choose from matinee or evening performances. The standard dinner menu includes chicken marsala, prime rib, and roast pork loin.

Musicians from Dave Brubeck to Bruce Springsteen have performed on the stage of the 1885 **Tarrytown Music Hall** (13 Main St., Tarrytown, box office 877/840-0457, www.tarrytownmusichall.org, 11am-6pm

Mon.-Thurs., 11am-4pm Fri.). A local non-profit rescued the theater from near demolition in the 1970s, and although the building is showing its age outside, it continues to host concerts, plays, musicals, operas, dance performances, and recordings inside. In 2004, the theater began showing movies again, after a 27-year hiatus. For tickets, call ahead or visit the box office up to two hours before a show.

Bars and Nightlife

In Katonah, **Willy Nick's Café** (17 Katonah Ave., Katonah, 914/232-8030, www.willynicks.com) is a good place to order a martini or two before heading out for a show.

Choose from more than 100 types of domestic and imported beer at **Horsefeathers** (94 N. Broadway, Tarrytown, 914/631-6606, www.horsefeathersny.com, 11:30am-9pm Sun.-Wed., 11:30am-10pm Thurs.-Sat.), including the local Saranac Pale Ale. The beautiful bar at **Sweet Grass Grill** (24 Main St., Tarrytown, 914/631-0000, www.sweetgrassgrill.com) was carved from an oak tree that was felled in the Rockefeller State Park Preserve. Enjoy a cocktail or microbrew before your meal.

Festivals

Caramoor International Summer Music Festival (149 Girdle Ridge Rd., Katonah, 914/232-1252, www.caramoor.org, July-Aug.) is a summer concert series with a wide range of productions from classical music to Latin jazz fusion. Many shows sell out, so check the website early for tickets. Arrive early to enjoy a stroll through the gardens before your performance begins.

Yonkers Hudson Riverfest (Yonkers Waterfront, Yonkers, 914/969-6660, www.yonkersriverfest.com) is a daylong environmental and multicultural festival held every September. Tens of thousands of visitors come each year. A new "ferry-go-round" provides ferry service to five communities for events, fireworks, and arts and crafts. Also on the river, the **Clearwater's Great Hudson River Revival** (www.clearwater.org) takes place at Croton Point Park in Croton-on-Hudson each June.

Once a year, Historic Hudson Valley invites artists of all ages and abilities to work on the grounds of Sunnyside, Washington Irving's estate during **Artists on the Hudson** (914/631-8200 ext. 618, www.hudsonvalley.org, free admission), which takes place in May. In April, the Rivertowns Arts Council hosts an **Annual RiverArts Studio Tour** that covers about 50 studios in Ardsley, Irvington, Hastings-on-Hudson, and Dobbs Ferry (914/412-5120, www.riverarts.org, free admission).

The Headless Horseman of Washington Irving's famous story, "The Legend of Sleepy Hollow," still rides at Philipsburg Manor a handful of evenings in October. Tickets are $20 weeknights and $25 on Saturdays. Contact **Historic Hudson Valley** (914/631-8200, www.hudsonvalley.org) for information.

SHOPPING

Westchester and shopping go all the way back to the Great Depression, when the first department store opened in White Plains. Today you can find it all, from antiques and flea markets to Neiman Marcus. If you're on a quest for unusual antiques, head to Bedford Hills, Cross River, Tarrytown, or Larchmont.

With more than 100 stores, the **Cross County Shopping Center** (8000 Mall Walk, 914/968-9570, www.crosscountycenter.com, 10am-9:30pm Mon.-Sat., 11am-7pm Sun.), in Yonkers, is one of the oldest and largest malls in the county, while **The Westchester** (125 Westchester Ave., 914/421-1333, www.simon.com, 10am-9pm Mon.-Sat., 11am-6:30pm Sunday), in White Plains, and **Vernon Hills Shopping Center** (700 White Plains Post Rd., 914/472-2000), in Eastchester, are among the most upscale.

In Katonah, the **Charles Department Store** (113 Katonah Ave., 914/232-5200, www.charlesdeptstore.com, 9am-6pm Mon.-Fri., 9am-5pm Sat.) is a throwback to the era of the family-owned department store. The store is managed by the grandsons of the founder

shops along Katonah Avenue

and sells everything from shoes to coffeepots. Closer to the train station, **The Gift Garage** (29 Katonah Ave., Katonah, 914/232-2322) is the place to buy creative gifts for kids—from princess shoes to Tegu magnetic blocks—or a stylish accent for your home.

Antiques and Galleries

Good finds in Larchmont include **Dualities Antiques and Art** (2056 Boston Post Rd., 914/834-2773, www.dualitiesantiquesandart.com, 10am-5pm Mon.-Sat.). In Tarrytown, look for the **Tarrytown Antiques Center** (25 Main St., 914/366-4613, noon-6pm Tues.-Thurs. and Sun., noon-10pm Fri.-Sat.) or **Belkind Bigi Antiques,** just up the street (21 Main St., Tarrytown, 914/524-9626, 11:30am-5pm Tues.-Sun.).

Yellow Monkey Antiques (Rte. 35, Cross River, 914/763-5848, www.yellowmonkey.com, 10am-5:30pm Tues.-Sat., noon-5pm Sun.) has more than 7,000 square feet of showrooms that focus on British pine antiques, shipped in large quantities from Europe. **The Eclectic Collector** (215 Katonah Ave., Katonah, 914/232-8700, www.theeclecticcollector.com, 10am-6pm Mon.-Sat., 11am-5pm Sun.) sells contemporary, folk, ceramic, and glass works from more than 300 artists.

Serious Toyz (1 Baltic Pl., Croton-on-Hudson, 866/653-8699 or 914/271-8699, www.serioustoyz.com, noon-5pm Fri.-Sat.) buys and sells an assortment of collectible toys, including tin, pressed steel, die cast, plastic, and character toys.

More than a dozen antiques shows take place year-round in Westchester County. Check www.westchestertourism.com for dates and locations. Each Sunday, hundreds of vendors set up outdoor booths at the **Yonkers Raceway Market** (914/963-3898, 9am-4pm Mar.-Dec.). Goods for sale include new merchandise, as well as antiques and collectibles. From the New York State Thruway, take Exit 2 northbound or Exit 4 southbound.

Riverrun Bookshop (12 Washington St., Hastings-on-Hudson, 914/478-1339, www.riverrunbookshop.com, daily 11am-4pm) is a haven for bibliophiles, with 200,000 titles in two stores and two warehouses. The collection includes signed books, vintage paperbacks, and modern first editions.

Peekskill's **Flat Iron Gallery** (105 S. Division St., Peekskill, 914/734-1894, www.flatiron.qpg.com, noon-6pm Thurs.-Sun.) specializes in contemporary fine art and handcrafted jewelry. This is a good place to look for Hudson River landscapes. More Hudson River art is found at **The Art Barn** (325 N. Highland Ave., Ossining, 914/762-4997, www.theartbarn.net, 10am-5:30pm Tues.-Sat.).

Farm Stands

In Tarrytown, family-owned **Mint Premium Foods** (18 Main St., Tarrytown, 914/703-6511, 11am-10pm Mon.-Sat.) carries gourmet cheeses, olive oils, and meats, as well as organic teas and honey. The **Tarrytown Farmers Market** (914/923-4837, 8:30am-1pm Sat. only, June-mid-Nov.) takes place at Patriot's Park off Route 9.

INFORMATION AND SERVICES

The **Westchester County Office of Tourism** (222 Mamaroneck Ave., White Plains, 800/833-9282, www.westchester-tourism.com) also runs a seasonal tourism information center in July and August at Exit 9 off the Bronx River Parkway, near Leewood Drive. Local commerce chambers in these towns can also provide visitor information:

- Greater Ossining Chamber of Commerce (914/941-0009, www.ossiningchamber.org)
- Sleepy Hollow/Tarrytown Chamber of Commerce (914/631-1705, www.greater-sleepyhollowtarrytown.com)
- Irvington-on-Hudson Chamber of Commerce (914/231-7779, www.irvington-nychamber.com)
- Dobbs Ferry Chamber of Commerce (www.dfchamber.com)
- Hastings-on-Hudson Chamber of Commerce (800/464-5809)
- Yonkers Chamber of Commerce (914/963-0332, www.yonkerschamber.com)

The **Katonah Village Library** (26 Bedford Rd., Katonah, 914/232-3508, www.katonahlibrary.org, 10am-8pm Mon. and Wed., 10am-6pm Tues. and Thurs., 10am-5:30pm Fri., 10am-5pm Sat., 1pm-5pm Sun.) has free Wi-Fi, visitor information, restrooms, and comfortable tables in a 1930 building that also houses the Katonah Historical Museum.

GETTING THERE AND AROUND

Bus

The **Bee-Line System** (914/813-7777, transportation.westchestergov.com) is a countywide bus service with more than 55 different routes and express service. Routes serve many of the county's recreational facilities and also provide connection to trains. The fare is $2.50 cash ($1.25 for seniors or disabled travelers) on most routes.

Train

It's hard to avoid the **Metro-North** (800/638-7646) commuter line in Westchester. It was practically built to serve this county's suburbs, and today, there are 43 station stops on three lines providing continual service to Manhattan's Grand Central Station and points within the county. Tarrytown, Croton-on-Hudson, and all of Westchester's riverside towns are easily accessible via the Hudson Line.

Car

You can rent a car at the **Westchester County Airport** in White Plains (240 Airport Rd., Suite 202, airport.westchestergov.com). But be forewarned: Traffic is bad and getting worse in Westchester—both from visitors' cars and those of local residents. The Tappan Zee Bridge regularly backs up during the rush hour commute. Drive off-peak when you can, and allow extra time to reach your destination at any time of day. Tune in to frequent metropolitan-area traffic reports on the radio at AM 880 "on the eights" (1:08, 1:18, 1:28, etc.) and AM 1010 "on the ones" (1:01, 1:11, 1:21, etc.).

Rockland County

With the Hudson River, New Jersey, and Orange County as its borders, Rockland County is the smallest county in the state, outside of the five boroughs of New York City. Located just 16 miles from New York City, Rockland has protected almost a third of its 176 square miles from development, thanks in part to generous donations from the wealthy families who built the first mansions along its riverbank. The terrain encompasses approximately 30 miles of Hudson River frontage, plus Bear Mountain and Harriman State Parks, which contain most of the Ramapo Mountain Range.

Rockland County's first European settlers arrived to join the Native American population in the 17th century. Initially a part of Orange County, Rockland separated in 1798 because the Ramapo Mountains made it difficult for residents to reach the county courthouse in Goshen.

Rockland communities endured two key battles during the Revolutionary War: British forces captured Fort Clinton at Bear Mountain in October 1777, but two years later, colonial forces overwhelmed the British at Stony Point. Benedict Arnold's partner in treason, British Major John André, was captured in Tarrytown across the river. In his possession were the plans for West Point that he had received from Arnold. André was taken to the village of Tappan for trial. A jury found him guilty, and he was hanged.

Like most of the neighboring Hudson River communities, Rockland grew around the industries of milling lumber, making bricks, harvesting ice, mining, and quarrying. In the 1920s, internationally accomplished artists and performers settled in the area, including painter and muralist Henry Varnum Poor, playwright Maxwell Anderson, and composer Kurt Weill. Artist Edward Hopper hailed from Nyack, along with actress Helen Hayes.

The opening of the Tappan Zee Bridge, Palisades Interstate Parkway, and New York State Thruway, all in the 1950s, ended Rockland's days as a rural getaway. The county began to absorb much of the sprawl from New York City, and business conference centers became plentiful. Fortunately, Rockland has managed to develop without compromising its treasured green space. Dozens of historic markers remind visitors of the churches, farms, cemeteries, and homes that hold a significant place in the American past. At the same time, numerous immigrant communities have helped create a vibrant scene for restaurants, performing arts, and museums. Several world-class shopping malls line the Route 59 corridor near Nanuet.

Four townships hold most of the county's historic and outdoor attractions: Clarkstown, Haverstraw, Ramapo, and Stony Point. New City is the county seat.

ALONG THE RIVER: ROUTE 9W

Rockland County begins about 10 miles north of the George Washington Bridge (I-95), a main artery out of New York City. From the bridge, the Palisades Interstate Parkway cuts diagonally across the county, and Route 9W hugs the riverbank. Near the New Jersey state line, the dramatic Palisades cliffs plunge into the river, creating a playground for geologists and rock climbers alike.

★ Piermont Village

Rockland's major river crossing, the Tappan Zee Bridge (I-287), is the longest span across the Hudson, connecting Rockland residents to Westchester County and points east. With 85,000 cars a day passing through, the bridge is the busiest crossing in the region.

Three miles south of the Tappan Zee Bridge, on a steep hillside between Route 9W and the riverbank, is the village of Piermont, where you can savor contemporary farm-to-table cuisine at **Xaviars at Piermont** (506 Piermont Ave., 845/359-7007, www.xaviars.com, 6pm-9pm Wed.-Sat., noon-2pm Fri. and Sun., 5pm-8pm Sun., prix fixe $90-100 pp), paddle a canoe through 1,000 acres of marsh, and then return to town for an evening of live music. Piermont has long been a haven for creative types. Woody Allen's 1985 film *The Purple Rose of Cairo* was filmed here, as was *At First Sight* (1999), starring Mira Sorvino and Val Kilmer.

These days, many residents also commute daily into Manhattan and ride their Italian-made bicycles on the weekends. A row of lively bistros and boutiques takes up most of Piermont Avenue in the village center, where a mile-long pier juts out over the marsh and into the Hudson.

Initially built to handle steamboat traffic, and later, railroad commerce, the **Piermont Pier** became the site of a successful paper mill during the 20th century. During World War II, tens of thousands of U.S. troops boarded ships to Normandy from the pier, earning it the name "Last Stop USA." The soldiers received their last training and inspections at **Camp Shanks,** four miles west of the pier. The camp also housed German and Italian prisoners of war until the end of the conflict. It's hard to get a sense of the magnitude of the camp from the small museum that remains today (South Greenbush Road, Orangeburg, 845/638-5419, noon-4pm Sat.-Sun.). Exhibits inside a model barracks depict life during the war.

Today, the Piermont Pier is a public park that attracts anglers, walkers, and anyone in search of a cool breeze. Just south of the pier is **Tallman Mountain State Park** (Rte. 9W, Bear Mountain, 845/359-0544, www.nysparks.com, vehicle entrance fee $6), a favorite spot for viewing birds and wildflowers on land that once belonged to John D. Rockefeller's Standard Oil Company. Additional facilities include a public pool and tennis courts. Take Exit 4 from the Palisades Interstate Parkway to reach the Piermont area.

Tappan

Students of the Revolutionary War must pay a visit to several sites in the village of Tappan, a few miles southwest from Piermont. George Washington turned the Dutch colonial **DeWint House** (20 Livingston Ave., 845/359-1359, www.dewinthouse.com, 10am-4pm daily, free admission)—now a National Historic Landmark and the oldest building in Rockland County—into temporary

Tappan Zee Bridge

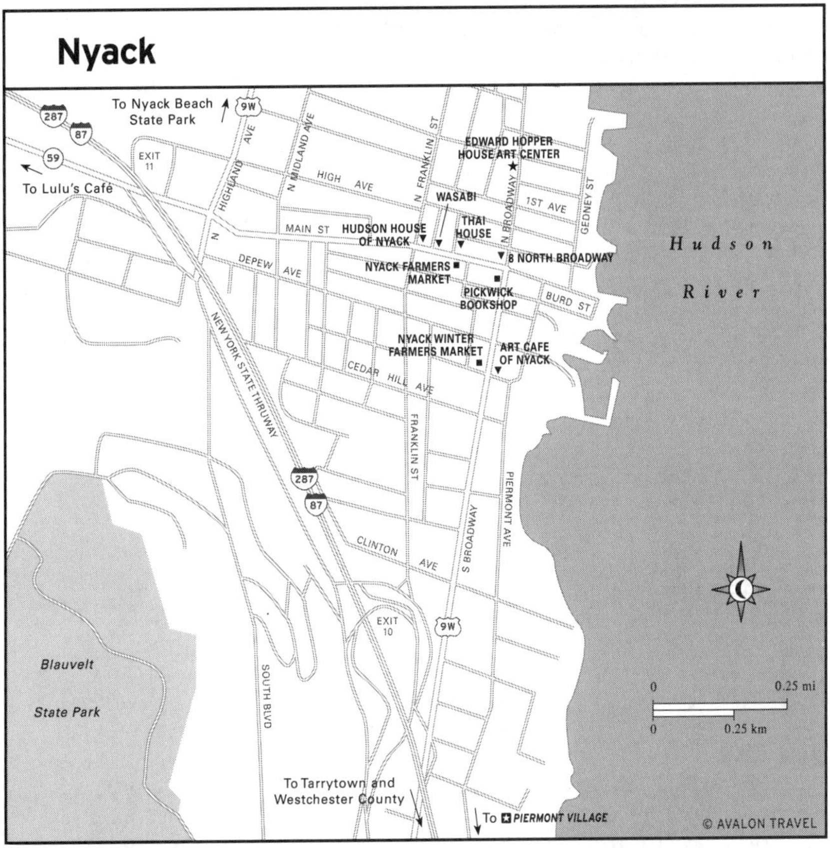

headquarters during the trial of Major John André, the British spy who was accused of conspiring with Benedict Arnold. The trial took place at the county courthouse, which stood on the Village Church Green, next door to the 1835 **Reformed Church of Tappan** that stands today.

Near a stoplight at the center of town is **The '76 House** (110 Main St., Tappan, 845/359-5476, www.76house.com, $19-30), built in 1755. André was held captive here until his execution. The building is now a restaurant and tavern.

Nyack

On the other side of the Tappan Zee Bridge lies the busier commercial center of Nyack (meaning Point of Land), part of the Clarkstown township. Home to a vibrant mix of artists, immigrants, and commuters (many of whom know each other by name), Nyack draws day-trippers out of the city with the **Edward Hopper House Art Center** (82 N. Broadway, Nyack, 845/358-0774, www.edwardhopperhouse.org, noon-5pm Thurs.-Sun., adults $6, seniors $4, students $2, 16 and under free), as well as dozens of galleries, shops, and restaurants. Most of the businesses are gathered around the intersection of Main Street (which slopes downhill toward the river), and Broadway, which runs parallel to it. Look for a visitors information booth near the Clock Tower, where Main Street crosses Cedar.

Realist painter Edward Hopper spent his childhood in a modest clapboard house on Broadway, a few blocks north of the main retail strip. After attending high school in Nyack, he moved to New York City but returned home frequently throughout his career. A small museum in the family home, now a restored New York State Historic Site, documents Hopper's life and displays works by local artists. In summer, jazz concerts are often held in the garden.

A short drive beyond the Edward Hopper House leads to a row of riverside mansions—many of them owned by celebrities, including Rosie O'Donnell—protected by imposing brick and stone fences. At the end of this exclusive neighborhood is **Nyack Beach State Park** (Broadway, 845/358-1316, www.nysparks.com, open year-round, vehicle entrance fee $8), where local residents come to walk, relax, and fish. A two-mile trail for jogging and biking follows the river north to Hook Mountain. Trains rumble in the distance, and to the south, you can see the Tappan Zee Bridge.

New City

Between Rockland Lake State Park and Haverstraw, Route 304 West leads to New City, where the **Historical Society of Rockland County** produces historical exhibits inside the **Jacob Blauvelt House** (20 Zukor Rd., New City, 845/634-9629, www.rocklandhistory.org, noon-4pm Wed.-Sun. during museum gallery exhibitions, admission $7). This two-story brick farmhouse was built in 1832 in the Dutch style with six rooms and an 1865 carriage house, which you can view on a guided walking tour of the property. Exhibits cover a broad span of time and address a range of topics relevant to the local experience. Native American culture, Dutch bibles, Civil War diaries, 19th-century furnishings, the agrarian lifestyle, and former industries (such as brickmaking, harvesting ice, mining, and quarrying) are all represented. To get there, take Exit 10 from the Palisades Interstate Parkway.

Haverstraw Bay

Natural resources and innovation in the process of brickmaking positioned Haverstraw at the forefront of the construction industry through most of the 19th century. In 1771, clay was discovered in the Hudson offshore from Haverstraw, and the ability to mold bricks into a standard size allowed Rockland County to play a pivotal role in the building of New York City. At its peak before the advent of steel and the Great Depression, the local industry supported 42 independent brickyards. The **Haverstraw Brick Museum** (12 Main St., Haverstraw, 845/947-3505, www.haverstrawbrickmuseum.org, 1pm-4pm Wed. and Sat.-Sun., admission $2), open three afternoons a week, documents the history of the industry. A ferry to the Ossining Metro-North station departs from Short Clove Road.

★ Stony Point Battlefield State Historical Site

Located on Haverstraw Bay is an all-important Revolutionary War site: the **Stony Point Battlefield State Historical Site** (Park Rd. off Rte. 9W, Stony Point, 845/786-2521, www.nysparks.com, 10am-5pm Wed.-Sat. and 1pm-5pm Sun. Apr. 15-Oct. 31, free admission) is a riverside park and museum that includes the oldest lighthouse on the Hudson (1826). On the night of July 15, 1779, Brigadier General Anthony Wayne led a small group of colonial soldiers in a midnight assault on the British troops who had taken control of the point. In a textbook operation, Wayne's men waded silently through marsh and mud to catch the British by surprise. A small but important win, the victory restored morale among American troops.

It takes about 10 minutes to walk from the parking lot to the lighthouse, where visitors are rewarded with a view of Haverstraw Bay. Interpretive signs inside the park document the battle, and staff members occasionally dress up in colonial costumes to set the mood. There are two entrances to the park from Route 9W: A historic marker indicates the southern turnoff, while the northern one is more difficult to spot.

THE RAMAPO MOUNTAINS

Rockland's greatest outdoor treasure is an enormous green space that straddles the border with Orange County, running southwest from the Bear Mountain Bridge almost to the New Jersey state line. Thanks in part to families including the Rockefellers, Vanderbilts, and Harrimans, more than 50,000 rugged acres are divided into two adjoining state parks: Harriman (46,000 acres) and Bear Mountain (5,000 acres).

★ Harriman State Park

The first section of the Appalachian Trail was cleared here in 1923, and today, hikers can access 200 miles of trails and more than 30 lakes and reservoirs inside the second largest park in the New York state system. Seven Lakes Drive runs the length of **Harriman State Park** (Rte. 9W, Bear Mountain, 845/786-2701, www.nysparks.com, fees vary by season) and provides access to the main recreation areas, including Lake Sebago, Lake Welch, Lake Tiorati, and the Anthony Wayne Recreation Area.

Camping, swimming, and picnics are permitted. Wilderness accommodations include shelters, cabins, and campsites. There are two entrances to the park: from Route 17 in Sloatsburg or from the Palisades Interstate Parkway near West Haverstraw. Park only in designated areas. The park often fills to capacity on busy holiday weekends; a midweek visit affords more tranquility, but if you do arrive with the masses, you can quickly escape by heading into the backcountry.

Bear Mountain State Park

Formed in 1910 as a reaction against the proposed relocation of Sing Sing prison from Ossining, the smaller but well-developed **Bear Mountain** (Rte. 9W, Bear Mountain, 845/786-2701, www.nysparks.com, dawn-dusk, vehicle entrance $8) sees as many visitors per year as the most popular national parks. The sprawling parking lot gives an indication of how crowded the park can get on hot summer weekends.

Near the entrance, a stone lodge overlooking Hessian Lake houses the **Bear Mountain Inn** (Bear Mountain, 845/786-2731, www.visitbearmountain.com, $189-450)—which was *the* place to stay in 1920s New York. Prospective guests had to complete

Bear Mountain Bridge

an application and provide a personal recommendation for the privilege of spending the night. The price of $3.50 a day bought a room with all meals. The lodge reopened in 2012 after a six-year closure for extensive renovations totaling $12 million. Changes include 15 new luxury guest rooms and suites, a restaurant, spa, 20,000-square-foot event space, and souvenir shop.

Behind the inn, Perkins Memorial Drive winds its way to the top of Bear Mountain and a commanding view of the highlands. Hikers can reach the summit in about three hours, starting at Hessian Lake. The **Bear Mountain Trailside Museum** (845/786-2701, www.trailsidezoo.org, 10am-4:30pm daily, ages 13 and up $1, 6-12 $0.50, under 5 free, parking $8) entertains kids with exhibits on black bears, beavers, coyotes, and other animals. The **merry-go-round** (845/786-2731, 10am-5pm Wed.-Sun. mid-June-Labor Day, other times of year open weekends and holidays only 10am-5pm, $1 per person per ride) is decorated with hand-painted scenes of the park and has 42 seats, each hand-carved in the shape of a native animal. Additional activities include swimming, paddleboats, ice-skating, and numerous seasonal festivals. Look for the entrance to Bear Mountain State Park on Route 9W, about half a mile from the traffic circle at the **Bear Mountain Bridge.**

Common wisdom said it would take the Bear Mountain Hudson River Bridge Company 30 years to build a span across the narrowest part of the Hudson—it was expected to be the longest suspension bridge in its day. Engineers finished in 20 months, and the first crossing over the river opened to traffic in 1924. The Appalachian Trail crosses the river at this point, and many hikers stop to admire the views of the highlands from the span.

THE ROUTE 59 CORRIDOR

The old Nyack Turnpike, built to transport manufactured goods from the Ramapo Mountains to the Hudson River, is now a busy thoroughfare that connects the towns of Suffern, Spring Valley, and Nanuet to Nyack. Along Route 59 are several suburban communities with sprawling shopping centers.

Historic **Suffern** has a handful of shops and restaurants, as well as Rockland County's largest movie complex, the 1927 **Lafayette Theatre** (Rte. 59 and Washington Ave., Suffern, 845/369-8234, www.lafayettetheater-suffern.com, adults $10, kids under 12 and seniors $8). The **Suffern Railroad Museum** (Orange Ave., Suffern, 845/369-7076) is housed in the original Wells Fargo Express Mail Depot, which was restored in 1998. For a faster east-west route, take I-287, which runs parallel to Route 59.

The **Holocaust Museum & Study Center** (145 College Rd., Brucker Hall, Room 6103, Suffern, 845/574-4099, www.holocauststudies.org, 9:30am-4pm Mon.-Thurs., 9:30am-noon Fri., noon-4pm Sun., closed Sundays in July and Aug., adults $5, students and seniors $3), now housed at the Rockland Community College in Suffern, displays documents, artifacts, and films as a powerful reminder of the tragedy. Particularly moving is the Children's Wall, built as a memorial to the youngest victims of the Holocaust.

SPORTS AND RECREATION

With two large state parks and several smaller green spaces, Rockland offers a surprising variety of possibilities for outdoor entertainment. You can do just about everything in Bear Mountain and Harriman State Parks: hike, bike, boat, camp, picnic, swim, fish, skate, ski, and play.

Winter Sports

When the Hudson ices over and snow blankets the highlands, cross-country skiers head to the two-mile trail at **Nyack Beach State Park** for a morning of exercise.

Hiking

Harriman State Park is a great place to hike in mid- to late fall, since no hunting is allowed within its boundaries. A number of daylong routes, including the scenic Lichen Trail, lead to the summit of Surebridge Mountain. Claudius Smith's Den is another popular excursion into the wilderness. The hike begins at the Tuxedo train station (Orange County) along the red-dot trail and ends at the hideout of a Revolutionary War-era outlaw.

For an overnight hike, head to the Cornell trailhead near the **Iona Island National Estuarine Sanctuary** off Route 9W, follow it to a ghost town called Doodletown, and camp at a shelter near Timp Brook. Maps are available from the **New York-New Jersey Trail Conference** (156 Ramapo Valley Rd., Mahwah, NJ, 201/512-9348, www.nynjtc.org). Park only in designated lots for hikers and camp only in public camping areas.

Hook Mountain State Park (Rte. 9W, Nyack, 845/268-3020, www.nynjtc.org, dawn-dusk, fees vary by season) is well known as a place to watch hawks soar above the treetops. Enter through Rockland Lake State Park and follow signs to the executive golf course. As a courtesy, park away from the clubhouse and look for a yellow mark on the curb next to the flagpole in the cul-de-sac. Proceed to the woods and follow the yellow-blazed trail to the blue blazed trail to the summit. Another entrance is found inside Nyack Beach State Park.

Cycling

Piermont's scenic roads are popular with cyclists, but beware of the steep fine for riding double file. Stop in to chat with the crew at **Piermont Bicycle Connection** (215 Ash St., Piermont, 845/365-0900, www.piermontbike.com, 11am-6pm Mon.-Fri., 9am-6pm Sat.-Sun.) and pick up maps and supplies before you ride. None of the shops in the area rent road bikes.

The **Rockland Bicycling Club** hosts a 3 Bridges Century ride in July, following a figure-eight route across the Hudson River and back. The ride starts at the Bear Mountain Bridge, and also crosses the Newburgh-Beacon Bridge and the Walkway Over the Hudson. Visit www.rocklandbike.org for information. The club also posts other routes and cue sheets for local and visiting cyclists.

Golf

Spook Rock Golf Course (233 Spook Rock Rd., Montebello, 845/357-6466, www.spookrockgolf.com, $55) has large, fast greens with tight fairways. The course consistently ranks in the top public courses in the state. **Rockland Lake State Park Golf Course** (Rte. 9W and Lake Rd., Congers, 845/268-7275, www.nysparks.com, weekends $22-39, weekdays $20-33) is a 6,864-yard, par 72 course with 18 holes. A second nine-hole executive course has plenty of bunkers to keep golfers on their toes.

Swimming and Boating

Piermont Marsh is a unique aquatic habitat within walking distance of Piermont's shops and restaurants. The best way to explore it is by canoe or kayak, which you can rent from Captain Bill at **Paradise Boats** (15 Paradise Ave., Piermont, 845/359-0073, www.paradisecanoeandkayak.com, 9am-5pm Sat.-Sun. and holidays May-June and Sept.-Oct., 8am-5pm Wed.-Sun. July-Aug., $15-24 per hour). Look for a sign at the corner of Piermont and Paradise. September and October are the best months to go for a paddle.

ENTERTAINMENT AND EVENTS

Performing Arts

Children's Shakespeare Theater (Palisades, 845/262-0278, www.childrensshakespeare.org) is an organization of children and teens (ages 8-18) who produce and present a number of Shakespeare plays each season, all with the intention of fostering an interest in the dramatic arts from a young age. Call or visit the website to inquire about current productions.

Bars and Nightlife

Turning Point (468 Piermont Ave., Piermont, 845/359-1089, www.turningpointcafe.com) lures acclaimed jazz performers to a cozy space in Piermont Village. You can have dinner on the porch before the show. Alternatively, the art deco **Freelance Café and Wine Bar** (506 Piermont Ave., Piermont, 845/365-3250, www.xaviars.com, lunch noon-3pm daily, dinner 5:30pm-10pm Tue.-Thurs., 5:30pm-10:30pm Fri., 5:30pm-11pm Sat., 5pm-10pm Sun., small plates $8-18, large plates $22-30) has a great selection of wines by the glass and a tempting menu of small plates, should hunger strike. **Hudson House of Nyack** (134 Main St., 845/353-1355, www.hudsonhousenyack.com, lunch 11:30am-3:30pm Thurs.-Sun., dinner 5:30pm-10pm Tues.-Thurs., 5:30pm-11pm Fri.-Sat., 4:30pm-9:30pm Sun., bar menu available between lunch and dinner, $12-31) offers jazz on Thursday nights to accompany its New American menu. Grab a stool at the curvy copper bar and sip a glass of wine or creative cocktail at **8 North Broadway** (8 N. Broadway, Nyack, 845/353-1200, www.8northbroadway.com).

For a family-friendly night out, **Grand Prix New York** (333 N. Bedford Rd., Mount Kisco, 914/241-3131, www.gpny.com, 3pm-10pm Mon.-Thurs., noon-midnight Fri., 10am-midnight Sat., 10am-9pm Sun.) is an indoor go-kart racing track and bowling alley. Racers have a choice of multiple tracks, including a kids track, and prices are $8-35 depending on the track and if you come during the track's peak hours Friday evening through Sunday. The bowling alley offers regular bowling along with leagues and private lessons, and there is a restaurant and full bar on-site. Other activities for kids include an arcade, art studio, and bounce house.

Festivals

Suffern produces the **Native American Festival** (845/786-2701) at Harriman State Park each August. More than 1,000 artists, performers, and educators participate. The event culminates in a dance competition that draws competitors from across North and South America. The **New York City Triathlon Club** (Apr.-Oct., www.nytc.org for races and dates) also runs a summer race series at Harriman. Entrants must be over 18.

Bear Mountain State Park puts on a lively **Octoberfest** (845/786-2701), with music and dancing in the crisp fall air. The **Rockland Audubon Society** (www.rocklandaudubon.org) runs field trips for wildlife observation.

SHOPPING

Farm Stands

Don't miss the twice-weekly summer **Nyack Farmers Market** (845/353-2221, www.nyackchamber.org, 8:30am-2:30pm Thurs. Apr. 1-Nov. 26 and 8am-1pm, June 7-Nov. 22), in the municipal parking lot at the corner of Main and Cedar Streets. You can buy 20 different types of mushrooms from a single grower, plus the usual assortment of locally grown fruits and vegetables. In winter, the **Nyack Winter Farmers Market** brings the party indoors at the Nyack Center (55 Depew Ave., 8am-2pm Thurs., Dec.-May). Also in Nyack, you can find specialty foods at the local health foods store, Back to Earth (3 S. Broadway, Nyack, 845/353-3311, www.back2earthonline.com).

Additional Rockland County farmers markets include:

- Wednesdays in Spring Valley (8:30am-3pm, July 9-Nov. 19)
- Saturdays at Stony Point (9am-2pm, July 5-Oct. 25) and Suffern (8:30am-1pm, May 17-Oct. 25)
- Sundays in the Village of Haverstraw (9am-1pm, July 5-Oct. 25) and Piermont (9:30am-3pm, May 11-Nov. 23)

Check www.rocklandtourism.com for current farmers market schedules, as hours and locations tend to change with every season.

Antiques and Galleries

Art galleries and antiques shops abound in Nyack and Piermont. In addition, the **Nyack Tobacco Company** (140 Main St., Nyack, 845/358-9300, 11am-6pm Mon., 11am-8pm Tues.-Thurs., 11am-10pm Fri.-Sat., 11am-6pm Sun.) carries one of the best selections

Antiques Advice

Collectors, casual shoppers, and bargain hunters all can find interesting shopping throughout the Hudson River Valley. The list includes vintage clothing, jewelry, furniture, artwork, glassware, home decorations, and more.

Some stores are set up as beautiful galleries, while others are run as auctions or sprawling multidealer affairs with a maze of different rooms to explore. A few even have cafés on-site.

Cold Spring, Hudson, and Millerton have a high concentration of upscale shops; the dealers in Tannersville, Warwick, and Saugerties meet a wider range of price points. Most businesses open during standard retail hours, but some are by appointment only. If you're looking for something specific, call ahead.

of handmade cigars outside of New York City. Its cigars are stored in a digitally controlled humidor. Meanwhile, book lovers will find contemporary and classic titles piled floor to ceiling at **Pickwick Bookshop** (8 S. Broadway, Nyack, 845/358-9126, pickwickbookshop.wordpress.com, 9:30am-7pm Mon.-Fri., 9:30am-8pm Sat., 11am-6pm Sun.).

On the Route 59 corridor, the **Palisades Center** (1000 Palisade Center Dr., West Nyack, 845/348-1000, www.palisadescenter.com, 10am-9:30pm Mon.-Sat., 11am-7pm Sun.) opened in 1998 as a four-level megamall with 250 stores, anchored by Lord & Taylor, Target, and H&M.

ACCOMMODATIONS

Accommodations with personality are surprisingly hard to come by in Rockland County. Like Westchester, Rockland has mostly conference centers and chains, from Marriott and Holiday Inn to Best Western and Super 8. Travelers who seek a unique lodging experience should continue on to Orange County or cross the river to Putnam.

$100-150

Next to Hessian Lake in the Bear Mountain State Park, the Bear Mountain Inn's **Overlook Lodge** (Bear Mountain, 845/786-2731, www.visitbearmountain.com, $150) has basic but comfortable motel-style rooms that are simply furnished with two double beds and private baths. The location and views are the most appealing quality of this property; however, be prepared for a noisy environment on weekends in the high season. Weekend rates are accordingly high, but if you can go midweek you might score a pretty good deal. Rates include continental breakfast.

FOOD

Along the River: Route 9W

The food scene in Nyack has blossomed of late. **Hudson House of Nyack** (134 Main St., Nyack, 845/353-1355, www.hudsonhousenyack.com, 4:30pm-9:30pm Sun., 5:30pm-10pm Tues.-Thurs., 5:30pm-11pm Fri.-Sat., brunch 11:30am-3:30pm Sat.-Sun., $15-33) prepares an outstanding Hudson River Valley duck breast. The restaurant occupies the former village hall and jailhouse. You might start with the arugula and endive chopped salad or the poached beet salad, then try the shrimp and grits or the steak au poivre.

Chef Doug Chi Nguyen heads **Wasabi** (110 Main St., Nyack, 845/358-7977, www.wasabichi.com, lunch noon-2:30pm Mon.-Fri., dinner 5pm-10pm Mon.-Thurs., 5pm-11pm Fri.-Sat., 4pm-9:30pm Sun., mains $20-30), a trendy sushi restaurant with a sister in New York City. Standouts on the menu include the truffle gyoza and the wasabi boat. Inquire about the nightly specials if you are feeling adventurous.

Though small and dark on the outside, **Thai House** (12 Park St., Nyack, 845/358-9100, www.thaihousenyack.com, lunch 11:30am-2:30pm Fri.-Sun., dinner 5pm-9:30pm Mon.-Thurs., 5pm-11pm Fri.,

2:30pm-11pm Sat., 2:30pm-9:30pm Sun., mains $15-20) is actually a nicely appointed restaurant serving a full Thai menu. The Massaman and Panang curries come highly recommended.

Since 2005, **Lulu's Café** (726 West Nyack Rd., Nyack, 845/358-5822, www.luluscafeny.com, 11:30am-9pm Tues.-Fri., 11am-9pm Sat., 9am-3pm Sun.) does homestyle cooking in a retro café setting. Weekend brunch draws the local crowd with huevos rancheros and whimsical treats like chunky monkey pancakes laden with bananas and chocolate chunks.

Xaviars at Piermont (506 Piermont Ave., 845/359-7007, www.xaviars.com, 6pm-9pm Wed.-Sat., noon-2pm Fri. and Sun., 5pm-8pm Sun., prix fixe $90-100 pp) is part of a group of New York State restaurants owned and run by Chef Peter Kelly. This is a formal affair, with multicourse tasting menus that emphasize locally grown ingredients. The service here is the best around, part of what makes the restaurant a popular venue for special occasions. Next door and run by the same entrepreneur, ★ **Freelance Café and Wine Bar** (506 Piermont Ave., Piermont, 845/365-3250, www.xaviars.com, lunch noon-3pm daily, dinner 5:30pm-10pm Tue.-Thurs., 5:30pm-10:30pm Fri., 5:30pm-11pm Sat., 5pm-10pm Sun., small plates $8-18, large plates $22-30), is the place to meet a friend for lunch or drinks. Order small plates like smoked trout salad or jumbo coconut shrimp, or large plates like a classic steak frites or Long Island fluke. And don't miss the duck fat roasted fingerling potatoes on the list of sides. Be prepared to wait for a table, as the café does not take reservations.

If you're passing through Nyack at lunchtime, centrally located **Art Café of Nyack** (65 S. Broadway, Nyack, 845/353-4230, www.artcafenyack.com) has Blue Bottle pour over coffee and Middle Eastern specialties like shakshooka (baked eggs) and labane (yogurt).

The '76 House (110 Main St., Tappan, 845/359-5476, www.76house.com, $19-30) is the oldest tavern in New York State. Highlights on the menu include wild boar sausage, locally raised rainbow trout, and a double-cut pork chop with apple marmalade. Listen to jazz on Saturday nights, or try the popular Sunday brunch (11am-3pm). Lunch and dinner hours are Monday to Saturday 11:30am-3pm and 5pm-9pm (Fridays until 9:30pm and Saturdays until 10pm). Dinner is served on Sunday 4pm-9pm.

The Ramapo Mountains

Just shy of the New Jersey state line, the **Mount Fuji Steakhouse** (296 Rte. 17, Hillburn, 845/357-4270, www.mtfujirestaurants.com, lunch noon-2:30pm Mon.-Fri., dinner 5pm-10pm Mon.-Thurs., 5pm-11pm Fri., 4pm-11pm Sat., 4pm-10pm Sun., $22-40) is perched on a hilltop above Route 17. Seating around a private hibachi station and servers tossing cleavers in the air make it the perfect venue to celebrate a birthday or a family reunion. You'll likely wait for a table, even with a reservation. Arrive in daylight to catch the mountain views.

At the southern end of Harriman State Park, the town of Sloatsburg has a handful of casual dining options. **Characters** (formerly The Glenwood, 94 Orange Turnpike, Sloatsburg, 845/753-5200, www.charactersresturant.com, 11:30am-10pm Sun.-Thurs., 11:30am-11pm Fri.-Sat., $8-10) prepares a comprehensive American menu of steaks, seafood, and chicken entrées. Another option is **Auntie El's Farm Market** (171 Rte. 17, Sloatsburg, 845/753-2122, 8am-6pm Mon.-Tues., 8am-7pm Wed.-Sun.), which takes the traditional farm stand to a new level. Pastries and pies are baked fresh daily, and a small store is stocked with fresh produce, candy, seasonal items, and small trinkets. Don't miss the apple cider doughnuts.

In a pinch, you can also grab a quick bite to eat at the concession stand at Lake Welch State Beach in Harriman State Park. For a greater variety of dining options, Suffern, at the southern edge of the park along Route 59, is the next closest town.

The Route 59 Corridor

Don't miss out on the best opportunity in the area for a sweet fix at **Rockland Bakery** (94 Demarest Mill Rd., Nanuet, 845/623-5800, www.rocklandbakery.com, 6am-10:30pm Sun.-Fri., 6am-midnight Sat.), which houses aisles of fresh-baked breads and pastries, from bagels to pies. Every variety of bread imaginable is available, but the challah in particular earns consistent praise.

Sakana Japanese Fusion (25 Rockland Plaza, Nanuet, 845/623-2882, www.sakanafusion.com, lunch 11:45am-3pm Mon.-Fri., dinner 4:45pm-10pm Mon.-Thurs., 4:45pm-11pm Fri., 1:15pm-11pm Sat., 1:15pm-9:30pm Sun., $12-25) offers a large and detailed menu of classic sushi dishes as well as unique creations like the angel roll--shrimp tempura topped with spicy tuna, tempura flakes, and black caviar. A number of cooked rolls, teriyaki dishes, and curries are also available.

For a traditional Indian lunch buffet, try **Priya** (36 Lafayette Ave., Suffern, 845/357-5700, www.priyaindiancuisineny.com, noon-3pm daily [à la carte menu on weekends], 5pm-10pm Tues.-Thurs., 5pm-11pm Fri.-Sat., 1pm-9:30pm Sun., $13-23).

Marcello's Ristorante of Suffern (21 Lafayette Ave., Suffern, 845/357-9108, www.marcellosgroup.com, noon-2:30pm Mon.-Sat., 5pm-9:30pm Mon.-Thurs., 5pm-10pm Fri.-Sat., 3pm-8:30pm Sun., $18-30) is a white linen affair with a menu of true Italian specialties. Look for the burgundy awning.

For casual, kid-friendly dining, **Pasta Cucina** (www.pastacucina.com, noon-10pm Mon.-Thurs., noon-11pm Fri., 5pm-11pm Sat., 4pm-9pm Sun., $10-16) offers great value on family-style meals in two Rockland County locations: Suffern (8 Airmont Rd., Suffern, 845/369-1313) and Stony Point (32 S. Liberty Dr., Stony Point, 845/786-6060).

INFORMATION AND SERVICES

The **Rockland County Office of Tourism** (18 New Hempstead Rd., New City, 845/708-7300 or 800/295-5723, www.rocktourism.com) is headquartered in New City. In Nyack, look for a visitors information booth by the Clock Tower at Main and Cedar.

GETTING THERE AND AROUND

Bus

Several companies run buses in Rockland County: **Transit of Rockland** (845/364-3333) and the **Spring Valley Jitney** (845/573-5800) provide local service, while ShortLine Bus and Adirondack Trailways connect to parts north.

Train

Metro-North (800/638-7646) and **New Jersey Transit** (201/762-5100) offer rail service to Rockland County. A ferry runs between Haverstraw and the **Hudson Line station** in Ossining (800/533-3779, www.nywaterway.com), and cabs are readily available in major towns, including Nyack. Stewart Airport is the best place to rent a car.

Car

The Palisades Interstate Parkway (Exits 4-15) connects Rockland County to the George Washington Bridge, and the Garden State Parkway heads to New Jersey. I-287 crosses the Tappan Zee Bridge to Westchester County. You can get frequent metropolitan area traffic reports on the radio at AM 880 and AM 1010.

The Hudson Highlands

Between the towns of Peekskill in Westchester County and Beacon in Dutchess County—a 15-mile stretch—a solid granite mountain range called the Appalachian Plateau crosses the Hudson. Here, the river has carved a narrow and deep path through the range to form the Hudson Highlands, a fairytale landscape that recalls the signature banks of the Rhine. Storm King Mountain on the west and Breakneck Ridge on the east rise up on opposite shores near Cold Spring and West Point, giving Orange and Putnam Counties some of the most beautiful vistas—and colorful history—of any county in the region.

It was here, in the narrowest part of the river, that American troops stretched an iron chain—each link measuring two feet long and weighing more than 140 pounds—across the entire width of the river. The goal was to prevent British ships from sailing north up the Hudson. Though it may well have been an effective deterrent, the chain was never tested because none of the British ships managed to advance as far as West Point after the chain was set.

A few miles north, where the river widens to form Newburgh Bay, tiny Pollepel Island has an abandoned Scottish-style castle and what remains of the former Bannerman Island Arsenal, an unusual family business that dealt in military supplies. You can see what remains of the fortress by taking river cruises and kayak tours that pass close by.

The Hudson Highlands area boasts four state parks, a section of the Appalachian Trail, the Black Dirt onion-growing region, and a lively summer scene around Greenwood Lake.

PLANNING YOUR TIME

Few travelers attempt to see the entire Hudson Highlands area in one trip. Weekend itineraries are best limited to one section. You might target several sights along the river, or plan to visit one of the expansive state parks. West Point, the Storm King Art Center, and Cold Spring Village are top destinations that can take from a few hours to a full day to explore. In summer, a day at Greenwood Lake followed by an evening of shopping and fine dining in Warwick make a good combination. Route 17 through western Orange County is a major access route to Sullivan County and the Catskill region.

Previous: Greenwood Lake, Orange County; Bannerman Castle. **Above:** Perkins Memorial Observatory at the summit of Bear Mountain.

Look for ★ to find recommended sights, activities, dining, and lodging.

Highlights

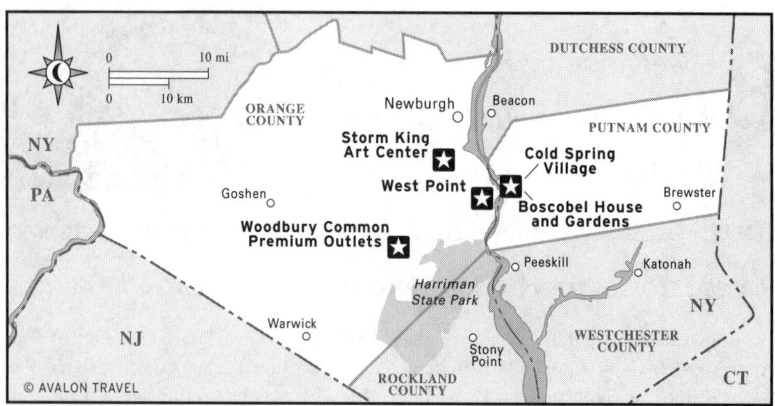

★ **West Point:** A gold mine of American military history sits in one of the most beautiful spots along the Hudson (page 64).

★ **Storm King Art Center:** This outdoor sculpture museum features works from well-known American and British artists (page 67).

★ **Woodbury Common Premium Outlets:** A sprawling complex of designer outlets draws shoppers from miles around (page 82).

★ **Boscobel House and Gardens:** The home of the annual Hudson Valley Shakespeare Festival is a restored neoclassical mansion called Boscobel (page 85).

★ **Cold Spring Village:** Visit antiques shops and gourmet restaurants just steps from the Metro-North commuter line (page 86).

The Hudson Highlands

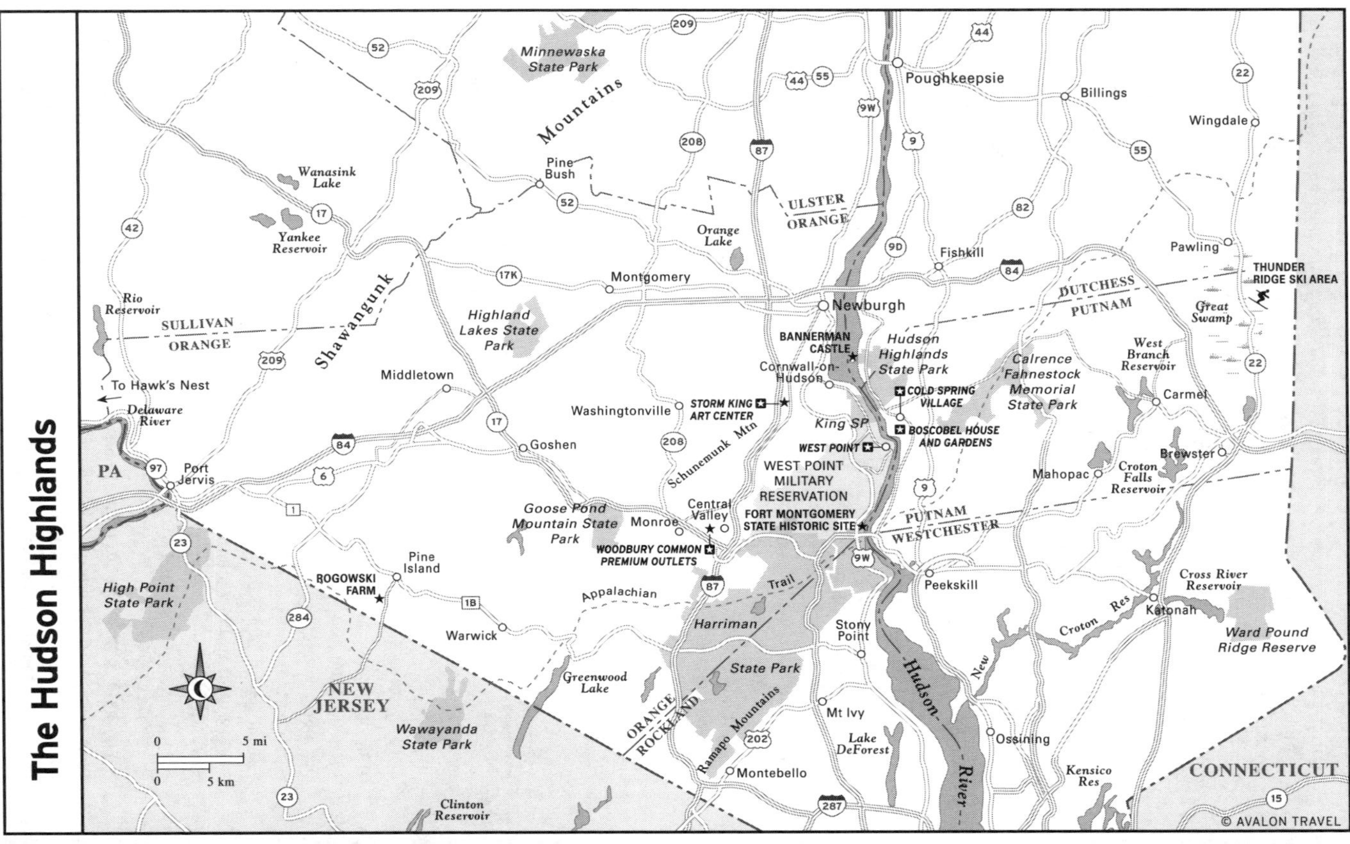

Putnam County measures less than 20 miles north to south and is well worth a full day's visit. Cold Spring is the county's most popular destination, and a day passes quickly in and around the riverside town. With an early start at the Bear Mountain Bridge, you'll have time for brief stops at Manitoga, Boscobel Restoration, and Constitution Marsh Center & Sanctuary, followed by a walk and a meal along Cold Spring's Main Street. Serious antiques shoppers will need more time, as will anyone who plans to hike the Hudson Highlands or paddle the river.

To add Clarence Fahnestock Memorial State Park and eastern Putnam County to the itinerary, follow Route 301 west out of Cold Spring through the towns of Kent, Carmel, and Brewster.

Scenic Drives

Route 9D in Putnam County, from Beacon to the Bear Mountain Bridge, winds its way through the dramatic Hudson Highlands. On the other side of the Hudson, Route 218 takes you over Storm King Mountain, with spectacular views of West Point and the Bear Mountain Bridge.

Orange County

The only county in the Hudson River Valley with frontage on both the Hudson and Delaware Rivers begins 50 miles north and across the river from New York City, encompassing 816 square miles of fertile fields, rolling hills, and quiet suburban communities. Orange County's largest commercial centers are Newburgh, Middletown, and Port Jervis. Goshen is the county seat.

History is one of the primary reasons travelers visit Orange County. It is home of the prestigious U.S. Military Academy at West Point and several related sights, which draw some three million visitors a year.

ALONG THE RIVER: ROUTE 9W

Orange and Rockland Counties share a border at the Bear Mountain Bridge on the west side of the Hudson River. Several thoroughfares meet here in a traffic circle at the approach to the bridge: Route 9W runs along the riverbank, the Palisades Interstate Parkway heads south toward New Jersey, and Route 6 runs west to join Route 17 (the Quickway). Appalachian Trail hikers also pass through on their way to or from Harriman State Park. (The AT crosses the Hudson at the Bear Mountain Bridge.)

Fort Montgomery State Historic Site

A few miles south of West Point, you can view the remains of an old fort, from which American soldiers sought—unsuccessfully—to prevent the British from advancing up the Hudson during the Revolutionary War. A visitors center contains artifacts found in the area of the fort, including shoe buckles and cuff links to glasses and flatware. Visits to **Fort Montgomery** (690 Route 9W, 845/446-2134, www.nysparks.com, grounds 8am-sunset daily, visitors center 9am-5pm Wed.-Sun., $3) begin with a short film about the site and its role in early American history.

★ West Point

A few miles north of the Bear Mountain Bridge, the Hudson flows through its narrowest and deepest stretch (more than 200 feet), creating the strategic military position of West Point. In revolutionary times, American forces strung a 40-ton chain 500 yards across the river to keep the British at bay. After the colonial victory, President Thomas Jefferson believed the young nation needed to build its own military capability and wean itself from dependence on foreign expertise. He signed

A Scene on the Banks of the Hudson

Cool shades and dews are round my way,
And silence of the early day;
Mid the dark rocks that watch his bed,
Glitters the mighty Hudson spread,
Unrippled, save by drops that fall
From shrubs that fringe his mountain wall;
And o'er the clear still water swells
The music of the Sabbath bells.
All, save this little nook of land,
Circled with trees, on which I stand;
All, save that line of hills which lie
Suspended in the mimic sky—
Seems a blue void, above, below,
Through which the white clouds come and go;
And from the green world's farthest steep
I gaze into the airy deep.
Loveliest of lovely things are they,
On earth, that soonest pass away.
The rose that lives its little hour
Is prized beyond the sculptured flower.
Even love, long tried and cherished long,
Becomes more tender and more strong
At thought of that insatiate grave
From which its yearnings cannot save.
River! in this still hour thou hast
Too much of heaven on earth to last;
Nor long may thy still waters lie,
An image of the glorious sky.
Thy fate and mine are not repose,
And ere another evening close,
Thou to thy tides shalt turn again,
And I to seek the crowd of men.

William Cullen Bryant (1827)

the United States Military Academy into law in 1802.

The academy's first curriculum produced civil engineers, who went on to build much of the nation's transportation infrastructure. West Point established its reputation for military excellence during the Civil War, when graduates including Robert E. Lee and Ulysses S. Grant fought against each other during almost every battle. Superintendents during the 20th century broadened the program to include academic, physical, and military education, and the first woman graduated from the academy in 1980.

Today, the academy runs guided bus tours daily, except on football Saturdays, holidays, and during graduation week. The one-hour tour ($14), led by **West Point Tours** (Highland Falls, 845/446-4724, www.westpointtours.com), begins at the visitors center, off the West Point Highway, where you can view a model cadet barracks room and gather information about the academy. A two-hour tour costs just two dollars more at $16 per person.

Behind the visitors center stands the **West Point Museum** (845/938-3590, www.usma.edu/museum, 10:30am-4:15pm daily, free), which houses four floors of warfare exhibits covering 135 military conflicts in the history of the United States. A large weapons display in the basement has a World War I tank, while the small weapons include axes, clubs, and swords that date all the way back to the Stone Age. Tours often stop at **Fort Putnam,** a key position in defending the fortress, with panoramic views of the river and campus. **Trophy Point** offers a postcard-perfect view of the Hudson Highlands.

Familiar names grace the monuments across the central part of the campus: Patton, Marshall, MacArthur, Eisenhower, Schwarzkopf. More than 2,000 names are inscribed on the massive granite shaft of the striking **Battle Monument** (1897), designed by Sanford White, who also built and furnished the opulent Vanderbilt Estate in Hyde Park). Nearby, the **Old Cadet Chapel** (8:15am-4:15pm daily), built in 1836, is one of the oldest buildings still used on campus.

Extended two-hour tours, offered twice daily June-October, include a stop at the **West Point Cemetery,** which holds graves that date back to 1782 and represent casualties of almost every war the academy's graduates have fought. Inquire about combination bus and river tours. The West Point Band plays on Sunday evenings in an outdoor amphitheater near the North Dock in West Point.

The Gothic **Thayer Hotel** (674 Thayer Rd., West Point, 845/446-4731, www.thethayerhotel.com, $150-175), built in 1926, overlooks the Hudson at the south entrance to West Point. It was named for Colonel Sylvanus Thayer, superintendent of West Point from 1817 to 1833. A $26 million facelift in 1996 restored the hotel to its former glory. Portraits of military leaders decorate the walls in the formal dining room, which is popular for holiday gatherings.

Call before you intend to arrive at West Point, because the visitors center may cancel tours at any time. Photo identification is required for entry, and your vehicle will also be searched. Allow extra time if you are taking a cruise or attending an event. To get there, exit the New York State Thruway at Exit 16.

From the back lawn of the hotel, you can see **Constitution Island** (845/446-8676, www.constitutionisland.org), the first place George Washington chose to fortify at West Point. Unfortunately, the British had the same idea and established a stronghold in 1777; the Americans won it back a year later. By the 1830s, the island fell into private hands. Henry

view of the South Fields at Storm King Art Center, all works by Mark di Suvero. Photograph by Jerry L. Thompson

Warner and his two daughters built a family estate, and for years the daughters invited cadets to the island to study the Bible. The Warners donated their house and gardens to the academy in 1908. Today's cadets complete many of their training exercises here.

Visitors must make a reservation to tour the 180-acre island. Tours take place at 1pm and 2pm on Wednesdays and Thursdays from late June through the end of September. Each tour takes about 2.25 hours. There is a suggested donation of $10. Boats depart from the South Dock inside West Point, past the Thayer Hotel. The nonprofit Constitution Island Association runs a shuttle bus from the Cold Spring rail station on select Saturdays during the summer, leaving every 10 minutes 10am-3pm.

Cornwall-on-Hudson

After West Point, Route 9W winds its way north to the base of Storm King Mountain and the quiet hamlet of Cornwall-on-Hudson. Alternatively, follow Route 218 north for a white-knuckle drive over Storm King Mountain, with gorgeous views of the fjord-like highlands. In Cornwall, the **Museum of the Hudson Highlands Nature Museum Outdoor Discovery Center** (20 Kenridge Farm Dr., Cornwall, The Boulevard, Cornwall-on-Hudson, 845/534-5506, www.scenichudson.org, noon-4pm Sat.-Sun.), hosts a variety of art and nature exhibits that explore the cultural and natural heritage of the area. The museum has two locations: At the Boulevard location near the river, the Ogden Gallery features local artists whose work focuses on the natural world. This location also has a gift shop and occasional live animal exhibits. A mile and a half away on Route 9W is the 177-acre Kenridge Farm, an outdoor classroom of native flora and fauna (Muser Drive, across from 174 Angola Rd.).

★ Storm King Art Center

The Quaker Avenue exit off Route 9W leads to the expansive sculpture gardens of the **Storm King Art Center** (1 Museum Rd., New Windsor, 845/534-3115, www.stormking.org, 10am-5:30pm Wed.-Sun. Apr. 1-Nov. 5, adults $15, seniors $12, ages 5-18 and students $8, children under 4 free). It's a perfect site for a summer picnic, but you'll have to just leave your barbecue, balls, Frisbees, pets, and radios at home. In this outdoor museum, you can walk along tree-lined paths and view larger-than-life sculptures against the dramatic landscape and ever-changing light of the Hudson Highlands. The collection represents British and American artists, both postwar and contemporary. Some of the sculptures were designed expressly for their sites in the 500-acre park. *The Arch,* one of Alexander Calder's "stabiles," measures 56 feet high. The *Joy of Life,* a monumental piece by Mark di Suvero, weighs 20 tons and stands 70 feet tall. Storm King is a popular place for organized singles' outings from New York City. The center offers guided, self-guided, and audio tours. On weekends during the summer, the center stays open until 8pm. Wear good walking shoes and dress for the weather. The museum café serves light lunch fare, including Applegate hot dogs, chicken kebabs, a hummus sandwich, and vegetarian soup.

Newburgh

Farther up the river at the intersection of Route 9W and I-84 lies Newburgh, a city that has struggled with its legacy as a manufacturing center. Jobs remain scarce, and many of the old buildings are run down, but underneath the layers of industrial age, the city retains a deep sense of history.

George Washington established **Washington's Headquarters,** his Revolutionary War headquarters, in the home of Jonathan Hasbrouck (84 Liberty St., Newburgh, 845/562-1195, www.nysparks.com, 10am-5pm Wed.-Sat., 1pm-5pm Sun. mid-Apr.-Oct., adults $4, seniors/students $3, children 12 and under free), a fieldstone fortress on a hill overlooking the river, and the building has been a national historic site since 1850. Guides in period dress lead groups through a half-hour tour of the house,

Tips for Exploring the Hudson River Valley

Proximity to a major metropolitan area brings large crowds to the best places in the region. Here are some tips to avoid the masses:

- **Get off the Thruway:** I-87 is straight with many lanes, and usually the fastest route through the valley, but older parkways and highways often make for a more pleasant drive.
- **Get out of the car:** Go ahead and stop at scenic overlooks and roadside stands. Follow handmade signs. They often lead to cool places.
- **Eat something fresh off the farm:** Try an heirloom tomato, fresh-picked strawberries, or an antique apple. You will taste the difference.
- **Talk to the innkeeper:** Bed-and-breakfast hosts in the country know a lot about the area—who's harvesting what that week, which businesses have opened and closed, and which have changed hands.
- **Get dirty:** Roll up your sleeves and feel the dirt. Volunteer on a farm, camp in the woods, or pick your own fruit.
- **Take to the river:** The land looks different when you're cruising on a small ship. Travel by boat to see fall colors, historic mansions, and birds of the Hudson.

which has been restored to reflect its setup as military headquarters. Before or after a tour, you can walk through a separate interpretive exhibit to learn more about the Revolutionary War. Across the lawn and overlooking the river is a monument built in the 1880s to honor the peace treaty that ended the Civil War.

The parking lot is somewhat tricky to find. If you're coming from I-84, follow Route 9W/32 south until Broadway. Turn left on Broadway and go about 10 blocks. Turn right on Liberty Street and after a block, look for the fenced lawn on the left and an alleyway just before Washington Street that leads to a parking lot.

The 1839 **Crawford House** (189 Montgomery St., Newburgh, 845/561-2585, www.newburghhistoricalsociety.com, 1pm-4pm Sun. Apr.-Oct., admission $5), once the residence of a shipping merchant, houses the Historical Society of Newburgh Bay and the Highlands. On display inside the classic revival building are 19th-century antiques and Hudson River School paintings. Views of Newburgh Bay are as memorable as the collection inside.

In addition to many private restorations under way, Newburgh has revived a section of its waterfront by turning several abandoned factories into an attractive boardwalk with a handful of upscale restaurants and shops. People now arrive at **Newburgh Landing** (Front St., Newburgh, 845/565-3297) by the boatful on summer weekends, where a variety of cuisines and trendy bars are just steps away from a slip in the marina. Fake palm trees—and some real ones too—are all part of the experience. Serious partiers often sleep on their boats after a night of revelry at one of the nearby clubs.

From the water's edge, you can see the beginning of the narrow Hudson Highlands to the south. Several river cruises depart from the landing. To reach the Newburgh Landing, exit I-84 at Route 9W and turn left at the second light onto North Plank Road. Go 1.25 miles and make a left onto 2nd Street to go under the train trestle.

If you continue on Route 9W instead of heading to the landing, you'll soon reach the intersection of South Street and the edge of Newburgh's onetime gem of a

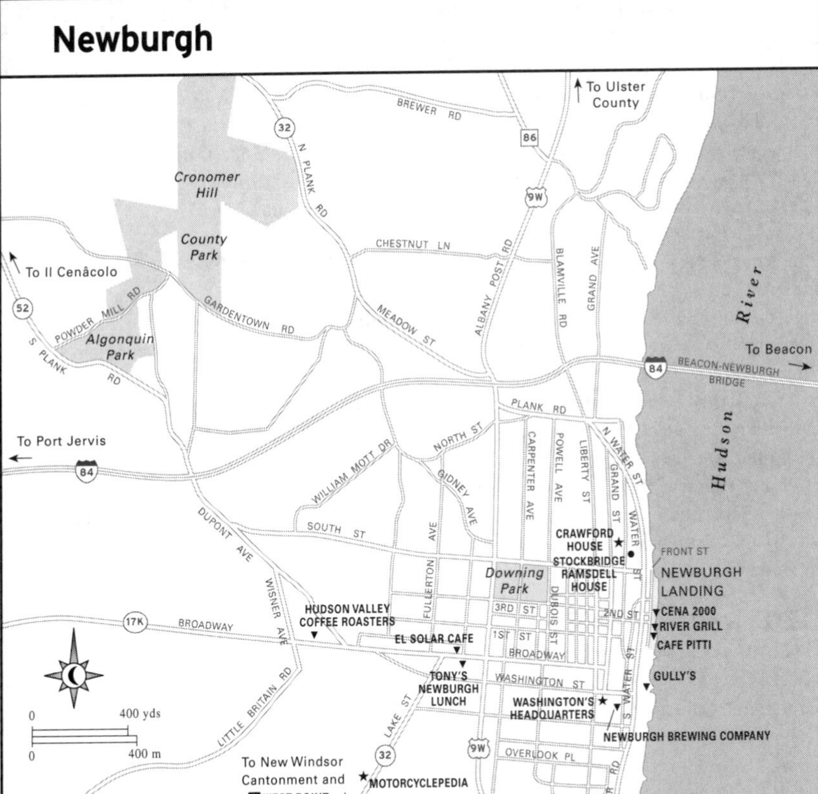

green space: 35-acre **Downing Park** (Rte. 9W and 3rd St., Newburgh, 845/565-5559, visitors center open year-round with summer hours 11am-5pm Wed.-Sun.), named for architect Andrew Jackson Downing and designed by Frederick Law Olmsted and Calvert Vaux, the creators of Central Park in New York City. The restored Downing Park Shelter House serves as the city's visitors center.

Motorcyclepedia (250 Lake St., Newburgh, 845/569-9065, www.motorcyclepediamuseum.org, 10am-5pm Fri.-Sun., $11) is a museum dedicated to two-wheeled transportation from 1897 to the present. There are some 500 choppers, vintage models, military, and police motorcycles on display.

New Windsor Cantonment and the National Purple Heart Hall of Honor

The history lesson continues a short drive from Newburgh, at the New Windsor Cantonment. George Washington's army stayed at the **New Windsor Cantonment State Historic Site** (Temple Hill Rd., Vails Gate, 845/561-1765, www.nysparks.com, 10am-5pm Mon.-Sat., 1pm-5pm Sun. Apr.-Oct.), which offers musket and artillery demonstrations and a tour of a replica of the Temple of Virtue, where Washington delivered one of his most moving speeches to troops who were losing faith in the war. The purposes of slanted bed frames, the use of charcoal for toothpaste, and the wonders of hard bread are just some of the trivia you'll pick up on a tour of the Cantonment.

With the addition of the **National Purple Heart Hall of Honor** (Temple Hill Rd., Vails Gate, 845/561-1765, www.thepurpleheart.com, 10am-5pm Mon.-Sat., 1pm-5pm Sun. Apr.-Oct.), the Cantonment offers an appealing blend of old and new. A visit to the Purple Heart Hall of Honor is an interactive experience that makes full use of the latest audiovisual technology. There are high-definition films to watch and interactive computer stations set up for visitors to find or add their loved ones. Although the hall is designed to honor all 1.7 million recipients collectively, museum staff bring individual stories to life through a series of Roll of Honor interviews recorded in an on-site video studio. An outdoor courtyard is set aside as ceremonial grounds for quiet reflection.

CENTRAL ORANGE COUNTY: ALONG ROUTE 17

Greenwood Lake

The Appalachian Trail enters New York State from New Jersey at Greenwood Lake, a long, narrow body of water that joins the two states. Surrounded by dense forest and mountains, the natural lake is shallow with a maximum depth of 57 feet and wetlands at each end. Visibility is generally good, except after heavy storms. A narrow local road hugs the eastern shore of the lake, and busy Route 210 heads into New Jersey on the western side.

The Erie Railroad brought the first wave of visitors to the lake in the 1870s, and Babe Ruth was a frequent vacationer. A number of year-round residences and second homes of city-dwellers crowd the shoreline today, but several access areas are open to the public for swimming and boating.

From Greenwood Lake, Route 17A climbs over Sterling Mountain to the east, winding through a 19,000-acre state park that is the site of a small ski resort and the annual Renaissance Faire before meeting up with Route 17 and the New York State Thruway at the town of Tuxedo.

Fifties-era billboards and diners like the battered Red Apple Rest line this stretch of Route 17. During the peak of the Catskill summer resorts in the 1960s, traffic leaving New York City poured through town en route to cooler air in the mountains.

Harriman State Park

Established in 1910 through a land grant from the Harriman family, Harriman State Park is the second largest park in the state of New York, with dozens of lakes, reservoirs, and ponds, and 200 miles of trails. Look for the entrance to **Harriman State Park** (Rte. 9W, Bear Mountain, 845/786-2701, www.nysparks.com, admission $8) on the east side of Route 17A. A much larger neighbor to Bear Mountain State Park at the Rockland County line, Harriman boasts the oldest stretch of the Appalachian Trail, which was cleared in 1923. The **Reeves Meadow Visitor Center** on Seven Lakes Drive near Sloatsburg on the west side of the park has maps, books, toys, and hiking essentials (845/753-5122, weekends and holidays 8am-5:30pm).

Because of its proximity to New York City, the park does tend to attract crowds on summer weekends. Most people head for the areas around Lake Welch, Bear Mountain, and Hessian Lake, and the network of trails that depart from Reeves Meadow. Avoid these areas, and you can find solitude in the woods. Dogs are allowed inside the park on leash.

The facilities at Lake Sebago have been closed since 2011 following damage from Hurricane Irene. Lake Welch has a popular swimming beach and cabins for camping. Lean-to shelters on a dozen of the trails are available on a first-come, first-served basis, free of charge.

You can get to the park by train from Harriman station, Tuxedo station, Manitou station (limited service), or Peekskill station ($25 cab ride to Bear Mountain). There is no entry fee to the park; however, parking in one of the larger lots costs $8 per day.

Warwick

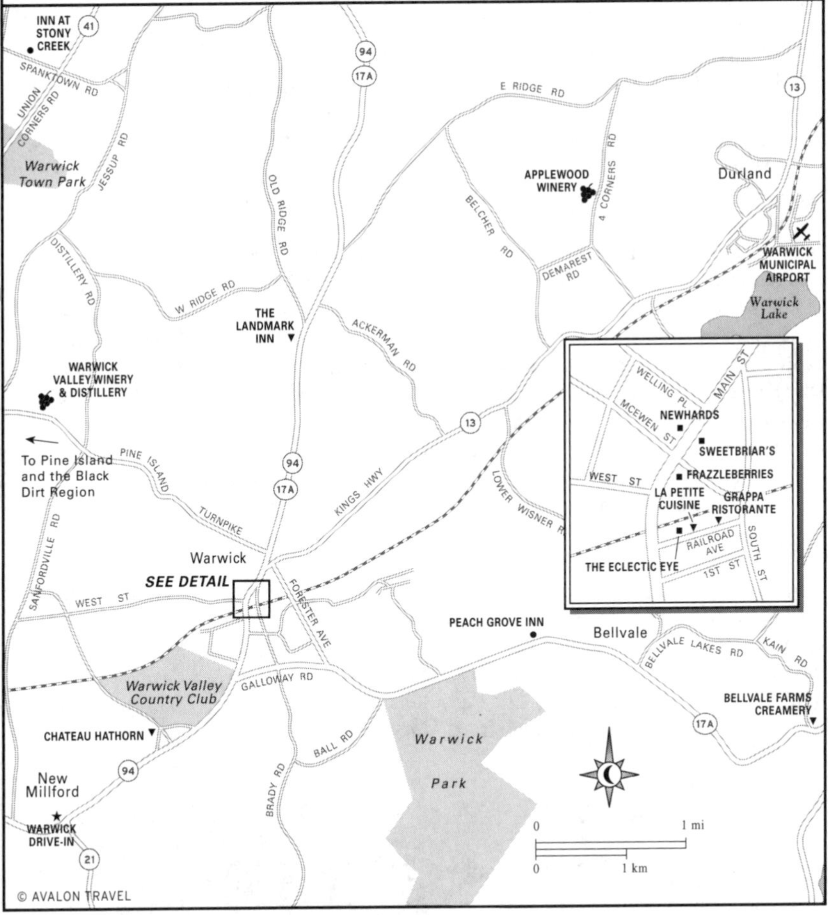

Warwick

In the opposite direction from Sterling Mountain on 17A—just minutes from the New Jersey state line—lies Warwick, a Victorian village with art galleries, antiques shops, and gourmet restaurants along its Main Street. The effect is a scaled-down but convincing imitation of New York City's SoHo district.

From May through December, the surrounding farmland produces a constant supply of freshly harvested treats: vegetables and berries in summer; pears, apples, and pumpkins in fall; evergreen Christmas trees in winter. The annual **Warwick Applefest** (www.warwickapplefest.com) in early October is not to be missed. And Warwick touts one of the best farmers markets around. Nightlife is lively, especially in summer when several local cafés and galleries offer live music. Parking will challenge even the most seasoned urbanites on weekends.

Black Dirt Region

The township of Warwick encompasses much

of the 14,000-acre Black Dirt Region, an agricultural anomaly formed by glacial activity some 12,000 years ago. Polish and German immigrants cleared fields in present-day Pine Island and Florida by hand in the 1880s and discovered that the soil was well suited to growing onions. The region still produces about a quarter of all the onions consumed in the United States. During the August harvest season, the sweet aroma seeps into the car the moment you cross into the area. You can sample the local harvest at the Pine Island Black Dirt Farmers Market, which takes place in Pine Island Town Park at the intersection of Kay Road and Treasure Lane 10am-2pm on Saturdays June-October. The annual **Black Dirt Feast** takes place in August, with area chefs preparing a five-course meal that celebrates local food and raises money for the community. In 2014, tickets cost $100 per person. Reservations required (Scheuermann Farms and Greenhouses, 73 Little York Rd., Warwick, www.pineislandny.com). **Rogowski Farm** (327-329 Glenwood Rd., Pine Island, 845/258-4574, www.rogowskifarm.com) opens the doors to its greenhouse, farm kitchen, and fields to show the public how real food grows.

To reach the Black Dirt Region from Warwick, follow the Pine Island Turnpike (Route 1B) west to Pine Island, or Route 17A north to Florida.

Monroe

Back on Route 17, schoolchildren have been visiting the historic **Museum Village at Old Smith's Clove** (1010 Rte. 17M, 845/782-8248, www.museumvillage.org) in Monroe since the 1940s to learn about the wonders of colonial life, such as making wagons and candles. Walk from the red barn to the firehouse, weaver, and blacksmith in the shade of stately sugar maples. The museum is located behind a park-and-ride lot off Exit 129. Turns are well marked from the exit ramp. The museum is open April-June and September-November. Self-guided tours are $3, and tours led by costumed interpreters are $5.

Farther west, off Route 17M, is the craft village of **Sugar Loaf** (Kings Highway, Sugar Loaf, 845/469-9181, www.sugarloafnewyork.com, hours vary by shop), a collection of boutique shops selling handmade goods including ceramics, clothes, and soaps. Pick up orange and eucalyptus loofah soaps at **Rosner Soap** (845/469-5931, www.rosnersoap.com). Find Native American art and artifacts at **Moondancer** (845/610-3740, www.mdancer.

orchard near Warwick

com). Browse the handcrafted leather goods at **Into Leather** (845/469-5519, www.sugarloafleather.com). Stores keep slightly different hours, but if you arrive between 11am and 5pm, you should be able to visit most of them. Some shops close on Mondays. Sugar Loaf hosts a fall festival on Columbus Day weekend in October with crafts, food, music, and more.

Harness racing fans head to Goshen for a tour of the sport's hall of fame. Housed in a 1913 Tudor stable, the **Harness Racing Museum & Hall of Fame** (240 Main St., Goshen, 845/294-6330, www.harnessmuseum.com, 10am-5pm daily, free) contains an extensive collection of Currier & Ives trotting prints, as well as photographs, trophies, and memorabilia. Interactive exhibits include a 3-D simulator and theaters.

Shawangunk Wine Trail

A 14-winery route through Orange and Ulster Counties meanders along country roads with stops in Warwick, Pine Island, Washingtonville, and Pine Bush. Tastings include barrel-fermented chardonnay, sweet ice wines, sparkling hard ciders, and locally distilled spirits paired with whatever is in season on nearby farms. Visit www.shawangunkwinetrail.com for information about live music and other events. **The Little Wine Bus** (917/414-7947, www.thelittlewinebus.com) shuttles tasters from one winery to the next, so you can leave your own car behind.

WESTERN ORANGE COUNTY: I-84 TO THE DELAWARE RIVER

From its intersection with Route 17, I-84 heads southwest toward Middletown and Port Jervis at the southern end of the Shawangunk Mountains. The Neversink and Delaware Rivers meet here, a stone's throw from both New Jersey and Pennsylvania.

A onetime hub for road, rail, and canal transportation, Port Jervis was named for John Bloomfield Jervis, an engineer who built the D&H Canal and Croton Aqueduct. Although the name suggests a major shipping port, the river is better suited to canoes than freighters. Today, a population of 10,000 supports several small- to mid-sized industrial businesses, and Port Jervis serves as a gateway to the Upper Delaware River in Sullivan and Delaware Counties. Beginning in the town of Sparrowbush, about five miles outside of Port Jervis, Route 97 twists and turns and climbs over the **Hawk's Nest** to present breathtaking views of New York, Pennsylvania, and the Delaware River in between. At a height of 150 feet above the river, the road has several lookouts called bay windows that were built into the original design. Car companies like to film commercials along this stretch of winding road.

SPORTS AND RECREATION

Although more developed than the Upper Hudson Valley, Orange County has preserved a number of open spaces that are ideal for a variety of mountain and aquatic adventures.

Winter Sports

Orange County enjoys a mild climate compared to other parts of the Hudson River Valley, receiving only a foot of snow on average each winter. But the Hudson Highlands and Ramapo Mountains create ideal terrain for beginner skiers, and several local ski areas offer weekend and evening entertainment for families. One of the four chairlifts at the **Tuxedo Ridge Ski Center at Sterling Forest** (581 Rte. 17A West, Sterling Lake Rd., Tuxedo, 845/351-1122, www.tuxedoridge.com, 10am-5pm Mon.-Fri. and 9am-5pm Sat.-Sun. Jan.-Feb., night skiing and riding until 10pm, adults $60, juniors $50, weekday rates $25/$18) crosses right over Route 17A. To the west of Greenwood Lake, also on Route 17A, is the smaller **Mount Peter Ski Area** (Rte. 17A, Warwick, 845/986-4940, www.mtpeter.com, adults $20-45, juniors $18-36).

Hiking

Backpackers can follow the **Appalachian**

Trail (AT) from the New Jersey state line at Greenwood Lake (Orange County) across the Bear Mountain Bridge to the Dutchess County line near Kent (Putnam County). Along the way is the oldest section of the AT, completed in 1923 in Harriman State Park. Moderate elevation changes provide valley and lake views. Besides the AT, Harriman State Park has 200 miles of hiking trails, with a dozen or so lean-tos for overnight camping. Visit www.myharriman.com for links to maps and recommended routes and directions. Trail maps are available from the **NY/NJ Trail Conference** (www.nynjtc.org).

In the western part of Sterling Forest above Greenwood Lake, the 5.3-mile **Sterling Ridge Trail** leads to views of Sterling Lake and the Sterling Fire Tower, while the four-mile Indian Loop Trail, an offshoot of the AT, climbs to views of Route 17 and the surrounding valley.

Bird-watchers have several good choices to explore in Orange County: The **Basha Kill Wildlife Management Area** (Rte. 209 South, Wurtsboro, 845/754-0743, www.thebashakill.org) is a bird sanctuary on 2,000 acres of state-owned wetlands, forests, fields, and abandoned orchards. And the **Eagle Institute** (Barryville, 845/557-6162, www.eagleinstitute.org) conservation group offers guided tours of bald eagle habitats along the Delaware and Hudson Rivers. The **Orange County Audubon Society** (www.orangecountynyaudubon.com) maintains another 62-acre sanctuary near the Heritage Trail, **6½ Station Road Sanctuary** (6½ Station Rd., Goshen, 845/744-6047).

Some parks are closed to hikers during hunting season in November and December. Contact the **Department of Conservation** for details (845/256-3000).

Cycling

On the access road to Museum Village is a treasure of a bikeway, the 15-mile Heritage Trail, which follows the bed of the old Erie Railroad, connecting Monroe to Goshen. You can rent bikes (or snowshoes in winter) at **Bryan's Bikes** (240 Main St., Cornwall, 845/534-5230, www.bryansbikes.com). The **Orange County Bicycle Club** (www.ocbicycleclub.org) meets every Saturday morning at the Dollar Tree store at the intersection of Route 17A and Route 94 in the town of Florida for rides of every level. Cue sheets for these rides are available on www.ridewithgps.com. The club also puts on the Country Roads Tour in September each year. In October, the Black Bear Century is a popular cycling event for exploring the western part of the county and into Pennsylvania. For a customized guided ride, contact **Hudson Valley Biking** (845/249-1987, www.hudsonvalleybiking.com).

Golf

A round of golf at the **Mansion Ridge Golf Club** (1292 Orange Tpke., Monroe, 845/782-7888, www.mansionridgegc.com, $25-129) begins in the stone barn clubhouse and meanders through forest and across hills, with incredible views of the countryside. The championship course is the only Jack Nicklaus Signature Design course in New York State that's open to the public. Another good option is the **Falkirk Estate and Country Club** (206 Smith Clove Rd., Central Valley, 845/928-8060, www.falkirkestate.com, $51-63), where golfers play with the Ramapo Mountains as a scenic backdrop.

Swimming and Boating

Orange County offers easy access to a host of aquatic activities. On the Delaware River, **Silver Canoe Raft Rentals** (37 South Maple Ave., Port Jervis, 800/724-8342, www.silvercanoe.com, 8am-7pm daily Apr.-Sept., $31-40) has canoes and kayaks for rent. Rates include transport and pickup.

Sailing and waterskiing are summer pastimes on Greenwood Lake. There are four marinas on the lake, and you can rent powerboats and personal watercraft at **Long Pond Marina** (634 Jersey Ave., Greenwood Lake, 845/477-8425, www.longpondmarina.com). There is a public beach on Windermere

Appalachian Trail

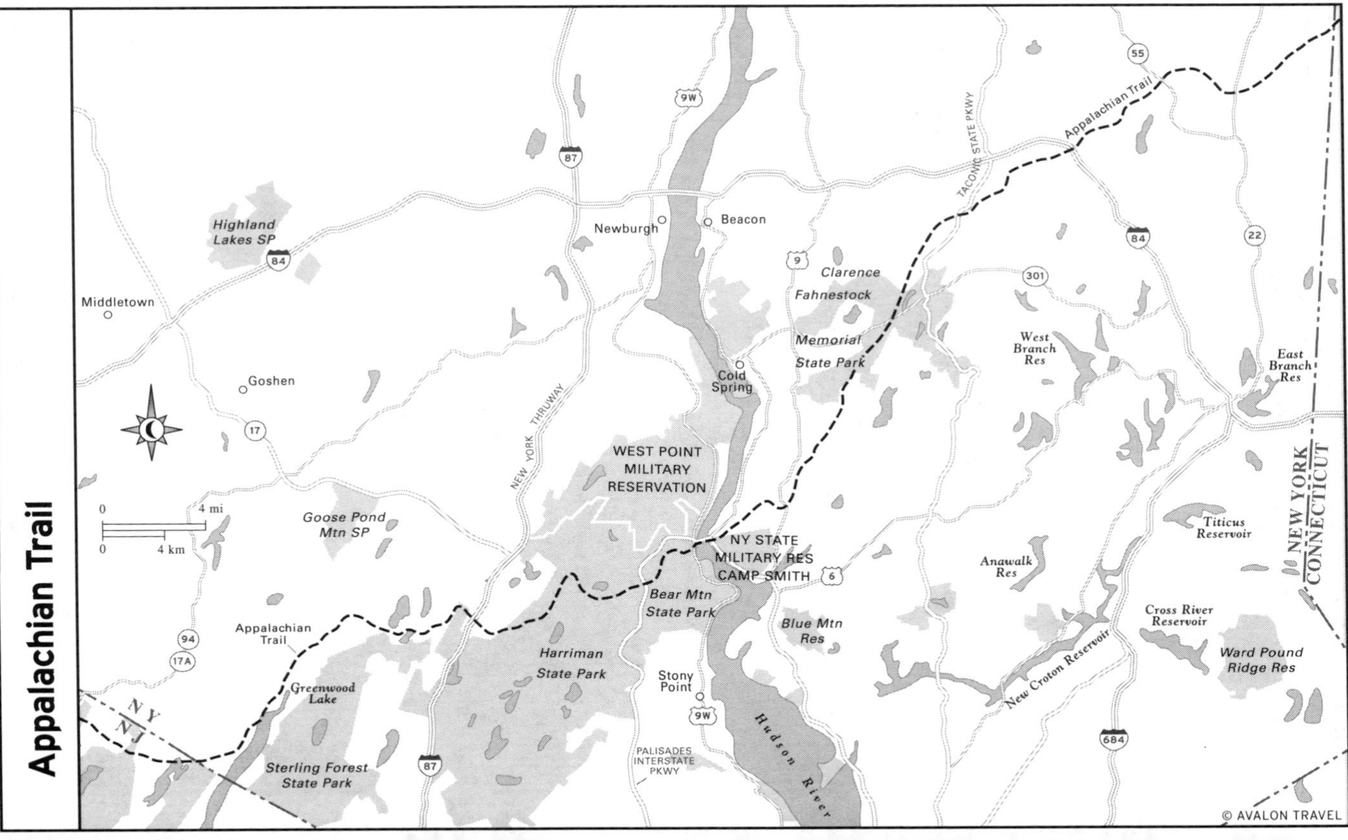

Avenue on the east shore. The **Greenwood Lake Triathlon,** held each year in mid-September, has become a popular race, drawing athletes from across the state.

Lake Welch in Harriman State Park is a popular destination for a summer swim or boating excursion. Several other lakes in the park offer swimming but not beaches or boating.

Several marinas along the Hudson River have boat ramps and services: **Highland Falls Marina** (72 Station Hill Rd., Highland Falls, 845/446-2402, 9am-9pm daily May-Oct.), within walking distance to West Point, has 44 slips and five moorings. In Newburgh, **Front Street Marina** (40 Front St., Newburgh, 845/661-4914, www.riverfrontmarinanewburgh.com) puts you at the doorstep of all the new restaurants and shops on the Newburgh waterfront. This is a state-of-the-art marina with all the amenities, including an ATM, but no fuel (bulk diesel is available dockside).

Storm King Adventure Tours (187 Hudson St., Cornwall-on-Hudson, 845/534-7800, www.stormkingadventuretours.com) will lead small groups on a guided paddle around Bannerman Castle, Storm King Mountain, and hidden coves along the river's edge. Tours range $60-100 for three- to four-hour paddles.

River Cruises

Pride of the Hudson (26 Front St., Newburgh, 845/220-2120, www.prideofthehudson.com) offers river cruises from Newburgh Landing. Boats depart on Wednesday-Friday afternoons and Saturday-Sunday afternoons and evenings (adults $22, seniors $20, children 4-11 $18, children under 3 free).

River Rose Cruises (70 Front St., Newburgh, 845/562-1067, www.riverrosecruises.com) runs tours on the River Rose, an authentic stern-driven Mississippi paddle wheeler. The two-hour sightseeing trip ($20 adults, $15 children) includes a full bar and heads south from Newburgh to view Bannerman Island, the Catskill Aqueduct, the village of Cold Spring, and West Point. Enjoy a special two-hour buffet brunch cruise on Sundays ($42 adults, $26 children). Nightly dinner cruises are another option ($48 adults, $26 children), as well as special dance party cruises ($30).

Another way to experience Bannerman Castle is a walking tour via boat service from Newburgh Landing with **Estuary Steward** (800/979-3370, www.bannermancastle.org). A two-hour trip includes close-up views of the abandoned Scottish-style castle and surrounding gardens. Tours run at 11am on Saturdays and Sundays, May-October. Visitors must be prepared to walk on rugged terrain.

Fishing and Hunting

Largemouth bass, chain pickerel, and panfish are the most popular catches in Orange County's lakes and ponds. The **Bait Bucket** (313 Rte. 211 West, Middletown, 845/361-4774, 6am-7pm daily) sells bait, equipment, and licenses and will point you to the best access points. **O&H Bait Shop** (209 Meadow Ave., Chester, 845/469-2566, 6am-6pm daily) is another option for fishing supplies.

For a guided trip on the Delaware, contact **Reel'em In Guide Service** (13 Fall St., Port Jervis, 845/856-3009, reservations required) to book a half-day trip for one or two people on a custom-made driftboat. Ice-fishing trips are an option in January and February.

To stock up on gear, visit **Gander Mountain** (Crystal Run Plaza, 100 N. Galleria Dr., Middletown, 845/692-5600, 9am-9pm Mon.-Fri., 8am-9pm Sat., 9am-8pm Sun.), a sprawling destination store for gear-hungry outdoors lovers.

Aviation

For a romantic morning adventure, take a hot air balloon flight with **Above the Clouds** (Middletown, 845/692-2556, www.abovethecloudsinc.com, May-Oct., reservations required, prices start at $179). Flights with **Fantasy Balloon Flights** (Middletown, 845/856-7103, www.fantasyfliers.com, prices start at $179) depart from Randall Airport and include a glass of champagne.

Horseback Riding

Several parks in Orange County offer the use of bridle paths by permit. Goosepond Mountain State Park in Chester and Highland Lakes State Park in Middletown both have extensive acreage of undeveloped woods to explore by horseback. **Juckas Stables** (Rtes. 302 & 17, Bullville, 845/361-1429, www.juckasstables.com) has 117 acres of trails and English and Western riding lessons on beautiful horses. Camping is available.

Spas

The Spa at Glenmere Mansion (624 Pine Hill Rd., Chester, 845/469-1939, www.glenmeremansion.com, 10am-7pm Wed.-Sat., 10am-5pm Sun.) offers an exhaustive menu of treatments from standard to traditional Turkish hammam experiences. The luxury comes with a hefty price tag; most 60-minute services run $165-260. If money is no object, make a weekend of it and stay in one of the inn's 18 guest rooms. Reservations required.

The Spa at Wellness Springs (489 Rte. 32, Highland Mills, 845/928-2898, www.wellness-springs.com) offers more affordable spa treatments, yoga classes, acupuncture, and other wellness programs to local residents as well as visitors.

ACCOMMODATIONS

The best places to stay in Orange County are clustered near Greenwood Lake and Warwick, and along the river between West Point and Cornwall. Small bed-and-breakfast inns are the most common type of accommodations, with an assortment of chain hotels located along I-84.

$100-150

The colonial ★ **Inn at Stony Creek** (34 Spanktown Rd., Warwick, 845/986-3660, www.innstonycreek.com, $119-175) has five guest rooms, each furnished and decorated with its own special touch, usually involving lace or floral fabrics. Choose among the brass, wrought iron, four-poster, and canopy beds. Enjoy fresh flowers and robes for your stay. The multicourse breakfast here may include fresh fruit smoothies, yogurt with granola, French toast with real maple syrup, or an omelette. Like many historic properties in the Hudson River Valley, this one attracts wedding parties during the summer months. The **New Continental Hotel** (15 Leo Ct., Greenwood Lake, 845/477-2456, www.thenewcontinentalhotel.com, $95-175) is a comfortable and affordable lakeside option. Its rooms have tiled private baths and lake views. Twin and double beds are available.

$150-200

Storm King Lodge (100 Pleasant Hill Rd., Mountainville, 845/534-9421, www.stormkinglodge.com, $160-190) offers four cozy rooms in a 19th-century lodge near Storm King Mountain. The Lavender and Pine rooms have fireplaces. Call ahead to schedule a massage appointment during your stay.

West Point's **Thayer Hotel** (674 Thayer Rd., West Point, 845/446-4731, www.thethayerhotel.com, $150-175) has 151 modern but cozy rooms decorated in 19th-century Americana style. Guest rooms and suites inside the imposing granite building offer campus, river, or mountain views. Amenities include cable TV, high-speed Internet access, and a renovated fitness center. The dining room, as well, recently got a much-needed face-lift.

Stockbridge Ramsdell House on Hudson (158 Montgomery St., Newburgh, 845/562-9310, www.stockbridgeramsdell.com, $175) treats guests to a Victorian-era stay in a brick mansion that was saved from demolition in the 1970s. The house was built in 1870 as the family home of the president of the Erie Railroad and later restored in the 1980s as a bed-and-breakfast inn. Five guest rooms are decorated tastefully in period furnishings, and some have river views. The surrounding neighborhood is home to a mix of artists and professionals who are committed to restoring the area. Some visitors may not feel at ease in the urban environment of present-day Newburgh, but the owners can help you avoid unsafe parts of town. They serve a full hot breakfast on the porch in summer and by the fire in winter. Walk to the Newburgh waterfront, or take a short drive to nearby wineries, historic sites, and the Dia:Beacon museum across the river. Children are welcome and Wi-Fi is available.

Over $200

A stay at the romantic ★ **Cromwell Manor** (174 Angola Rd., Cornwall, 845/534-7136, www.cromwellmanor.com, $165-380), located five miles from West Point, includes a gourmet breakfast and help-yourself anytime coffee/tea/snacks. Choose one of nine guest rooms in the main house, an 1820 brick manor, or one of four rooms in the 1764 Chimneys Cottage. The cottage has a delightful collection of antiques, and Internet access is a plus for travelers who need to stay in touch with the real world.

Canopy beds and working fireplaces set an elegant mood at the meticulously restored ★ **Peach Grove Inn** (205 Rte. 17A, Warwick, 845/986-7411, www.peachgroveinn.net, $195-245). Its six rooms occupy a stately 1850 Greek Revival building tastefully furnished with 19th-century antiques throughout. The two downstairs rooms have whirlpool tubs and televisions. The back porch looks out over the original 285-acre property.

Owners John and Dena serve up a legendary multicourse breakfast every morning at **Caldwell House Bed and Breakfast** (25 Orrs Mills Rd., Salisbury Mills, 845/496-2954, www.caldwellhouse.com, $195-275). Its 10 rooms are all private and comfortably appointed with antique furniture and modern amenities. Hot drinks, goodies, and a roaring fire are available all day in the parlor, and the common rooms are all stocked with books and games for guest entertainment.

Catlin Gardens (2865 Rte. 6, Slate Hill, 845/355-3555, www.catlingardens.com, $175-300) houses 40 rooms and suites and is a popular wedding venue. Rooms are comfortable with standard amenities. Over five acres of well-maintained grounds include an outdoor bar, fountains, waterfalls, and a half mile of pathways to stroll. The hotel is also home to Jack's Pub and Restaurant.

Eighteen guest rooms, including five premium suites, comprise the luxury accommodations at **Glenmere Mansion** (634 Pine Hill Rd., Chester, 845/469-1900, www.glenmeremansion.com, rates start at $750). This boutique resort opened in 2010 and caters to an exclusive clientele. Originally built in 1911 as the country retreat of industrialist Robert Goelet, the property now serves as a luxurious hideaway, complete with a full-service spa, its own restaurant, and 150 acres of gardens and grounds. Guests often arrive via helicopter landing on the front lawn. Reservations are required for any activity here; security is tight, and accommodations are strictly limited to guests who are 18 or older.

Campgrounds

Oakland Valley Campground (399 Oakland Valley Rd., Cuddebackville, 845/754-8732, www.oaklandvalleycampground.com, May-Oct., $30-55) has large wooded sites for tents, trailers, and motor homes. Amenities include water and electric hookups, flush toilets, firewood, cable TV, swimming pool, and free hot showers. **Otisville Campground** (298 Grange Rd., Otisville, 845/386-5104, open year-round) has tent sites next to a small pond, with wooded trails, telephone hookups, hot showers, and a laundry.

FOOD

Along the River: Route 9W

Centrally located near West Point, Storm King, and the Brotherhood Winery, **Painter's** (266 Hudson St., Cornwall-on-Hudson, 845/534-2109, www.painters-restaurant.com, lunch 11am-4pm Mon.-Sat., dinner until 10pm Mon.-Thurs., until 10:30pm Fri.-Sat., and until 9pm Sun., brunch 10:30am-3pm Sun., $10-27) is a favorite for summer dining. The theme seems to be eating around the world: a little American, a little Mexican, mixed with some Japanese, and Italian food. You might start with a kale salad served with summer berries, sample the Mediterranean plate, or go for the grilled hanger steak. There are plenty of vegetarian and gluten-free options, and kids may order from an extensive children's menu. Do save room for dessert.

Inside the Thayer Hotel at West Point, the buffet-style champagne brunch at **MacArthur's Riverview Restaurant** is a memorable experience for a special occasion (www.thethayerhotel.com, 10am-2pm Sun., $36.95 pp). The highlight, of course, is the bubbly. Enjoy bottomless sparkling wine, mimosas, and Bloody Mary cocktails while you graze from station to station. The rest of the week, the restaurant serves American fare from land, air, and sea. Crab and lobster appear in several main dishes, alongside American onion soup and various cuts of steaks. For Friday seafood nights, the buffet presents four types of fish, linguini and clam sauce, king crab legs, and fried clams and shrimp.

★ **Woody's Farm to Table** (30 Quaker Ave., Cornwall, 845/534-1111, www.woodysfarmtotable.com, 11:30am-8:30pm daily) is not your average burger joint. Ground beef comes from a co-op of small farmers in Maine, and just about everything else comes from Hudson River Valley farms. This is also one of few places in the Hudson River Valley where you'll find a lobster roll on the menu. Vegetarian options include a beet burger, along with a selection of organic soups and salads. Must-try items: onion hay, fried pickles, and a thick milkshake.

In Newburgh, rub elbows with the locals over the famous hot dogs slathered in "Texas sauce" at **Tony's Newburgh Lunch** (348 Broadway, Newburgh, 845/562-9660, www.tonysnewburghlunch.com, 6:30am-4pm Mon.-Wed., 6:30am-5pm Thurs.-Sat., mains $2-3). Tony's family will turn you down if you dare ask for the sauce recipe, but if you must bring it home, you can order some online. Besides the hot dogs and burgers, there is a soup of the day.

A trio of Italian restaurants serve Tuscan fare at the Newburgh waterfront: **Cena 2000** (50 Front St., Newburgh, 845/561-7676, www.cena2000.com, lunch noon-3pm daily, dinner 5pm-10pm Mon.-Thurs., 5pm-11pm Fri.-Sat., 5pm-9pm Sun., $18-29) has an outdoor oyster bar and the best river views. **Café Pitti** (40 Front St., Newburgh, 845/565-1444, www.cafepitti.com, 11:30am-10pm Mon.-Thurs., 11:30am-11pm Fri.-Sat., noon-9pm Sun., $9-13) serves antipasti, panini, and pizzettes under a bright yellow awning. The most intimate of the bunch is **Il Cenácolo** (228 S. Plank Rd., Newburgh, 845/564-4494, www.ilcenacolorestaurant.com, lunch noon-2:30pm Mon. and Wed.-Fri., dinner 5pm-9pm Mon., Wed., Thurs., 5:30pm-11pm Fri.-Sat., 4pm-9pm Sun., $19-28). The menu here is a carnivore's delight, with choices like house-made egg pasta with lamb sauce, calves liver sautéed in brown butter and sage, and a roasted lemon chicken.

★ **Newburgh Brewing Company** (88 South Colden St., Newburgh, 845/569-2337, www.newburghbrewing.com, 4pm-9pm Wed., 4pm-11pm Thurs., 4pm-midnight Fri., noon-midnight Sat., noon-5pm Sun., mains $3-15) makes craft beers from locally sourced hops in a converted 1850s-era box factory. More than a dozen beers are on tap most nights. Besides the brews, there are local wines to sip, and you can take the edge off by ordering small plates made from locally sourced ingredients. Rosemary and garlic fries with house-made mayo are a must.

River Grill (40 Front St., Newburgh, 845/561-9444, www.therivergrill.com, lunch 11:30am-3:30pm daily, dinner 5pm-9pm Mon.-Thurs. and Sun., 5pm-10pm Fri.-Sat., $16-29) does surf and turf with a Latin twist. Try the seafood paella special while you take in the river views. At the end of the road at Newburgh Landing, a large dirt parking lot announces **Gully's** (2 Washington St., Newburgh, 845/565-0077, 11:30am-midnight Sun.-Wed., 11:30am-1:30am Thurs.-Sat., $10-32), a two-story bar and restaurant on an old barge. The atmosphere is super casual, and the floor slopes with the tide. This is the place to order a bowl of steamers or a plate of surf and turf. On weekend nights, the upstairs bar stays open until the wee hours of the morning.

El Solar Café (346 Broadway, Newburgh, 845/561-3498, daily 11am-11pm, mains $15) brings Latin, Spanish, and Mediterranean flavors to downtown Newburgh. That means dishes like plantain and shrimp salad, saffron risotto, and wild-caught sea bass prepared whole and filleted tableside.

Central Orange County: Along Route 17

New restaurants are opening at a fast clip in the Warwick area. But the **Landmark Inn** (Rte. 94, North Warwick, 845/986-5444, www.landmarkinnwarwick.com, 5pm-9:30pm Tues.-Thurs., 5pm-10pm Fri.-Sat., 3:30pm-8pm Sun., $20-28) remains a local favorite for casual American cuisine and evening cocktails. Sit in the main dining room or the cozier pub. Daily specials put the local harvest in the spotlight. The crab cakes are usually a hit.

Out-of-towners head to the fancier **Chateau Hathorn** (33 Hathorn Rd., Warwick, 845/986-6099, www.chateauhathorn.com, 5pm-9:30pm Wed.-Sat., 3pm-8pm Sun., $20-33) for Swiss and French cuisine in a storybook mansion from the 18th century. Start with frog legs a la Provencal or smoked trout, and then move on to the rack of lamb or the Wiener schnitzel. For a more casual taste of Europe, visit **La Petite Cuisine** (20 Railroad Ave., Warwick, 845/988-0988, www.lapetitecuisine.biz, 10am-4pm Tues.-Sat., 9am-4pm Sun., breakfast $4-8, lunch/dinner $8-15) next door for brunch or lunch. Fresh-baked bread is a treat here, especially when it's part of a grilled sandwich.

Grappa Ristorante (22B Railroad Ave., Warwick, 845/987-7373, www.grapparistorante.com, noon-10pm Tues.-Thurs., noon-11pm Fri.-Sat., noon-9pm Sun., $20-30) brings northern Italian fare prepared by a graduate of the Culinary Institute of America to hungry restaurant-goers in Warwick. Dip warm bread in olive oil to start, then move on to cold or hot antipasti such as beets and goat cheese or eggplant rollatini. Mains include a variety of chicken cutlets, veal, and fresh fish. Gluten-free pasta is available, and the chef can sometimes modify other dishes to meet dietary needs.

At Greenwood Lake, the most popular choices for lakeside dining are **Emerald Point** (40 Sterling Rd., Greenwood Lake, 845/477-2275, www.emeraldpnt.com, noon-close daily, $13-24)—which has a wood-fired pizza oven and makes legendary bacon wrapped shrimp—and the **Breezy Point Inn** (620 Jersey Ave., Greenwood Lake, 845/477-8100, www.breezypointinn.com, lunch and dinner daily, $17-26), with a raw bar and German-influenced menu.

On the drive between Warwick and Greenwood Lake, don't miss the homemade ice cream, fresh-baked waffle cones, and valley views at the hilltop ★ **Bellvale Farms Creamery** (1390 Rte. 17A, 845/988-1818, www.bellvalefarms.com, open daily noon-9pm Apr.-Oct., with reduced hours in the early and late season). Choose from 50 flavors, including maple cinnamon and the Black Dirt Blast, a chocolate lover's delight. Locals stockpile the cookies and cream by the quart in their freezers. The creamery also has a pumpkin patch open weekends only in October from 11am until dusk.

Glenmere Mansion (634 Pine Hill Rd., Chester, 845/469-1900 or 866/772-2982, www.glenmeremansion.com) has two dining options, the more casual Frogs End Tavern and the ultraformal Supper Room. Tavern fare includes soups, salads, and flatbread pizzas ($8-19) for starters and entrées in the form of sandwiches, pasta dishes, and fish or beef specials ($14-38). The Supper Room serves dinner Thursday, Friday, and Saturday (prix fixe $85) with seasonal risottos, lobster bouillabaisse, and dark chocolate mousse. Additionally, guests may order a seven-course tasting menu (prix fixe $145) specially prepared by the executive chef and pastry chef.

ENTERTAINMENT AND EVENTS

Performing Arts

West Point's **Eisenhower Hall Theatre** (Eisenhower Hall Theatre Box Office, Bldg. 655, West Point, 845/938-4159, www.ikehall.com) is a top-notch venue for a range of performances, from the musical *Spamalot* to John Tesh around the holidays.

Walkill River School of Art (232 Ward St., Montgomery, www.wallkillriverschool.com, 9am-6pm) is a nonprofit artists' cooperative that runs an art school and fine art gallery as well as a plein air art workshop series on local farms and open spaces. The gallery represents about 40 local Orange County-based artists, and classes are available for both adults and children in a range of mediums.

Bars and Nightlife

Zulu Time Rooftop Bar and Lounge at the Thayer Hotel (674 Thayer Rd., West Point, 845/446-4731, www.thethayerhotel.com, 4pm-last call Wed.-Sat., noon-10pm Sun.) overlooks the Hudson River and offers a few appetizers and entrées to accompany your drinks. The signature drink from the fully stocked bar is The Double Tap, a 16-ounce beer with a shot of tequila, a souvenir cup, and a T-shirt.

Newburgh Landing puts on a lively—and sometimes downright rowdy—nightlife. **Gully's** (2 Washington St., Newburgh, 845/565-0077, 11:30am-midnight Sun.-Wed., 11:30am-1:30am Thurs.-Sat, meals $10-32), has a two-story bar and restaurant on an old barge. On weekend nights, the upstairs bar is open late.

For a mellower scene, Warwick locals gather at the bar inside **The Landmark Inn** (Rte. 94, North Warwick, 845/986-5444, www.landmarkinnwarwick.com). Keep an eye out for live music performances at Warwick's wineries and cafés. The family-owned, 1950s-era **Warwick Drive-In Theater** (Rte. 94, 845/986-4440, www.warwickdrivein.com, adults $10, seniors and children 4-11 $6, under 4 free) is also packed on summer nights.

Applewood Winery (82 Four Corners Rd., Warwick, 845/988-9292, www.applewoodwinery.com, 11am-5pm Sun.-Fri., 11am-6pm Sat.) produces chardonnay, cabernet franc, and a hard cider called Naked Flock. And **Warwick Valley Winery & Distillery** (114 Little York Rd., Warwick, 845/258-4858, www.wvwinery.com, 11am-6pm daily) makes riesling and pinot noir wines, as well as apple and pear ciders (Doc's Hard Cider) and a variety of baked goods.

Brotherhood Winery (100 Brotherhood Plaza Dr., Washingtonville, 845/496-3661, www.brotherhood-winery.com) was established in 1839—hence the self-appointed designation, "America's Oldest Winery." Its network of underground cellars holds more than 200 oak barrels. If you're new to wine trail travel, take the guided tour to learn how the different labels are made. Then head upstairs and put your newly acquired knowledge to the test in the tasting room. The tour and tasting flight runs $10. A large reception hall is available to host weddings, and there is also a restaurant and small café on-site. This place is very popular with the tour buses.

Festivals and Events

Nothing quite tops the spirited rivalry of an Army vs. Navy football game at West Point. West Point Football Saturdays take place at Michie Stadium, with a parade, cannon salute, and cadet review to kick off the event. Ferry service is available from Tarrytown.

Cars line the sides of Route 17A over Sterling Mountain during the popular **New York Renaissance Faire** (Sterling Forest, Tuxedo, 845/351-5171, www.renfair.com, 10am-7pm Sat.-Sun. Aug.-Sept., adults $24, children $11) each year. The **Orange County Fair** (100 Carpenter Ave., Middletown, 845/343-4826, www.orangecountyfair.com) takes place in Middletown each July.

Rogowski Farm on Pine Island hosts an **Heirloom Tomato Festival** in August (845/258-4574, www.rogowskifarm.com),

Where to Take the Kids

Young travelers find many opportunities for entertainment and recreation in the Hudson River Valley, from hiking and swimming to apple and berry picking to tours of historic homes and museums. Here are a few family-friendly destinations:

- **Children's Museum of Science and Technology, Troy:** In Rensselaer County, view the 75-foot-long Living Indoor Hudson River exhibit, which models the river from the Adirondacks to the Atlantic. (250 Jordan Rd., Troy, 518/235-2120, www.cmost.org, 10am-5pm Mon.-Sat., $5)
- **Museum Village at Old Smith's Clove, Monroe:** In Orange County, you can experience life in the 19th century; learn to make a candle, and tour the blacksmith, printing, and pottery shops. (1010 New York 17M, Monroe, 845/782-8248, www.museumvillage.org, 11am-4pm Sat.-Sun., adults $10, seniors $8, children 4-12 $8, under 4 free)
- **New Windsor Cantonment State Historic Site, Valatie:** Columbia County offers the opportunity to imagine what it was like to be a soldier in the Revolutionary War as you walk the grounds where George Washington's troops spent their final winter and spring. (374 Temple Hill Rd., New Windsor, 845/561-1765, www.nysparks.com, 10am-5pm Wed.-Sat., 1pm-5pm Sun.)
- **Old Chatham Sheepherding Company, Chatham:** Also in Columbia County is a chance to stop by and help feed the sheep at 3pm daily. (155 Shaker Museum Rd., Old Chatham, 518/794-7733, www.blacksheepcheese.com)
- **Zoom Flume, East Durham:** Cool off in the pools and slides of the area's biggest water park. (Shady Glen Rd. off Rte. 145, East Durham, 800/888-3586, www.zoomflume.com, 10am-6pm June-Sept., some weekends until 7pm, adults $27.99, kids 7 and under $20.99, infants 2 and under free)
- **Stone Barns Center for Food and Agriculture, Pocantico Hills:** Help gather eggs, walk the trails, and explore this farm in Westchester County. (630 Bedford Rd., Pocantico Hills, 914/366-9600, www.bluehillfarm.com)
- **Taconic Outdoor Education Center, Cold Spring:** Located inside Clarence Fahnestock Memorial State Park in Putnam County, the center offers a variety of summer and winter programs for kids as well as adults. (75 Mountain Laurel Ln., Cold Spring, 845/265-3773, www.nysparks.com)
- **Mid-Hudson Children's Museum, Poughkeepsie:** Set on the banks of the Hudson in downtown Poughkeepsie in Dutchess County, the museum has a mastodon skeleton, solar and wind energy exhibits, and a horizontal rock climbing wall. (75 N. Water St., Poughkeepsie, 845/471-0589, www.mhcm.org, 9:30am-5pm Mon.-Sat., 11am-5pm Sun., $8)

while Warwick puts on the **October Applefest** (845/987-2731, www.warwickapplefest.com). Another popular October event is the **Sugar Loaf Fall Festival** (845/469-9181, www.sugarloafnewyork.com).

The **Bear Mountain Native American Festival** (Anthony Wayne Recreation Area, Harriman State Park, www.redhawkcouncil.org) takes place in Harriman State Park in August with singing, dancing, food, crafts, and educational programs.

SHOPPING

Orange County has everything a shopper could desire, from mega-chains and discount outlets to one-of-a-kind boutiques. One of the county's unique finds is Sugar Loaf, a small village of artisans who craft handmade ceramics, soaps, and other goods.

★ Woodbury Common Premium Outlets

Bargain hunters flock to the **Woodbury**

Common Premium Outlets (498 Red Apple Ct., Rte. 32, Central Valley, 845/928-4000, www.premiumoutlets.com, 10am-9pm daily), at the edge of Harriman State Park (Exit 16 off I-87). Dozens of stores are arranged in a campus-like setting, making it less-than-ideal for rainy-day retail therapy. Look for significant discounts on name brands from Coach and Fendi to Banana Republic and Gap. American Eagle Outfitters, Dunhill, Moncler, Theory, and Esprit are among the newest additions to the complex. Beware, the long list of stores and often-deep discounts draw crowds on holiday weekends. **Shortline Bus** (201/529-3666, www.coachusa.com) offers weekday service to the outlets (adults $42, children $21), as well as daily "shop and stay" packages that include accommodations at one of several local hotels (double room $140 per person).

Farm Stands

Orange County made national TV in February 2004 when the Food Network produced a Hudson River Valley episode of *FoodNation with Bobby Flay,* featuring several local eateries. Among them was the **Quaker Creek Store** (757 Pulaski Hwy., Goshen, 845/258-4570, www.quakercreekstore.com, 7am-6pm Mon.-Fri., 7am-4pm Sat.) in Pine Island, a must-try for homemade sausages and smoked meats made by a third-generation owner and CIA graduate. The family-run business has evolved from a 1940s sandwich shop to a gourmet treasure. Onion rings are made from the bounty that makes the region famous.

Chances are, you'll have to wait for a parking space at the **Warwick Valley Farmers Market** (South St. parking lot off Main St., Warwick, www.warwickvalleyfarmersmarket.org, 9am-2pm Sun. mid-May-mid-Nov.). Local businesses sell homemade pies and candies, as well as fresh-picked produce. The entire town of Warwick shuts down for the wildly popular **Applefest** every September.

Elsewhere around the county, at least a dozen other municipal farmers markets take place each week in Cornwall, Monroe, Newburgh, Pine Bush, and other towns. Locations and hours vary with each growing season. Visit www.orangetourism.org for the latest details.

Family-run **Overlook Farm Market and Country Store** (5417 Rte. 9W, Newburgh, 845/562-5780, www.overlookfarmmarket.com, 8am-6pm Wed.-Mon.) sells a variety of fresh produce, eggs, dairy, honey, syrup, and jams that are ideal for a picnic lunch. Behind the market is a pick-your-own orchard, and the property is also home to a bakery, deli, garden center, and petting zoo. The deli famously serves a $1 turkey sandwich.

Orchard Hill Cider Mill (29 Soons Circle, New Hampton, 845/374-2468, www.orchard-hillcidermill.com) is a new farm winery that makes hard cider from the Soons Orchard apple harvest. Located next to the market at Soons, the cidery makes a convenient all-in-one farm stand experience.

Several you-pick farms open during the fall apple-picking season. **Applewood Orchards** (82 Four Corners Rd., Warwick, 845/986-1684, www.applewoodorchards.com, 10am-5pm daily Sept.-Oct.) and **Apple Ridge Orchards** (101 Jessup Rd., Warwick, 845/987-7717 www.appleridgeorchards.com, 9am-5pm daily Sept.-Oct.) are both great places to take the kids for a farm-to-food experience.

Antiques, Galleries, and Boutiques

Main Street in Warwick has a treasure trove of antiques dealers selling everything old, from toys to rugs to lace, as well as several contemporary boutiques. Most stores close by 6pm, although some stay open until 8pm on Fridays.

The Eclectic Eye (16-18 Railroad Ave., 845/986-5520, www.theeclecticeye.com, 11am-4pm Mon., 11am-5pm Tues.-Wed., 11am-6pm Thurs., 11am-8:30pm Fri.-Sat., 9:30am-5pm Sun.) has Glidden pottery, couture clothing, fine lithographs, and items the owner simply calls "worthies." **1809 House** (210 South Rte. 94, Warwick, 845/986-1809, weekends and most weekdays May-Oct.) has a large collection of restored Victorian furniture for sale. Country is the theme at **Harvest Antique Barn** (293 Rte. 94 South, Warwick, 845/986-7979, 10am-5pm Thurs.-Sun.), where you'll find timeworn farm tables, corner cupboards, hutches, and the like.

One of Warwick's top boutiques is **Frazzleberries** (24 Main St., Warwick, 845/988-5080, www.frazzleberries.com, 10am-5:30pm Mon.-Wed., 10am-8pm Thurs.-Fri., 10am-6pm Sat., 11am-4:30pm Sun.), known for cute country furnishings and festive seasonal displays. The store is stocked with quilted bags and smells like apples. Another tempting store is **Newhard's** (39 Main St., Warwick, 845/986-4544, www.newhards.com, 10am-6pm Mon.-Sat. [Friday until 8pm], 11am-5pm Sun.), which stocks upscale kitchen equipment and supplies, including pottery and cookbooks, plus a good selection of toys and games. On Railroad Avenue, **Sweetbriar's** (26 Railroad Ave., Warwick, 845/986-5700, 10am-6pm Tues.-Sat., 10am-5pm Sun.-Mon.) has outdoor table service with a menu of chocolate fondue, s'mores, and gourmet hot chocolate and coffee. Inside is a broader selection of chocolates, truffles, and candy apples.

One of the oldest glassblowing operations in the country is open to the public in Port Jervis. **Gillinder Glass** (39 Erie St., Port Jervis, 845/856-5375, www.gillinderglassstore.com, 9:30am-5:30pm Mon.-Fri., 9:30am-4pm Sat., noon-4pm Sun., $5 demonstration and tour) offers demonstrations, tours, and a gift store where you can find that one-of-a-kind gift for a special occasion.

INFORMATION AND SERVICES

A network of 10 tourist information centers serve Orange County visitors; several of them open seasonally. The **Orange County Tourism** (124 Main St., Goshen, 845/615-3860, www.orangetourism.org, 8am-5pm Mon.-Fri.) office can provide a wealth of information before or during a visit. The **Palisades Parkway Tourist Information Center** (between Exits 16 and 17, Palisades Interstate Parkway, 845/786-5003, 8am-6pm daily Apr.-Oct., 8am-5pm daily Nov.-Mar.) stocks a variety of trail guides, local interest books, road maps, and all things Hudson River Valley. This is also the place to pick up your New York State fishing license.

GETTING THERE AND AROUND

Bus

Adirondack Trailways (800/776-7548, www.trailwaysny.com) stops in Newburgh, while **Shortline Bus** (201/529-3666, www.coachusa.com) stops include Monroe, Middletown, Newburgh, Goshen, Chester, and Central Valley. **Main Line Trolley Bus** (800/631-8405) offers local service to Chester, Goshen, Harriman, Middletown, Monroe, and Woodbury Common. **New Jersey Transit** (973/275-5555, www.njtransit.com) also runs bus service to Greenwood Lake and Warwick.

Train

The Metro-North Port Jervis Line stops in western Orange County between Port Jervis and Suffern, with connecting service to Newark Liberty International Airport in New Jersey and Penn Station in New York City. Alternatively, Beacon station along the Hudson Line is a short cab or shuttle ride across the river from Newburgh. The Newburgh Beacon Shuttle bus connects the Beacon station, downtown Newburgh, and Stewart International Airport.

Car

In the eastern part of Orange County, Route 17, I-87, and I-84 form a triangle that encloses many of the most popular attractions in the area. More than a dozen taxi services cover Orange County, including West Point, Monroe, Warwick, and Greenwood Lake—but only two service all points in the county: **All Family Taxi** (845/565-1616) and **ASAP TXI**

(845/294-7433). Car rentals are available at Stewart International Airport (www.panynj.gov) including Avis, Budget, Enterprise, and Hertz.

Boat

The **Newburgh-Beacon Ferry** (212/532-4900, www.nywaterway.com, adults $1.75, seniors and children $1) connects the cities of Newburgh and Beacon on opposite sides of the Hudson River and provides convenient access to the Metro-North train station in Beacon. Although it's primarily run for commuters, travelers who want to experience both the **Dia:Beacon Museum** (3 Beekman St., Beacon, 845/440-0100, www.diaart.org) and Newburgh Landing may find the ferry service to be a good way to avoid driving.

Putnam County

Squeezed between the large and densely populated counties of Westchester to the south and Dutchess to the north are 231 square miles of the most dramatic landscape along the Hudson. On overcast days, a dreamy mist clings to the jagged ridgeline of the Hudson Highlands, producing a landscape reminiscent of a tale from the Brothers Grimm. Just 50 miles from Manhattan and easily accessible by rail, romantic Putnam County features two Victorian-era towns along the river, two large state parks, and hundreds of miles of wilderness trails. The county's many lakes and streams provide a vital source of freshwater for the New York City reservoir system.

Putnam does not have a Hudson River crossing of its own—its borders extend from just above the Bear Mountain Bridge to a point south of the Newburgh-Beacon Bridge—however, two Metro-North rail lines make Putnam an easy day trip from New York City. The Hudson Line stops in Garrison and Cold Spring along the river, while the Harlem Line stops in Brewster. From Brewster, it's about a 90-minute ride to Grand Central.

In addition to the train tracks, a 20-mile stretch of the Appalachian Trail crosses diagonally through Putnam County, from the Bear Mountain Bridge and Hudson Highlands State Park in the southwest to Clarence Fahnestock Memorial State Park and the Dutchess County line in the northeast.

Anthony's Nose at the Bear Mountain Bridge makes a logical starting point for a Putnam County tour. Follow Route 9D north from Westchester County or Route 301 east from I-84.

ALONG THE RIVER: ROUTE 9D

★ Boscobel House and Gardens

Two rows of apple trees frame the view of the Hudson from the entrance to Boscobel (Beautiful Wood), a restored neoclassical mansion dating back to the 19th century. Named after an English manor, the home belonged to colonial loyalist States Morris Dyckman, a contemporary of Chancellor Robert Livingston.

The building originally sat on a 250-acre farm in Montrose, about 15 miles south of its present-day location. It was nearly lost to history when the federal government sold it to a demolition contractor in the 1950s for $35. Fortunately, a group of private citizens came to the rescue and moved the building, piece by piece, to a scenic bluff in Garrison.

The structure and details of the home create a light and airy feel that is unique among the Hudson River Valley's riverside mansions. On the outside, wood-carved drapery, complete with bow ties and tassels, decorates the space between columns on the 2nd-floor balcony. Inside, Dyckman furnished Boscobel with exquisite silver, china, and glassware that he purchased in London in the late 18th century.

Home to a number of cultural events throughout the year, **Boscobel House and Gardens** (Rte. 9D, Garrison, 845/265-3638, www.boscobel.org, 9:30am-5pm Wed.-Mon. Apr.-Oct., 9:30am-4pm Wed.-Mon. Nov.-Dec., adults $17, seniors $14, children under 14 $8, under 6 free, grounds only adults $11, seniors $8, children under 14 $5, under 6 free) hosts the annual Hudson Valley Shakespeare Festival. The museum runs a free shuttle from the Cold Spring Metro-North station on designated weekends. Call for exact dates. Visitors must pay an entrance fee to wander the formal gardens and the mile-long Woodland Trail, but the variety of roses (more than 150 types) and the views of West Point across the river are well worth the donation.

Directly below Boscobel, the National Audubon Society operates the **Constitution Marsh Center & Sanctuary** (Rte. 9D/Indian Brook Rd., Garrison, 914/265-2601, www.constitutionmarsh.org). A short but steep and rocky path leads from the parking lot to a nature center and boardwalk that spans a large section of tidal marsh—an ideal setting for bird-watchers. The center offers guided canoe trips in summer months. The parking lot off Route 9D can accommodate only eight cars at a time, so be prepared to change plans if the sign says Full.

To the east of Route 9D in Garrison, Manitoga (Place of the Great Spirit of Algonquin) and the **Russel Wright Design Center** are a one-of-a-kind nature retreat and residence created by nationally acclaimed designer Russel Wright. With his unique and practical designs for the home, Wright championed easier living and pioneered lifestyle marketing. Beginning in 1942, he transformed an abandoned quarry and lumberyard in Garrison into a 75-acre masterpiece of ecological design, featuring native plants, stones, and streams. Dragon Rock, his experimental home, sits on a rock ledge, surrounded by four miles of trails that connect to the Appalachian Trail. Visitors can tour the home and grounds beginning at 11am on selected weekdays, 11am and 1:30pm weekends (Rte. 9D, Garrison, 845/424-3812, www.russelwrightcenter.org, office open 9am-5pm Mon.-Fri., adults $20, seniors $15, children 12 and under $10).

Another place to stroll in Garrison is the **Graymoor Spiritual Life Center** (Rte. 9, Garrison, 845/424-3671, www.atonementfriars.org), the headquarters of the Franciscan Friars of the Atonement. Open to the public, the grounds offer a serene vantage for scenic river views.

★ Cold Spring Village

The timeless village of Cold Spring lies in the shadow of Storm King Mountain, which rises 1,000 feet across the Hudson at the narrowest and deepest stretch of the river. A haven for antiques-lovers, Cold Spring's Main Street is divided into upper and lower sections that slope downhill toward an inviting gazebo at the river's edge—the site of many a marriage proposal. Adjoining it is the Foundry Dock Park, with access to the river. Pedestrians can cross the tracks via an underpass, but drivers must take a detour to the south to reach lower Main Street and the riverfront. An easy day trip for city dwellers, Cold Spring lures hikers, shoppers, and diners by the trainful. Treasures from vintage toys to designer jewelry await within walking distance of the station. There is a new visitors center booth located directly above the station, next to the Cold Spring Depot.

Nearby, the **Putnam County Historical Society** and **Foundry School Museum** (63 Chestnut St., Cold Spring, 845/265-4010, www.pchs-fsm.org, 11am-5pm Wed.-Sun., adults $5, seniors and students $2, children free) is a popular field trip for area schoolchildren. The building was constructed in 1817, when America was reeling from the War of 1812 and the realization that it needed a domestic source of iron to defend its borders, and now contains a collection of tools, letters, blueprints, and decorative ironworks, such as the ornate Washington Irving bench. Other

Cold Spring Village

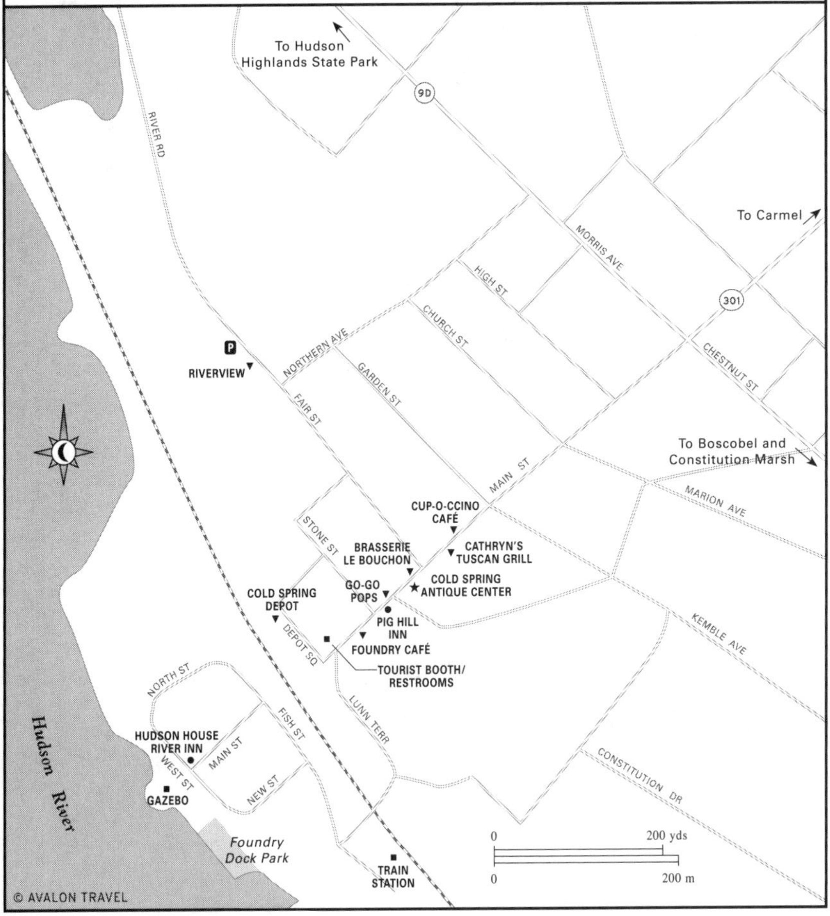

highlights include a famous painting by John Ferguson Weir called *The Gun Foundry* and the Civil War-era *Parrot Gun.*

Outdoor activities are readily accessible from Cold Spring: The most popular pastimes include paddling the river and the Constitution Marsh and hiking trails in the 4,200-acre Hudson Highlands State Park.

Hudson Highlands State Park

Extending the length of Putnam County, from Westchester to Dutchess, **Hudson Highlands State Park** (Rte. 9D, Beacon, 845/225-7207, www.nysparks.com, sunrise-sunset) offers 25 miles of hiking trails that meander along the ridgeline of the Hudson Highland range. Views of the river here are among the best anywhere in the region.

Bird-watchers frequent 900-foot-high Anthony's Nose at the Westchester County line to watch hawks, eagles, and vultures hover over the Bear Mountain Bridge. A route to the summit of South Beacon Mountain, six miles round-trip, brings hikers to the highest point along the range. Look for the trailhead on Route 9D, four miles north of Cold Spring. For a more challenging hike (5.5 miles round-trip), try the Breakneck Ridge Trail, which begins north of the tunnel on Route 9D, two miles north of Cold Spring. This trail covers some of the steepest terrain and most striking views in the park; however, it can be dangerous during inclement weather. Choose a different route in wet or windy conditions.

As a symbol of its commitment to preserving open space along the river, the New York State government added 240 acres to this park in 2002. Camping, campfires, bikes, and motorized vehicles are not permitted within the park. Fishing and boating are, however, permitted along the shoreline.

Bannerman Castle

As the river widens to form Newburgh Bay, a small island appears just north of Storm King Mountain and about four miles north of West Point. At less than seven acres, the island is made mostly of rock and sits about 1,000 feet from the river's eastern shore. (Though Bannerman Island lies technically within Dutchess County, it is most often viewed from Hudson Highlands itineraries.) It played a role in colonial history, first as part of a plan to stop the British from advancing north along the Hudson, and later as a designated military prison that was built but never used.

The island's most interesting story, however, is connected with a Scottish American entrepreneur named Frank (Francis) Bannerman VI, who collected and sold military goods acquired at government auctions. When he needed a place to store ammunition from the Spanish American War, Bannerman Island Arsenal came to be.

Bannerman acquired the island formerly known as Pollepel from the state of New York in 1900 and built a Scottish-style castle, complete with crenellated towers and turrets. The fortress housed the family business until 1967, when the Bannermans sold the island back to New York State. State officials had planned to open the island to visitors, but a fire in 1969 severely damaged many of the buildings, and the island remained off-limits for four decades, making it the subject of much speculation and mystery.

Today, what remains of the castle is managed by the **Bannerman Castle Trust** (www.bannermancastle.org), which offers guided walking tours May-October by boat

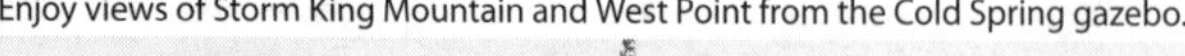

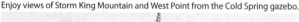

Enjoy views of Storm King Mountain and West Point from the Cold Spring gazebo.

The Amateur Geologist

Unless you are a professional geologist, it's hard to imagine that a good part of the Hudson River Valley was once a tropical sea. Over the course of hundreds of millions of years, a continual process of uplift and erosion—and four different ice ages—shaped the mountains and rivers we know today. As a result, geological sites abound along highways, in state parks, and on mountaintops across the region, offering insight for both professional and amateur scientists into the natural forces that have defined the topography over time.

WHERE TO GO

Hudson Highlands

Head first to Harriman State Park in search of rocky exposures along trails in the western part of the park. You can reach the trails directly from the Metro North station in Tuxedo. Plan for several hours of hiking to reach the best views and geological sites. Nearby, swing through Bear Mountain State Park to view examples of resilient Storm King Granite. Then cross the Bear Mountain Bridge to view the roadcuts along Route 9D near Anthony's Nose.

Upper Hudson

Start with the roadcuts along Route 23 between the towns of Leeds and Cairo in Greene County (New York State Thruway Exit 21), a popular destination for college fieldtrips. Continue northwest to Kaaterskill Falls on Route 23A to get an idea of the power of water erosion. In the Albany area, the "Indian Ladder" is a striking 80-foot-high limestone cliff inside John Boyd Thacher State Park.

WHAT TO LOOK FOR

In the Hudson Highlands, you'll encounter glacier-scoured exposures of bedrock, granite gneiss (combinations of sandstone and shale) cut by small veins of quartz, and abandoned iron mines. In the Catskills, look for fossils of ferns, root systems, and marine life, as well as ripple marks in shale layers.

WHERE TO LEARN MORE

The U.S. Geological Survey (USGS) has published a thorough guide to New York geological sites online, as well as an overview of geological fundamentals at http://3dparks.wr.usgs.gov. In addition, see local geologist Robert Titus's *The Catskills: A Geological Guide* (Fleischmann's, NY: Purple Mountain Press, 1998).

or kayak. Tours depart from nearby towns of Beacon, Cold Spring, Cornwall, and Newburgh. You can get a glimpse of the island and its abandoned castle from a river cruise or kayak tour—but paddlers, beware of strong currents around the island. Contact **Hudson River Adventures** (Newburgh/Beacon, 845/220-2120, www.prideofthehudson.com, $22) for sightseeing cruises, or **Hudson River Expeditions** (Cold Spring, 845/809-5935, www.hudsonriverexpeditions.com, $130) and **Storm King Adventure Tours** (Cornwall, 845/534-7800, www.stormkingadventuretours.com, $120) for guided paddling trips.

CENTRAL PUTNAM COUNTY: ALONG THE TACONIC STATE PARKWAY

Clarence Fahnestock Memorial State Park

The white sand beach at Canopus Lake in central Putnam County arrived by truck from Long Island in the late 1970s. Today, the completed waterfront complex has everything beach-goers need, save the salty air. A concession stand sells burgers and hot dogs, and there are showers, picnic tables, a boat launch, and campsites.

The beach sits within Putnam County's

second state park, **Clarence Fahnestock Memorial State Park** (1498 Rte. 301, Carmel, 845/225-7207, www.nysparks.com, call ahead as hours vary, $7/vehicle), which covers 10,000 acres extending from a few miles east of Cold Spring to beyond the Taconic State Parkway. Several lakes and ponds are suitable for boating and fishing.

Hikes on 42 miles of wooded trails range from easy to moderately strenuous. The Three Lakes Loop is a popular route that follows the bed of an old railroad line and meets up with the Appalachian Trail at the end. Along the way, hikers meander through forest, wetlands, and dense patches of mountain laurel (3.2 or 5.9 miles, depending on shortcuts). Mountain bikers and horseback riders have access to additional trails and bridle paths. Access the park from Route 301, which connects Route 9 along the Hudson River to the Taconic State Parkway.

Also inside the park, **Taconic Outdoor Education Center** (75 Mountain Laurel Rd., Cold Spring, 845/265-3773, www.nysparks.com, year-round for group use by reservation) has wildlife exhibits and runs geology, aquatic ecology, astronomy, and outdoor skills programs for groups only. Guests stay in nine heated log cabins. In winter, the center has more than nine miles of groomed cross-country ski trails, along with equipment rentals and lessons. A little farther east on Route 301, **Canopus Lake** has more trails for cross-country skiing. It's about a two-mile drive to the center from Route 301, and the turnoff is well marked.

EASTERN PUTNAM COUNTY: ALONG I-84

Brewster

Named for a local contractor, Walter Brewster, who built a station for the Harlem Line Railroad in the 1850s, this village thrived as an early thoroughfare between New York City and Danbury, Connecticut. Today, however, the town is a mixed bag of 19th-century homes and run-down storefronts.

Unique among regional museums, Brewster's **Southeast Museum** (67 Main St., 845/279-7500, www.southeastmuseum.org, 10am-4pm Tues.-Sat. Apr.-Dec., admission free) documents a number of seemingly unrelated developments—from the arrival of the early American circus and the Borden Condensed Milk factory to the engineering of the Harlem Line Railroad and the Croton Reservoir—that took place in and around the town of Southeast. Located in a historic building in downtown Brewster, the museum also displays a collection of antique farm equipment, quilts, and other Americana in rotating exhibits throughout the year.

Carmel and Mahopac

On the shores of a small lake at the intersection of Route 6 and Route 301 is Carmel (CAR-mel), the Putnam County seat since 1812. It is home to the second-oldest courthouse in New York State, a Greek Revival structure built in 1814.

Suburban Mahopac sits on the shores of Lake Mahopac, once a large resort community. Today, local residents water-ski, sail, and fish the lake during summer months. The town has two marinas for launching and servicing powerboats.

Nearby in Kent is a more unusual sight: the peaceful **Chuang Yen Monastery** (2020 Rte. 301, Kent, 845/225-1819, www.baus.org, 9am-5pm daily Apr.-Dec.), a Dharma education center featuring the largest Buddha statue in the Western Hemisphere. The 37-foot Buddha Vairocana towers over thousands of smaller statues inside the Great Buddha Hall, a pagoda-like structure that was built around the giant statue in the style of the Tang dynasty era (AD 618-917). The Woo Ju Memorial Library on the premises contains 70,0000 Buddhist reference texts in many different languages. A pleasant reading room faces Seven Jewels Lake and is open to the public.

Great Swamp

The **Great Swamp** (Patterson, www.frogs-ny.org) covers more than 6,000 acres of wetlands in Dutchess and Putnam Counties. Wildlife sightings include 185 species of birds, turtles, beaver dams, and otters. Most of the land is privately owned and in danger of being developed over time; however, local and national environmental organizations are working to raise awareness of the sensitive habitat and the important role it plays in the New York City watershed. The Appalachian Trail traverses the swamp in Dutchess County near Pawling. The best way to explore the swamp is by kayak. Paddlers can launch at **Green Chimneys School** (400 Doansburg Rd., at the Southeast-Patterson town line, 845/279-2995). Another, more challenging option is the **Patterson Environmental Park** (South St., Patterson, 845/878-6500).

SPORTS AND RECREATION

Putnam County offers a remarkable variety of outdoor activities, given its proximity to the urban sprawl of New York City. Much of the county's land and water is protected from development by the state park system. Trails are well maintained, and rental gear and professional instruction are readily available for a range of sports, including hiking, skiing, paddling, and horseback riding.

Winter Sports

During winter, Clarence Fahnestock Memorial State Park becomes a playground for Nordic skiing, snowshoeing, ice-skating, ice fishing, and snowmobiling. **Thunder Ridge Ski Area** (Rte. 22, Patterson, 845/878-4100, www.thunderridgeski.com, 10am-9pm Mon.-Fri., 9am-9pm Sat., 9am-5pm Sun., adults $40-50, juniors $25-37) is a family-run business with easy slopes that are ideal for beginners. The mountain runs a free shuttle from the Patterson train station during the peak season. They also offer babysitting services for a reasonable price.

Hiking

Both Hudson Highlands and Clarence Fahnestock state parks maintain extensive trail systems for hikers, including well-traveled stretches of the Appalachian Trail. Water found on the trails within these parks is not safe to drink. Bring your own. Except for the designated camping area at Canopus Lake, camping and campfires are not permitted within the parks.

The **Putnam Trailway** follows the route of the old New York Central Railroad, connecting Mahopac to Carmel and Brewster. From 1881 until 1958, the "Old Put" ushered passengers between the Bronx and Brewster. Today, the tracks are a paved bike- and footpath. Many sections are still under construction.

Cycling

Putnam's annual **Tour de Putnam Cycling & Mountain Biking Festival** (845/225-0381, www.visitputnam.org) takes place in late August. The races (15-100 miles) start and finish in Kent, covering miles of Putnam's pretty countryside. The Putnam Trailway is a 12-mile paved path along the route of the former New York Central Railroad. It begins at Baldwin Place in Westchester County and runs to Brewster at the Dutchess County line. A trail map is available at www.putnamcountyny.com.

Golf

Golfers can choose from four public golf courses in Garrison, Mahopac, and Carmel. The **Highlands Golf Club** (955 Rte. 9D, Garrison, 845/424-3254, www.highlandscountryclub.net, $28-35) has river views. It's open to the public daily in spring and fall. In summer, Saturday mornings and Sunday afternoons are reserved for members only. The **Garrison Golf Club** (2015 Rte. 9, Garrison, 845/424-4747, www.thegarrison.com, weekdays $55, weekends $80 for 18 holes) is open to the public daily April through November. Non-golfers can visit the spa instead. The **Putnam National Golf Club** (187 Hill St., Mahopac, 845/628-4200, www.putnamnational.com, $20-70 for 18 holes) also is open daily from mid-March through December. **The Centennial Golf Club** (185 John

Simpson Rd., Carmel, 845/225-5700, www.centennialgolf.com, $100-135 for 18 holes) has five lakes on the course and is open daily April through November.

Swimming and Boating

Putnam County offers aquatic activities on the Hudson and in several natural lakes located in its two state parks. For a sandy beach, head to Canopus Lake in Clarence Fahnestock Memorial State Park.

Hudson River Expeditions (14 Market St., Cold Spring, 845/809-5935, www.hudsonriverexpeditions.com, 11am-6pm Mon.-Fri., 9am-6pm Sat.-Sun.) runs beginner- to advanced-level kayak trips on the Hudson to Constitution Marsh, Bannerman Castle, and overnight destinations, as well guided hikes through the Hudson Highlands. You can also rent kayaks, but contact the shop at least a day in advance to find out about the tides for the hours when you want to paddle. You can only enter the marsh during low tide due to a railroad bridge that you need to paddle under. The **Constitution Marsh Center & Sanctuary** (Rte. 9D/Indian Brook Rd., Garrison, 914/265-2601, www.constitutionmarsh.org) offers guided canoe trips in summer months for $25 per adult or $15 per child age 7-15. Children under 7 are not permitted on canoe trips.

Fishing and Hunting

Anglers head to the lakes to catch bass, perch, pickerel, and trout. **Stillwater Lake** in Clarence Fahnestock Memorial State Park is stocked with rainbow and brook trout each spring. Brown trout are common in the streams that feed the New York City Watershed. Thirteen miles of water are open to the public, and the season typically runs April 1-September 30. Regulations vary by location and are more protective in Putnam County than elsewhere in New York State. In designated areas, size limits may be higher, daily limits may be lower, and artificial lures may be required. Bow hunting for deer and wild turkey hunting are permitted during limited seasons.

Water tumbles from the Hudson Highlands to the marsh and river below.

Horseback Riding

There are bridle paths in Clarence Fahnestock Memorial State Park, and **Hollow Brook Riding Academy** (890 Peekskill Hollow Rd., Putnam Valley, 845/526-8357, www.hollowbrookriding.com) offers lessons to new and experienced riders. **Chessfield Farm** (240 Washington Rd., Carmel, 914/227-5337, www.chessfieldfarm.com) is another option for riding and lessons.

ACCOMMODATIONS

Putnam County accommodations are extremely limited these days with the closure of two historic properties, The Plumbush Inn and the Bird & Bottle Inn. Besides these three choices in Cold Spring, budget motels near the interstate are the only other options. Happily, it's a short drive to more lodging choices in Orange and Dutchess Counties.

Fresh-fruit ice pops at Go-Go Pops are a delight on a hot summer day.

Under $100

Clean and affordable, the **Countryside Motel** (3577 Rte. 9, Cold Spring, 845/265-2090, www.countrysidemotelny.com, $75) has 22 rooms with full- or queen-size beds and in-room AC units. Some rooms have kitchenettes; two are suites with whirlpool tubs. The location on busy Route 9 may be noisy at times, and it's five miles from the Metro North station in Cold Spring. Plan on taking a cab if you arrive by train. The Wi-Fi is free here.

$150-250

The lobby of the three-story red brick ★ **Pig Hill Inn** (73 Main St., Cold Spring, 845/265-9247, www.pighillinn.com, $150-250) doubles as an antiques shop, and the effect is a cozy and historical feel. All nine rooms are individually appointed in Victorian decor and have private baths—some with marble tile and basins; several have poster beds, whirlpool tubs, and fireplaces or tiny woodstoves. After a comfortable night's sleep, enjoy breakfast made to order in the atrium. This is the place for a peaceful and intimate getaway.

At the bottom of Cold Spring's Main Street, the 1832 **Hudson House River Inn** (2 Main St., Cold Spring, 845/265-9355, www.hudsonhouseinn.com, $170-250) has 11 simply furnished guest rooms and 2 suites. Lodging comes with private bath, television, and breakfast. Some rooms have balconies with views of the Hudson River, which is steps away from the building. Others have small terraces that face Main Street. You can walk to antiques shopping and more fine dining along Main Street, as well as the Metro North station. The rooms are fairly basic for the price, but a stay here is worth it for the convenient location, historical appeal, and the convenience of a good restaurant on-site.

Campgrounds

The best place to pitch a tent in Putnam County is the shores of Canopus Lake in **Clarence Fahnestock Memorial State Park** (1498 Rte. 301, Carmel, 845/225-7207, $15-19 camping fee per night).

FOOD

Putnam County restaurants excel at blending farm-fresh ingredients with international cuisine to please the cosmopolitan palate.

Along the River: Route 9D

Kick off a day of antiquing with a fresh-baked scone at the **Foundry Café** (55 Main St., Cold Spring, 845/265-4504, $5-10), a popular gathering place for local residents on weekday mornings. **Cup-O-Ccino Café** (92 Main St., Cold Spring, 845/809-5574, www.cupoccino.com, 6am-6pm Mon.-Fri., 8am-7pm Sat.-Sun.) serves locally roasted organic and fair trade coffee and espresso drinks. You can also order smoothies, bagels, panini, soups, and ice cream.

Another place for a frozen treat is ★ **Go-Go Pops** (64 Main St., Cold Spring, 845/809-5600). Choose a fresh fruit ice pop made by hand on the premises. Flavors change frequently; at any given time there are usually more than a dozen to choose from. Recent faves include lime mojito, blueberry buttermilk, and pumpkin pie. You can also order bubble teas, soups, and fresh-squeezed juices. A little farther up Main Street, **Cathryn's Tuscan Grill** (91 Main St., Cold Spring, 845/265-5582, www.tuscangrill.com, lunch noon-5pm, dinner 5pm-10:30pm daily, brunch noon-3pm Sun., lunch $10-21, dinner $15-29) is a longtime favorite for an Italian-style lunch or dinner of spinach ravioli, linguini with clams, sautéed calamari, and other Italian dishes. Vegetarians report plenty of options on the wide-ranging menu. On a warm day, ask for a table in the courtyard. **Brasserie Le Bouchon** (76 Main St., Cold Spring, 845/265-7676, noon-10pm daily, $15-25) is a popular bistro with garden seating in warm weather and a few tables on the porch, from where you can watch the action on Main Street. On the menu are pâté, terrines, three different preparations of mussels, escargot, steak frites, cassoulet, and bouillabaisse. Be prepared for cozy seating indoors, as the dining room is very small.

The **Cold Spring Depot** (1 Main St., Depot Square, Cold Spring, 845/265-5000, www.coldspringdepot.com, 11:30am-9pm Sun.-Thurs., 11:30am-10pm Fri.-Sat., $10-23), at the foot of Main, has pleasant patio seating and a separate clam bar. A Dixieland band plays live music on weekends. Tucked away on a side street near the depot is a small gray building that houses **The Village Scoop** (1 Railroad Ave., 845/265-5000), a refreshing find on a hot summer day. **Moo Moo's Creamery** (32 West St., Cold Spring, 845/554-3666, www.moomooscreamery.com, 2pm-9pm Mon.-Fri., noon-9pm Sat.-Sun.), makes its ice cream fresh daily on-site. Flavors change daily and usually aim to surprise the palate. Try the fig walnut, pomegranate chip, or chai tea if you see them on the menu.

Hudson Hil's Café and Market (129-131 Main St., Cold Spring, 845/265-9471, www.hudsonhils.com, 8am-4pm Wed.-Mon.) serves breakfast and lunch with ingredients sourced from Hudson River Valley farms. A large porch offers good people-watching when the weather cooperates. This is a great place to fill your picnic basket with treats from the bakery and small market stocked with organic and gourmet foods including syrups, raw natural honey, premade salads, and teas. Another option: Choose from a menu of prepared meals at Boscobel House and Gardens, which partners with Hudson Hil's, and enjoy the riverside scenery.

A short walk from Main Street, **Riverview** (45 Fair St., Cold Spring, 845/265-4778, www.riverdining.com, noon-2:30pm and 5:30pm-9:30pm Tues.-Fri., noon-4pm and 5pm-10pm Sat., noon-9pm Sunday, $15-25, cash only) occupies an unassuming building with an enclosed terrace. Fresh fish, scallops, and oysters top the list of seafood specials. Starters include a large Caesar salad or beet and arugula salad. In business since 1941, the restaurant is located next to a large municipal lot for easy parking.

Hudson House River Inn (2 Main St., Cold Spring, 845/265-9355, www.hudsonhouseinn.com, lunch 11:30am-3:30pm daily, dinner 5pm-9pm Mon.-Thurs., 5pm-10pm Fri.-Sat., and 3:30pm-8pm Sun., $22-38) is the place for an old-world dining experience. Executive chef John Guerrero serves dishes including sesame-crusted sashimi tuna and rosemary loin of pork. The restaurant is affiliated with two Dutchess County eateries: Hudson's Ribs & Fish and Union House, both in Fishkill. A prix fixe Sunday brunch begins with an appetizer or fresh fruit martini and costs $33.

Another CIA-trained chef runs the kitchen at ★ **Valley Restaurant at The Garrison** (2015 Rte. 9 at Snake Hill Rd., Garrison, 845/424-3604, www.thegarrison.com, 5pm-9pm Thurs.-Sat. and 11:30am-2:30pm Sun. Mar.-Dec., $29-36), a golf and spa resort nestled among the Hudson Highlands. Farm-fresh ingredients are paired with creative sauces: shishito peppers with a miso aioli, raw oysters with an unusual black grape mignonette, softshell crab with a fava bean puree. Eggplant, chives, peas, carrots, potatoes, fennel, lettuce, spinach, and other vegetables are grown on-site in Garrison Farm's kitchen garden.

Guadalajara (2 Union St., Briarcliff Manor, 914/944-4380, www.guadalajaramexny.com, 11:30am-10pm Mon.-Thurs., 11:30am-11pm Fri.-Sun., $13-22) pours some of the best margaritas around at the bar in a mustard-yellow stucco building. Tile floors and bright colors complete the ambience inside. Order chiles rellenos, taquitos al carbon, tostadas, or bistec. Servers prepare guacamole at the table. Enjoy live music on Fridays and Saturdays.

Eastern Putnam County: Along I-84

You can't miss the red-and-white striped ★ **Red Rooster Drive-In** (1566 Rte. 22, Brewster, 845/279-8046, 10am-11pm Mon.-Thurs., 10am-1am Fri.-Sat., 10am-midnight Sun.) when driving along Route 22 through Brewster. This is a true retro eating experience: classic burgers, fries, onion rings, shakes, and ice cream too. Wait it out for a picnic table on the lawn and dig in.

For an evening of house-cured gravlax, grilled antelope medallions, or roasted baby pheasant, head to **The Arch** (Rte. 22N, Brewster, 845/279-5011, www.archrestaurant.com, $23-32, $40 prix fixe brunch, noon-2:30pm and 6pm-9pm Wed.-Fri., 6pm-9pm Sat., noon-8pm Sun., Sun. brunch until 3pm). For spicier fare, try **Jaipore Royal Indian Cuisine** (280 Rte. 22, Brewster, 845/277-3549, www.jaiporenyc.com, noon-3pm and 5pm-10pm daily, buffet $11-20), located in an 1856 mansion that was once a speakeasy. Known locally for its lunch buffet, the restaurant has several dining rooms, including an outdoor porch and patio.

Locals stop for burgers and hot dogs at **Forrest Side Street Café** (6 Old Rte. 22, Patterson, 845/878-6571, 11am-3pm Wed.-Sun.), near Pawling and the Dutchess County line, where a friendly couple serves food from a converted truck on the west side of Route 22.

In Mahopac, ★ **Il Laghetto** (825 S. Lake Blvd., Mahopac, 845/621-5200, www.theterraceclubrestaurant.com, Wed.-Sun. for lunch and dinner, Sun. brunch from 11am, $16-24) has revived the 1940s supper club scene and draws loyal patrons from several counties away. Guests are treated to a bowl of truffled popcorn while perusing the menu. Try the Meyer lemon Ceasar salad or Maryland crab cake, then move on to hanger steak frites or pan-seared grouper served with a horseradish and spring onion risotto. Terrace seating and lake views combined with good American-style foods at reasonable prices make for a memorable dining experience.

If you're out for a ride on the North County Trailway and need a bite to eat, hold out for the **Freight House Café** (609 Rte. 6, Mahopac, 845/628-1872, www.thefreighthousecafe.com, 8am-5pm Mon.-Thurs., 8am-10pm Fri., 9am-3pm Sat.), located just off the bike path on the site of the first building constructed for the New York Central & Hudson River Railroad branch, in 1872. The menu includes house-made granola, smoothies, wraps, espresso, and the like.

ENTERTAINMENT AND EVENTS

Performing Arts

The theater event of the summer in Putnam County is the **Hudson Valley Shakespeare Festival** (845/265-9575, www.hvshakespeare.org, $30-50), which started in 1987 and has staged *Hamlet, The Comedy of Errors,* and *Around the World in 80 Days.* This is a world-renowned festival that attracts more than 250,000 people each year. Performances take place under a tent at Boscobel House and Gardens. Special offerings include a beer garden, lawn parties, wine and cheese tastings, and family nights. Shows are performed from mid-June through early September at 6pm Sundays, 7pm Tuesdays through Thursdays, and 8pm Fridays and Saturdays. Children must be five or older to attend and no pets are allowed. Locals also adore the **Philipstown Depot Theatre** (Lower Station Rd., Garrison,

845/424-3900, www.philipstowndepottheatre.org) at Garrison Landing, a historic venue that dates back to 1892. The theater produces plays, children's programs, poetry readings, chamber music, cabaret, film, and other community programs.

Festivals

Dozens of dealers participate in the **Cold Spring Antiques Show** (97 Main St., Cold Spring, 845/265-4414) held each summer (past shows have been in June or July) in Mayor's Park on Fair Street.

Winterfest takes place at the Taconic Outdoor Education Center on National Winter Trails Days in January, with snowshoeing, nature walks, and crafts. In March, the center celebrates the maple sugaring season with a Maple Sunday Pancake Breakfast and hands-on demonstration of tapping trees and boiling sap into syrup. Call 845/265-3773 or visit www.nysparks.com for details. Brewster and Mahopac hold street fairs in October. Boscobel holds candlelight tours in December.

Events

The **New York Triathlon Club** (www.nytri.org) hosts the annual Tri 'n Du Putnam sprint distance triathlon in Carmel in July. The annual **Tour de Putnam Cycling & Mountain Biking Festival** (845/225-0381, www.putnamcycling.com) takes place in late August. The races (15-100 miles) start and finish in Kent, covering many miles of Putnam's pretty countryside.

Bars

Sports fans can view 22 TVs and a most impressive collection of memorabilia at **The Stadium** (1308 Rte. 9, Garrison, 845/734-4000, www.stadiumbarrest.com, 11:30am-10pm daily, bar stays open late). Unique treasures represent the essential all-American pastimes: football, baseball, basketball, and hockey, including two Heisman trophies, Mickey Mantle's Triple Crown award, and more. The restaurant serves pub fare 11:30am-10pm, and the bar stays open late with 16 beers on tap. The U-shaped bar at the **Cold Spring Depot** (1 Main St., Depot Square, Cold Spring, 845/265-5000, www.coldspringdepot.com, 11:30am-9pm Sun.-Thurs., 11:30am-10pm Fri.-Sat.) makes for a popular local watering hole, with Irish nights, jazz music, and acoustic guitar performances. A Dixieland band plays live music on weekends. Its annual Oktoberfest celebration features live oompah bands and Spaten beer on five weekends beginning in late September.

SHOPPING

Farm Stands

The Hudson River Valley's orchards aren't far away from Putnam County. **Brewster** (208 E. Main St. at Routes 22 & 6, 914/671-6262, www.brewsterfarmersmarket.com, 9am-2pm Wed. and Sat. mid-June-late Nov.) and **Cold Spring** (The Nest, 44 Chestnut St., 845/265-3611 8:30am-1:30pm Sat. May-Oct.) host two of the most popular farmers markets around. **Cascade Farm and Farm School** (124 Harmony Rd., Patterson, 845/878-3258, offers a community-supported agriculture program with shares of produce during the growing season, as well as a farm stand that's open to the public 8am-noon Saturdays. Everything here is grown without the use of chemicals or pesticides. Pick up honey, syrup, eggs, and other seasonal treats along with your fruits and veggies. **Kessman Brothers** (Cornwall Hill Rd., Patterson, 845/878-6071) has pumpkins and corn.

Antiques and Galleries

Casual and serious antiques collectors flock to Cold Spring for a day of retail adventure. Dozens of shops line Main Street, inviting shoppers with window displays of vintage toys, coins, jewelry, and home furnishings. Most stores close by 6pm, with some open later on weekend evenings. Many are also closed on Tuesdays.

The **Cold Spring Antiques Center & Odd Things** (77 East Main St., Cold Spring, 845/265-5050, 11am-5pm Thurs.-Mon.) is located just a few doors up from the Pig Hill Inn in a 19th-century bank building. Here you'll find furniture, records, dolls, toys, silver, jewelry, art glass, and other vintage items from multiple dealers. **Bijou Galleries** (50 Main St., Cold Spring, 845/265-4337, www.bijougalleries.com, 11am-5pm most days) represents 30 dealers of antiques, collectibles, and art. **Art & Antiques/Downtown Gallery** (40 Main St., Cold Spring, 845/265-4866, www.artantiquegallery.com, 11am-5pm Thurs.-Mon.), another multidealer shop, specializes in vintage clothing, books, magazines, comic books, records, lighting, prints, and costume jewelry. You can easily spend a few hours here reminiscing about the past.

For modern gifts for children or the home, visit the **Country Goose** (115 Main St., Cold Spring, 845/265-2122, www.countrygoose-highlands.com, 11am-6pm daily). A friendly British proprietor has everything from retro calendar towels and candles to games, coffee, and other knicknacks. She also prepares beautiful country gift baskets for a loyal clientele.

Mahopac's **Kitch 'n' Kaffe** (985 Rte. 6, Mahopac, 845/276-0072, www.kitch-n-kaffe.com, 9am-7pm Mon.-Fri., 10am-6pm Sat.-Sun.) sells high-end cooking equipment and ingredients, in addition to offering cooking classes for home chefs.

INFORMATION AND SERVICES

The **Putnam Visitors Bureau** (110 Old Rte. 6, Bldg. 3, Carmel, 800/470-4854 or 845/225-0381, www.visitputnam.org) is headquartered in Carmel, and its website contains detailed information on major destinations and sights in the county. The **Brewster Chamber of Commerce** (16 Mount Ebo Rd. S., Suite 12A, 845/279-2477, www.brewsterchamber.com) is located near the Southeast Museum. You can also pick up maps and brochures at the new Cold Spring visitors center, located directly above the pedestrian train track crossing at the foot of Main Street.

GETTING THERE AND AROUND

Bus

Putnam Area Rapid Transit (845/878-7433, www.putnamcountyny.com, $2.50 one-way) covers major towns throughout the county with four lines, but the **Metro-North rail lines** are a more reliable way to get around. A trolley is available for transportation to **Boscobel and Garrison Landing** (845/878-7433). A ride costs $1, and you can flag the trolley down anywhere you see one. Inquire at the Cold Spring visitors booth above the pedestrian train track crossing at the foot of Main Street.

Train

Two Metro-North rail lines serve Putnam County: The Hudson Line stops in Garrison and Cold Spring along the river, while the Harlem Line runs to Brewster on its way from Grand Central Station to Dover Plains in Dutchess County. Taxis are generally available from the stations.

Car

The easiest way to see Putnam County is by car, and the fastest routes are I-84 and the Taconic State Parkway. On busy weekend days in Cold Spring, look for free parking in a large municipal lot on Fair Street.

Mid-Hudson Valley and the Southern Catskills

North of the Hudson Highlands, the river widens once again, and the surrounding terrain forms rolling hills, babbling brooks, and expansive orchards. Fenced horse farms, fields of wildflowers, and ranks of wood stacked for winter heat are common sightings along the back roads of Dutchess and Ulster Counties. The two counties share 40 miles of coastline along this stretch of the Hudson, with four points of connection: the Newburgh-Beacon, Mid-Hudson, and Kingston-Rhinecliff Bridges—plus the new Walkway Over the Hudson pedestrian park, which connects Highland in Ulster County to Poughkeepsie in Dutchess County. A strong focus on the arts and abundant opportunities for farm-to-table dining draw visitors for weekends and longer stays—and are reviving once-prosperous towns that suffered from the decline of manufacturing along the river.

Cultural highlights in the Mid-Hudson region include the Frances Lehman Loeb Art Center at Vassar College, the Dia:Beacon museum, and the prestigious Culinary Institute of America (CIA). To complement the cuisine, a handful of wineries on both sides of the river produce award-winning chardonnay, pinot noir, merlot, and cabernet franc wines.

Several large state parks, including the southern region of the Catskill Forest Preserve and Minnewaska State Park Preserve, offer leaf-peepers a prime setting for viewing the annual display of fall colors. If you aren't afraid of heights, head to the Shawangunk Ridge in Ulster County for a day of rock climbing. And if you are inclined to stay at sea level, there are miles of country roads to explore by bicycle and trails to wander by foot.

PLANNING YOUR TIME

By far the most popular destination in the region is the bustling college town of New Paltz and the surrounding countryside. You can walk the town center in a few hours, but to absorb the alternative vibe, you'll want at least a couple of days. Plan a hike or a bike ride and then enjoy a meal at one of the area's outstanding

Previous: a wooden footbridge, Lake Minnewaska; a shaded overloop at Lake Minnewaska. **Above:** Skytop Tower in New Paltz.

Look for ★ to find recommended sights, activities, dining, and lodging.

Highlights

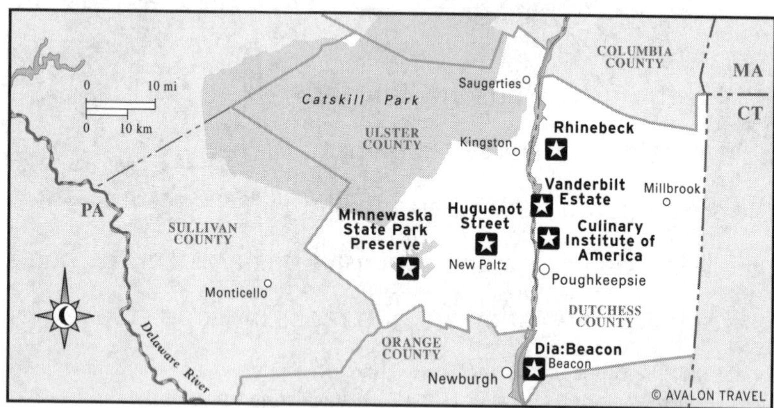

★ **Dia:Beacon:** Dutchess County's hottest contemporary art museum draws art aficionados out of New York City for a refreshing change of pace. Expansive single-artist galleries flooded with natural light hold paintings, sculptures, and installations from the 1960s to the present (page 102).

★ **Vanderbilt Estate:** The 50-room home of Frederick and Louise Vanderbilt exhibits a range of design influences, from Renaissance to Rococo. A carved wooden ceiling in the formal dining room is one of many European antiques found by designer Stanford White (page 108).

★ **Culinary Institute of America:** Set on a picturesque riverside campus, the CIA trains aspiring professionals and enthusiasts in the art of fine cuisine. Tour the grounds at sunset before eating in one of the five public restaurants on campus (page 109).

★ **Rhinebeck:** Rhinebeck stands out as an upscale enclave in an otherwise rural county. Victorian, Colonial, and Greek Revival buildings line several blocks of boutique stores, country inns, and gourmet eateries (page 109).

★ **Huguenot Street:** Named for the French Huguenots who came to America to escape persecution, Huguenot Street in New Paltz features stone dwellings now more than 300 years old (page 136).

★ **Minnewaska State Park Preserve:** Ulster County's gem of a park covers 12,000 acres of the Shawangunk Ridge with a sparkling glacial lake (page 137).

Mid-Hudson Valley and the Southern Catskills

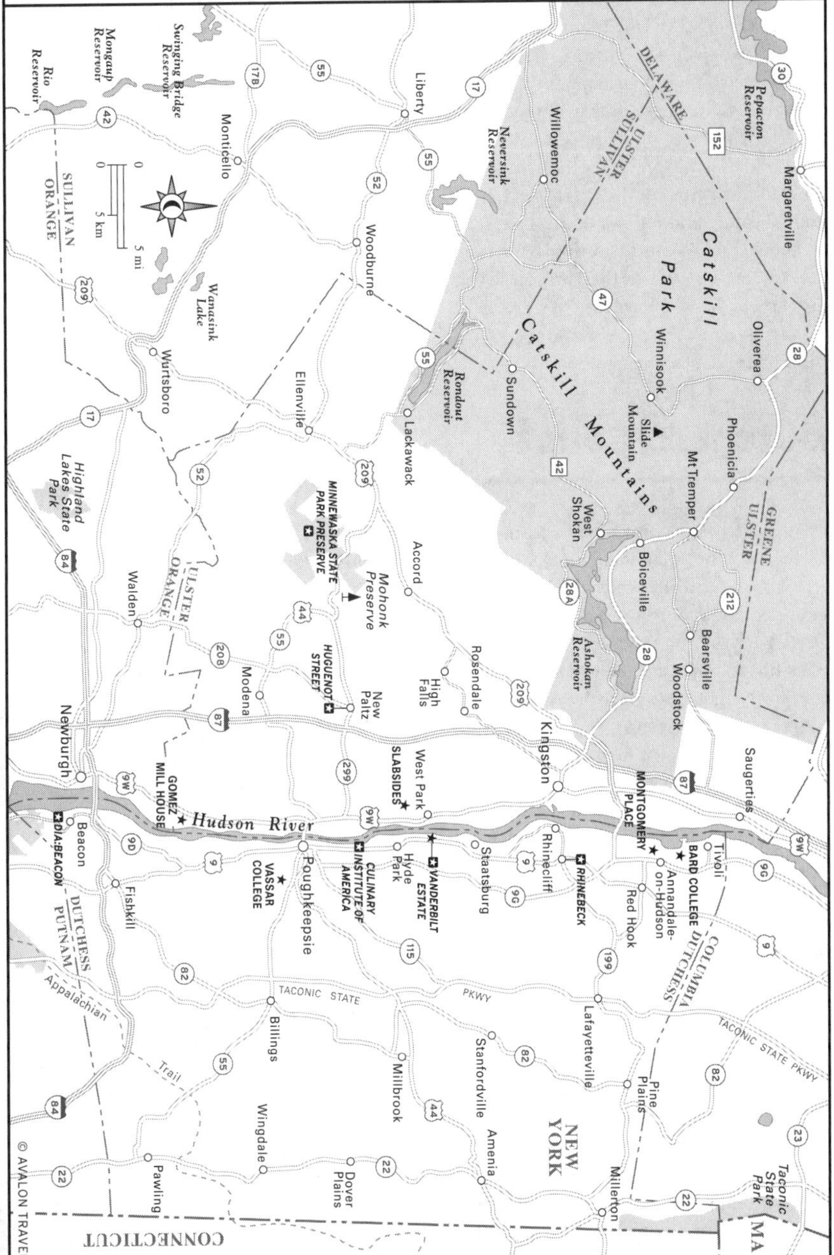

Catskill Park
Catskill Mountains
DELAWARE
ULSTER
SULLIVAN
GREENE
ORANGE
DUTCHESS
PUTNAM
COLUMBIA
NEW YORK
CONNECTICUT
MA
Pepacton Reservoir
Margaretville
Willowemoc
Neversink Reservoir
Liberty
Monticello
Mongaup Reservoir
Swinging Bridge Reservoir
Rio Reservoir
Wanasink Lake
Woodburne
Wurtsboro
Ellenville
Rondout Reservoir
Sundown
Lackawack
Winnisook
Slide Mountain
Oliverea
Phoenicia
Mt Tremper
West Shokan
Boiceville
Bearsville
Woodstock
Ashokan Reservoir
Saugerties
Kingston
Rosendale
High Falls
Accord
Mohonk Preserve
MINNEWASKA STATE PARK PRESERVE
HUGUENOT STREET
New Paltz
Modena
Walden
Highland Lakes State Park
Newburgh
Beacon
DIA:BEACON
GOMEZ MILL HOUSE
Hudson River
West Park
SLABSIDES
MONTGOMERY PLACE
Tivoli
BARD COLLEGE
Annandale-on-Hudson
Red Hook
Rhinecliff
RHINEBECK
Staatsburg
VANDERBILT ESTATE
Hyde Park
CULINARY INSTITUTE OF AMERICA
Poughkeepsie
VASSAR COLLEGE
Fishkill
Appalachian Trail
TACONIC STATE PKWY
Billings
Millbrook
Stanfordville
Lafayetteville
Pine Plains
Wingdale
Dover Plains
Amenia
Millerton
Pawling
Taconic State Park
0 5 mi
0 5 km

eateries. Rock climbers will want to spend the week scaling the ledges of the Gunks.

Poughkeepsie and Kingston, the largest cities in the area, are not destinations per se; however, you won't be wasting your time if you stop to stroll or dine along their historic waterfronts. History buffs may want to make a special trip to tour the many preserved sites.

In northern Dutchess County, a 60-mile loop begins at the train station in Poughkeepsie and follows Route 44 east to Millbook, then Route 22 north to Millerton, and Route 199 west to the Hudson River. From there, Route 9 hugs the riverbank back to Poughkeepsie. The drive should take two to three hours, depending on stops.

Ulster is a large county, and there are several options for scenic driving routes. One approach is to begin at the Mid-Hudson Bridge and follow Route 9D north to Kingston. Then take Route 28 west to Mount Tremper. A short loop along Route 212 heading northeast takes you through Woodstock and Saugerties and eventually back to Route 9W. Or you can continue along Route 28 to Belleayre Mountain and Delaware County beyond. Closer to Kingston, Route 209 south off Route 28 goes to New Paltz and Minnewaska State Park Preserve. Allow about half an hour to drive from New Paltz to Kingston on local roads, and an hour to cross the county from east to west.

Dutchess County

Scenic Dutchess County offers a telling mix of restored historic landmarks and nearly deserted manufacturing centers, bedroom communities, and progressive towns that attract weekenders by the thousands. A sampling of its historic riverside mansions should anchor every first-time visitor's itinerary. The county seat, Poughkeepsie, was designated the New York state capital in 1777, a distinction it held for about a decade. IBM set up shop in the 1950s, and despite the massive layoffs of the early 1990s, the company remains the county's dominant employer.

Poughkeepsie and Dover Plains mark the northern ends of the Metro-North commuter lines. But while the southern half of Dutchess County has succumbed to the congestion of suburban sprawl, the northern part retains an idyllic charm.

ALONG THE RIVER: ROUTE 9

★ Dia:Beacon

A flight along the Hudson in search of a new museum space resulted in the creation of a major new cultural attraction for Dutchess County, and a positive influence on the surrounding town. Michael Govan, then the director of New York City-based Dia Center for the Arts, reportedly spotted the 75-year-old printing plant from the air and immediately chose the site to house the museum's permanent collection. The result is an enormous contemporary art museum, **Dia:Beacon** (3 Beekman St., Beacon, 845/440-0100, www.diabeacon.org, 11am-6pm Thurs.-Mon. Apr.-Oct., limited winter hours, adults $12, seniors $10, students $8, children under 12 free), with constantly changing exhibits that draw art aficionados out of New York City for a refreshing change of pace. Spacious single-artist galleries flooded with natural light hold paintings, sculptures, and installations from the 1960s to the present. Don't miss Richard Serra's *Torqued Ellipses* on the lower level. The towering pieces look especially dramatic at sunset, when they catch the light streaming in through frosted-glass windows. Outside, the West Garden presents sweeping river views.

Beacon

The Dia:Beacon is located outside the small city of Beacon, which began to show early

Beacon

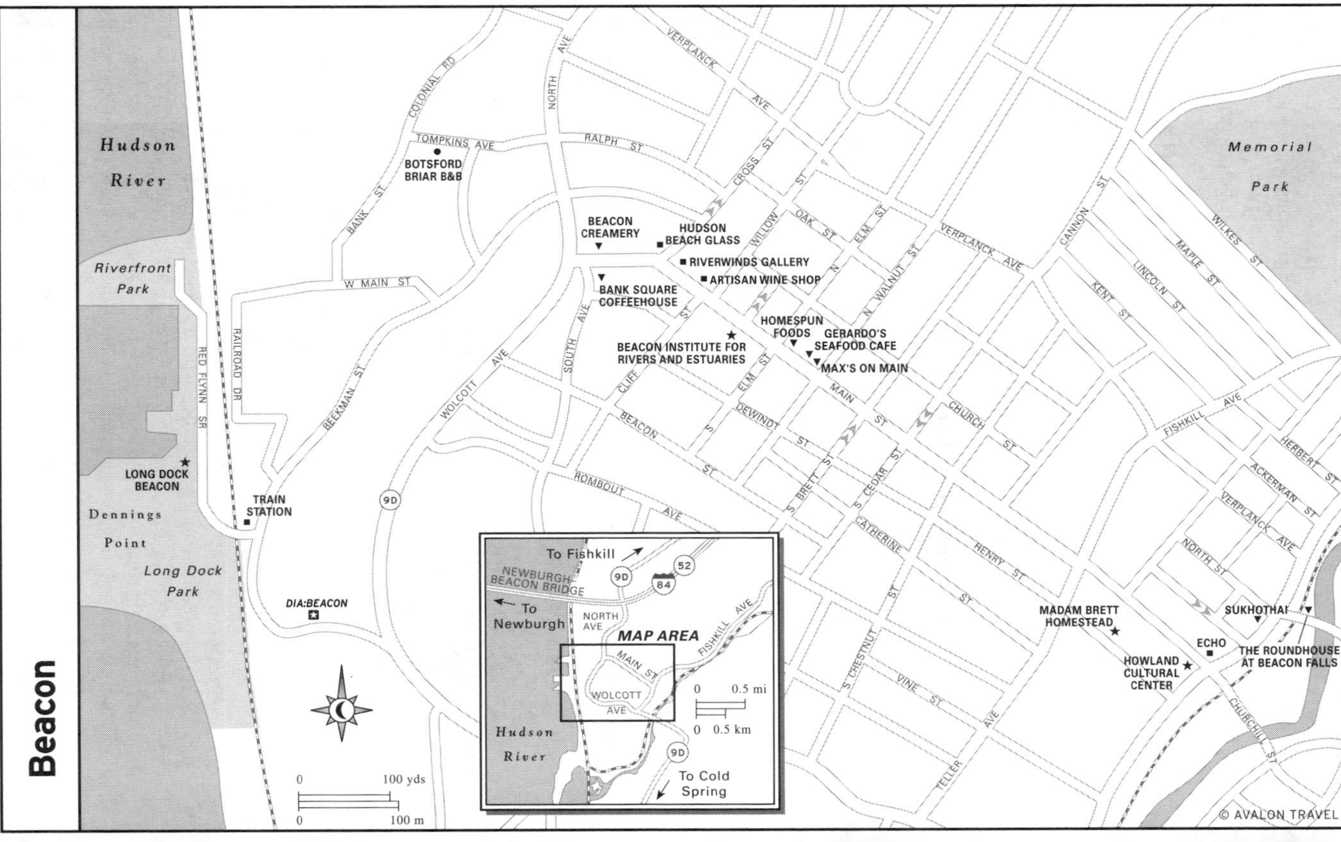
Hudson River
Riverfront Park
LONG DOCK BEACON
Dennings Point
Long Dock Park
RED FLYNN SR
RAILROAD DR
TRAIN STATION
DIA:BEACON
BEEKMAN ST
W MAIN ST
BANK ST
COLONIAL RD
TOMPKINS AVE
BOTSFORD BRIAR B&B
NORTH AVE
RALPH ST
VERPLANCK AVE
CROSS ST
WILLOW ST
OAK ST
ELM ST
BEACON CREAMERY
HUDSON BEACH GLASS
RIVERWINDS GALLERY
ARTISAN WINE SHOP
BANK SQUARE COFFEEHOUSE
SOUTH AVE
WOLCOTT AVE
9D
N WALNUT ST
HOMESPUN FOODS
GERARDO'S SEAFOOD CAFE
MAX'S ON MAIN
BEACON INSTITUTE FOR RIVERS AND ESTUARIES
CLIFF ST
ELM ST
MAIN ST
BEACON ST
DEWINDT ST
S ST
CHURCH ST
ROMBOUT AVE
S BRETT ST
S CEDAR ST
CATHERINE ST
HENRY ST
S CHESTNUT ST
VINE ST
TELLER AVE
CANNON ST
KENT ST
LINCOLN ST
MAPLE ST
WILKES ST
Memorial Park
FISHKILL AVE
HERBERT ST
ACKERMAN ST
VERPLANCK AVE
NORTH ST
MADAM BRETT HOMESTEAD
HOWLAND CULTURAL CENTER
ECHO
SUKHOTHAI
THE ROUNDHOUSE AT BEACON FALLS
CHURCHILL ST
0 100 yds
0 100 m
To Fishkill
NEWBURGH-BEACON BRIDGE
To Newburgh
NORTH AVE
MAP AREA
MAIN ST
WOLCOTT AVE
FISHKILL AVE
52
84
9D
0 0.5 mi
0 0.5 km
Hudson River
To Cold Spring
© AVALON TRAVEL

signs of revival in the 1990s with the restoration of a stretch of East Main Street, now the city's antiques district. Its 15,500 residents are nestled between Mount Beacon (which one can hike in under an hour), a recent extension of the Hudson Highlands State Park, and the eastern bank of the Hudson. Today, nearly the entire 1.5-mile street has been developed, from Route 9D to Wappinger Creek—with only a few older buildings remaining in the middle stretch. More than 100 artists have opened studios in town, plus there are galleries, cafés, shops, and restaurants to explore. Real estate prices have soared as the town builds a new profile.

One historic sight, well maintained over the years, is the 1709 **Madam Brett Homestead** (50 Van Nydeck Ave., Beacon, 845/831-6533, melzingah.awardspace.com/id5.htm, tours given on the second Saturday each month 1pm-4pm Apr.-Dec. or by appointment, adults $5, students $2), another George Washington haunt and Dutchess County's oldest dwelling. Visitors can tour 17 rooms filled with antiques, artwork, and seven generations' worth of Brett family memorabilia. On the National Historic Register, the **Howland Cultural Center** (477 Main St., Beacon, 845/831-4988, www.howlandculturalcenter.org) houses the Beacon Historical Society and hosts art exhibits, performances, and other events. A sign/trail map and small dirt parking lot at the north end of town on Route 9D mark the starting point for a hike up Mount Beacon, one of the toughest stair workouts around.

Farther north on Route 9D, the **Mount Gulian Historic Site** (145 Sterling St., Beacon, 845/831-8172, www.mountgulian.org, 1pm-5pm Wed.-Fri. and Sun. mid-Apr.-Oct., adults $8, seniors $6, children $4) appears at the end of a row of modern townhouses. The 18th-century Dutch stone barn and 44 acres of gardens descending to the riverbank belonged to the Verplanck family and served as the headquarters of influential Revolutionary War General Friedrich Wilhelm Augustus von Steuben, a German volunteer who led the Americans to a critical victory at Freehold, New Jersey, in 1778.

Beacon has also become a hub of environmental activity, with the opening of the **Beacon Institute for Rivers and Estuaries** (199 Main St., Beacon, 845/838-1600, www.bire.org), formed to study and protect rivers, estuaries, and watersheds such as the Hudson River. Folk singer Pete Seeger, owner of the Hudson River sloop ***Clearwater*** (www.clearwater.org), lived in town until his death in early 2014. And Scenic Hudson's **Long Dock Park** (Long Dock Rd., open dawn-dusk year-round) is a cleaned-up waterfront green space with a kayak launch and new sculpture called *Beacon Point*. A one-mile trail connects the park to the Beacon train station and Denning's Point State Park.

Fishkill and Wappingers Falls

Two miles east of Beacon, the signature steeple of the **First Reformed Church** (55 Main St., Fishkill, 845/896-9836, www.fishkillreformed.org) marks the village center of Fishkill (Fisherman's Creek), a major hub of wartime activity during the American Revolution. The church dates to 1731 and served as both a New York State government meeting place and a prison. Today, the town primarily hosts business travelers en route to IBM.

One mile south of town at the highway interchange of I-84 and Route 9, the **Van Wyck Homestead Museum** (504 Rte. 9 at I-84, Fishkill, 845/896-9560, 1pm-4pm Sat.-Sun. June-Oct., donations accepted) stands out among the surrounding group of chain hotels. Army officers and heads of state convened here during the American Revolution. The barracks and blacksmith shop that once surrounded the home are lost to history, but the town historical society continues to restore the inside with original documents and period furnishings.

Stony Kill Farm Environmental Center (79 Farmstead Ln., Wappingers Falls, 845/831-1617, www.stonykill.org, sunrise-sunset daily), run by the New York Department of

Environmental Conservation, is a good place to stop for a picnic and a refresher in environmental science. Look for one of two entrances off Route 9D (Exit 11 from I-84). A tree-lined driveway leads to the Manor House and surrounding gardens. Inside, a visitors center houses an extensive library with titles on a wide variety of nature topics, including acid rain, wildlife management, and environmental literature.

Visit the Common Ground Farm on the property to learn about the model of community-supported agriculture (CSA). Historic buildings associated with the farm include a 19th-century barn and farmhouse and an 18th-century Dutch stone house.

Several interpretive trails, ranging from 0.5 to 2.5 miles long, lead walkers though evergreen and hardwood forests, across fields, and around ponds. Brochures for self-guided tours are available at each trailhead. The center holds special events throughout the year, including maple sugaring demonstrations, wildflower walks, and programs for children.

Poughkeepsie

Poughkeepsie has suffered the fate of postindustrial contraction worse than most. In a textbook case of urban decay, the majority of the city's middle-class residents fled the city center for the suburbs during the late 20th century, leaving once-beautiful homes boarded up and a six-lane arterial in their wake. When IBM slashed its workforce by two-thirds in the early 1990s, scores of small businesses went under, and the local economy never fully recovered. Though this city of 32,700 has a few historical gems, well-meaning locals continue to steer travelers north to Rhinebeck for a decent night's sleep.

That said, there are encouraging signs of recovery, notably, the opening of the long-awaited **Walkway Over the Hudson State Historic Park** (www.walkway.org, 7am-sunset daily), a 1.3-mile-long span that connects downtown Poughkeepsie to Highland across the Hudson River. Once an abandoned railroad bridge, the area's newest pedestrian park holds the distinction of being the longest elevated pedestrian bridge in the world. It is wheelchair accessible from both sides, and motorized scooters or power-assisted vehicles are allowed for visitors with mobility needs. To start at the east side, drive Route 9 to Route 9G north. Bear right onto Washington Street and continue for half a mile. Turn left on Route 9G/Parker Avenue and park at the lot on the left (61 Parker Ave., $5).

Walkway Over the Hudson State Historic Park

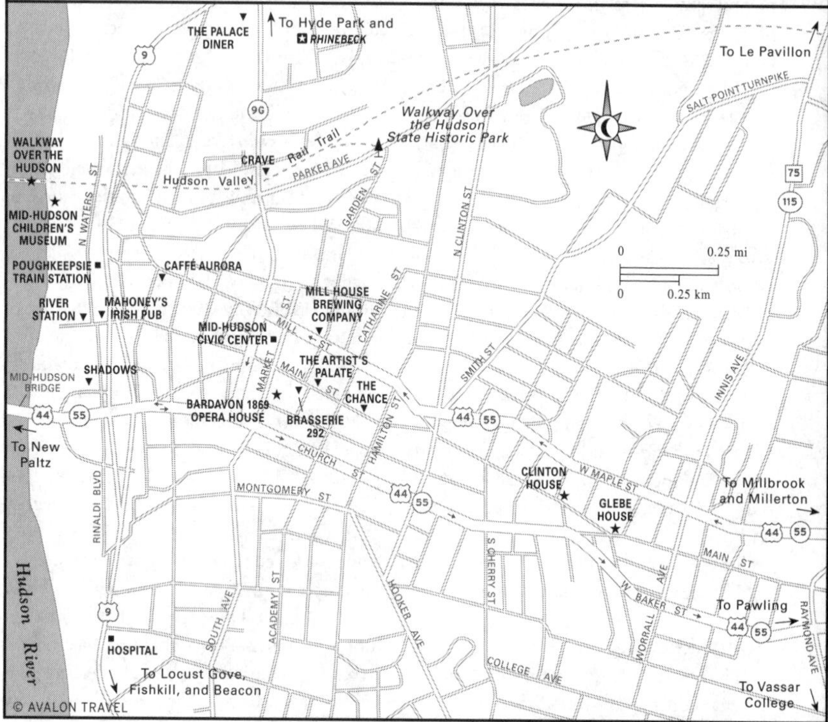

Poughkeepsie has reopened its Main Street to car traffic to draw retail businesses back, and the old storefronts are getting new tenants and a fresh coat of paint. And the Bardavon 1869 Opera House continues to stage first-rate theater performances. With the influence of Vassar College, New York City commuters, and the **Culinary Institute of America** (1946 Campus Dr., Hyde Park, 845/451-1588 or 845/452-9600, www.ciachef.edu), Poughkeepsie has an appealing mix of culture and diversity. Like Newburgh to the south and Kingston to the north, its recovery hinges on making the waterfront an attractive place for residents and visitors alike.

Poughkeepsie's Main Street begins at Waryas Park under the Mid-Hudson Bridge and runs east-west between the two legs of the arterial (Rtes. 44/55) until it reaches the town of Arlington. The Hudson River Sloop *Clearwater* and its sister vessel, *Mystic Whaler*, dock here when they are in the area, as Poughkeepsie is the headquarters for the nonprofit environmental organization that runs them. Modeled after the Dutch vessels that sailed the Hudson in the late 18th century, *Clearwater* was conceived in the 1960s as a call to action to clean up the river before it was too late. In a unique classroom setting, *Clearwater* volunteers educate local residents about the importance of environmental awareness and conservation. Since 1966, the watchdog organization has battled GE on the dumping of PCBs into the river, prosecuted Clean Water Act offenders, and pioneered the model of encouraging environmental advocacy through a hands-on sailing experience.

Moving away from the riverfront, a number of historic sites are clustered in the downtown area near Academy Street. The **Clinton House** (549 Main St., Poughkeepsie, 845/471-1630, www.nysparks.com, 10am-3pm Tues.-Fri. by appointment) holds the offices and library of the Dutchess County Historical Society. This stone building hosted the New York State government briefly in 1777 and was rebuilt after a fire in 1783. The society also runs the neighboring **Glebe House** (635 Main St., Poughkeepsie, 845/454-0605, www.dutchesscountyhistoricalsociety.org, tours by appointment only), a restored home dating back to 1767.

The **Bardavon 1869 Opera House** (35 Market St., Poughkeepsie, 845/473-5288, box office 845/338-6088, www.bardavon.org) escaped demolition in the mid-1970s only to become listed on the National Register of Historic Places. With its original pipe organ (a 1928 Wurlitzer theater organ), and an interior dome that dates to 1920, the Bardavon is one of the oldest surviving theaters in the United States. Legendary performers from Mark Twain to Frank Sinatra have appeared on its stage. Today, the theater hosts the Hudson Valley Philharmonic and a full schedule of musical, dance, film, and theater productions by contemporary artists.

Samuel B. Morse became a household name in the 1840s when he developed the first commercial telegraph, sending the famous words "What hath God wrought" across the line. With money earned from the venture, Morse bought **Locust Grove** (2683 South Rd., Poughkeepsie, 845/454-4500, www.lgny.org, 10am-5pm daily Apr.-Dec., 10am-5pm Mon.-Fri. Jan.-Mar., adults $10, children $6), a 100-acre property south of the Mid-Hudson Bridge that is now a National Historic Landmark. The Italianate villa houses an informative exhibit on telegraph technology, as well as American and European furniture and many of Morse's own paintings. The surrounding woods and gardens are open to the public year-round.

Vassar College

Between downtown Poughkeepsie and Arlington is the ivory tower of Vassar College, a top-ranked liberal arts school that draws students from across the country and around the world. Vassar's attractive campus is spread over 1,000 acres with some 200 varieties of trees interspersed among inviting lawns. English brewer Matthew Vassar founded the college in 1861 in an effort to provide young women with courses in science, math, art history, and music to rival those of the best men's schools in the country. Vassar remained a women's college until 1969, when the first coed class was admitted.

Vassar prides itself on being first among U.S. colleges to have established its own art gallery. Today, the **Frances Lehman Loeb Art Center** (124 Raymond Ave., Poughkeepsie, 845/437-5632 or 845/437-5237, fllac.vassar.edu, 10am-5pm Tues.-Wed. and Fri.-Sat., 10am-9pm Thurs., 1pm-5pm Sun., free admission) holds a varied permanent collection, from ancient Egyptian sculptures of marble and red granite to contemporary American paintings. The museum stays open late on Thursday evenings, until 9pm. Enter the gallery near the main gate on Raymond Avenue.

East of Vassar College, where Route 55 meets the Taconic State Parkway, is **James Baird State Park** (845/452-1489, www.nysparks.com, hours vary) with an 18-hole golf course, tennis courts, picnic areas, and hiking trails. Its wooded trails are popular with local runners, while families use the playground and attend programs at the nature center on summer weekends.

Back at the river's edge, Matthew Vassar's former home is now the **Springside National Historic Site** (185 Academy St., Poughkeepsie, 845/454-2060, info@springsidelandmark.org, www.springsidelandmark.org, dawn-dusk), preserved as the last standing design of landscape architect Andrew Jackson Downing. Most of the estate's 44 acres belong to a private condominium complex now, but visitors can view the restored gatehouse and wander along old carriage roads. Look for the entrance on Academy Street, on the west side of Route 9.

Hyde Park

Hyde Park offers a strong lineup for students of history and visitors who travel to eat. For starters, the **Home of Franklin D. Roosevelt National Historic Site** (Rte. 9, Hyde Park, 845/229-5320 or 800/337-8474, www.nps.gov/hofr, tour times vary, adults $18, 15 and under free, grounds open dawn-dusk daily, no fee), where the four-term president lived all his life, houses FDR's presidential library and museum. Exhibits inside chronicle the president's and first lady's achievements. Visitors can also tour **Top Cottage** (7097 Albany Post Rd., Rte. 9, Hyde Park, 845/229-5320, www.nps.gov/hofr, open daily May-Oct.), the hilltop retreat where FDR met with international heads of state. Trails on 300 acres lead to the river's edge.

Eleanor Roosevelt spent many quiet years at the unassuming Val-Kill Cottage after FDR's death. Today, the **Eleanor Roosevelt National Historic Site—Val-Kill** (Rte. 9G, Hyde Park, 845/229-9422, www.nps.gov/elro, 9am-5pm daily May-Oct., tours at 1pm and 3pm only Thurs.-Mon., Nov.-Apr., admission $10) welcomes visitors with guided home tours and 180 acres of beautifully landscaped grounds.

Between Hyde Park and Rhinebeck along Route 9 stands a tribute to the Gilded Age: the former residence of Ogden Mills—a financier and philanthropist—and Ruth Livingston Mills, a descendent of the Livingston family, who first settled much of Columbia County. The home began as a 25-room Greek Revival in 1832. Subsequent renovations by the same architectural firm that built the Vanderbilt Estate turned it into a massive 65-room estate adorned with exquisite furnishings from Europe and Asia. The property was handed over to the State of New York in 1938 to become the **Staatsburgh State Historic Site** (Old Post Rd., Staatsburg, 845/889-8851, www.nysparks.com, 11am-4pm Sat.-Sun. Jan.-Mar., 11am-5pm Tues.-Sun. Apr.-Oct., call for Nov.-Dec. holiday schedule, adults $8, seniors and students $6, 12 and under free).

If you are a train enthusiast, save time to visit the tiny **Hyde Park Railroad Station** (34 River Rd., Hyde Park, 845/229-2338, www.hydeparkstation.com, 5pm-9pm Mon. year-round, noon-5pm Sat.-Sun. and holidays June-Sept., adults $5, children $4). Built in 1914, the station was restored by the Hudson Valley Railroad Society and holds a treasured place on the National Register of Historic Places. Follow River Road from Route 9 in Hyde Park.

★ Vanderbilt Estate

A tour inside the **Vanderbilt Estate** (Rte. 9, Hyde Park, 845/229-7770, www.nps.gov/vama, 9am-5pm daily, adults $10, 15 and under free) will also send you straight back to the days of robber barons, railroad monopolies, and American capitalism run amok. A fine product of the Gilded Age, the 50-room home of Frederick and Louise Vanderbilt exhibits a variety of interior design influences, from Renaissance to Rococo. A carved wooden ceiling in the formal dining room is one of many European antiques found by designer Stanford White.

Though they only spent a few weeks per year at the estate, the Vanderbilts enjoyed it as a place to entertain guests, who arrived by boat, rail, or private car. Thirteen rooms on the third floor were reserved as quarters for the maids of lady visitors. Outside, the property remains as beautiful today as it did a century ago. Local residents meet here on weekends to play Frisbee and picnic on the lawn. Contemporary artists often set up canvases to paint the river and surrounding landscape. The grounds are open 7am-sunset and there is no admission fee. The Hyde Park Trail system connects the Roosevelt and Vanderbilt estates along the river. Inquire at any of the homes for a trail map.

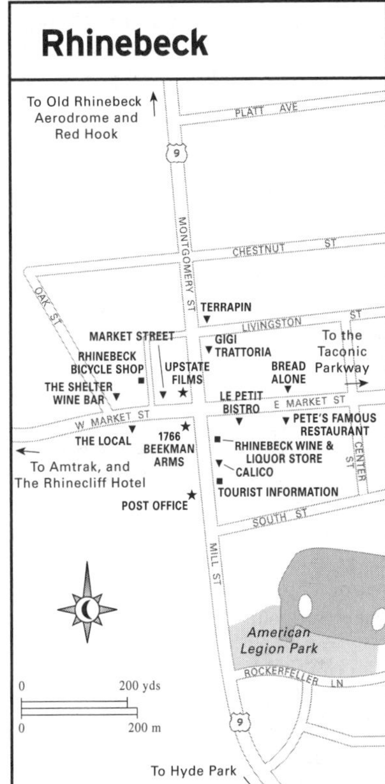

★ Culinary Institute of America

Since 1970, Hyde Park has been home to the oldest culinary college in the United States, the prestigious **Culinary Institute of America** (1946 Campus Dr., Hyde Park, 845/451-1588, www.ciachef.edu, tours 10am and 4pm Mon., 4pm Tues.-Fri., $6, reservations required). Set on a picturesque riverside campus, formerly the site of a Jesuit seminary, the CIA trains aspiring professionals and enthusiasts in the art of fine cuisine. Its facilities include 41 kitchens and the largest collection of culinary books and reference materials of any library in the country. Among the school's best-known graduates is Anthony Bourdain, author of the bestseller *Kitchen Confidential* and chef-at-large of Les Halles in New York City.

Tour the grounds at sunset before dining in one of the five public restaurants on campus. Better yet, enroll in one of the CIA's Boot Camp programs, which are multiday intensive courses geared toward cooking enthusiasts. Classes cover a variety of rotating topics, such as French cuisine, baking, and healthy cooking. Tuition is steep at $895 for two days and $2,195 for five days.

★ Rhinebeck

Continuing north on Route 9, Rhinebeck stands out as an upscale enclave in an otherwise rural region. Victorian, Colonial, and Greek Revival buildings line several blocks of boutique stores, country inns, and gourmet restaurants expanding out from the intersection of Routes 9 and 308. (Route 9 is called Mill Street south of Route 308, and Montgomery Street north of Route 308; Route 308 is also called Market Street.)

At the center of all the activity is the 1766 **Beekman Arms** (Rte. 9, Rhinebeck, 845/876-7077, www.beekmandelamaterinn.com), reportedly the oldest continuously operating inn in the United States and where many guests stayed for Chelsea Clinton's wedding in 2010. Indeed, colonial history and political intrigue rise from every creak in the floorboards. George Washington, Philip Schuyler, Benedict Arnold, and Alexander Hamilton are among the most famous overnight guests. Local townspeople gathered inside for safety while the British burned Kingston to the ground across the Hudson.

As Rhinebeck grew into a commercial crossroads, the inn became a popular venue for political and cultural discussion. FDR even delivered several victory speeches from the front porch. The inn has expanded over the years, but much of the original building remains intact, including the oak beams and pine plank floor. The place is worth a peek, whether or not you plan to stay the night.

Next door to the Beekman Arms, FDR oversaw construction of the **Rhinebeck Post Office** (6383 Mill St.) through the Works Progress Administration (WPA). The building was designed to commemorate the first house in Rhinebeck. Inside, a series of murals chronicle the town's history. The **Dutch Reformed Church** (16 Albany Post Rd., Hyde Park, 845/229-5354), across Route 9 from the post office, was built in 1808.

Idyllic family farms and grand country estates surround the town of Rhinebeck. **Wilderstein** (330 Morton Rd., Rhinebeck, 845/876-4818, www.wilderstein.org, noon-4pm Thurs.-Sun. May-Oct. and weekends in Dec., group tours by reservation, adults $10, students/seniors $9, children under 12 free), a riverside mansion located south of town on Route 9, has a five-story round tower that juts upward from its center, offering views of an equally dramatic landscape. With ties to the prominent Beekman and Livingston families, this fanciful Queen Anne country home began as an Italianate villa in the mid-19th century. Carefully planned trails, vistas, and lawns around the property reflect the Romantic-era aesthetic.

North of town, the Dutchess County Fairgrounds holds antique car shows and the annual Dutchess County Fair. Amtrak services the train station in Rhinecliff, three miles to the west.

Red Hook

The sleepy town of Red Hook received its name when early Dutch explorers ventured up the Hudson to find red sumac and Virginia creeper in full bloom. The Dutch called it Red Hoek (Red Peninsula), and the name has stuck ever since. A modern-day bedroom community, Red Hook encompasses the Village of Tivoli and hamlet of Annandale-on-Hudson on the banks of the river, as well as Bard College and the Village of Red Hook to the east. A small commercial district fans out from the intersection of Routes 9 and 199, with a John Deere store, CVC pharmacy, Stewarts, and a few casual eateries.

A rocker on the North Porch is the best seat in the house at **Montgomery Place** (River Rd., Annandale-on-Hudson, 845/758-5461, www.hudsonvalley.org, 10am-4pm Thurs.-Sun. May-Oct., adults $10, children under 5 free, grounds only free). Nestled among 434 acres of woodlands with views of the Catskill Mountains across the Hudson, Montgomery Place is a stunning riverside estate conceived in the Federal style. Located in Annandale-on-Hudson, the home has been restored with period furnishings and enchanting gardens. Fruit from the estate orchards is available in season at the Montgomery Place Orchards Farm Stand.

Many of the undergraduate students at **Bard College** (Rte. 9G, Annandale, 845/758-6822, www.bard.edu) have views of the Hudson and Catskill Mountains from their dorms. An affiliate of Columbia University, the liberal arts school is set on 500 acres of lawns and woodlands. A variety of music and performing arts programs are open to the public year-round.

CENTRAL DUTCHESS COUNTY: ROUTES 44 AND 22

Pawling

Routes 22 and 55 meet at Pawling, in the southeastern corner of Dutchess County. Named after Colonel Henry Beekman's daughter, Catherine Pawling, the town has been a crossroads of commercial activity since colonial days. Pawling's early settlers were Quakers, as documented by the display of artifacts in the **Quaker Museum, Akin Free Library** (378 Old Quaker Hill Rd., Pawling, 845/855-5099, 2pm-4pm Sat.-Sun.). The 1764 Oblong Friends Meeting House served as a temporary hospital for George Washington's troops in 1778. And Washington set up headquarters in the John Kane House. Inside is a replica of the village from the year 1948, complete with moving trains.

Today, Pawling attracts New York City commuters, Appalachian Trail hikers, and celebrities seeking privacy. Keep an eye out for permanent resident James Earl Jones if you pass through town.

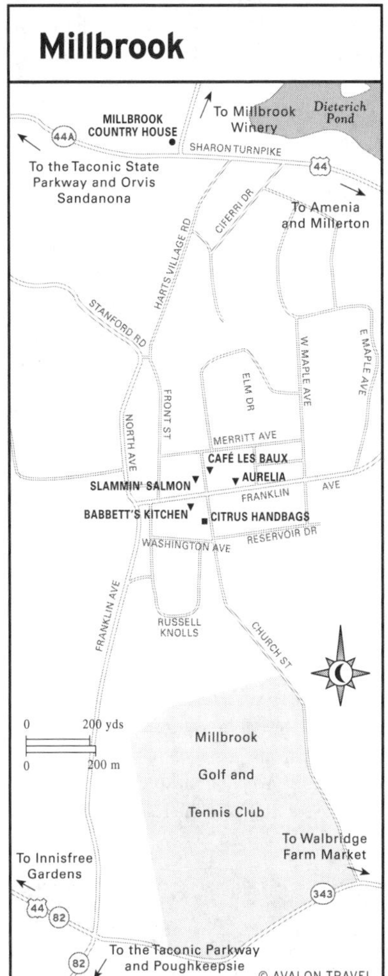

Millbrook

Once known for celebrity residents, boarding schools, and exclusive hunting, fishing, and horseback riding clubs, Millbrook seems to be quieter these days—though it is still the kind of place where restaurants raise their menu prices on weekends, figuring the Fortune 500 CEOs and Hollywood types who own second homes in the area can pay a little more for their burgers. In summer, the village's preserved Greek Revival homes hide behind a canopy of oak and maple trees. Several boutiques and restaurants are worth a visit, but there are four B&Bs and one motel to stay right in town; other options are located a few miles away.

Innisfree Garden (Tyrrell Rd., Millbrook, 845/677-8000, www.innisfreegarden.org, 11am-5pm Sat.-Sun., 10am-4pm Wed.-Fri. May 7-Oct. 20, admission Wed.-Fri. $6, Sat.-Sun. $7) is a popular green space for locals and visitors alike. Petronella Collins, president of the Innisfree Foundation, has called the park "a textbook of tips for the home gardener." Inspired by ancient Chinese gardens, the 200-acre property applies Chinese ideas of design and motion to a decidedly American landscape. The result is a lush display of flora ranging from lotus blossoms to daffodils. When the bugs aren't too bad, you can slip into an Adirondack chair beside the pond and read a book or simply watch and think. Picnic tables are provided.

The scenic rural roads that surround Millbrook's town center are ideal for running and cycling. A popular route is to follow the Dutchess Wine Trail, which isn't exactly a trail, but a joint marketing effort of several local vineyards, located on different roads in different towns. While it's a far cry from the Silverado Trail in California's Napa Valley, the roads connecting Alison Wines, Clinton Vineyards, and Millbrook Vineyards & Winery cover miles of pretty countryside. Meanwhile, the wineries themselves produce some of the highest-quality labels in New York State.

Millbrook Vineyards & Winery (26 Wing Rd., Millbrook, 800/662-9463 or 845/677.8383, www.millbrookwine.com, noon-5pm daily Sept.-May, 11am-6pm Memorial Day-Labor Day) introduced French hybrid grapes to the region and makes an outstanding chardonnay. A few miles away, **Clinton Vineyards** (450 Shultzville Rd., Clinton Corners, 845/266-5372, www.clintonvineyards.com, noon-5pm Sun.-Fri. May-Oct.) is known for its seyval blanc. **Oak Summit Vineyard** (372 Oak Summit Rd.,

Millbrook, 845/677-9522, www.oaksummit-vineyard.com) bottles an organic pinot noir made in the burgundy style, from its six-acre vineyard. Tastings are available by appointment only ($45 pp), and they include a personalized tour led by the owners, John and Nancy Bruno.

The Harlem Valley

Continuing northeast from Millbrook, Route 44 enters the scenic Harlem Valley, which follows the west side of the Taconic Range and the Connecticut border from Pawling to Pine Plains. The land here is sparsely populated, with only a few thousand residents per town, and much of it is permanently protected from development. Taconic State Park, Stissing Mountain Forest, and the Harlem Valley Rail Trail are among the largest wilderness areas.

From the west, Route 44 winds downhill to meet Route 22 at the rural town of Amenia and the **Troutbeck Inn and Conference Center** (515 Leedsville Rd., Amenia, 845/373-9681, www.troutbeck.com). Named in 1765 for its counterpart in England, Troutbeck was founded by literary-minded farmers who knew the likes of Emerson and Thoreau. Sycamore trees and flower gardens surround the original stone house. In the early 20th century, Sinclair Lewis, Ernest Hemingway, and Theodore Roosevelt were frequent guests of Troutbeck's second owners, Joel and Amy Spingarn. Joel Spingarn was instrumental in the founding of the NAACP and served as the organization's second president. Although the inn no longer attracts the same kind of movers and shakers—today's guests are primarily conference and wedding attendees—it still offers good food and comfortable accommodations in a tranquil setting.

Nearby, **Cascade Mountain Winery & Restaurant** (835 Cascade Mountain Rd., Amenia, 845/373-9021, www.cascademt.com, weekends and Monday holidays, 11am-5pm) pioneered the concept of producing high-quality wines in the Hudson River Valley back in the 1970s. Today, the farm opens a seasonal tasting room and restaurant and gives farm tours to visitors. Picnics are encouraged, and Wi-Fi is available for those who want to spend the afternoon. Try the dry white seyval blanc and the newer coeur de lion, a beaujolais-style red.

South of Amenia on Route 22 is Wassaic and the terminus for the Harlem Valley Line

a row of Adirondack chairs on the lawn at Innisfree Garden

riding along the paved Harlem Valley Rail Trail between Wassaic and Millerton

of the Metro-North commuter rail. The ride to Grand Central Station takes about two hours, with a transfer in Southeast.

Next stop is the **Webatuck Craft Village** (Rte. 55, Wingdale), on Route 55 off Route 22 near Wingdale, where resident artists work in copper, tin, clay, glass, and wood. The village consists of half a dozen buildings, and visitors shop here for one-of-a-kind handmade items, from furniture and stained glass windows to ceramics and vintage toys.

Millerton

A scenic location in the Harlem Valley, close proximity to the Housatonic River in Connecticut, and a bevy of antiques stores have turned Millerton into one of the newest Hudson River Valley hot spots. The much-loved Harney & Sons tea company occupies a prominent location next to a small town park, which is also the site of the Saturday morning farmers market. Several farms, restaurants, and boutique shops have opened their doors to greet visitors who wander into town by car or by bike, along the Harlem Valley Rail Trail.

SPORTS AND RECREATION

Winter Sports

Cross-country skiing is permitted on the golf course at Baird Park and along the Harlem Valley Rail Trail. The **McCann Ice Arena** (Mid-Hudson Civic Center, 14 Civic Center Plaza, Poughkeepsie, 845/454-5800, www.midhudsonciviccenter.com, 10am-5:30pm Mon.-Fri., noon-4pm Sat.) offers public skating sessions year-round.

Hiking

A 30-mile stretch of the Appalachian Trail passes through the hills of Dutchess County, connecting the towns of East Fishkill, Dover Plains, Beekman, and Pawling along the way. Several well-marked access areas have trailside parking. In Stormville, find one on Route 52, three miles east of the Taconic State Parkway. In Poughquag, the area is at the intersection of Routes 55 and 216 or Depot Hill Road, off Route 216. In Pawling, it's on Route 22, north of town. Note that mountain bikes are not allowed on the trail.

Additional areas for hiking include the **Pawling Nature Reserve** (Quaker Lake Rd., Pawling, 914/244-3271, www.pawlingnaturereserve.org), on 1,000 acres, and Poughkeepsie's **Bowdoin Park** (85 Sheafe Rd., Wappingers Falls, 845/298-4600, www.nynjtc.org/park/bowdoin-park), on 300 acres near the riverfront.

Cycling

Whether you are riding off-road or on, Dutchess County offers terrain to suit all levels. The scenery alternates between rolling hills, village streets, and Hudson River views. The **Mid-Hudson Bicycle Club** (www.midhudsonbicycle.org) organizes area rides through the summer and fall. The **Dutchess County Rail Trail** (www.dutchessrailtrail.com) is a 13-mile paved path that begins at the former Hopewell Junction train depot and

Millerton

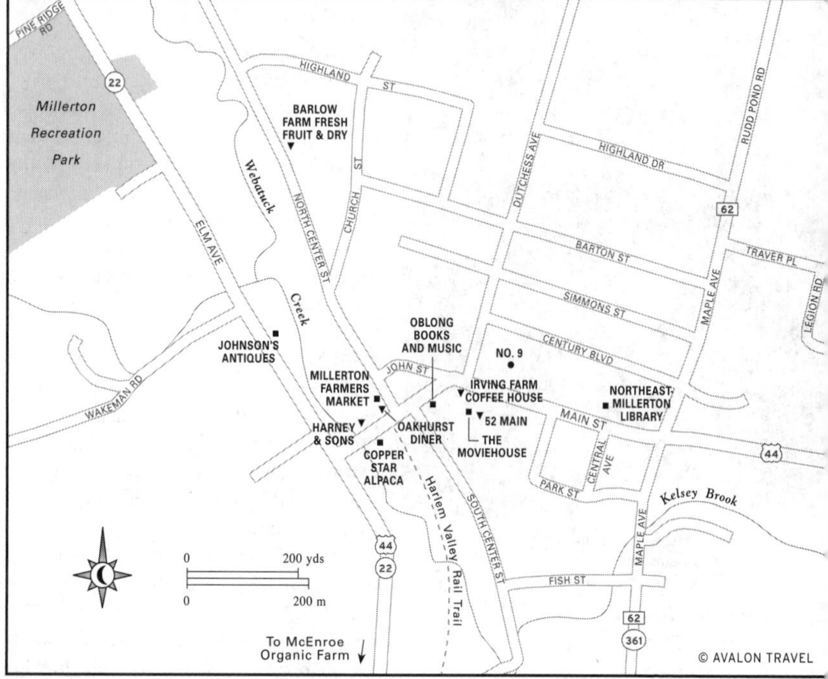

connects to the Walkway Over the Hudson (www.walkway.org). From the river, cyclists can continue another four miles into Ulster County. Road crossings are well marked, and there are several parking areas along the trail.

A 10-mile section of the more remote **Harlem Valley Rail Trail** (51 S. Center St., Millerton, 518/789-9591, www.hvrt.org) begins at the Wassaic train station on Route 22 and reaches Millerton near the Harney & Sons tea shop. The path follows the tracks of the old New York and Harlem Railroad, through wooded forests, grassy meadows, and pastured farmland. It has fewer road crossings than the Dutchess County Rail Trail and is paved the entire way for foot and bike traffic.

The always busy **Bikeway** (1581 Rte. 376, Wappingers Falls, 845/463-7433, www.bikeway.com, 10am-8pm Mon., 10am-6pm Tues.-Wed., 11am-8pm Thurs., 10am-6pm Fri.-Sat.) is the biggest shop around and most convenient to the Dutchess County Rail Trail, but it does not have rentals. Farther north, **Rhinebeck Bicycle Shop** (10 Garden St., Rhinebeck, 845/876-4025, www.rhinebeckbicycleshop.com, 10am-6pm Mon.-Fri., 10am-4pm Sat.) is a Fuji and Giant dealer, and offers repairs and rentals. It has a second location in Kingston called **The Famous Bike Brothers** (139 Boices Ln., 845/336-5581, www.bikebrosny.com). In the eastern part of the county, **Pawling Cycle and Sport** (3198 Rte. 22, Patterson, www.pawlingcycle.com, 10am-6pm Tues.-Sat., noon-4pm Sun.) rents hybrid bikes made by Raleigh for $20/day, helmet included. The shop also leads guided tours for $30/hour.

Golf

Golfers have a dozen or more courses to choose from in Dutchess County. Foremost among them is the swanky **Trump National Golf Course** (178 Stormville Rd., Hopewell Junction, 845/223-1600, www.trumpnationalhudsonvalley.com, $125-200). Formerly known as Branton Woods, it was acquired by Donald Trump in 2010 and renovated to cater to an even more exclusive clientele. The best course for the money in Dutchess County is **The Links at Union Vale** (153 N. Parliman Rd., LaGrangeville, 845/223-1000, www.thelinksatunionvale.com, 6am-dark daily, $39-49 or $49-65 with cart Mon.-Fri., $49-76 or $65-92 with cart Sat.-Sun. and holidays). Another good option is the **Beekman Country Club** (11 Country Club Rd., Hopewell Junction, 845/226-7700, www.beekmangolf.com, opens at 6am Sat.-Sun. and at 7am Mon.-Fri., weekends $47-75, weekdays $42-52, seniors $37-47).

Swimming and Boating

Kids love to slip and slide down the tubes at **SplashDown Beach Water Park** (16 Old Rte. 9, West Fishkill, 845/897-9600, www.splashdownbeach.com, 10am-6pm daily May-mid-June and 10am-7pm late June-Labor Day, adults $33, children under 42 inches and seniors $28). "Beach" is a misnomer, however; there is no water here aside from that in the park's own pools, and the place gets crazy crowded on weekends.

Kayakers can paddle lakes, ponds, creeks, and the Hudson River in Dutchess County. **The River Connection** (9 W. Market St., Hyde Park, 845/229-0595 or 845/242-4731, www.the-river-connection.com) offers water sports instruction, as well as equipment sales and rentals. Certified instructors lead trips from various launch points along the river, including Norrie Point (Staatsburg), Tivoli, Croton Point, and Poughkeepsie ($120 pp). Experienced paddlers may join the guided day trips from Athens to Saugerties, Saugerties to Norrie Point, and Cold Spring to Annsville Creek, which make up the annual Great Hudson River Paddle (ages 16 and up only, $120 pp).

Fishing and Hunting

Anglers will be hard-pressed to choose among the many streams, lakes, and ponds in Dutchess County. And then there's also the Hudson River itself. Outside of Millbrook, **Orvis Sandanona** (311 Sharon Tpke., Millbrook, 845/677-9701, www.orvis.com, 9am-5pm daily) offers fly-fishing lessons (Apr.-Oct.) and instruction in the English Churchill method of shooting clays

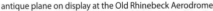

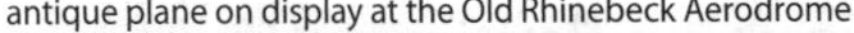
antique plane on display at the Old Rhinebeck Aerodrome

(year-round). The club hosts a competitive shooting event each Orvis Cup.

Aviation

Aviators must plan a weekend visit to the **Old Rhinebeck Aerodrome** (Stone Church Rd., Rhinebeck, 845/758-8610, www.oldrhinebeck.org, museum hours 10am-5pm daily mid-June-mid-Oct., adults $20 weekends, $10 weekdays), which hosts dazzling air shows during summer and fall (at 2pm every Saturday and Sunday), complete with vintage fashion shows. The museum's collection of antique aircraft includes working models dating back to the early 20th century.

Blue Sky Balloons (99 Teller Ave., Beacon, 845/831-6917, www.blueskyballoons.com, sunrise-sunset daily, $225 per person) tours are a special way to watch the sun rise or set over the valley. A guide will happily meet you at the Beacon or Poughkeepsie train station.

Yoga and Spas

The Rhinebeck campus of the nationally known **Omega Institute for Holistic Studies** (150 Lake Dr., Rhinebeck, 877/944-2002 or 845/266-4444, www.eomega.org) offers wellness weeks, yoga retreats, and spiritual programs throughout the year. A massage or body wrap at **Haven Spa** (6464 Montgomery St., Rhinebeck, 845/876-7369, www.havenrhinebeck.com, Wed.-Mon. by appointment) rejuvenates mind and body after a day of farm touring and wine tasting.

ACCOMMODATIONS

Business travelers congregate around corporate headquarters in southern Dutchess County, while the more distinctive inns—mostly of the bed-and-breakfast variety—are found in the northeastern part of the county. Book early around major events. Hotels are known to fill up as far as a year in advance.

$100-150

Le Chambord (2737 Rte. 52, Hopewell Junction, 845/221-1941, www.lechambord.com, $104) has been a longtime favorite for elegant affairs. Set in an 1863 mansion, the inn has nine ornate rooms in the main building, and 16 more in a newer wing—all large with high ceilings and white tiled baths. Chef Lenny Mott prepares classic French fare for lunch and dinner ($16-39).

$150-200

Built in 1824, the six-room **Red Hook Inn** (7460 S. Broadway, Red Hook, 845/758-8445, www.theredhookinn.com, $149-215), is a midpriced option that's close to area wineries. Lace curtains let in plenty of natural light. Hardwood floors, antique furnishings, and floral bedspreads complete the look.

Botsford Briar B&B (19 High St., Beacon, 845/831-6099, www.botsfordbriar.com, $165-210) provided the setting for Melanie Griffith's house in the 1994 film *Nobody's Fool*. The owner once hosted quilting retreats in this 1889 Victorian. The home has wicker furniture on the front porch, original hardwood floors, lace curtains, English faucets, and antique furnishings. The top-floor room has a river view and enclosed porch; the downstairs Gentleman's Parlor has a cozy fireplace for winter getaways. The B&B is located across Route 9D from Main Street, near the Beacon train station.

Spotless and welcoming, the ★ **Journey Inn** (1 Sherwood Pl., Hyde Park, 845/229-8972, www.journeyinn.com, $160-240) is a bed-and-breakfast with seven rooms located across from the Vanderbilt Estate. A multicourse breakfast is a highlight of the day. European soaps add a fine touch, and wireless Internet is available throughout. Also close to the CIA, and run by a graduate and beekeeper, **The Willows Bed & Breakfast** (53 Travis Rd., Hyde Park, 845/471-6115, www.willowsbnb.com, $140-165) occupies a white 1765 Colonial farmhouse with red shutters. Two air-conditioned rooms appointed in country style come with a breakfast that takes homemade to a new level. Cozy and quiet, **Inn the Woods** (32 Howard Blvd., Hyde Park, 845/229-9331, www.innthewoods.com,

$120-210) has just three guest rooms, and breakfast comes with homemade jam, cheese, yogurt, and sausage. **Le Petit Chateau Inn** (38 W. Dorsey Ln., Hyde Park, 845/437-4688, www.lepetitchateauinn.com, $155-275) has four guest rooms, each named for a wine region in France, in a renovated farmhouse. A stay here begins with a cheese plate and wine, and a gracious host tends to guests' needs. Breakfast is as local as it gets, and cooking classes with the inn's CIA-graduate chef are available as a package.

You won't forget an overnight stay at the historic 1766 **Beekman Arms** (6387 Mill St., Rhinebeck, 845/876-7077, www.beekmandelamaterinn.com, $155-185). Ask for one of the 13 rooms in the main house, where the ceilings are low and the floors creak with every step. Soundproof it is not. It's been more than a decade since the last major renovations, but the rooms are standing the test of time. For more modern accommodations (but much less character), the inn has a total of 13 buildings and 74 rooms—some of them apartment-like. Skip the included breakfast and try one of the reputable eateries in town. Securing a reservation for when the auto shows come to town may be futile. Repeat visitors reserve every room on the premises more than a year in advance.

For more secluded lodging, check out ★ **Whistlewood Farm Bed and Breakfast** (52 Pells Rd., Rhinebeck, 845/876-6838, www.whistlewood.com, $150-310), which has four rooms in the main house and three more in a renovated barn. The owners serve a hearty farmers' breakfast. Oak and pine furnishings, gas fireplace stoves, and accents including an elkhorn chandelier create a distinctly rustic feel. Some rooms have a four-poster bed, whirlpool, and/or private patio. All have air-conditioning and Wi-Fi. Afternoon coffee, tea, pie, and cake are included with your stay.

Owner and innkeeper Barbara Lanman renovated an 1860s home in the Queen Anne style and opened the **Pawling House Bed and Breakfast** (105 W. Main St. at Dykeman St., Pawling, 845/855-3851, www.pawlinghouse.com, $150-200) in late 2007. Its four guest rooms have private baths, and the location is close to restaurants, shops, and the Pawling train station.

Near the Amtrak station in Rhinecliff and only two miles from the village of Rhinebeck, ★ **The Rhinecliff** (4 Grinnell St., Rhinecliff, 845/876-0590, www.therhinecliff.com, $200) has undergone a five-year transformation from a run-down bar into a showcase hotel and restaurant at the river's edge. The building dates to 1854 and is now on the National Register of Historic Places. Wood floors, beams, doors, fireplaces, even the original oak bar all have been preserved and restored. Its nine guest rooms all have river views, king-size beds, flatscreen TVs, iPod docks, whirlpool tubs, and rain showers. Common areas are wheelchair accessible. Noise-sensitive visitors may want to bring earplugs or white noise, as the freight trains run until midnight. The brasserie-style restaurant (entrées $14-26) is run by a CIA graduate and is open daily from 7am until late night; a light bar menu is available between meal times; the Sunday jazz brunch has become a popular local tradition. Enjoy a cold beer or classic cocktail on the patio, such as a pisco sour or cucumber gimlet, and order the oysters on the half shell, served with a cucumber mignonette. Entrées include hanger steak, fish-and-chips, and leg of lamb.

Over $200

On Route 9G a few miles north of the village of Rhinebeck, the 1745 **Olde Rhinebeck Inn** (340 Wurtemburg Rd., Rhinebeck, 845/871-1745, www.rhinebeckinn.com, $225-325) is another property that's listed on the National Register of Historic Places. The owners have worked to preserve its original character; the wide-plank hardwood floors, exposed beams, and four-poster beds will send you back in time. Guests stay in one of four rooms, and can lounge in Adirondack chairs beside the pond or swing in a hammock under the willow trees. Amenities include Wi-Fi, air-conditioning, in-room refrigerators, robes, and fresh-cut flowers. The owners also rent out the nearby **Apple Blossom Cottage** ($250-295 per night, two-night minimum), set amid three acres in an old apple orchard.

A stay at the three-bedroom **Cottage at Sprout Creek Farm** (34 Lauer Rd., 845/485-8438, www.sproutcreekfarm.org) in LaGrange, comes with a selection of cheeses made on-site at the working farm. The cottage has a full kitchen, fireplace, and garden. Weekend rentals (two nights) are $575, and each additional night after that is $225.

Marble baths, French antiques, and ornate silk fabrics set the Gilded Age tone at **Belvedere Mansion** (10 Old Rte. 9, Staatsburg, 845/889-8000, www.belvederemansion.com, $150-275), a riverside getaway located between Hyde Park and Rhinebeck. Rooms in the neoclassical mansion, restored in 1993, run $225-275. Individually decorated rooms in the Carriage House have king-size beds for $150-195. Smaller rooms, called Cozies ($105-125), are a good way to get affordable lodging at an upscale venue. Suites in the Hunting Lodge cost $250-450, and rooms in the Zen Lodge cost $125-175.

At the edge of the village, the **Millbrook Country House** (3244 Sharon Tpke., Millbrook, 845/677-9570, www.millbrookcountryhouse.com, $175-275) blends American Colonial architecture with 18th-century Italian decor. Journalist Lorraine Alexander and her husband, Giancarlo Grisi, moved from a Mediterranean town in Italy to open the bed-and-breakfast in 2002. The elegant furnishings and linens in their four guest rooms reflect the tastes of experienced world travelers. Behind the house is a white-picket-fenced flower and herb garden.

Ten minutes from the village, ★ **The Millbrook Inn** (3 Gifford Rd., Millbrook, 845/605-1120, www.themillbrookinn.com, $240-400) opened in 2011 with eight rooms in a turn-of-the-century building that was once part of Hope Farm School. Neutral colors and dark wood accents the rooms; there are no floral prints here. For breakfast the innkeeper serves farm eggs and bacon, fresh fruit, and yogurt. This inn makes a great home base for a weekend of leaf-peeping and wine tasting.

No. 9 (53 Main St., Millerton, 518/592-1299, www.number9millerton.com, $170-250) has six guest rooms on the second floor of a farm-to-table restaurant. Crisp white sheets and duvets contrast with floral wallpaper and area rugs. The house has a fabulous front porch and you're within walking distance to all that Millerton has to offer.

Campgrounds

Ideal for a family car camping trip, **Wilcox Memorial Park** (Rte. 199, Stanfordville, 845/758-6100, $25-32 for nonresidents) has two small lakes with fishing, boat rentals, and swimming, Memorial Day-Labor Day. Kids can safely explore miles of trails by foot or on bikes. The park is open 9am-4pm Monday through Friday January 2-May 27 and September 6-December 31, 9am-7pm weekdays and 9am-8pm weekends and holidays May 28-September 5.

FOOD

Dutchess County eateries range from classic diners and American bistros to game-inspired, farm-fresh menus, and the occasional international delight. New places are opening at a fast clip, and as elsewhere in the Hudson River Valley, farm-to-table dining experiences are all the rage.

Along the River: Route 9

Beacon

Friendly service makes for a wonderful meal at **Gerardo's Seafood Café** (244 Main St., Beacon, 845/831-8500, 11am-9pm Wed.-Mon., $11-30) Order the clam chowder, crab cakes, or fish tacos. Bring your own bottle of wine. The kitchen at **Max's on Main** (246 Main St., Beacon, 845/838-6297, www.maxsonmain.com, open daily for lunch and dinner) stays open late when most others have closed for the night. Comfort food is the theme. Flank steak marinated in a sweet soy maple glaze hits the spot.

The restaurant scene has blossomed in

Beacon in recent years, thanks to the influx of Dia:Beacon visitors and a new community of resident artists. In between gallery visits, stop for pad thai, green curry, or other Thai specialties at ★ **Sukhothai** (516 Main St., Beacon, 845/790-5375, www.sukhothainy.com, 11:30am-9:30pm Mon.-Thurs. and Sun., 11:30am-10:30pm Fri.-Sat., lunch $9, dinner $13-26). This restaurant serves the most authentic Thai cuisine in the area. Follow Main Street all the way past the Howland Cultural Center and look for the restaurant across from the abandoned factory on Wappinger Creek. There are a few sidewalk tables outside, and a pleasant air-conditioned dining room inside.

Stock up for a picnic or eat in the café at **Homespun Foods** (232 Main St., Beacon, 845/831-5096, www.homespunfoods.com, 11am-5pm Mon.-Fri., 8am-5pm Sat.-Sun.) House-made pastries are a memorable treat. Near the intersection of Main Street and Route 9D, **Bank Square Coffeehouse** (129 Main St., Beacon, 845/440-7165, www.banksquarecoffeehouse.com, 6am-10pm Mon.-Thurs., 7am-10pm Sun., 6am-9pm Fri.-Sat.) has a full menu of coffee and espresso drinks from beans roasted at Coffee Labs Roasters in Tarrytown, as well as pastries from a local bakery in Fishkill. If you like dark coffee, try the only-in-Beacon Mt. Beacon roast. Across the street is **Beacon Creamery** (Main St., Beacon, www.janesicecream.com, 3pm-8pm Tues.-Thurs., 1pm-9pm Fri., noon-9pm Sat., noon-6pm Sun.), a satellite of the Kingston-based wholesaler, Jane's Ice Cream.

After extensive renovations, a one-time textile mill and lawnmower factory has been transformed into **The Roundhouse at Beacon Falls** (2 E. Main St., Beacon, 845/765-8369, www.roundhousebeacon.com), which serves lobster rolls, Caesar salads, and portobello burgers on a patio overlooking Fishkill Creek. Grab a table for a round of craft beers after a day at Dia:Beacon. (Its 23 guest rooms are oddly arranged and overpriced; best stick with the food.)

Fishkill and Wappingers Falls

★ **Il Barilotto Enoteca** (1113 Main St., Fishkill, 845/897-4300, www.ilbarilottorestaurant.com, 11am-2:30pm and 5pm-10pm Mon.-Sat., until 11pm Fri.-Sat., $18-28) gets food, setting, and service right with remarkable consistency. Seasonal appetizers such as squash blossoms are a treat. Italian entrées include the Long Island breast of duck in a cherry-grappa sauce and veal scaloppine with a leek fondue. Gluten-free pasta is an option for most of the main dishes. Meals at **Hudson's Ribs & Fish** (1099 Rte. 9, Fishkill, 845/297-5002, www.hudsonsribsandfish.com, 4pm-10pm Mon.-Sat., 2pm-9pm Sun., $18-35) come with a piping hot popover on the side.

★ **Aroma Osteria** (114 Old Post Rd., Wappingers Falls, 845/298-6790, www.aromaosteriarestaurant.com, 11:30am-2:30pm and 5pm-10pm Tues.-Sat., until 11pm Fri.-Sat., 4pm-9pm Sun., $18-27), run by the same owners as Il Barilotto, is good enough to remind you of a trip to Italy. Start with the heirloom tomato salad in summer, and then try a pasta course of spaghetti with baby clams or mushroom ravioli in a creamy porcini sauce.

Le Chambord (2737 Rte. 52, Hopewell Junction, 845/221-1941, www.lechambord.com, 11:30am-2:30pm and 6pm-10pm Mon.-Fri., 6pm-11pm Sat., 11am-3pm brunch and 3pm-9pm Sun., $16-39) prepares classic French dishes in a formal setting. Tournedos, chateaubriand, venison, and sea scallops are featured dishes.

Poughkeepsie

Many of the trendiest restaurants in Poughkeepsie are located in an attractive new plaza called Dooley Square, which is next to the train station. Shepherd's pie, corned beef and cabbage, and fish-and-chips will fill you up at **Mahoney's Irish Pub & Restaurant** (35 Main St., Poughkeepsie, 845/471-7026, www.mahoneysirishpub.com, lunch 11am-5pm daily, dinner 5pm-10pm Mon.-Thurs, 5pm-11pm Sat., 4pm-9pm Sun., pub open late, $15-26).

Inside a historic department store building

in downtown Poughkeepsie, ★ **The Artist's Palate** (307 Main St., Poughkeepsie, 845/483-8074, www.theartistspalate.biz, lunch from 11am Mon.-Fri., dinner from 5pm Mon.-Sat., $15-25) feels like someone lifted it right out of Lower Manhattan. Sophisticated and hip, the dining room creates an ideal stage for a culinary adventure. The menu emphasizes contemporary American cuisine with a few surprises. The Nestor's Salad features a red Bartlett pear "carpaccio," baby arugula, house-made Hudson River Valley duck prosciutto, ricotta salata, and cider vinaigrette. Maine blue mussels come with a saffron mayo, while the baby bluefish sudado hints of South America. Meat eaters can choose the New York strip (grass-fed angus beef), heritage breed pork chop, or braised rabbit.

Newer ★ **Brasserie 292** (292 Main St., Poughkeepsie, 845/473-0292, www.brasserie292.com, lunch 11am-4pm Tues.-Fri., dinner 5pm-9:30pm Tues.-Thurs., 5pm-10:30pm Fri., 2pm-9pm Sat., 4pm-9pm Sun., brunch 11am-4pm Sun., mains $18-26) is a variation on the same theme. It turns ingredients from nearby Sprout Creek, Coach, and Fazio farms into traditional entrées including cassoulet, bouillabaisse, and braised short ribs. The shaved vegetable salad turns familiar fruits and veggies into something of a surprise. Roasted bone marrow comes with onion jam and toasted sourdough. Mussels and fries hit the spot. Manhattans have their own section of the cocktail menu, and Punch Bowl Service is a novel way to order drinks for a crowd.

The **River Station** (25 Main St. or 1 N. Water St., Poughkeepsie, 845/452-9207, www.riverstationrest.com, 11:30am-9pm Sun.-Thurs., 11:30am-10pm Fri.-Sat., $18-29) serves dependable surf and turf on a pleasant outdoor terrace that overlooks the Hudson. A few blocks away, **Caffé Aurora** (145 Mill St., Poughkeepsie, 845/454-1900, www.caffeaurora.com) serves legendary Italian pastries made on the premises by a family that has run the business since 1941.

Nearby, overlooking the river, **Shadows** (176 Rinaldi Blvd., Poughkeepsie, 845/486-9500, www.shadowsonthehudson.com, $12-39) is a mammoth brick dining and events complex. Shadows caters to a business crowd during weekday lunch hours and turns into a trendy nightclub on weekends. You'll likely catch views of the Mid-Hudson Bridge from your table, but don't expect a cozy, romantic feel. Surf and turf defines the menu, but you can also choose from a list of filling sandwiches and salads. The bistro steak salad, for example, comes with marinated portobello mushrooms sliced on top. Lobster mac 'n cheese is one of the more creative entrées on the pasta list. Shadows is open 11:30am-9pm Monday-Thursday with late-night snacks and cocktails served until 10pm, 11:30am-10pm Friday-Saturday with late-night snacks and cocktails served until 2am, and 11am-9pm Sunday.

Ask a group of locals to name the best diner in town and you'll spark a heated debate. **The Palace Diner** (194 Washington St., Poughkeepsie, 854/473-1576, www.thepalacediner.com, 24 hours daily, $16-19) has the best food. But the **Daily Planet** (1202 Rte. 55, LaGrangeville, 845/452-0110, www.dailyplanetdiner.com, 5am-midnight daily, $11-14), near Arlington High School, kicks it up a notch with unexpected dishes like Crabwiches and The Wrap of Khan (grilled portobello mushroom).

Saigon Cafe (6A LaGrange Ave., Poughkeepsie, 845/473-1392, www.saigon-cafe.net, noon-3pm and 5pm-10pm weekdays, noon-10pm Sat., 5pm-9:30pm Sun., $7-10) serves passable Vietnamese pho in a small but air-conditioned space just off the Vassar College campus. Nearby, the **Beech Tree Grill** (1 Collegeview Ave., Poughkeepsie, 845/471-7279, www.beechtreegrillpk.com, 5pm-10pm Mon., 11:30am-11pm Tues.-Sun., $17-19) has a decent wine and beer list, with an inviting bar and a dinner menu of hearty pub fare. On the same block, **Gusto** (15 Collegeview Ave., Poughkeepsie, 845/454-8200, www.gustopk.com, $13-28) satisfies the need for butternut squash soup and lacinato kale salad. The brown rice bowl comes on a plate, but is otherwise healthy and fresh. Do not under any circumstances skip the butterscotch budino. It's open for dinner, but the casual atmosphere seems better suited to a nice lunch.

Under the footbridge to the Walkway Over the Hudson, a CIA-graduate opened **Crave Restaurant and Lounge** (129 Washington St., Poughkeepsie, 845/452-3501, www.caverestaurantandlounge.com, 4pm-10pm Wed.-Sat., 4pm-9pm Sun., brunch 11:30am-3pm Sun., mains $24-28). It's a cozy eatery with barbecue octopus, lamb meatballs, and a kale Caesar salad on the small plates menu. More substantial dishes include duck cavatelli, wild boar Bolognese, and salmon cooked in beet dashi and served with pineapple kimchi.

Hyde Park

CIA sophomores run the kitchens in four campus restaurants at the **Culinary Institute of America** (1946 Campus Dr., Hyde Park, www.ciachef.edu). It's a toss-up to say which of the two formal dining restaurants is the best. **American Bounty** (845/471-6608, www.americanbountyrestaurant.com, 11:30am-1pm and 6pm-8:30pm Tues.-Sat., $18-28) is a white tablecloth affair that aims to please the locavore audience with creative soups, garden-fresh salads, and entrées from land and sea. The Berskshire porkchop doubles up on meat with housemade sausage on the side. Ricotta meatballs feature Meiller Farm beef and Wild Hive polenta. Roasted chicken comes with crunchy mac 'n cheese and red cabbage slaw.

Named for the father of modern French cuisine, Chef Paul Bocuse, **The Bocuse Restaurant** (1946 Campus Dr., Hyde Park, 845/471-6608, www.bocuserestaurant.com, 11:30am-1pm and 6pm-8:30pm Tues.-Sat., $26-34) replaced the former Escoffier with a here-and-now approach to classic French cuisine. A sous vide station, wine list on an iPad, and liquid nitrogen for freezing tableside ice cream are a few of the high-tech innovations on display. Think crispy sweetbreads, foie gras with apricot compote, olive oil poached halibut, and braised rabbit, and you'll have a good idea of the menu.

Elegant **Ristorante Caterina de' Medici** (Colavita Center for Italian Food and Wine, 1946 Campus Dr., Hyde Park, 845/471-6608, www.ristorantecaterinademedici.com, 11:30am-1pm and 6pm-8:30pm Mon.-Fri., $18-25) serves regional Italian specialties under a Venetian chandelier. You might order a terrine of summer vegetables, a Tuscan-style tomato and bread soup, or the sautéed pork tenderloin with capers and escarole. For a more casual dining experience, ask to be seated in the Al Forno Trattoria.

Casual and fairly priced, the ★ **Apple Pie Bakery Café** (1946 Campus Dr., Roth Hall, 845/905-4500, www.ciarestaurantgroup.com, 7:30am-5pm Mon.-Fri., $6-13) bakes strawberry almond scones, sticky buns, and salted caramel doughnuts. Needless to say, it's a favorite among the locals.

When making reservations, note that CIA restaurants are only open when the school is in session. And if everything isn't just perfect, remember it's a training restaurant after all.

Rhinebeck

★ **Calico Restaurant & Patisserie** (6384 Mill St., Rhinebeck, 845/876-2749, www.calicorhinebeck.com, bakery opens at 8am, lunch 11am-2pm, dinner from 5:30pm Wed.-Sat., brunch 11am-2pm Sun., pastries $4, lunch $9-10, dinner $19-26) has less than a dozen tables, so the atmosphere is cozy, and you'll likely have to wait to be seated. But it's worth the wait for the bouillabaisse or the saffron-flavored monkfish. If it's not time for dinner, at least try a macaroon at the bakery.

Housed inside an old church in the center of town, **Terrapin** (6426 Montgomery St., Rhinebeck, 845/876-3330, www.terrapinrestaurant.com, 5pm-8:30pm Sun.-Thurs., 5pm-9pm Fri.-Sat., $21-37) remains a hot spot for creative New American cuisine, including a grilled double-thick pork chop with rhubarb demi-glace, rack of spring lamb, Peking duck, and several vegetarian entrées. Its sister establishment, Terrapin Red, is a cozy bar and bistro that's open daily for lunch and dinner. On the same block, the refreshing blend of Italian, Mediterranean, and Hudson River Valley dishes at **Gigi Trattoria** (6422 Montgomery St., Ste. 1, Rhinebeck, 845/876-1007, www.gigitrattoria.com, 11:30am-9pm Tues.-Thurs. and Sun., 11:30am-10pm Fri.-Sat., $15-30) has impressed travelers from all around the country, and weekend residents and visitors fill the place night after night. Another graduate of the CIA turns out flatbread pizzas, creative pastas, and a range of hearty second courses.

★ **Le Petit Bistro** (8 E. Market St., Rhinebeck, 845/876-7400, www.lepetitbistro.com, 5pm-9pm Thurs.-Mon., $25-35) still ranks among the top French restaurants in the entire Hudson River Valley. Whether you order sea scallops, English Dover sole, frog legs, duck, or steak au poivre, the meal should come perfectly prepared.

The Local (39 W. Market St., Rhinebeck, 845/876-2214, www.thelocalrestaurantandbar.com, 5:30pm-10pm Tues.-Sat., $24-32) sources food from more than 30 farms across the Hudson River Valley, so if you can only dine here, rest assured you're getting a taste of all there is to eat. Weekly comfort specials include taco Tuesday, linguine white clam sauce Wednesday, meatloaf Thursday, fish-n-chips Friday, and southern fried chicken Saturday. You can add sunny-side up quail eggs, ewe's goat cheese, or roasted garlic crust to any dish for $5.

Part of a trio of Hudson River Valley restaurants, **Market Street** (19 W. Market St., Rhinebeck, 845/876-7200, www.marketstrhinebeck.com, $15-33) cranks out thin-crust pizzas from a wood-fired oven. Gluten-free pasta is an option. The chicken is free-range and the beef is grass-fed.

The menu at **Pete's Famous Restaurant** (34 E. Market St., 845/876-7271, 6am-9pm Mon.-Sat., 5am-5pm Sun., $10) covers a lot of ground, from French toast with bacon and eggs to burgers and veal liver. It's a local chain with additional restaurants in Hyde Park (4204 Albany Post Rd., 845/229-1475), and on Hooker Avenue in Poughkeepsie, near Vassar College. **Bread Alone** (45 E. Market St., Rhinebeck, 845/876-3108, www.breadalone.com, 7am-5pm daily, $9-16) has opened a Rhinebeck location to serve its legendary breads, pastries, and sandwiches.

Red Hook

Red Hook boasts a few casual eateries: At the corner of Routes 9 and 199, across from the Merritt Bookstore, **J&J Gourmet Catering** (1 E. Market St., 845/758-9030, www.jandjgourmet.com, 7am-5pm Mon.-Fri., 8am-4:30pm Sat., 9am-4pm Sun., $6-10) has a window display of old cans and tins from brands like Ritz crackers, Life Savers, Coca-Cola, Hershey's, and Maxwell House. Inside is a gourmet deli that makes homemade soups and sandwiches. And on the same block, farther east, **Mercato Osteria & Enoteca** (61 E. Market St., 845/758-5879, www.mercatoredhook.com, 11:30am-2:30pm Fri.-Sun., dinner from 5:30pm Wed.-Sat. and from 5pm Sun., $15-30) lets fresh ingredients shine in simple Italian dishes served in a homey and sometimes noisy setting.

South of town, there's barbecue and more barbecue to be found at **Max's Memphis Barbecue** (736 S. Broadway, Red Hook, 845/758-6297, www.maxsbbq.com, 5pm-10pm Tues.-Sun., $16).

At the northern edge of the county, Bard College students frequent **Santa Fe** (52 Broadway off Rte. 9G, Tivoli, 845/757-4100, www.santafetivoli.com, dinner Tues.-Sun. from 5pm, $14-19) for tacos and burritos, margaritas and mojitos. Also in Tivoli, ★ **Luna 61** (55 Broadway, Tivoli, 845/758-0061, www.luna61.com, 5:30pm-9pm Thurs., 5:30pm-10pm Fri.-Sat., 5:30pm-9pm Sun., no Sunday dinner in January, $9-16) is one of the best vegetarian eateries around. The Farm Plate delivers all the protein you need in a platter of quinoa, black beans, and steamed greens, while several Asian-inspired dishes pack in the fresh veggies. Falafel, burritos, and several more sandwiches complete the menu.

Hudson River Valley Wineries

Enterprising Hudson River Valley farmers planted the first French-American hybrid grapes in the 1970s, and the quality and popularity of their wines have been rising steadily ever since to meet the demands of increasingly sophisticated local consumers. Today, the Hudson River Valley is the smallest of four major wine regions in New York State, with about 20 producers. (The others are Long Island, the Finger Lakes, and Great Lakes regions.) Dutchess, Ulster, and Columbia Counties have several wineries with tasting rooms open to the public. Millbrook Vineyards & Winery has one of the largest operations in the area, while Oak Summit Winery offers a more intimate wine-tasting experience (by appointment only).

Unlike the hot, dry climate that nurtures California zinfandel, merlot, and cabernet sauvignon grapes, cooler temperatures in the Hudson River Valley are well suited for growing the types of grapes you find in Burgundy, Germany, and northern Italy: chardonnay, aligote, dornfelder, and pinot noir. The resulting wines are earthy, crisp, and clean with a moderate alcohol content.

Grape	European Growing Region	Hudson River Valley Wineries
Pinot noir	Burgundy (France)	Oak Summit Vineyard, Millbrook Winery & Vineyard
Seyval blanc	French-American hybrid	Clinton Vineyards, Cascade Mountain Winery
Tocai friulano	Friuli (Northern Italy)	Millbrook Winery

Central Dutchess County: Routes 44 and 22

Pawling

Pawling residents know ★ **McKinney & Doyle** as simply, The Bakery (10 Charles Colman Blvd., Pawling, 845/855-3875, www.mckinneyanddoyle.com, lunch 11:30am-3pm Tues.-Fri., dinner 5pm-9pm Wed.-Thurs. and Sun. and until 9:30pm Fri.-Sat., brunch 9am-3pm Sat.-Sun., lunch $8-17, dinner $20-29). Enter through the bakery and try not to drool at all the treats behind the glass counter. Grab a booth or table in the adjoining air-conditioned restaurant, which has brick walls and worn wood floors. Try the meatloaf sandwich served on rye with melted cheese, a crab cake burger, rough chop Cobb salad, or roasted turkey cranberry with crisp fried asparagus on top. The bakery and soda fountain/ice cream shop are open daily, unfortunately (6:30am-7pm Mon., 6:30am-9pm Tues.-Fri., 7am-9pm Sat., 7am-7pm Sun.). Old-fashioned sodas, egg creams, and ice cream sodas add a retro touch.

Around the corner from the train station, **Petite on Main** (10 E. Main St., Pawling, 845/418-6959, www.petiteonmain.com, 8am-8pm Mon. and Wed.-Sat., 8am-3pm Sun., $10) offers a variety of savory crepes ranging from traditional to unique, like the beet, mesclun, orange, and feta crepe. Dessert crepes include s'mores, nutella, and fig butter/goat cheese. During the summer months, teens build strong arm muscles scooping homemade ice cream at **Heinchon's Old Farmhouse & Ice Cream Parlor** (Rte. 22, Pawling, 845/878-6262, noon-10pm early May-Labor Day, until 9pm thereafter). The family's dairy farm has been in business since the 1920s. They no longer deliver by horse and wagon, but they do make the hot fudge and whipped cream in-house, as well as the ice cream itself.

Just north of Pawling in Wingdale, ★ **Big W's Roadside Bar B Que** (1475 Rte. 22, Wingdale, 845/832-6200, www.bigwsbbq.com, $7-14) does dry rub right. This is the place to stop for slow-smoked spareribs, pulled pork, and beef brisket, but plan to get there early, as the restaurant often runs out of ribs by 8pm. The owner likes to show off the 1.5-ton tank smoker.

Millbrook

Whether you order a croque monsieur, a bowl of steamed mussels, or *le steak frites,* Millbrook's ★ **Café Les Baux** (152 Church St., Millbrook, 845/677-8166 www.cafelesbaux.com, noon-3pm and 5pm-9pm Wed.-Thurs. and Sun.-Mon., until 10pm Fri.-Sat., $9-29) will give you that authentic French bistro dining experience. Open since 2002, it serves lunch and dinner in a warm and cozy dining room located in the center of town.

Order a chicken salad sandwich at tiny **Babbett's Kitchen** (3293 Franklin Ave., Millbrook, 845/677-8602, www.babetteskitchen.com, 7am-5pm Mon., 7am-6pm Wed.-Sat., 8am-4pm Sun.) after a walk around Innisfree Garden. The café/bakery makes muffins, scones, and buttermilk biscuits daily.

Slammin' Salmon (3267 Franklin Ave., Millbrook, 845/677-5400, www.slamminsalmon.com, 10am-5pm Tues.-Thurs., 9am-5pm Fri.-Sat.) gets fresh seafood deliveries on Tuesday and Friday, and the inventory sells out fast. Fresh-picked veggies from local farms arrive daily. The fridge holds organic eggs and dairy from Ronnybrook and Hudson River Valley Fresh. Shelves in the center of the shop hold the essentials for a picnic lunch or gourmet dinner. Behind the counter, the same ingredients appear in a variety of salads and prepared dishes. Order a salmon sandwich to eat at a patio table outside, or take it to go.

Aurelia (3299 Franklin Ave., Millbrook, 845/677-4720, www.aureliarestaurant.com, noon-9pm Wed.-Mon., mains $15-25) adds a new venue for al fresco dining in the village Millbrook. Dishes range from marinated beets with toasted pistachios to crispy tofu with couscous and capers. It's a great stop for a leisurely lunch after a morning round of golf.

Just outside of town **Charlotte's** (4258 Rte. 44, Millbrook, 845/677-5888, www.charlottesny.com, 5pm-9pm Wed.-Thurs., 5pm-10:30pm Fri., 11:30am-10:30pm Sat., 11:30am-8:30pm Sun., $20-28), delights even the most discerning of diners with a New American menu that changes daily. The converted 200-year-old church is a romantic venue for celebrating anniversaries and other special occasions.

Continuing up the Taconic State Parkway, the **Fireside BBQ and Grill** (1920 Salt Point Tpke., Salt Point, 845/266-3440, www.firesidebbqgrill.com, from 4pm Tues.-Fri., from 11:30am Sat.-Sun., $9-22) serves 25-ounce beers in frosted mugs. It's been around for generations and has a friendly staff that

the Harney & Sons Tea Tasting Room in Millerton

serves tasty baby back ribs, barbecue, tri-tip, and prime rib on weekends.

Millerton

Taste the latest imported teas along with lunch at the **Harney & Sons Tea Tasting Room** (1 Railroad Plaza, Millerton, 518/789-2121, www.harney.com, 10am-5pm Mon.-Sat., 11am-4pm Sun.) after a walk on the Harlem Valley Rail Trail, which passes right through town. The **Irving Farm Coffee House** (44 Main St., Millerton, 518/789-2020, www.irvingfarm.com, 6am-5pm Mon.-Thurs., 6am-8pm Fri., 7am-8pm Sat., 8am-5pm Sun.) serves its own espresso, roasted in a converted 19th-century carriage house nearby. You can also order wine, beer, and light snacks besides the usual menu of frothy coffee drinks.

The farm-to-table menu at ★ **No. 9** (53 Main St., Millerton, 518/592-1299, www.number9millerton.com, 5pm-10pm Tues.-Sat., mains $23-29) combines a taste of France and a taste of Austria with a whole lot of Hudson River Valley flavors. Wiener schnitzel, hanger steak, and Long Island duck breast won't disappoint. Chef Tim Cocheo even finds time for the occasional cooking demo at the local farmers market. Inquire about the restaurant's Local Farm Dinners, when the menu highlights ingredients from a specific farm.

52 Main (52 Main St., Millerton, 518/789-0252, www.52main.com, 4pm-10pm Tues.-Thurs., 4pm-11pm Fri., 11:30am-11pm Sat., 11:30am-10pm Sun.) is a tapas place in theory, but aside from the olive tapenade, Serrano ham, and a rare white rioja on the wine list, it's not particularly Spanish. The **Oakhurst Diner** (19 Main St., Millerton, 518/592-1313, 7am-9pm Thurs.-Mon., $8-18) is a contemporary diner that does best with breakfast fare, which it serves until 5pm daily. In summer, air-conditioning seems to be all or nothing. **Barlow Farm Fresh Fruit & Dairy** (56C S. Center St., Millerton, 518/592-1440, Apr.-Sep.) is a seasonal ice cream stand known for smoothies made with real local fruit, milkshakes, and frozen coffees. There is nothing artificial about the soft-serve either.

ENTERTAINMENT AND EVENTS

Performing Arts

The 1869 **Bardavon Opera House** (35 Market St., Poughkeepsie, 845/473-2072, www.bardavon.org) is one of the top performing arts venues in Dutchess County. It hosts the Hudson Valley Philharmonic and a full schedule of musical, dance, film, and theater productions by contemporary artists.

At the other end of the architectural spectrum, the **Fisher Center for the Performing Arts** (Rte. 9G, Annandale, 845/758-7900, fishercenter.bard.edu, box office 10am-5pm Mon.-Fri.) is housed in a modern, stainless-steel building on the Bard College campus. Designed by Frank Gehry and opened in 2003, its shows include orchestra, chamber, and jazz music, as well as modern theater, dance, and opera. The **Bard Music Festival** (Rte. 9G Bard College, Annandale-on-Hudson, 845/758-7900, fishercenter.bard.edu/bmf) focuses on a single composer each year.

The Rhinebeck Theatre Society and other local groups perform at the **Center for the Performing Arts at Rhinebeck** (661 Rte. 308, Rhinebeck, 845/876-3080, www.centerforperformingarts.org, box office noon-5pm Tues.-Fri., 1pm-5pm Sat.). Also in Rhinebeck, **Upstate Films** (6415 Montgomery St. at Rte. 9, Rhinebeck, 845/876-2515 or 866/345-6688, www.upstatefilms.org, $10 regular, $8 students and seniors 62 and over, $6 members) has been showing indie films since 1972. Regulars can't resist the homemade treats at the candy counter.

Bars and Nightlife

Poughkeepsie's proximity to New York City means that well-known performers come to town on a fairly regular basis. Most popular among the city's nightclubs is **The Chance** (6 Crannell St., Poughkeepsie, 845/471-1966, www.thechancetheater.com), which offers live music. The Chance is part of an entertainment complex that includes four different clubs all in one building. The others are Club

Crannell Street, The Loft (for DJ music), and the Platinum Lounge.

Bananas Comedy Club (Umberto's Restaurant, 2245 South Rd., Poughkeepsie, 845/462-3333, www.bananaspk.com, Fri.-Sat. admission $25) is the place to go for a good laugh.

In Rhinebeck, the wood-paneled Colonial **Tap Room** at the Beekman Arms (6387 Mill St., Rhinebeck, 845/876-1766, www.beekmandelamaterinn.com) offers a cozy and historic atmosphere for enjoying a cold draft beer. Alternatively, the **Rhinebeck Wine & Liquor Store** (41 E. Market St., Rhinebeck, 845/876-6264, www.rhinebeckwineandliquor.com, 9am-7pm Mon.-Sat., noon-7pm Sun.) offers free tastings 4pm-7pm on Friday and Saturday.

Across the road from the FDR National Historic Site, the **Hyde Park Brewing Company** (4076 Albany Post Rd., Hyde Park, 845/229-8277, www.hydeparkbrewing.com, 4pm-10pm Mon.-Tues., 11am-10pm Wed.-Thurs., 11am-midnight Fri.-Sat., 11am-9pm Sun.) brews its own ales and lagers on the premises. Enjoy a three-hour-long weekday Happy Hour 4pm-7pm and $11 pitchers several other times during the week. Mahoney's Irish Pub in Poughkeepsie also has live music several nights a week.

Mill House Brewing Company (289 Mill St., Poughkeepsie, 845/485-2739, www.millhousebrewing.com, noon-9:30pm Sun.-Thurs., noon-11pm Fri.-Sat., mains $16-26) introduced its first beer, The Calibrator (IPA), in 2013. Its most recent creation, Albany Ale, is a vintage brew that took a year and a half to research. The bar is set in a historic building in downtown Poughkeepsie. Tasty bar bites include deviled eggs, fried brussels sprouts, and mussels steamed in beer, of course.

Run by the owners of The Local restaurant and tucked away in a basement bar, **The Shelter Wine Bar** (47 E. Market St., Rhinebeck, 845/876-1500, www.shelterwinebar.com, 5pm-midnight Tues.-Thurs., 5pm-2am Fri.-Sat.) mixes dependable cocktails from the Underground Old Fashioned to the 5 Finger Milk Punch. A dozen wines by the glass all come from Spain or Portugal.

Festivals

Summer in Dutchess County brings one food, wine, auto, and art festival after another. Kids get excited when the **Dutchess County Fair** (Rte. 9, Dutchess County Fairgrounds, Rhinebeck, 845/876-4000, www.dutchessfair.com) comes to town in August. One of the largest antique car shows in the Northeast is also held at the fairgrounds: The **Hudson River Valley Antique Auto Association's Annual Car Show & Swap Meet** (Rte. 9, Dutchess County Fair Grounds, 845/876-4001, www.rhinebeckcarshow.com) arrives in May.

Wineries from the Hudson River Valley and across New York State gather at Greig Farm each September for the **Hudson Valley Wine Fest** (Dutchess County Fair Grounds, 845/658-7181, www.hudsonvalleywinefest.com, one-day tasting $40, weekend tasting $70), a weekend of gourmet food, crafts, wine seminars, cooking demos, and live music. Also in September, the Culinary Institute of America in Hyde Park hosts an **International Wine Showcase & Auction** (845/658-7181, www.greystoneprograms.org). A who's who of Hudson River Valley chefs participate in the annual **Taste of the Hudson Valley** (845/431-8707, www.tastehv.org, $200 pp), pairing their most creative dishes with wines from New York, California, Europe, and beyond. With a 22-year history, this event draws attendees from across the Northeast.

The Beacon Arts Community Association organizes a monthly event, **Beacon Second Saturday** (845/546-6222, www.beaconarts.org), during which galleries and shops stay open until 9pm.

Pawling hosts its **Annual Pawling Triathlon** (845/247-0271, www.nytc.org) each May that draws competitors from around the Tri-State area.

Spectator Sports

For an evening of all-American fun, head to **Dutchess Stadium** (1500 Rte. 9D, Wappingers Falls, 845/838-0094, admission $5-9) to watch the Hudson Valley Renegades play minor league baseball. Tickets are easy to come by, and fireworks often follow the games.

SHOPPING

A busy commercial zone crowds Route 9 from Fishkill to Hyde Park, with one shopping mall after another. Head for the hills to avoid the chains.

Citrus Handbags (141 Church St., Millbrook, 845/677-9660) also has a unique selection of clothing, jewelry, headbands, and ribbon watches, and Bette Midler is an occasional customer. If you're in the market (and have the budget) for a one-of-a-kind beaded and jeweled dress, **Rowena Gill** (24 North Ave., Millbrook, 845/702-4280, www.rowenagill.com, 10am-4pm Tues.-Fri., 10am-12:30pm Sat.) is the designer for you. Stop by her showroom to see these exquisite works of art. **Punch** (3262 Franklin Ave., Millbrook, 845/677-6796, www.shoppunchnow.com, 10am-5pm Mon.-Thurs., 9am-7pm Fri.-Sat., 11am-4pm Sun.) has a selection of the finer things for country living, from cashmere sweaters to designer hunter boots.

Copper Star Alpaca (20 Main St., Millerton, 518/592-1414, 11am-5pm Wed.-Thurs., 10am-6pm Fri.-Mon.) sells capes and wraps, sweaters, bags, and blankets—all made of fleece shorn from the farm's herd of alpacas.

Rhinebeck has a handful of imaginative boutique shops. **EB's Hudson Valley Finds** (41 E. Market St., Rhinebeck, 845/876-3020, www.hudsonvalleyfinds.com, noon-6pm Wed.-Thurs., 11am-6pm Fri.-Sat., 11am-5pm Sun.), next to the Bread Alone bakery, has everything from trendy tote bags to designer jewelry to paintings to candlesticks, honey, and the occasional piece of furniture—all locally made somewhere in the Hudson River Valley. Chief Finder Evelyn Bartin takes great pleasure in seeking out the whimsical and the unusual, and she puts it all together in a storefront that feels like an art gallery. **Periwinkles** (24 E. Market St., Rhinebeck, 845/876-4014, www.periwinklesatrhinebeck.com, 10am-5pm Sun., noon-5pm Mon.-Fri., 10am-6pm Sat.,) sells Sally Spicer handbags, Yankee Candles, and the usual assortment of kitchen and bath accessories. A few doors closer to the intersection with Route 9, **Winter Sun & Summer Moon** (10-14 E. Market St., Rhinebeck, 845/876-3555, www.wintersun-summermoon.com) carries everything from Tibetan player flags to Dr. Hauschka skincare products and Putumayo World Music.

Stop by the handy **Cabin Fever Outfitters** (6423 Montgomery St., Rhinebeck, 845/876-6005, www.cabinfeveroutfitters.com, 11am-6pm Mon.-Sat., 11am-5pm Sun.) for any gear you left behind. The **Rhinebeck Bicycle Shop** is on Garden Street, open 10am-5:30pm Monday-Saturday.

In Red Hook, **Basic French** (17 Metzger Rd., Red Hook, 845/758-0399, www.basicfrenchonline.com) is a Francophile place with French-milled soaps, Petit Bateau baby clothes, and the like.

Beacon has a trendy women's boutique and toy store in **Echo** (470 Main St., Beacon, 845/440-0047, www.echobeacon.com, 10am-7pm Mon.-Sat., 10am-6pm Sun.). This is a great place to find gifts for children such as wooden alphabet blocks, dollhouse furnishings, musical instruments, and books or games. The women's boutique side has wraps, shoes, designer tees, handbags, and other stylish must-haves.

Wine

Beacon's **Artisan Wine Shop** (180 Main St., Beacon, 845/440-6923, www.artisanwine-shop.com, 10am-7pm Mon.-Sat., noon-5pm Sun.) has the chilled white wine you need for a riverside picnic after a Dia:Beacon visit. The **Rhinebeck Wine & Liquor Store** (41 E. Market St., Rhinebeck, 845/876-6264, www.rhinebeckwineandliquor.com, 9am-7pm Mon.-Sat., noon-7pm Sun.) carries labels from near and far and offers free tastings 4pm-7pm on Fridays and Saturdays. You can also purchase locally made wines at the individual winery tasting rooms.

Farm Stands

The after-work stop for fresh-picked veggies at a local farm stand is a way of life for Dutchess County residents. True connoisseurs can tell from the first bite if their corn was picked in the morning or afternoon. You can often find these stands at major local intersections, such as at Routes 9 and 9G near Rhinebeck. If you have more time on your hands, pick your own produce at an orchard like **Fishkill Farms** (9 Fishkill Farm Rd., Hopewell Junction, 845/897-4377, www.fishkillfarms.com), which has been growing apples for 75 years. At **Montgomery Place Orchards** (8 Davis Way, Red Hook, 845/758-6338, www.mporchards.com, 9am-6pm Wed.-Sun.), you can combine your picking with a tour of the historic Montgomery Place mansion.

Greig Farm (223 Pitcher Ln., Red Hook, 845/758-1234, www.greigfarm.com, 8am-7pm daily) has evolved from a standard apple-picking operation to a year-round marketplace and bakery.

Walbridge Farm Market (538 Rte. 343, Millbrook, 845/677-6221, www.walbridgefarm.com, 10am-5pm Mon., Thurs. Fri., 9am-5pm Sat., noon-5pm Sun.) has one of the best-stocked farm stores of anyone in the county. It's worth the short drive from town to pick up grass-fed beef, Ronnybrook yogurt, pastured eggs, and a selection of locally made treats. The farmers also host a popular festival in mid-July with hayrides, face painting, and live music. Say hello to the herd if you go.

Sawkill Farm (7782 Albany Post Rd., Red Hook, 845/514-4562, www.sawkillfarm.com, 10am-5pm Thurs.-Sun.) has two large chest freezers full of grass-fed beef, pasture-raised pork, lamb, and chicken. The fridge holds farm eggs and organic vegetables, all grown on-site. In the works is a new kitchen for making sausage, stocks, soups, and pot pies. The stores stay open until 6pm when it's warm.

During the summer and fall harvest, more than 10 farmers markets spring to life, most on the weekends, but a few take place on weekday afternoons. For example, the **Millbrook Farmers Market** (Front St. and Franklin Ave., Millbrook, www.millbrooknyfarmersmarket.com) is open 9am-1pm each Saturday May-October. **Beacon** (www.thebeaconfarmersmarket.org) has a Sunday riverfront farmers market 11am-3pm. Other options include **Fishkill** (Grand Union parking lot,

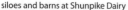

siloes and barns at Shunpike Dairy

The Birth of American Art: The Hudson River School of Painters

In the early 19th century, America's first generation of artists began to discover and explore the wilderness of the Hudson River Valley, Catskills, and Adirondack Mountains. Inspired by what they saw—lush forests, cascading waterfalls, fall foliage, and 4,000-foot peaks—they began to paint a new kind of landscape.

Led by Thomas Cole (1801-1848), the movement found roots in European Romanticism and later became known as the Hudson River School. These painters, contemporaries of writers including Emerson, Thoreau, William Cullen Bryant, and Whitman, shaped a young nation's first artistic movement, leading to the start of the Romantic era.

From his home and studio in Catskill, Cole painted Kaaterskill Falls, Catskill Creek, the Catskill Peaks, and other wilderness areas in the valley. Asher B. Durand (1796-1886), a contemporary and friend of Cole's, and Frederic Edwin Church, Cole's student, are also associated with the movement.

Today, you can view these works of art at the Frances Lehman Loeb Art Center at Vassar College in Poughkeepsie, the Olana State Historic Site (Church's home) near Hudson, and the Albany Institute of History and Art in Albany—as well as other museums and libraries in New York City and out of state.

Guided hikes from the Thomas Cole National Historic Site at Cedar Grove in the town of Catskill are another way to experience the works of these artists. Visitors can hike to Kaaterskill Clove, the site of the famous Catskill Mountain House hotel, and Sunset Rock—places that are as beautiful and moving today as they were two centuries ago.

Rte. 52, 845/897-4430, 10am-2pm Thurs. July-Oct.); **Hyde Park** (Hyde Park Drive-In, Rt. 9, Hyde Park, 845/229-9111, www.hydeparkfarmersmarket.org, 9am-2pm Sat. June-Oct.); **Millerton** (Dutchess Ave., just off Main St., Millerton, 518/789-4613, www.millertonfarmersmarket.org, 10am-2pm Sat. May-Sept.); **Pawling** (Charles Colman Blvd., next to the Pawling Chamber of Commerce Building, Pawling, 917/224-4801, www.pawlingfarmersmarket.org, 9am-noon Sat. July-Oct.); and **Rhinebeck** (municipal parking lot, 23 E. Market St., Rhinebeck, 845/876-7756, www.rhinebeckfarmersmarket.com, 10am-2pm Sun. May-Nov.). These weekly farmers markets allow you sample the local bounty and also find plants, honey, crafts, baked goods, and the like.

Dykeman Farm (823 W. Dover Rd., Wingdale, 845/832-6068, www.dykemanfarm.com, 9am-6pm daily July 1-Oct. 31, 10am-5pm daily after Labor Day) grows sweet corn and tomatoes and offers pick-your-own pumpkins in the fall. Northeast of Amenia, the **McEnroe Organic Farm Market** (5409 Rte. 22 Millerton, 518/789-4191, www.mcenroeorganicfarm.com, 9am-6pm Sat.-Thurs. and 9am-6:30pm Fri. early Mar.-early Nov., 9am-5pm Sat.-Thurs. and 9am-5:30pm Fri. early Nov.-early Mar.) offers organic produce in season, plus pick-your-own herbs and flowers.

Pick up fine teas and accessories for friends back home at the **Harney & Sons Tea Shop** in Millerton (13 Main St., Railroad Plaza, Millerton, www.harney.com, 10am-5pm Mon.-Sat., 11am-4pm Sun.).

Shunpike Dairy (1328 Shunpike Rd., Millbrook, 845/702-6224) is a secret stop for raw milk. Serve yourself from a tank in the barn and leave cash in the box. Pay a few dollars more if you need to use one of their jars.

Adams Fairacre Farms (765 Dutchess Turnpike/Rte. 44, Poughkeepsie, 845/454-4330, www.adamsfarms.com, 8am-9pm Mon.-Fri., 8am-8pm Sat., 8am-7pm Sun.) began as a roadside stand in 1932, selling homegrown fruits and vegetables to

Poughkeepsie residents. Today, the company is a local phenomenon with 650 employees operating three large supermarkets in Poughkeepsie, Kingston, and Newburgh. In addition to fresh produce, Adams sells gourmet cheese, breads, coffee, and meats, including many locally made products. Expect long lines on weekends.

Antiques and Galleries

Every town in Dutchess County has its share of antique treasures. Twenty-five such places are found under one art deco roof at Red Hook's **Annex Antiques Center** (23 E. Market St., Red Hook, 845/758-2843, 11am-5pm daily). Watch artisans at work in half a dozen shops along the Ten Mile River at the **Webatuck Craft Village** (Rte. 55, Wingdale, 845/832-6601). Handmade crafts include blown glass, pottery, and objects made of copper, tin, and wood. Most of the shops are open 10am-5pm daily except Tuesday.

Hudson Beach Glass (162 Main St., Beacon, 845/440-0068, www.hudsonbeachglass.com, 10am-6pm Mon.-Sat., 11am-6pm Sun.) carries jewelry, vases, bowls, and other glass works created by several local artists. It is one of the only glassworks galleries of its size in upstate New York. **Riverwinds Gallery** (172 Main St, Beacon, 845/838-2880, www.riverwindsgallery.com, noon-6pm Wed.-Mon.) displays paintings and photography as well as jewelry, pottery, ceramics, lamps, sculpture, porcelain, and glass.

The **Hyde Park Antiques Center** (4192 Albany Post Rd., Hyde Park, 845/229-8200, www.hydeparkantiques.net, 10am-5pm daily) represents more than 50 dealers with antiques that span the 18th, 19th, and 20th centuries. Allow plenty of time to wander through the maze of rooms, which contain vintage toys, jewelry, porcelain, pottery, and more. Best of all, there's something for every price point.

The huge showroom at **Johnson's Antiques** (Route 22 North, 518/789-3848, www.johnsonsantiquesbarn.com, 10am-5pm Fri.-Sun.) has used furniture, a dedicated garden center, and all kinds of new-to-you gift ideas.

Bookstores

Booklovers will find both big chains and independent treasure chests across the county. For example, **Merritt Bookstore** (57 Front St., Millbrook, 845/677-5857, www.merrittbooks.com, 9am-6pm Mon.-Sat., 10am-5pm Sun.) sells new fiction and nonfiction. **The Book Cove** (22 Charles Colman Blvd.,

Browse the Merritt Bookstore for books by local authors.

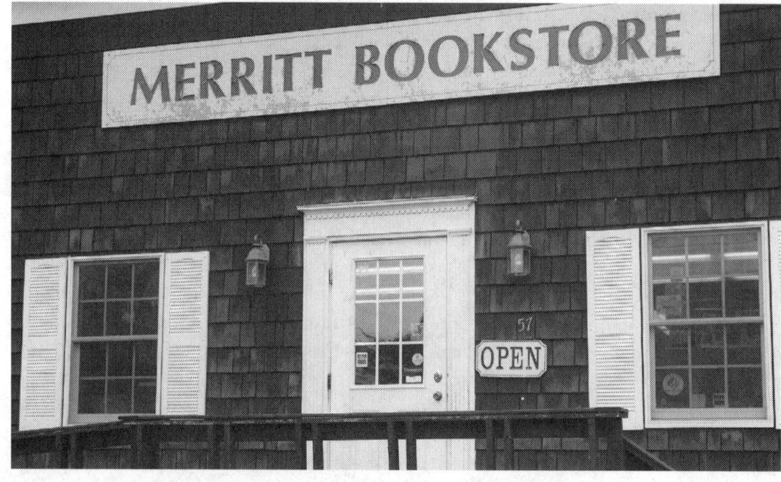

Pawling, 845/855-9590, www.pawlingbookcove.com, 10am-6pm Tues.-Fri., 10am-5pm Sat., 11am-3pm Sun.) also sells a great collection of children's books, toys, CDs, and stationery. After a Harney & Sons tea tasting, browse the regional books, best sellers, and signed copies at **Oblong Books & Music** (26 Main St., Millerton, 518/789-3797, www.oblongbooks.com, 10am-6pm Sun.-Thurs, 10am-8pm Fri.-Sat.).

INFORMATION AND SERVICES

The **Dutchess County Tourism Promotion Agency** (3 Neptune Rd., Ste. Q-17, Poughkeepsie, 845/463-4000 or 800/445-3131, www.dutchesstourism.com) can provide a wealth of information on places to see across the county. Several of the smaller towns have visitors centers as well: **Rhinebeck Chamber of Commerce** (23F E. Market St., Rhinebeck, 845/876-5904, www.rhinebeckchamber.com, 10am-4pm Wed.-Sat., noon-4pm Sun.) and **Red Hook Area Chamber of Commerce** (P.O. Box 254, Red Hook, 845/758-0824, www.redhookchamber.org, 9:30am-12:30pm Mon.-Fri.).

GETTING THERE AND AROUND

Bus

Shortline Bus (800/631-8405, www.coachusa.com) provides daily service to Poughkeepsie, Hyde Park, and Rhinebeck from New York City ($44-50 adult round-trip fare), Long Island, and New Jersey. **Adirondack Trailways** (800/858-8555, www.escapemaker.com) also runs buses between Poughkeepsie and New York City. The **Dutchess County Loop Bus System** (14 Commerce St., Poughkeepsie, 845/485-4690, www.co.dutchess.ny.us) covers major destinations, including Dutchess County Community College, Marist College, and the Poughkeepsie Train Station. In Poughkeepsie, a city bus system with six lines services all parts of the city.

Train

Amtrak and Metro-North offer frequent connections to the Poughkeepsie Train Station, and taxis are usually waiting. On weekdays, the parking lot overflows with commuter vehicles. Amtrak also stops in Rhinecliff to the north. And the Metro-North Hudson Line stops in Beacon to the south, while the Harlem Line services Pawling, Dover Plains, and Wassaic.

Car

The most direct routes through Dutchess County are the Taconic State Parkway and Route 22. Route 9 follows the Hudson River through the most densely populated areas of the county. I-84 runs east-west, connecting motorists to I-87, the New York State Thruway. Avis and Hertz have rental car offices off Route 9, near the IBM complex in Poughkeepsie. Budget, Enterprise, and Sears also have rental facilities in the area. Each major town in the county has at least one taxi service.

Ulster County

The Esopus Indians were the first people to settle mountainous Ulster County. European invasion began with a Dutch trading post in 1614, and a series of battles with the Native American population ensued for the next few decades. A group of French Huguenots arrived in 1663, fleeing religious persecution on the continent. One hundred years later came the British, who would burn the county seat of Kingston to the ground during the Revolutionary War.

Ulster's early industries were the production of cement and bluestone; its communities also prospered as the terminus for the

Delaware and Ulster Canal, which delivered coal from mines in Pennsylvania to the Eastern Seaboard.

Covering more than a thousand square miles of riverfront, foothills, and two distinct mountain ranges, modern-day Ulster County is a haven for hikers, rock climbers, organic farmers, foodies, and lovers of nature. The state university at New Paltz and nearby Minnewaska State Park Preserve attract a young and active crowd that supports an abundance of cafés, bookstores, restaurants, and gear shops. Farther west lie bohemian Woodstock, the Esopus Creek, and a few of the summer boarding houses that were popular in the 1960s.

Ulster boasts the highest peak in the Catskills: Slide Mountain, which rises 4,180 feet above the town of Oliverea. The Ashokan Reservoir, completed in 1917 in a major engineering feat, supplies more than half of New York City's water.

ALONG THE RIVER: ROUTE 9W

One of the oldest and prettiest spans across the Hudson, the Mid-Hudson Bridge, connects southern Ulster County to downtown Poughkeepsie. To the north of the auto bridge, a long abandoned railroad bridge opened in 2009 as a pedestrian park, known as Walkway over the Hudson (www.walkway.org). The span is 1.3 miles long and connects the town of Highland to Poughkeepsie's waterfront. There is parking at both ends of the span. To get to the west side of the walkway, follow Havelin Drive off Route 9W to a small park that connects to the bridge.

Ten miles south of the Mid-Hudson Bridge, **Gomez Mill House** (11 Millhouse Rd., Marlboro, 845/236-3126, www.gomez.org, 10am-4pm Wed.-Sun. mid-Apr.-early Nov., adults $8, seniors $6, students and children $3) boasts a multicultural past that reaches all the way back to the time of the Spanish Inquisition. Luis Moises Gomez, a Sephardi, or descendant of the Jews who settled Spain and Portugal in the Middle Ages, fled persecution in the early 18th century and built a trading post in Marlboro in 1714. Subsequent owners of the fieldstone home were Patriots of the American Revolution, farmers, writers, artisans, and environmentalists. Today, the building is the oldest surviving Jewish homestead in North America. Tours of the inside are available, and the museum holds cultural events and lectures through the summer season.

Slabsides Burroughs Sanctuary

Naturalist John Burroughs wrote hundreds of essays over the span of his career, many of them from a log cabin tucked away in the woods near present-day West Park. A student of Whitman and Thoreau, Burroughs treasured the simple things in life: books, friends, and above all, nature. Of a summer hike in the southern Catskills, he wrote, "An ideal trout brook was this, now hurrying, now loitering, now deepening around a great boulder, now gliding evenly over a pavement of green-gray stone and pebbles; no sediment or stain of any kind, but white and sparkling as snow-water, and nearly as cool."

A visit to the Burroughs retreat, called **Slabsides** (Burroughs Dr., West Park, 845/384-6320, www.johnburroughsassociation.org), will bring out the nature writer in any traveler. The John Burroughs Association, formed soon after Burroughs died in 1921, maintains the grounds of the 180-acre Slabsides Burroughs Sanctuary and opens the 1895 cabin to the public twice each year, on the third Saturday in May and the first Saturday in October. Allow about 20 minutes to walk from the parking lot to the cabin.

Kingston

As the third most important Dutch trading post (after New Amsterdam/Manhattan and Fort Orange/Albany), Kingston played a pivotal role in the establishment of New York State. But early settlers paid dearly for their independence: During the American Revolution, the British retaliated against the

Kingston

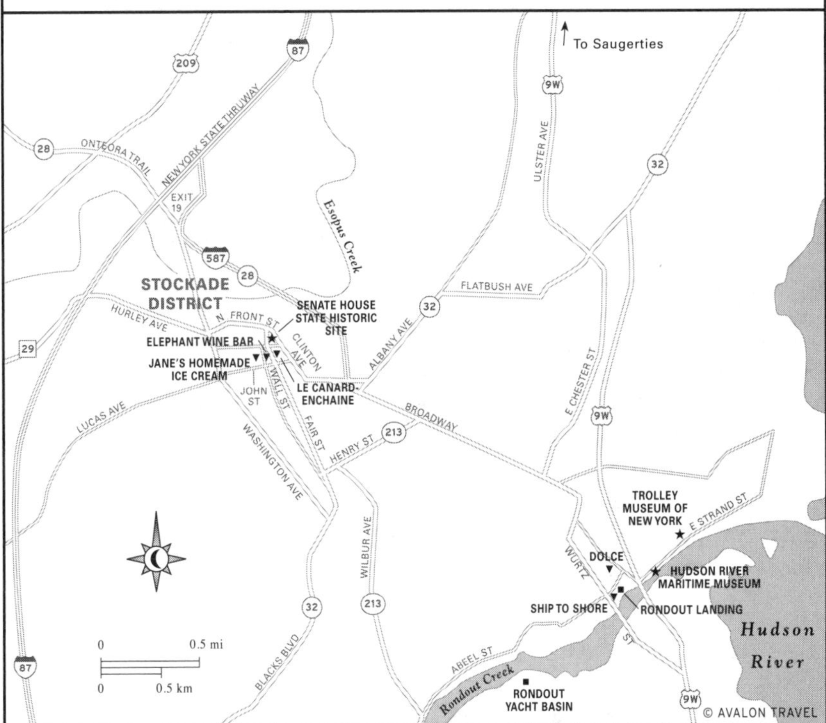

colonists by burning the city to the ground. The tragedy left its mark, and no story is repeated more often as one tours the Hudson River Valley's historic sights.

Like Saugerties to its north, Kingston developed around a strategic watershed: where the Rondout Creek meets the Hudson River. Settlers traded cement, bricks, and bluestone, and Kingston served as a transportation hub during the steam and rail eras. Today, greater Kingston (population 23,800) is a sea of huge retail stores with some interesting pockets of culture and history. A variety of architectural styles have been preserved, from Federal, Georgian, and Greek Revival to Romanesque, Italianate, neoclassical, and art deco. Two areas are of interest to the traveler: the Stockade District and the revitalized Rondout Village.

Colorful brick facades of mauve, orange, and lima-bean green line Wall Street inside the old stockade, originally built to keep Native Americans out. Many of the homes in this district are private residences, but a few are open to the public. A gorgeous **Federal home** at the corner of Main and Wall Streets was saved in the late 1930s by Fred J. Johnston (63 Main St., Kingston, 845/339-0720, www.fohk.org, 1pm-4pm Sat.-Sun. May-Oct., adults $5, children $2), an antique and restoration specialist. Johnston deeded the home and collection of 18th- and 19th-century furnishings to a local nonprofit organization, and the building is open to the public.

Up the street stands the **Old Dutch Church** (272 Wall St., Kingston, 845/338-6759, www.olddutchchurch.org), dating back to the 18th century. George Clinton, the first governor of New York and vice president to Jefferson and Madison, is buried here. Hoffman House, at the north end of Front Street, is a Dutch Colonial structure dating back to 1679. A pair of entrepreneurs renovated the building in the mid-1970s and turned it into **Hoffman House Tavern** (94 N. Front St., Kingston, 845/338-2626, www.hoffmanhousetavern.com, 11:30am-9pm Mon.-Thurs., 11:30am-10pm Sat., lunch $9-12, dinner $19-27).

In 1777, a group of local political leaders gathered in Kingston to draft the New York State constitution. The first senate convened at 296 Fair Street, now the **Senate House State Historic Site** (845/338-2786, www.nysparks.com, 10am-5pm Wed.-Sat., 1pm-5pm Sun., adults $4, seniors $3, under 12 free). A historical exhibit contains paintings by Kingston's own John Vanderlyn.

For a guided tour of the Stockade District homes and the Senate House, contact **1658 Stockade District Walking Tours** (63 Main St., 845/339-0720, www.fohk.org, adults $10, children $5). Tours are offered the first Saturday of the month July-October starting at 1pm, or by special appointment. Stop by the **Tourism Information Caboose** on Washington Avenue (800/331-1518, www.kingston-ny.gov) to pick up a self-guided brochure. Take New York State Thruway Exit 19 to reach downtown Kingston.

When you leave the Stockade District, follow Broadway to its end at the edge of the Rondout Creek, where a handful of upscale restaurants, including Mariner's Harbor, have revitalized Rondout Village, a cluster of restored brick buildings near the Route 9W crossing. In summer, you can dine in one of the landing's trendy eateries and finish the evening with a stroll along the waterfront.

The **Hudson River Maritime Museum** (50 Rondout Landing, 845/338-0071, www.hrmm.org, 11am-5pm daily May-Oct., adults $7, seniors and children $5) opens here each spring. A restored 1898 steam tug named *Mathilda* takes up most of the museum's yard. Inside are a 100-year-old shad boat and a number of model ships. A collection of paintings, prints, photos, blueprints, and artifacts document the maritime history of the river—from sloops and iceboats to steam engines and tugs—and the industries it has supported throughout the years.

For a taste of life during the railroad era, visit the **Trolley Museum of New York** (89 E. Strand St., 845/331-3399, www.tmny.org, noon-5pm Sat.-Sun. Memorial Day-Columbus Day, adults $6, seniors and children 5-12 $4, under 5 free) at Rondout Landing and take a short ride along the original tracks of the Delaware and Ulster Railroad. The trolley stops at Kingston Point Park on the Hudson River. Exhibits inside the museum trace the history of rail transportation, and visitors can watch restorations in progress in the workshop below.

Saugerties

The Esopus Creek empties into the Hudson at Saugerties. Water rushing out of the mountains once powered a mill that led the town to the forefront of the paper industry. Recognition on the National Register of Historic Places has put Saugerties on the map once again, with an eight-block stretch of 18th- and 19th-century homes, antiques shops, and top-notch restaurants that appeal to collectors and food travelers.

The restored **Saugerties Lighthouse** (168 Lighthouse Dr. off Mynderse St., 845/247-0656, www.saugertieslighthouse.com), built in 1869, stands at the mouth of the Esopus Creek. Access is via a half-mile-long walk along a nature path that can be flooded at high tide, or by personal boat. Now a two-room bed-and-breakfast, the house is furnished in 1920s-era style. Guided tours are available noon-3pm on Sundays Memorial Day-Labor Day (adults $5 donation, children $3 donation). Plan a picnic along the shoreline and enjoy the secluded river views.

Plan to arrive in Saugerties on a weekend afternoon, with time to browse the **Hope Farm Press and Bookshop** (15 Jane St.,

Saugerties

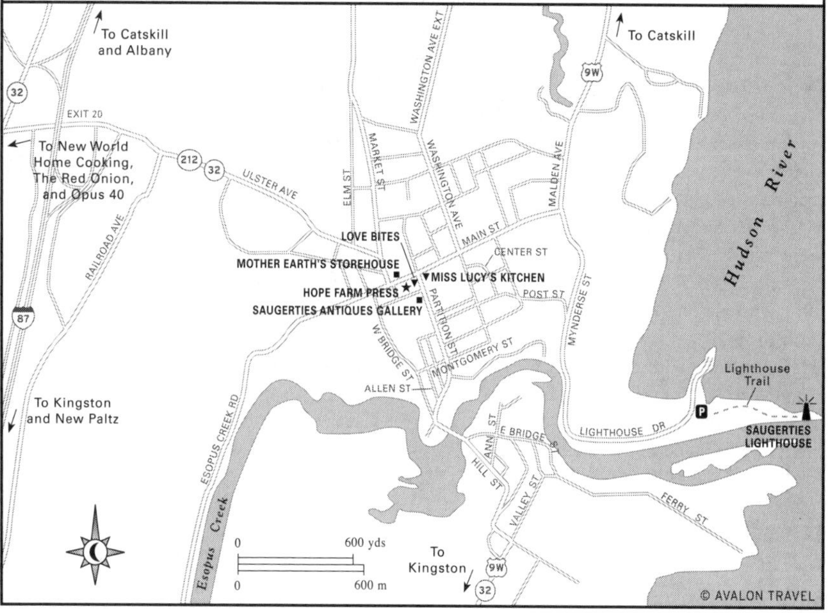

845/246-3522, www.hopefarm.com, noon-6pm Mon.-Sat.).

Tucked away on a narrow country lane between Saugerties and Woodstock is a vestige of the bluestone era. Over four decades, sculpture artist Harvey Fite turned an abandoned quarry behind his house and studio into a six-acre sculpture garden that's open to the public on weekends throughout the summer. A small gallery on-site holds a collection of quarryman's tools. Look for the turnoff to **Opus 40** (50 Fite Rd., Saugerties, 845/246-3400, www.opus40.org, Memorial Day weekend through Columbus Day weekend, Fri.-Sun. and holiday Mondays, 11am-5:30pm, adults $10, students and seniors $7, children $3, under 6 free) at The Red Onion restaurant on Route 212.

NEW PALTZ AND SURROUNDINGS

More than any other community in the Hudson River Valley, New Paltz offers travelers a healthy dose of alternative culture. Within walking distance from the town center, the SUNY New Paltz campus fosters a vibrant student community.

New Paltz has deep roots in protecting groups who face discrimination. The town owes its name to a group of French Huguenots from Mannheim, Germany—part of a region called Die Pfalz—who came to the New World in 1677 to escape religious persecution. These early settlers built homes above the Wallkill River on present-day Huguenot Street.

A short walk uphill from Huguenot Street puts you on Main Street in striking distance of most of the shops and restaurants in town. The **Wallkill Valley Rail Trail** (www.gorail-trail.org) crosses Main Street just below Route 32, making this an ideal stopover for walkers or cyclists following the length of the 12.2-mile trail from Wallkill to Rosendale. Drivers should take Exit 18 from the New York State Thruway to reach New Paltz (parking is available at the Huguenot Historical Society's lot at 18 Broadhead Ave., two blocks north of Rte.

299/Main St., as well as the Village of New Paltz municipal parking lot off Huguenot St. north of Rte. 299/Main St). Expect traffic jams and difficult parking on summer weekends.

★ Huguenot Street

Several of the six original stone buildings on this street have survived more than three centuries of evolution in the community. The original structures of the Bevier-Elting, Jean Hasbrouck, and Abraham Hasbrouck Houses were built in the 1680s, and these homes are preserved as they would have looked in the 18th century. The 1799 LeFevre House was built in the Federal style, and the museum has furnished it with 19th-century accoutrements. The Deyo House is designed to portray an 1890s aesthetic, while the Colonial Freer House was remodeled in the 1940s.

The Huguenot Historical Society runs guided tours from its visitors center in the **DuBois Fort** (18 Broadhead Ave., New Paltz, 845/255-1660, www.huguenotstreet.org, 9:30am-4:30pm Sat.-Sun., 10:30am-4:30pm Mon., Thurs. and Fri. June-Oct.). Tours run 50 or 90 minutes and cost $16 for adults, $15 for seniors and students, and $10 for children, with reduced rates for the abbreviated tour.

The organization also maintains **Locust Lawn** (Rte. 32, Gardiner, 845/255-1660, www.huguenotstreet.org, tours by appointment only), an 1814 Federal mansion that belonged to the prominent Hasbrouck family. A collection of family memorabilia is on display inside.

The Shawangunk Ridge

Between New Paltz and the Catskill Mountains lies another mountain range with its own geologic history, the Shawangunk Ridge. The result of a continental collision, the exposed sedimentary rock of the Shawangunks offers amateur and professional geologists an accessible, living laboratory to study the formation of the Appalachian Mountains—an eroded range that once stretched as high as the Himalayas.

The Shawangunk Ridge runs from the town of Rosendale all the way to New Jersey and Pennsylvania. From the spotted salamander to the black bear, it supports a delicate habitat for dozens of endangered plants and animals, among them the dwarf pitch pine, which grows on bedrock, and the peregrine falcon. Shale cliffs and dramatic overhangs also form ideal pitches for serious rock climbers, who know the area as The Gunks. The climbers arrive by the hundreds on clear

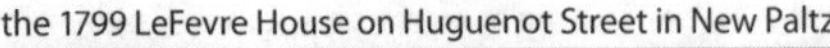

the 1799 LeFevre House on Huguenot Street in New Paltz

New Paltz

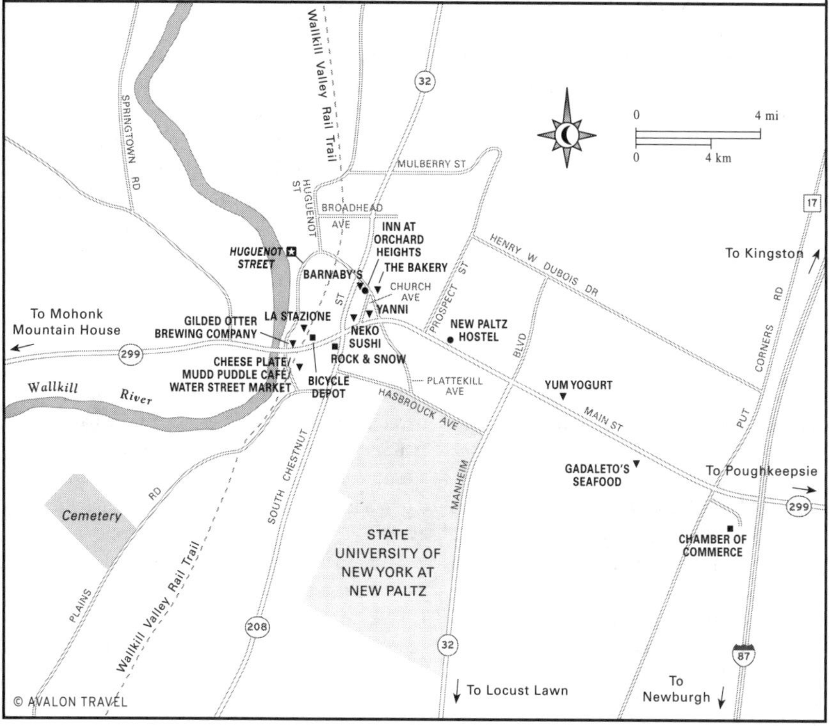

summer days, with their ropes, harnesses, and chalk in tow.

Three protected wilderness areas cover a large portion of the Shawangunk Ridge: Minnewaska State Park Preserve, the Mohonk Preserve, and Sam's Point Preserve.

★ Minnewaska State Park Preserve

Acquired by New York State in 1987, **Minnewaska State Park Preserve** (5281 Rte. 44/55, New Paltz, 845/255-0752, www.nysparks.com, open year-round for day use, $8 per vehicle) encompasses 12,000 acres with a main entrance at Lake Minnewaska, off Route 44/55. Though the elevation here is about 2,000 feet, the scrubby pines, precipitous cliffs, and sparkling water might trick you into thinking you are above 10,000.

Swimming normally is permitted in the lake, but in 2014 the lake was closed for several weeks due to a problem with leeches. Hikers have a full menu of options within Minnewaska, from easy two-mile routes to challenging 10-mile loops. You can actually follow the ridgeline by foot from the Appalachian Trail at the New Jersey state line all the way to Wurtsboro and the Basha Kill preserve, in Sullivan County. Climbers will want to head to the Peter's Kill escarpment, a good alternative to the crowds at the Mohonk Preserve. Bicycles are allowed on the carriage paths only, not on the trails.

In addition to the Lake Minnewaska parking lot, Minnewaska has parking and trailheads at Peter's Kill to the east and Awosting to the west. A word of caution: To protect the fragile ecosystem, the park service limits the number of visitors allowed in Minnewaska at once. On summer weekends, the lots often fill immediately after opening. It's a good idea to arrive with a backup plan in mind, such as exploring the Wallkill Valley Rail Trail. Minnewaska is a day-use park only; there are no overnight accommodations, and visitors must pack out all trash.

Mohonk Preserve

Adjoining Minnewaska to the north is the **Mohonk Preserve** (3197 Rts. 44/55, New Paltz, 845/255-0919, www.mohonkpreserve.org), set aside by the environmentally aware Smiley family. Climbers flock here to choose from 1,000 different routes through world-class crags and crevices. Hikers have 65 miles of trails to explore. Follow Route 199 from New Paltz to find the Mohonk visitors center. Climbers will want to continue past the center to the West Trapps trailhead. Parking lots fill quickly on weekend mornings. Entrance fees are $12 for hikers and $17 for climbers and cyclists.

At the intersection of Minnewaska and Mohonk lies the fairytale **Mohonk Mountain House** (1000 Mountain Rest Rd., New Paltz, 855/883-3798, www.mohonk.com), whose story begins with 280 acres of land, a 10-room inn, and a pair of Quaker twins. In the late 19th century, Albert and Alfred Smiley built rival country inns on the ridgeline, which grew to accommodate hundreds of guests at a time. A network of carriage paths connected the properties and provided the ideal setting for quiet contemplation. One of the original buildings burned down, but to this day, the historic Mohonk Mountain House, on the shores of Lake Mohonk, is owned and run by descendants of the Smiley family.

In its heyday, this sprawling hotel entertained a slew of famous guests, among them John Burroughs, Andrew Carnegie, and Theodore Roosevelt. Mohonk is no longer the remote and elegant wilderness getaway it was in the 19th century, but the property remains as beautiful as ever and continues to draw a steady crowd of tourists. Today, it serves as a popular venue for weddings and corporate events.

South of Minnewaska is the 4,600-acre **Sam's Point Preserve** (Sam's Point Rd., Cragsmoor, 845/647-7989, 9am-5pm Thurs.-Mon., $10 parking fee), created in 1997 to protect the rare ridgetop dwarf pine barrens that define the landscape. Trails lead to numerous valley vistas, and the moderately strenuous

Lake Minnewaska in summer

Lake Mohonk

7.6-mile hike to Verkeerderkill Falls takes about five hours round-trip. Follow Route 52 to Cragsmoor.

Rosendale

Surrounding New Paltz are several smaller but equally charming towns: Route 32 north takes you to Rosendale, home of the internationally acclaimed Rosendale Cement Company, whose "natural cement" limestone was used in nearly every major construction project undertaken in the 19th century: Rosendale cement found its way into the Brooklyn Bridge, the wings of the U.S. Capitol, the pedestal of the Statue of Liberty, the Washington Monument, Grand Central Terminal, and even the Panama Canal.

Geologists head to Rosendale's abandoned mines for clues about the past. The **Widow Jane Mine** (688 Rte. 213, 845/658-9900, www.centuryhouse.org, 1pm-4pm Sun. May 8-Sept. 25 or by appointment, adults $3, children $1), run by the Century House Historical Society, is a rare horizontal mine that is open to the public. Since its operational days ended, the mine has been used to grow mushrooms and trout, and as a venue for musical performances.

The society also operates the former estate of farmer-turned-businessman A. J. Snyder, an 1809 home that's listed on the National Register of Historic Places. A tour of the **Snyder Estate** (668 Rte. 213, 845/658-9900, www.centuryhouse.org, 1pm-4pm Sundays May 8-Sept. 25 or by appointment, adults $3, children $1) covers the house and mine, as well as a visit to the Delaware and Hudson Canal and a look at the old cement kilns.

High Falls

About 15 minutes from New Paltz by car, High Falls is the kind of place where locals give you funny looks when you try to get a cell phone signal. Hidden in the Shawangunk Mountains, on the south shore of the swift-flowing Rondout Creek, High Falls has found a niche in accommodating the spillover of weekenders from New Paltz. Many residents here started as weekenders, evolved into part-time commuters, and eventually moved in for good. A two-block stretch of businesses includes a handful of boutique stores and eateries, including the exclusive **DePuy Canal House** (103 Main St., 845/687-7700, www.depuycanalhouse.com, 5pm-10pm Fri., 10am-3pm and 5pm-10pm Sat., 10am-4pm Sun., dinner $18-34).

It was a cold January day in 1825 when the founders of the Delaware and Hudson Canal Company began their company's public offering with a show-and-tell on Wall Street: the burning of anthracite coal. In the midst of the War of 1812, the country faced its first energy crisis and needed an alternative to bituminous coal, which the British had been supplying. Pennsylvania coal offered an alternative; the challenge was getting it from inland hills to coastal settlements.

The offering succeeded and thus began the construction of the Delaware and Hudson Canal. Built by Irish immigrants on the heels of the Erie Canal (by the same architect), it measured 108 miles long, 4 feet deep, and 32 feet wide. Along the way, the canal passed through 108 locks and crossed 137 bridges. At its terminus, it had to drop 70 feet to sea level in Rondout Creek—a series of five locks did the trick.

Today, the **D&H Canal Museum** (23 Mohonk Rd., 845/687-9311, www.canalmuseum.org, 11am-5pm Sat.-Sun. May-Oct., adults $5, children $3), housed in the former St. John's Episcopal Church, is a National Historic Landmark offering lock demonstrations and a collection of documents and artifacts that trace the history of canal and railroad transportation.

Traveling Route 209 from High Falls toward Kingston, you'll pass through Marbletown, where the **Ulster County Historical Society** (2682 Rte. 209, Marbletown, 845/338-5614, www.ulstercountyhs.org, noon-5pm Thurs.-Sun. May-Oct., adults $6, seniors $5, children 12 and under $4, under 5 free) maintains a stone farmhouse with an exhibit of 18th- and 19th-century furniture and farming tools. Five generations of Davenports have farmed the land in neighboring Stone Ridge. Today, the family's farm market, greenhouse, and pick-your-own crops are a favorite local supply station.

THE SOUTHERN CATSKILL MOUNTAINS: ROUTE 28

Ashokan Reservoir

Route 28 west out of Kingston leads to the Ashokan Reservoir, the southern Catskill Mountains, and many of the old resorts that made the region world famous. Completed in 1915, the second-oldest reservoir in the New York City watershed (Croton is the oldest) holds 123 billion gallons in an artificially constructed lake that covers 253 square miles. Nine villages were flooded in its making, and an entire cemetery of Revolutionary War graves were dug up and relocated.

Woodstock

Follow the turnoff for Route 375 to reach the mountain town of Woodstock, a onetime artists' colony with deep roots in folk and rock music. (Bob Dylan was a longtime resident.) Unlike some of the Hudson River Valley's river towns, Woodstock has not reinvented itself overnight to appeal to a new demographic. Its busy cafés and art galleries give the impression of a genuine place with a passion for the arts.

Present-day Woodstock attracts a creative and outdoor-oriented crowd, including many New York City escapees. Woodstock is also one of the few towns in the region that have inviting accommodations within walking distance of shops and restaurants.

A popular day hike from Woodstock is the **Overlook Mountain Fire Tower** (34 Wardwell Ln., 845/679-2580) at 3,150 feet elevation. On clear days, the summit rewards hikers with a sweeping view of the Hudson River to the east. The trail (2.4 miles one-way) passes the remains of the Overlook Mountain House, another of the Catskills' 19th-century inns. Listen for the rattle of the endangered timber rattlesnake along the way. To reach the trailhead from Woodstock, follow Rock City Road from Route 212 and cross Route 33, where the name changes to Meads Mountain Road. The trailhead is about 1.5 miles up the mountain.

Across from the trailhead, one of Woodstock's old inns, the former Mead Mountain House, is now a Tibetan Buddhist monastery called the **Karma Triyana Dharmachakra** (335 Meads Mountain Rd., 845/679-5906, www.kagyu.org, office@kagyu.org, main shrine 2pm-6pm Mon.-Fri., weekend shrine hours vary, guided tours at 1pm Sat.-Sun.). It may be the only monastery in the world located in a 19th-century farmhouse. Visitors can tour the main shrine room, which contains one of the largest Shakyamuni Buddha statues in North America. A library and bookstore are also open to the public.

Beyond the Ashokan Reservoir and just minutes from Woodstock, a cluster of new buildings stand out on Route 28, looking much like the set of a Hollywood film. Centered on a converted 1841 barn in the hamlet of Mount Tremper, they are the shops and restaurants of **Catskill Corners Marketplace** (5340 Rte. 28, Mount Tremper, 845/688-5800), an upscale commercial plaza that seems out of place in the otherwise bohemian countryside. The main attraction for those passing through is a giant kaleidoscope.

Phoenicia

Farther along Route 28 are Phoenicia and the Catskill Mountain Railroad, which offers rides along the Esopus Creek. A better way to tour the creek, however, is by inner tube. On hot summer days, visitors line up at several rental shops in town to rent tubes that will float them down the gentle creek.

Train aficionados will want to check out the **Empire State Railway Museum** (Ulster & Delaware Railroad Station, 70 Lower High St., 845/688-7501, www.esrm.com, 11am-4pm Sat.-Sun. Memorial Day-October, admission by donation), which houses artifacts, photographs, and films that document the history of rail travel in the area.

Slide Mountain

A few miles past Phoenicia in the town of Shandaken, Route 42 turns north to Greene County. And soon after, in Big Indian, comes the turn for Route 47, or Oliverea Slide Mountain Road. This road leads to Frost Valley and the base of Slide Mountain. It's an eight-mile drive along Route 47 to the Winnisook Club and the Slide Mountain parking lot.

Naturalist John Burroughs spent long hours contemplating the highest peak in the Catskills. In an essay about the southern Catskills, he wrote that the peak looked like the back and shoulders of a gigantic horse: "The horse has got his head down grazing; the shoulders are high, and the descent from them down his neck very steep; if he were to lift up his head, one sees that it would be carried far above all other peaks, and that the noble beast might gaze straight to his peers in the Adirondacks or the White Mountains."

Burroughs spent many years fishing the streams that drained the mountain and camping on all sides of the peak before he attempted a summit. On approaching Slide at last from a spruce grove on the north side, he wrote, "The mountain rose like a huge, rock-bound fortress from this plain-like expanse. It was ledge upon ledge, precipice upon precipice, up which and over which we made our way slowly and with great labor, now pulling ourselves up by our hands, then cautiously finding niches for our feet and zigzagging right and left from shelf to shelf."

It's much easier to access Slide Mountain today, but the hike remains one of the most difficult in the Catskill Forest Preserve. A strenuous five-mile route from the parking lot leads to the top. There are no views from the summit proper, but from a ridge that connects Slide to neighboring Wittenberg, you can see all but one of the thirty-four Catskill High Peaks that rise above 3,500 feet (Thomas Cole peak is obscured by Hunter Mountain). Allow four or five hours to complete the hike.

Belleayre Ski Center

Past the turnoff for Oliverea, Route 28 begins to climb until it reaches the base of the **Belleayre Ski Center** (Rte. 28, Highmount, 845/254-5600 or 800/942-6904, www.belleayre.com, 9am-4pm daily Nov.-Mar.) in Pine Hill. With ideal terrain for intermediate skiers, Belleayre is located within the Catskill Forest Preserve. Skiers began carving turns down its slopes as early as the 1930s, and in 1949, the New York State Department of Environmental Conservation cleared a network of trails and opened the area to the public. Today, Belleayre sponsors outdoor and cultural programs year-round, including the **Belleayre Music Festival** in summer.

SPORTS AND RECREATION

Winter Sports

With an annual base of 75 to 165 inches of snow and the highest skiable peak in the Catskills, Belleayre offers the most varied terrain for downhill skiers and snowboarders in Ulster County. It is especially popular with families. In addition, the mountain boasts the only snowcat skiing in the Catskills and grooms 9.2 kilometers of cross-country ski trails. Adult tickets cost $60 on weekends and $48 midweek, with multiday discounts. Lifts run 9am-4pm daily.

Beginners or families with young kids may prefer the considerably smaller **Sawkill Family Ski Center** (167 Hill Rd. off Sawkill and Jockey Hill Rd., Kingston, 845/336-6977, www.sawkillski.com, 10am-4pm Sat.-Sun. and holidays late June-Labor Day, adult full day $40, half day $30, one-hour tubing $15).

The **Frost Valley YMCA** (2000 Frost Valley Rd., Claryville, 845/985-2291, www.frostvalley.org) in the shadow of Slide Mountain, provides access to 35 kilometers of cross-country ski trails, including several cable bridge crossings. Strung high above a swift-flowing creek, these "bridges" are made of three single cables in an inverted triangle: one for your feet and the other two for your hands. Choose a different route if you are at all afraid of heights. Ideal for groups, Frost Valley has cabins on the premises with hot showers and flush toilets. Some are in better shape than others. Meals are included with your stay, and reservations are required.

For the most extensive network of cross-country ski trails, head to Minnewaska State Park Preserve. The Mohonk Preserve and Mohonk Mountain House also groom trails for skiers. Rent your gear on the way in at **Rock & Snow** (44 Main St., New Paltz, 845/255-1311, www.rocksnow.com, 9am-6pm Mon.-Thurs., 9am-8pm Fri., 8am-8pm Sat., 8am-7pm Sun.).

Belleayre Mountain Statistics

- Base: 2,025 feet
- Summit: 3,429 feet
- Vertical: 1,404 feet
- Trails: 38
- Lifts: 8
- Skiable acres: 171
- Snowmaking: 96 percent
- Snow report: 800/942-6904

Hiking

Hikers will find endless miles of beautiful terrain in the Shawangunks, at Minnewaska, Sam's Point, and Mohonk Preserve (65 miles of trails). Note, there is no camping in Minnewaska. And other than a hot dog stand that occasionally sets up at the top of the Minnewaska parking lot, food and water are not readily available near the trailheads. Stock up on supplies before you head into the park. At the river's edge, **Black Creek Preserve** (Winding Brook Acres Rd., off Route 9W, 7.6 miles north of the Mid-Hudson Bridge, year-round dawn-dusk) has two miles of trails on a 130-acre property managed by Scenic Hudson.

For a moderately challenging day hike near Woodstock, head to the base of Overlook Mountain, on Meads Mountain Road (www.catskillcenter.org) For a more strenuous route, head west to climb the highest peak in the range: Slide Mountain. John Burroughs called Slide a "shy mountain" because it was difficult to spot until he got very close, and even on the ascent, it was difficult to find the peak.

Cycling

New Paltz is a mecca for avid cyclists. Surrounding country roads have terrain to match all levels: flat fields, rolling hills, and steep climbs. Stop by the **Bicycle Depot** (15 Main St., New Paltz, 845/255-3859, www.bicycledepot.com, 10am-6pm Mon. and Wed.-Fri., 10am-5pm Sat.-Sun.) at the bottom of Main Street for route advice. This is also one of the only shops in the area that rents decent road bikes. The gear is in good condition and prices are reasonable.

Mountain bikers can choose between

gentle rail trails and more aggressive single track. Woodstock and New Paltz both have convenient access to trailheads. The **Wallkill Valley Rail Trail** is a favorite route for trail riding, jogging, and walking. This 12-mile trail connects the towns of New Paltz, Rosendale, and Gardiner. All trail signs have maps on the back.

Try **Overlook Mountain Bikes** (93 Tinker St., Woodstock, 845/679-2122, www.overlookmountainbikes.com, 11am-6pm Mon. and Wed.-Sat., 11am-5pm Sun.) or **Catskill Mountain Bicycle** (3 Church St., New Paltz, 845/255-3859) for maps and gear. **Favata's Table Rock Tours and Bicycles** (386 Main St., Rosendale, 845/658-7832, www.trtbicycles.com, 11am-6pm Mon. and Wed., 11am-7pm Thurs. and Fri., 11am-5pm Sat., noon-5pm Sun.) offers one- and two-day bike tours of Ulster County.

Golf

More than a dozen golf courses are scattered along the base of the Shawangunks in Ulster County. One of the prettiest, **Apple Greens Golf** (161 South St., 845/883-5500, www.applegreens.com, $34-53), is set on an apple orchard. It also offers one of the best deals in the area for 18 holes.

Swimming and Boating

Ulster County offers access to several unusual water sports: For starters, a day of drifting along the Esopus Creek is practically a mandatory activity for anyone who lives within a day's drive of Phoenicia. Time your visit on the one day a month when the water is released, and you'll be in for a real whitewater adventure. **F-S Tube and Raft Rental** (29 Main St., Phoenicia, 845/688-7633, www.fstuberental.com, 10am-6pm daily May-Sept., $20) offers transportation and rentals. **Town Tinker Tube Rental** (10 Bridge St., Phoenicia, 845/688-5553, www.towntinker.com, 9am-6pm daily, $35/day full gear rental) offers tubing courses for beginners and experts. It takes about two hours to travel 2.5 miles along the river.

Planning a trip to the Caribbean and need to get certified to dive? Spend two weekends with **Deep-Six Underwater Systems** (14 Deerpath Dr., New Paltz, 845/255-7446 or 888/901-5780, www.deep-six.com, 9am-5pm Mon.-Sat.) and you'll be good to go. Training dives take place at Diver's Cove in Lake Minnewaska, where the Mid-Hudson Diving Association has set up a bench and drying racks for fellow divers.

Lake Minnewaska is hands-down the most beautiful place to swim in Ulster County. In summer, the surface temperature climbs to a refreshing 75°F. Visibility is not as good as it once was (10-12 feet on average), but underwater cliffs and a maximum depth of 72 feet make for an interesting dive in a safe environment. Expect a thermocline at about 30 feet. In summer 2014, the lake was closed for several weeks due to a problem with leeches.

Hudson River Cruises (Rondout Landing, Kingston, 845/340-4700, www.hudsonrivercruises.com, adults $21, seniors $19, children 4-11 $13) offers tours aboard the *Rip Van Winkle* from Rondout Landing. Passengers are able to see the historic Rondout and Esopus lighthouses and the Vanderbilt, Staatsburg, and Wilderstein estates from the shaded deck in spring, summer, and fall. This is a unique way to experience the fall colors. Inquire about dinner and brunch cruises.

Fishing and Hunting

Anglers primarily use nymphs and streamers to fish the lower Esopus Creek, since it gets less water pressure than the Delaware, Willowemoc, and Beaver Kill. As a tailwater, the Esopus offers the best conditions late in the season. Access the stream near Boiceville.

Fly-fishing with Bert (P.O. Box 153, Tillson, 845/658-9784, www.flyfishwithbert.com) offers fly-fishing instruction and guide services on the Catskills' trout streams in May, June, and September.

Aviation

Learn to glide at the **Mountain Wings Hang Gliding Center** (77 Hang Glider Rd.,

Ellenville, 845/647-3377, www.mtnwings.com), where an introductory program costs $220. The course is certified by USHGA (United States Hang Gliding Association) and includes one day of training with videos and a simulator, followed by supervised flights.

You can jump from 13,500 feet and free-fall to 6,000 with **Skydive the Ranch** (55 Sandhill Rd., Gardiner, 845/255-4033, www.skydivetheranch.com, $219 per jump including gear, $119 additional for a video of the skydive). Repeat visitors can complete all 13 levels of the Instructor-Assisted Freefall (IAF) skydiver training program. Group rates are also available.

Rock Climbing

When the weather cooperates, climbers descend on the **Mohonk Preserve** (West Trapps trailhead, admission $10) to scale several of the 1,000 world-class pitches in the preserve. A good alternative to climbing in the Mohonk Preserve is the **Peter's Kill Area** (Rte. 44/55, New Paltz, 845/255-0752, www.nysparks.com, open at 9am daily, $8/day) in Minnewaska State Park Preserve. Located five miles west of the junction of Routes 299 and 44/55, and one mile east of the main park entrance, Peter's Kill boasts some of the best bouldering anywhere in the northeast. You'll climb on quartz conglomerate cliffs found a half-mile walk from the parking lot. A range of single-pitch climbs will suit various levels. The area has a daily limit of 70 climbers.

Before you go, pick up a helmet, shoes, chalk, and a climbing harness at **Rock & Snow** (44 Main St., New Paltz, 845/255-1311, www.rocksnow.com, 9am-6pm Mon.-Thurs., 9am-8pm Fri., 8am-8pm Sat., 8am-7pm Sun.). Brush up on your skills at **The Inner Wall** (234 Main St., New Paltz, 845/255-7625, www.theinnerwall.com, noon-9pm Tues.-Sat., noon-6pm Sun., $6-15), an indoor climbing gym.

High Angle Adventures (178 Hardenburgh Rd., Ulster Park, 800/777-2546, www.highangle.com) offers a range of classes, including classes for women, lead training, and transition courses from indoor to outdoor environments. Locals also recommend **Mountain Skills** (Stone Ridge, 845/853-5450, www.mountainskills.biz, single climber $275, two climbers $195 each, three climbers $165 each, four climbers $140 each) for climbing instruction.

You can also rent climbing shoes and camping equipment at the **Eastern Mountain Sports** (EMS) store (3124 Rte. 44/55, Gardiner, 845/255-3280 or 800/310-4504, www.emsclimb.com, 8:30am-5pm daily) at the intersection of Routes 299 and 44/55. Unlike other EMS locations, this one is a designated Climbing Specialty Store that offers classes, rental gear, and repair services. Note that the center does not rent harnesses, helmets, ropes, or protective gear.

Spa Treatments

Buttermilk Falls Inn and Spa (220 North Rd., Milton, 845/795-1310, www.buttermilkfallsinn.com) offers a full menu of spa treatments, including aromatherapy massage, hot stone massage, reflexology, and a variety of facials. A one-hour massage costs $110-135.

A 30,000-square-foot spa at the **Mohonk Mountain House** (877/877-2664, www.mohonk.com) has 200 windows overlooking Lake Mohonk and the hotel's 2,200-acre mountaintop estate. The spa was built with environmental conservation in mind: Excavated stone was recycled into walls and fireplaces, a geothermal system regulates temperature inside, and a 2,000-square-foot garden terrace functions as a green roof. Choose from a menu of 50 treatments, including the signature Mohonk Red massage, which incorporates indigenous Mohonk Red witch hazel into the treatment, or the Shawangunk Grit exfoliation, which involves fine quartz grains from the surrounding cliffs. A private couples treatment room has a fireplace. The spa is open year-round, and in 2013, Condé Nast named it the #1 resort spa in the United States.

Another place to indulge in a luxurious spa treatment is the **Emerson Resort and Spa** (5340 Rte. 28, Mt. Tremper, 877/688-2828 or

845/688-2828, www.emersonresort.com, 9am-5pm Sun.-Mon., 10am-5pm Tues.-Thurs., 9am-6pm Fri., 9am-7pm Sat.) near Woodstock. Fifty-minute treatments range $95-110. The Emerson Signature Massage involves warm ginseng-infused oil and two therapists.

ACCOMMODATIONS

Ulster accommodations conjure images of historical mountain houses, rustic country inns, and wooded campgrounds. There are surprisingly few places to stay in downtown New Paltz, but many bed-and-breakfast inns dot the surrounding countryside.

Under $100

True to its reputation as a university town, New Paltz has one of the few hostel accommodations in the Hudson River Valley. Stay from one night to two weeks at the **New Paltz Hostel** (145 Main St., New Paltz, 845/255-6676, www.newpaltzhostel.com, $30-90), within walking distance to public transportation, university buildings, and stores and restaurants of downtown New Paltz. The hostel closes during the day between 10am and 4pm.

$100-150

Private porches and a central location are defining features of **The Inn at Orchard Heights** (20 Church St., New Paltz, 845/255-6792, www.innatorchardheights.com, $135-200). Owners Janet and Darryl Greene offer five rooms in their 1888 Queen Anne Victorian. Some are on the small side and not all have private baths, but you can't beat the convenient location.

Wood paneling and stone fireplaces lend a rustic feel to rooms and cabins at the **Woodstock Lodge** (20 Country Club Ln., Woodstock, 845/679-2814, www.woodstock-lodge.com, $100-130). Enjoy the outdoor pool in summer, and warm your toes by the tavern fireplace in winter.

Closer yet to the action are nine basic but affordable rooms at **Twin Gables** (73 Tinker St., Woodstock, 845/679-9479, www.twingableswoodstockny.com, $90-184), which has been open more than 50 years. Some rooms have private baths, while others share.

★ **The Woodstock Inn on the Millstream** (48 Tannery Brook Rd., Woodstock, 800/420-4707, www.woodstock-inn-ny.com, $129-249) has 18 well-appointed rooms and studios in three creekside buildings that are walking distance from town, yet comfortably removed from the daily bustle. Amenities include private baths, exterior entrances, cable television, air-conditioning, and Wi-Fi. Guests can relax in hammocks or deck chairs on the lawn or in the shade of the maple trees beside the water.

$150-200

A picturesque stream meanders through the property at **Captain Schoonmaker's** (913 Rte. 213, High Falls, 945/687-7946, www.captainschoonmakers.com, $140-195). The inn is a 1760 stone house; rooms are located in the carriage house with private balconies and air-conditioning. The owners are animal lovers; a posse of cats and dogs roam the grounds at all times.

The **ElmRock Inn** (4496 Rte. 209, Stone Ridge, 845/687-4492, www.elmrockinn.com, $125-265) changed hands from the Sparrow Hawk Bed and Breakfast in 2012. Set among a stand of black locust trees just off busy Route 209, the inn is 15 minutes from downtown New Paltz. The 1770 brick Colonial was renovated during the management change. Cozy—and immaculate—guest rooms have air-conditioning and high-quality linens; a gourmet breakfast of homemade frittatas starts the day right.

In the southern Catskills, the **Enchanted Manor of Woodstock** (23 Rowe Rd., Woodstock, 845/679-9012, www.enchanted-manorinn.com, $170-250) is set on eight acres. Each of the five rooms has a private bath (one is a stand-alone cottage). Guests can swim in the saltwater pool, relax on the deck, or soak in the hot tub. One of the owners is a licensed massage therapist (treatments $95/hour), and the inn offers outdoor yoga during the summer.

For Victorian ambience in a mountain setting, reserve a room at ★ **The Wild Rose Inn** (66 Rock City Rd., Woodstock, 845/679-8783, www.thewildroseinn.com, $175-300). Its five floral-themed rooms all have private baths and have hosted the likes of Uma Thurman, Ethan Hawke, and Chevy Chase. The owners serve a gourmet continental breakfast each morning, and you can walk to shops in town.

Over $200

One of the most inviting places to stay anywhere in the Hudson River Valley sits at the edge of the Shawangunks with views of sheer cliff walls right outside the window. Built in 2001, the ★ **Minnewaska Lodge** (3116 Rte. 44/55, Gardiner, 845/255-1110, www.minnewaskalodge.com, $179-255) has 26 modern but cozy rooms with a fitness center and a spacious, ground-floor breakfast room. Trails lead right from the back porch, and the restaurants and shops of New Paltz are just six miles away.

Weekend reservations are difficult to secure at the two-room **Saugerties Lighthouse** (168 Lighthouse Dr., off Mynderse St., Saugerties, 845/247-0656, www.saugertieslighthouse.com, $225, breakfast included). Accommodations are rustic, with a shared bath and limited electricity.

The historic **Mohonk Mountain House** (1000 Mountain Rest Rd., New Paltz, 845/255-1000 or 800/772-6646, www.mohonk.com, $540-700) reportedly spent more than $30 million on a new spa and other renovations in recent years. Rates include buffet-style breakfast and lunch and a four-course dinner, as well as afternoon tea and cookies. Jackets are still required for dinner service, but once-strict alcohol policies have been relaxed. Rooms, suites, and cottages represent a variety of styles. Some create the feeling of a cozy mountain lodge, while others feature elaborate Victorian fabrics. Optional extras include balconies, fireplaces, or views. Televisions are available in some public areas.

The Inn at Stone Ridge/Hasbrouck House (3805 Main St., Stone Ridge, 845/687-0736, www.innatstoneridge.com, $195-350) has five suites in a handsome 18th-century Dutch Colonial set on 150 acres of woods and gardens between New Paltz and Kingston. Rooms are decorated in warm tones and country quilts. The Carriage House is a separate two-bedroom apartment for $395 per night.

Once a 17th-century trading post, ★ **Buttermilk Falls Inn and Spa** (220 North Rd., Milton, 845/795-1310, www.

a wedding reception at Buttermilk Falls Inn and Spa

buttermilkfallsinn.com, $250-375) now caters to a different kind of traveler: Thirteen individually decorated guest rooms in three carriage houses have fireplaces, private baths, cable TV, high-speed Internet, and air-conditioning. Most important, all have river, garden, or pond and field views. The owners maintain 70 acres of riverside trails that meander through woods, fields, and gardens. Breakfast includes such treats as freshly baked croissants, and guests may also enjoy afternoon tea service. Spa packages are available.

Soon after it opened for the first time in 2003, the **Emerson Resort and Spa** (146 Mt. Pleasant Rd., Mt. Tremper, 877/688-2828 or 845/688-2828, www.emersonresort.com, $199-439) was severely damaged by a fire and had to be rebuilt. The new resort opened in 2007 with 26 luxury guest suites that blend Silk Road decor with mountain ambience. All have soaking tubs, flat-screen TVs, in-room wine refrigerators, private decks, and fireplaces. The adjoining **Emerson Lodge** ($159-299) is geared toward families with suites of varying sizes. Also in the Mt. Tremper complex are an award-winning spa, upscale country store, and a New American-Asian fusion restaurant called Phoenix.

Campgrounds

Campers have all kinds of options in Ulster County. **Yogi Bear's Jellystone Camp-Resort** (50 Bevier Rd., Gardiner, 848/255-5193 or 800/558-2954, www.campjellystone.com, Apr. 28-early Oct.) is a large but well-run operation with two locations, Lazy River in Gardiner and Birchwood Acres in Woodridge. Amenities include canoe rentals, showers, and swimming pools.

The **Saugerties/Woodstock KOA Kampground** (882 Rte. 212, Saugerties, 845/246-4089 or 800/562-4081, www.koa.com, late March-Oct.) has 90 sites, a camp store, children's play area, dumping station, flush toilets, showers, laundry room, wireless Internet, swimming pool, and fishing. Cabins are available, and you can bring your pooch along too.

FOOD

Ulster County holds some culinary surprises, as well as a number of mainstay establishments.

Along the River: Route 9W

By many accounts, the **Raccoon Saloon** (1330 Rte. 9W, Marlborough, 845/236-7872, www.raccoonsaloonny.com, 11:30am-9:30pm Sun.-Thurs., 11:30am-11pm Fri.-Sat.) serves the best burger in the region, if not more broadly speaking. Tucked away on a hill in a suburban neighborhood, **The Would** (120 North Rd., Highland, 845/691-9883, www.thewould.com, dinner nightly, $15-35) occupies the site of a 1920s-era summer resort. Its New American menu has some surprises. Appetizers range from nachos to foie gras to the pulled pork and mac-n-cheese spring roll. Main dishes could be fennel salmon, mushroom strudel, or maple-chipotle pork tenderloin.

A CIA grad oversees the surf-and-turf menu at ★ **Ship to Shore** (15 W. Strand St., Rondout Landing, Kingston, 845/334-8887, www.shiptoshorehudsonvalley.com, lunch and dinner daily and Sunday brunch, $14-36). Enjoy live jazz on Saturday evenings. House-made lobster ravioli are actually lobster and peas in a pink tomato cream sauce all wrppaed in a wonton skin. You could also keep it simple and stick to the beer-battered fish-and-chips. In a brick building a few doors up the hill from the waterfront, **Dolce** (27 Broadway, Kingston, 845/339-0921, $8-15) serves innovative crepes (order a house combo or build your own), panini, and a dependable selection of coffee and tea to warm you on a rainy day.

In Kingston's Stockade District, pop into **Jane's Homemade Ice Cream** (307 Wall St., Kingston, 845/338-1801) for a milkshake or quick lunch. For fine dining, **Le Canard Enchaine** (276 Fair St., Kingston, 845/339-2003, www.le-canardenchaine.com, noon-9:30pm Mon.-Tues. and Thurs., noon-10:30pm Fri.-Sat., 2pm-9:30pm Sun., $18-38, prix fixe lunch $15) is an authentic French

Five Places for a Summer Picnic

- **Boscobel House and Gardens:** Picnic among the roses on the grounds of an 18th-century Federal-style mansion in the Hudson Highlands.
- **Lake Minnewaska:** Put on your hiking shoes and spread a blanket along the rocky shoreline of Lake Minnewaska. Bring your own drinking water and pack out your trash.
- **Kaaterskill Falls:** Bring a sketch pad—and your lunch—to the place that inspired Thomas Cole and the Hudson River School of painters.
- **Storm King Art Center:** What goes better together than art and food? Stroll the expansive grounds of this outdoor museum and enjoy a quiet picnic on the lawn, or order from the on-site café.
- **Saratoga Performing Arts Center:** Bring a lawn chair and settle in for a concert, ballet, or symphony performance in this outdoor amphitheater.

bistro serving classics including cassoulet and reasonably priced wines.

★ **Elephant Wine Bar** (310 Wall St., Kingston, 845/339-9310, www.elephantwinebar.com, 5pm-10pm Tues.-Sat.) is a wine and tapas bar that matches local ingredients with the food, music, and wine of northern Spain. Wines from across Spain, Italy, Argentina, and France make up the selection. Pair your glass with Marcona almonds roasted with Moorish spices, *tacos al pastor* made of Mexican-style pork belly, or local burrata and peaches. A section of the menu is dedicated to "swine of the week" such as Serrano ham and chorizo. And the dairy bar lists several unusual offerings made of raw sheep's milk and raw cows' milk.

In Saugerties, **Love Bites Cafe** (85 Partition St., Saugerties, 845/246-1795, 8:30am-4:30pm Thurs.-Tues., $5-10) serves breakfast (carrot coconut bread French toast, vegan pancakes) and creative sandwiches for lunch six days a week. **Miss Lucy's Kitchen** (90 Partition St., Saugerties, 845/246-9240, www.misslucyskitchen.com, noon-3pm Wed.-Fri., 11am-3pm Sat.-Sun., 5pm-9pm Wed.-Thurs. and Sun., until 10pm Fri.-Sat., $17-24) serves hearty American dinners, such as a country-style veal stew, made of local ingredients.

Between Saugerties and Woodstock, a colorful decor and central bar complement a menu of Cajun jerk chicken, ahi tuna, Thai mussel stew, and churrasco-style grilled meats at **New World Home Cooking** (1411 Rte. 212, Saugerties, 845/246-0900, www.ricorlando.com/nwhc, 5pm-9:30pm Mon.-Thurs., 5pm-11pm Fri., 5pm-10pm Sat., 5pm-9pm Sun., $19-30). Located in an 1830s farmhouse, **Red Onion** (1654 Rte. 212, Saugerties, 845/679-1223, www.redonionrestaurant.com, 5pm-9pm Sun.-Thurs., 5pm-10pm Fri.-Sat., $17-25) serves international fare and a Sunday brunch at half a dozen tables arranged around a cozy bar. Mussels can be prepared three ways: roasted with butter and lemon, steamed with a lime leaf and coconut milk, or steamed in white wine and herbs. Arctic char comes with leeks and shitake mushrooms; spicy yellow Thai curry is served with basmati rice.

New Paltz and Surroundings

New Paltz just about has it all when it comes to food: sushi, Mediterranean, haute cuisine, frozen yogurt, and cheese. For breakfast or a quick bite to eat at lunchtime, head to **The Bakery** (13A N. Front St., New Paltz, 845/255-8840, www.ilovethebakery.com, 7am-7pm daily, $4-8). Soups and sandwiches change daily, and there are a handful of tables in a courtyard outside. Service is slow, but the baked goods are worth the wait.

At the end of Main Street in New Paltz is

the **Gilded Otter Brewing Company** (3 Main St., Rte. 299, New Paltz, 845/256-1700, www.gildedotter.com, 11:30am-10pm Mon.-Thurs., 11:30am-10:30pm Fri.-Sat., noon-9pm Sun., $9-18), with a good selection of wursts and schnitzels and freshly brewed beers to wash them down. The bar stays open until 2am.

Gadaleto's Seafood (246 Main St., Cherry Hill Shopping Center, New Paltz, 845/255-1717, www.gadaletos.com, 11am-9pm Wed.-Sun., $15-25) is a local institution that supplies many area restaurants with their fresh catch. Sample the shellfish at the raw bar or place an order for fish-and-chips or crab cakes. Be prepared to wait; the casual restaurant can get crowded, and service tends to be slow.

Located just steps away from the Wallkill Valley Rail Trail, the **Cheese Plate** (10 Main St., Ste. 302, New Paltz, 845/255-2444, www.cheeseplatenewpaltz.com) is the perfect place to stop for picnic supplies. It carries an outstanding selection of local and imported cheeses, from Sprout Creek Farm across the river to the Pyrenees of Spain and France. Next door, the **Mudd Puddle Café** (10 Main St., Ste. 312, New Paltz, 845/255-3436, www.muddpuddlecoffee.com, call ahead as hours vary) roasts its own coffee and serves homemade soups and sandwiches. The $5.45 "best deal" includes a cup of soup and half-panini. Also near the trail, **La Stazione** (5 Main St., New Paltz, 845/256-9447, www.lastazioneny.com, 11:30am-10:30pm Tues.-Thurs., 11:30am-11pm Fri.-Sat., 1pm-10pm Sun.) takes its name from the train station it converted into an eatery. Student servers staff the dining room, and the menu consists of reasonably priced Italian dishes.

A landlocked location is no obstacle to culinary creativity at **Neko Sushi** (49 Main St., New Paltz, 845/255-0162, www.thenekosushi.com), where the chef presents an artistic variety of raw fish and maki rolls each evening. Two doors up, **Yanni Restaurant & Café** (51 Main St., New Paltz, 845/256-0988, 11:30am-11pm daily, $6-14) offers a late-night menu of gyros, Greek salad, spanakopita, and other specialties to a clientele of students and weekend tourists. Greek TV is an added highlight.

Yum Yogurt (215 Main St., New Paltz, no tel., noon-10pm daily) is a self-serve frozen yogurt shop with all the requisite toppings to pile on top—even seasonal ones like pomegranate seeds. Flavors rotate seasonally from strawberry to pumpkin to espresso, but sea salt caramel is a permanent fixture on the menu.

High Falls claims one of the region's most exclusive fine-dining establishments in the **DePuy Canal House** (103 Main St., High Falls, 845/687-7700, www.depuycanalhouse.com, brunch 10am-3pm Sat.-Sun., lunch and dinner 11am-10pm Fri.-Sat., $18-34). Guests can choose from the "little plates" menu or full entrées such as trout and fennel puree on spinach or duck breast medallion and foie gras sauté.

If the southwestern food at **The Egg's Nest** (Rte. 213, High Falls, 845/687-7255, www.theeggsnest.com, 11:30am-11pm daily, $6-12) doesn't leave an impression, the funky decor certainly will. Toasters hang from the ceiling, and tinfoil is stuck on the walls. Everything about the place is intentionally mismatched. Enjoy the huge portions, and save room for dessert.

★ **Mountain Brauhaus** (Rtes. 44/55 and 299, Gardiner, 845/255-9766, www.mountainbrauhaus.com, 11:30am-9pm Wed.-Sat., 11:30am-8:30pm Sun., $16-25) is an informal restaurant that welcomes hikers from The Gunks. Sauerbraten, schnitzels, and Swabian rostbraten are all prepared in traditional German fashion. The difference is the produce is mostly organic, eggs come from nearby Feather Farm, and deep-frying is done with oil free of trans fats. Don't forget to order the spaetzle on the side.

Southern Catskill Mountains: Route 28

For a casual meal and a memorable experience, try a homemade muffin at **Bread Alone** (22 Mill Hill Rd., Woodstock, 845/679-2108, www.breadalone.com, 7am-5pm daily), a European-style organic bakery and café with additional locations in Kingston, Rhinebeck, and Boiceville. The owner, Daniel Leader, is a CIA graduate who traveled from Paris to the Pyrenees to learn what gives European breads their hearty flavor. He now produces 15 tons of fresh bread per week from twin ovens that were custom-built by a Parisian oven mason. At headquarters in Boiceville, you can take an impromptu tour of the bakery while you sip a frothy cappuccino.

★ **Oriole 9** (17 Tinker St., Woodstock, 845/679-5763, www.oriole9.com, 8:30am-4:30pm daily, $7-17) is a slow food kind of place where you can order Feather Ridge eggs, tofu hash, a prosciutto and brie press, or falafel. The owners have partnered with a local school to start an organic garden and teach children about healthy food.

For dinner in Woodstock, try **Joshua's Café** (51 Tinker St., Woodstock, 845/679-5533, www.joshuascafe.com, 11am-10pm Sun.-Tues. and Thurs.-Fri., 10am-11pm Sat., $21-28), a local institution for more than four decades. Dishes from the Middle East are the theme, with accents from around the world.

Another breakfast mainstay, famous for its variety of supersized pancakes and equally tasty French toast, lies farther west in Phoenicia. **Sweet Sue's** (49 Main St., Phoenicia, 845/688-7852, 7am-3pm Thurs.-Mon., $5-15) is the perfect place to start or end a day of tubing on the Esopus Creek. Be prepared to wait it out for a table.

Celebrity sightings are common among the trendsetters who dine creekside at **The Bear** (295 Tinker St./Rte. 212, Bearsville, 845/679-5555, www.bearcafe.com, 11am-2:30pm Sun., 5pm-9pm Sun. and Wed.-Thurs, 5pm-10pm Fri.-Sat., $18-34). Entrées range from grilled tofu to filet mignon and from Caesar salad to a half-pound hamburger.

Locals drive from near and far to dine at **Peekamoose Restaurant & Tap Room** (8373 State Rte. 28, Big Indian, 845/254-6500, www.peekamooserestaurant.com, 4pm-10pm Thurs.-Mon.). Choose the fisherman stew or house-made local charcuterie to start. Then move on to the pan-seared Beaverkill Hatchery rainbow trout or slow-braised short ribs with roasted parsnips. The Tap Room and lounge are open until midnight on Friday and Saturday nights.

Try the crispy squid appetizer and grilled lamb chops in a farmhouse setting at **Cucina** (109 Mill Hill Rd., Woodstock, 845/679-9800, www.cucinawoodstock.com, $14-33).

ENTERTAINMENT AND EVENTS

Performing Arts

In Woodstock, the **Colony Café** (22 Rock City Rd., Woodstock, 845/679-8639, www.colonycafewoodstock.com, from 7pm Thurs.-Tues.) stages music concerts and poetry readings inside a historic dinner theater. The **Ulster Performing Arts Center** (601 Broadway, Kingston, 845/339-6088, www.bardavon.org) is managed by the Bardavon theater in Poughkeepsie across the river. It is the home of the Hudson Valley Philharmonic, as well as the Ulster Ballet Company and the Catskill Ballet.

Bars and Nightlife

New Paltz and Kingston's Rondout Landing have the most variety for nightlife. About a dozen bars line a short stretch of Main Street in New Paltz, a town that allows its watering holes to stay open until 4am. Many, though by no means all, of them are student hangouts. Open-mic Wednesdays are a popular feature at **Oasis** (58 Main St., New Paltz, 845/255-3400, www.cabaloosa.com). **Bacchus** (4 S. Chestnut St., New Paltz, 845/255-8636, www.bacchusnewpaltz.com), near the corner of Main and Chestnut, keeps 300 beers on hand to accompany a menu of Southwestern fare. Students and local residents alike enjoy the late-night appetizer menu until 11pm Sunday-Wednesday and until 1am Thursday-Saturday.

Buffalo wings and a dozen TVs are a hit at **McGillicuddy's Restaurant & Tap House** (84 Main St., New Paltz, 845/256-9289, www.cuddysny.com, 11am-4am daily, Fri.-Sat.

A Wave of Farm Distilleries

In 2008, New York State passed the Farm Distillery Bill allowing the sale of distilled products on-site for the first time since Prohibition, provided the makers source 70 percent of their materials from the state's agricultural market. The Hudson River Valley was a major grower of barley and rye in the 19th century, and more than 1,000 farms produced regional whiskey and gin. After a long dry spell, a wave of new microdistilleries has caught the attention of farmers, restaurants, travelers, and aficionados. With copper stills and on-site malt houses, at least six distilleries are open for business today.

Tuthilltown Spirits (14 Grist Mill Ln., Gardiner, 845/255-1527, www.tuthilltown.com, 11am-6pm Mon.-Sat., noon-6pm Sun.) is the first of its kind in the New York State. Tours are offered on the weekend noon-5pm on the hour. Besides the signature Hudson Single Malt Whiskey, Hudson Manhattan Rye, and Hudson Baby Bourbon Whiskey, the company makes a cassis liqueur, aged rum, and its own bitters.

Hillrock Estate Distillery (408 Pooles Hill Rd., Ancram, 518/329-1023, www.hillrockdistillery.com) is the creation of the former head distiller of Maker's Mark, who is experimenting with the Solera system of aging whiskey to get the complex flavors that connoisseurs desire. The spirit is then finished in 20-year-old oloroso sherry casks to add the final touch. Barley for the bourbon is grown on the farm, and the entire production process takes place here as well.

The **Catskill Distilling Company** (2037 Rte. 17B, Bethel, 845/583-8569, www.catskilldistillingcompany.com, 2pm-6pm Tues.-Sun. Memorial Day-Labor Day, off-season 2pm-6pm Fri.-Sun., or call for an appointment) blends Catskill Mountain water and locally grown grains, fruit, and botanicals in a creative mix of craft spirits, including bourbon, vodka, and gin.

Albany Distilling Company (78 Montgomery St., Albany, 518/621-7191, www.albanydistilling.com, tours and tastings 4pm-8pm Tues. and noon-8pm Sat.) is a small operation in downtown Albany, producing one batch of spirits at a time. Products include the Ironweed whiskey and Quackenbush Still House rum labels. It is the first licensed distillery in Albany since Prohibition.

Although some local malting facilities have opened recently, the founders of **Coppersea Distilling** (1592 Broadway, Rte. 9W, West Park, 845/444-1044, www.coppersea.com) prefers to malt its own grain seeds.

The **Warwick Valley Winery & Distillery** (114 Little York Rd., Warwick, 845/258-4858, www.wvwinery.com, 11am-6pm daily) makes a rustic gin, as well as apple and pear brandies.

night cover $3-5), which also has a pool table and dance floor.

P&G Restaurant (91 Main St., New Paltz, 845/255-6161, www.pandgs.com, 9am-4am Mon.-Sat., noon-4am Sun.), affectionately known as "Pigs," is a New Paltz institution among students and alumni. Nightly specials include $2 pitchers of Newcastle beer and a menu of casual pub fare.

At the legendary **Country Inn** (1380 County Road 2, Krumville, 845/657-8956, www.krumville.com), in a southern Catskill hamlet, choose from hundreds of beers among a crowd of locals and travelers.

Tuthilltown Spirits (14 Grist Mill Ln., Gardiner, 845/255-1527, www.tuthilltown.com, 11am-6pm Mon.-Sat., noon-6pm Sun.) is the first of its kind in New York State—a farm distillery making spirits from local grains and fruits. Tours are offered on the weekend noon-5pm on the hour. Besides the signature Hudson Single Malt Whiskey, Hudson Manhattan Rye, and Hudson Baby Bourbon Whiskey, the company makes a cassis liqueur, aged rum, and its own bitters.

Festivals

The **Belleayre Music Festival** (800/942-6904, ext. 1344, or 845/254-5600, ext. 1344, www.belleayremusic.org) draws a large crowd of music lovers to the Catskills each summer. Popular with kids in October is the **Headless Horseman Hayrides & Haunted Houses** (778 Broadway, Ulster Park, 845/339-2666, www.headlesshorseman.com) on Route 9W between Highland and Kingston. The attraction is open during the last two weekends in September and every weekend in October. Reservations are required.

The 100-year-old **Ulster County Fair** (249 Libertyville Rd., 845/255-1380, www.ulstercountyfair.com, $15 admission) takes place in August each year, with music, amusement rides, and fireworks. The fairgrounds are located two miles outside of New Paltz.

The **Woodstock Film Festival** (845/810-0131, www.woodstockfilmfestival.com) is gaining on its sixtieth anniversary. The September festival draws a number of leading filmmakers and critics to watch a selection of the industry's newest and boldest independent films.

Hardneck garlic is indigenous to the Saugerties area; July is the harvest season. Some say it's more bitter than what you buy at the grocery store; others disagree. See for yourself during the last weekend in September, when Saugerties hosts the annual **Hudson Valley Garlic Festival** (Pavilion St., Saugerties, 845/246-3090, www.hvgf.org, $10 per person per day, under 12 free). Local musicians, guest chefs, and a long list of food vendors all participate.

SHOPPING

Clothing

The **Groovy Blueberry** (1 Water St. and 57 Main St., New Paltz, 845/256-0873, www.groovyblueberry.com) is a one-of-a-kind shop for locally made tie-dye T-shirts and hoodies.

Farm Stands

Davenport Farms (3411 Rte. 209, Stone Ridge, 845/687-0051, www.davenportfarms.com, 6am-7pm daily) operates a popular farmers market, greenhouse, and pick-your-own field on Route 209 in Stone Ridge. To pick your own strawberries, head to **Kelder's Farm** (5755 Rte. 209, Kerhonkson, 845/626-7137, www.kelderfarm.com, 10am-8pm daily, winter hours 10am-4pm Mon., Wed., Fri., and Sat.) in early June.

shops in the Water Street Market of New Paltz

Meadow View Farm (105 Phillies Bridge Rd., New Paltz, www.meadowviewfarmstand.com) farms without pesticides, herbicides, fertilizers, or GMOs. You can buy its produce as well as grass-fed beef, farm eggs, and fresh goat cheese.

With three locations in Kingston (300 Kings Mall Ct.), Saugerties (249 Main St.), and Poughkeepsie (1955 South Rd.), **Mother Earth's Storehouse** (www.motherearthstorehouse.com) organic grocer is a sight for sore eyes after a long search for healthy food. The deli counter packs a crowd at lunchtime, and the staff really knows their stuff. Inexpensive it is not.

Not really a farm, but locally made just the same, **Fruition Chocolate** (3091 Rte. 28, Shokan, 845/657-6717, www.tastefruition.com, 11am-5pm Fri.-Sun.) makes small batches of specialty bars that wow even the most seasoned tasters. Chocolatier Bryan Graham is a former sous chef of the Apple Pie Bakery Café at the CIA in Hyde Park. The beans come from Peru and everything else happens in the workshop in Shokan.

Antiques and Galleries

There are dozens of antiques shops and art galleries across Ulster County, many of them clustered around Saugerties and Rosendale. The **Woodstock School of Art** (2470 Rte. 212, Woodstock, 845/679-2388, www.woodstockschoolofart.org) holds auctions and exhibitions during summer months. The **Center for Photography at Woodstock** (59 Tinker St., Woodstock, 845/679-9957, www.cpw.org, noon-5pm Wed.-Sun.) shows contemporary works in a small gallery. It also runs workshops, auctions, and lectures.

A number of home furnishing stores have opened in High Falls and Stone Ridge, selling both new and old pieces. **Lounge Furniture** (8 2nd St., High Falls, 845/336-4324, www.loungefurniture.com) has couches, area rugs, lighting, and other accents.

Most of the 30 antiques shops in Saugerties are located within the eight-block commercial area on Main, Market, and Partition Streets. At **Saugerties Antiques Gallery** (104 Partition St., Saugerties, 845/246-2323, 9am-5pm Mon.-Sat.), owner Pat Guariglia caters to other dealers with a two-floor showroom of European and American antiques.

Outdated: An Antique Café (314 Wall St., Kingston, 845/331-0030, 8am-5pm Mon. and Wed.-Sat., 9am-3pm Sun.) brings shopping together with food in a funky café atmosphere. You might find a vintage puzzle, or set of rubber indoor horseshoes. Find the store on Etsy or Facebook.

Bookstores

Anyone with more than a passing interest in New York State history should plan a visit to Saugerties to browse the extensive collection of titles at the **Hope Farm Press and Bookshop** (15 Jane St., Saugerties, 845/246-3522, www.hopefarmbooks.com, noon-6pm Mon.-Sat.). Owner Richard Frisbie houses two sister bookshops in one location—the larger sign over the door says Booktrader, which is a general-interest bookstore, and a smaller sign in the window reads Hope Farm Press & Bookshop.

Across from the Bread Alone Bakery, **Mirabai Books** (23 Mill Hill Rd., Woodstock, 845/679-2100, www.mirabai.com, 11am-7pm daily) stocks a unique collection of metaphysical books, music, and jewelry, all related to inspiring, transforming, and healing. The owners have added a two-room apartment above the shop, so you can absorb the good vibes all night long.

The **Emerson Country Store** (5340 Rte. 28 at Mt. Pleasant Rd., Mt. Tremper, 845/688-5800, www.emersonresort.com, 10am-5pm Thurs.-Mon.), at the Emerson Resort and Spa, sells jewelry, home accents, and gourmet foods. The adjoining Emerson Coffee Bar is open daily 9am-5pm.

Wineries

Like Dutchess County, Ulster has a handful of small wineries producing white and red bottles. You can hit each of them by driving a 30-mile loop called the **Shawangunk Wine Trail** (845/256-8456, www.shawangunkwinetrail.com). Better yet, ride a bike. Try the black currant blend at Adair Vineyards in New Paltz (www.adairwine.com) or the cabernet franc at Benmarl Winery (Marlboro). This group of nine family-owned wineries is scattered along the back roads connecting the New York State Thruway, I-84, and Highway 17 between New Paltz and Warwick in Orange County. A trail map is available online and at any of the member wineries.

INFORMATION AND SERVICES

The **Kingston Heritage Area Visitor Centers,** located at 20 Broadway and 308 Clinton Avenue (845/331-7517 or 800/331-1518, www.ci.kingston.ny.us, 8:30am-4:30pm Mon.-Fri., also 11am-5pm weekends May-Oct.) can provide information about Kingston's past and present. This is the place to pick up brochures, maps, and schedules of events.

Alternatively, look for the **Kingston**

Tourism Caboose in the traffic circle off I-87 Exit 19 (800/331-1518). In Saugerties, stop by the McDonald's on Route 212, I-87 Exit 20 (845/246-5816). A tourist information center at **Belleayre Mountain** also has a wealth of information for travelers (845/254-5600 or 800/942-6904, www.belleayre.com).

GETTING THERE AND AROUND

Bus

Ulster County Area Transit (845/340-3333) serves major towns and rural areas across the county. Routes and schedules are available online at www.co.ulster.ny.us. In addition, **Adirondack Trailways** (800/858-8555, www.trailwaysny.com) runs connector services to and from other destinations in the region.

Kingston has its own reliable public transportation system called **CiTiBus** (845/331-3725, www.ci.kingston.ny.us, $1.25), with three city routes. The closest train station is at Rhinecliff (Hutton and Charles Streets) directly across the Hudson River.

Car

Car rentals can be found at the Stewart and Albany airports. **Blue Mountain Limousine** is another way to get to and from the airport (845/389-4404). Taxis are also available at the airports, bus terminals, and at the Rhinecliff train station. Kingston gets congested by Ulster County standards, and the narrow streets downtown can be disorienting. But with a little patience, it's easy enough to find your way around.

Western Catskills to the Delaware River

Look for ★ to find recommended sights, activities, dining, and lodging.

Highlights

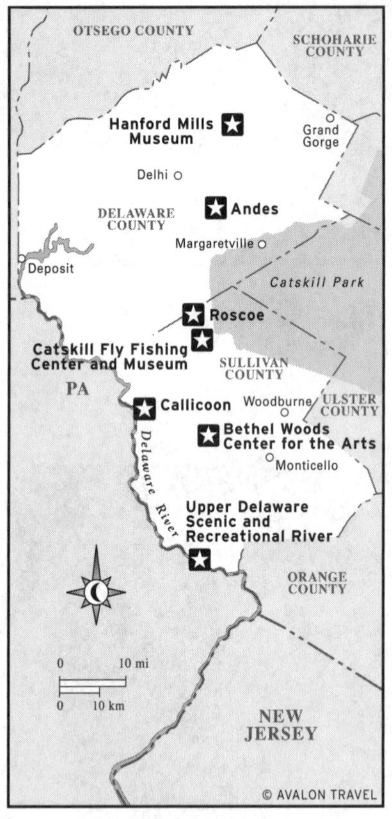

★ **Bethel Woods Center for the Arts:** Relive Woodstock and the 1960s at this museum and performing arts center on the site of the original Woodstock Music Festival (page 161).

★ **Catskill Fly Fishing Center and Museum:** Located in the heart of some of the country's best fly-fishing, the museum celebrates the art and sport of the catch (page 163).

★ **Roscoe:** They call it Trout Town USA for a good reason. A haven for anglers and outdoor enthusiasts of all kinds, Roscoe lies at the junction of the Beaver Kill river and Willowemoc Creek, on land that provoked many a battle between the Iroquois and Algonquin nations (page 164).

★ **Upper Delaware Scenic and Recreational River:** This winding stretch of Route 97 begins near the Orange/Sullivan county line and leads to breathtaking views of New York, Pennsylvania, and the Delaware River (page 164).

★ **Callicoon:** Anglers and leaf peepers congregate in Callicoon along the Delaware River, a stone's throw from Pennsylvania and the Delaware County line (page 166).

★ **Andes:** The best stopover for a bite to eat and plenty of antiques shopping in Delaware County (page 176).

★ **Hanford Mills Museum:** Watch a historic sawmill turn logs into lumber and see how a 19th-century water turbine generates power (page 178).

In the days before air-conditioning, the promise of lively entertainment, kosher food, and a cool mountain breeze lured hundreds of thousands of families out of the sweltering New York City heat and into the perennial weekend traffic jam on slow and winding Route 17. Their destination was the western Catskills, where a handful of grand resorts delivered wholesome family fun.

During the 1950s and '60s, dozens of stand-up comedians launched their careers in this land of bungalows and boarding houses. George Burns, Rodney Dangerfield, and Don Rickles all performed in the Borscht Belt—at places like Grossinger's, the Concord, the Nevele, and Kutsher's. But just as these resorts had reached their prime, affordable jet travel intervened, and travelers began to skip the Catskills in favor of more exotic destinations.

It's been a few decades since Grossinger's resort closed its doors. At its peak, the 1,200-acre resort served 150,000 guests a year. All that remains of the original property today is a golf course. Meanwhile, the last of the family-owned resorts, Kutsher's, was leveled in 2014 to make way for a new wellness resort.

And yet, even as the old guard fades quietly into history, a new wave of visitors has arrived to take its place. After several decades of neglect and decline, the Catskills are once again in vogue. The market for second homes is booming, and once-forgotten towns like Andes and Livingston Manor are getting makeovers seemingly overnight as artists, chefs, and other creative types make their way north to enjoy a simpler, more sustainable way of life. They come for the hiking and the fly-fishing, real food and yoga retreats. The heady days of the Borscht Belt may never happen again, but a new era of food-inspired travel is taking shape. Farmers are opening one-of-a-kind eateries and tiny inns, to help people get connected to the source of their food.

PLANNING YOUR TIME

Although sleepy Sullivan and Delaware Counties do not directly border the Hudson River, they make a natural extension to many Hudson River Valley itineraries. The busiest

Previous: site of the 1969 Woodstock music festival in Bethel, New York; Delaware & Ulster Railroad depot in Arkville, New York. **Above:** a maple sugar house in the off season.

Western Catskills to the Delaware River

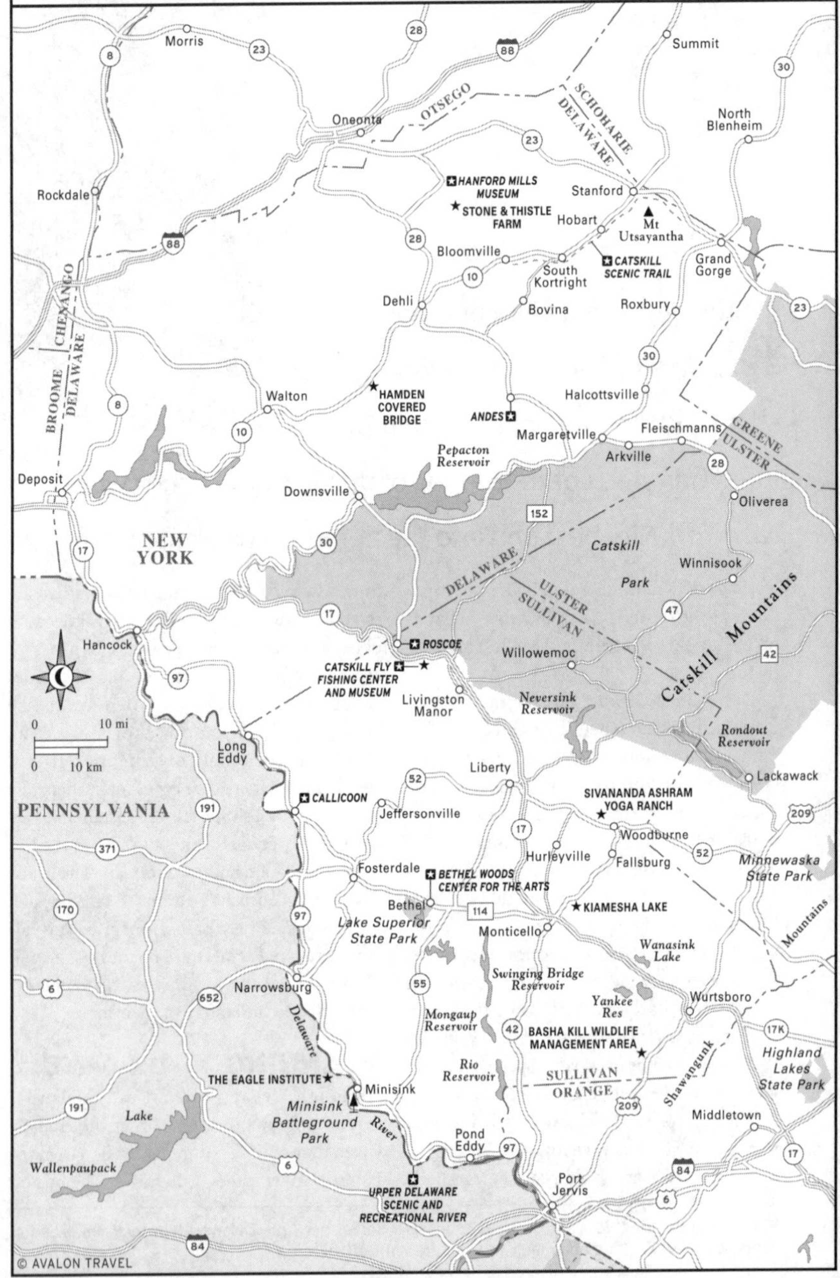

WESTERN CATSKILLS

seasons in the western Catskills correspond to peak fishing conditions: April-June and September-October. In July and August, many inns fill with parents visiting their children at local summer camps. Hunters arrive in November, and most towns are quiet January-March.

It takes less than an hour to drive the length of the Quickway (Route 17) from Wurtsboro to Rockland, but there are many back roads to explore along the way. A weekend stay allows time for both sightseeing and recreation. Most Sullivan County itineraries center on a specific activity, such as fishing, yoga, or antiques shopping. Head here to enjoy the serenity of a quiet morning on the Beaver Kill or to visit a selection of the three dozen shops along the Sullivan County Antiques Trail.

Popular itineraries in Delaware County include self-guided barn and farm stand tours, daylong bike rides, and multiday hikes and canoe trips. No major highways cross the county, and it takes about three hours to drive the perimeter. Add a half-day stop to pick your own fresh berries or bid on rare antiques in a country auction.

Sullivan County

Home to many of the family resorts that made the Catskills famous during the early to mid-20th century, Sullivan County stretches from the Orange and Ulster county lines in the east to the Delaware River and state of Pennsylvania to the west, covering a total area of about 1,000 square miles. The northern part of Sullivan County lies within the Catskill Preserve, but the terrain is more hilly than mountainous, with many of the same exposed rock ledges that characterize other parts of the Catskill region.

With a low population density (though not as low as Delaware County), Sullivan County supports a diverse ecosystem, including a growing number of bald eagles that make an annual winter appearance. Abundant trout in two famous rivers, the Willowemoc and Beaver Kill, attract diehard fly-fishers, while two large reservoirs at Neversink and Rondout send freshwater to New York City, 90 miles to the southeast. Despite its outdoor treasures, Sullivan County is best known as the site of the original 1969 Woodstock Music Festival, a three-day extravaganza that took place in the town of Bethel.

Sullivan County separated from Ulster County in 1809, borrowing its name from the controversial Revolutionary War General John Sullivan. In 1779, Sullivan led a devastating attack against the remaining Native American settlements in New York and Pennsylvania. He later became the first governor of New Hampshire.

Early Dutch settlers in Sullivan County built tanneries, bluestone quarries, sawmills, and gristmills to compensate for the lack of arable land. Irish and German immigrants later arrived to build a canal and two railroads connecting Pennsylvania and its stores of natural resources to New York City. Novelist and local resident Stephen Crane popularized Sullivan County in the 1890s with a series of *Sullivan County Sketches*. Around 1900, the Jewish Agricultural Society began to encourage Jewish farmers to move to Sullivan County from New York City. But when the new residents found the land difficult to farm, they supplemented their income by turning their farmhouses into boarding houses. Thus began the Borsch Belt and its history of famous resort hotels, most of which are lost to history.

Today, Sullivan County consists of 15 townships and no large cities. Monticello is the county seat.

ALONG THE QUICKWAY

Wurtsboro

Wurtsboro moves at the comfortably slow pace of a rural community. A string of inviting shops and cafés lines a two-block stretch of Sullivan Street, off Route 209.

Aviation enthusiasts will want to meet the pilots at the family-run **Wurtsboro Airport** (Rte. 209, 845/888-2791, www.wurtsboroairport.net, 9am-5pm Thurs.-Mon.), one of the oldest soaring sites in the country. A low ridge of the Catskills passes through the town, creating the ideal updraft for flying sans motor. In fact, pilots have soared as far as Georgia in one day from this tiny airstrip. A sailplane ride begins with an exhilarating tow on the runway. Most flights pass over the **Basha Kill Wildlife Management Area** (Rte. 209 South, Wurtsboro, 845/754-0743, www.thebashakill.org) outside of town, a prime location for viewing bald eagles. The airport is located on Route 209, two miles north of town. Call to schedule a tour or lesson.

Monticello

Sullivan County's largest township and government headquarters, Monticello is the next major stop on the Quickway. Many of the storefronts along Broadway are showing signs of age and neglect, but the imposing **Sullivan County Courthouse** (414 Broadway), made of sandstone in 1909, is a notable exception. Aside from a handful of food and gas options, the only attraction that calls for a longer stop is the **Monticello Casino & Raceway** (204 Rte. 17B, 845/794-4100, www.monticellocasinoandraceway.com, 10am-2am Mon.-Thurs., 10am-4am Fri.-Sun.), which opened in 2004. Its investors battled authorities for several decades to secure permission to open the casino.

For rail travelers, Monticello is located a half hour from the Middletown train station on the Port Jervis Line. Several hotels provide transportation to the racetrack. Take Exit 104 off Route 17.

Kiamesha Lake and Fallsburg

Follow Route 42 northeast out of Monticello to reach Kiamesha Lake, a popular fishing destination, where smallmouth bass, perch, and panfish are the most common catches. The lakeside **Concord Resort & Golf Club** (219 Concord Rd., Kiamesha Lake, 888/448-9686, www.concordresort.com, $35-95) once numbered among the most famous resorts in the Catskills. Long abandoned, the remains of the original hotel were torn down in 2008, and the property owners are in negotiations to build a new $600 million casino/resort.

At the **Shree Muktananda Ashram** (371 Brickman Rd., South Fallsburg, 845/434-2000, www.siddhayoga.org, opens 9am daily), in the

site of the original Woodstock Music Festival in Bethel

next town over, students of Siddha yoga congregate for a healthy dose of spiritual development and renewal. In recent decades, the center has turned three abandoned hotels into a vibrant community. Day visitors are welcome to participate in meditations, hatha yoga classes, and meals. A large temple dedicated to Bhagawan Nityananda, spiritual founder of the Siddha yoga discipline, is also open to the public. If you visit the grounds, respect the modest dress code and quiet atmosphere of the center.

Continuing along Route 42, the weathered buildings that line the streets of Fallsburg were once rows of pristine stucco hotels drawing visitors all the way from the Atlantic coast. Tough times have lingered in the area since the advent of air-conditioning and airplane travel, and the largest employers are now three county prisons in neighboring Woodbourne. That said, local residents are taking steps to revive their quiet town. Long-abandoned hotels and bungalows are disappearing from sight. And a new overlook at the Neversink River offers visitors a place to enjoy the falls that provided waterpower for the mills and tanneries that sustained the town in its earlier days.

Sivananda Ashram Yoga Ranch

Every Friday after work, a group of harried city dwellers gathers at a busy yoga center in Manhattan for a ride to a weekend escape at the **Sivananda Ashram Yoga Ranch** (500 Budd Rd., Woodbourne, 845/436-6492, www.sivananda.org) in northern Sullivan County. A getaway here promises ample time for relaxing and rejuvenating.

Located 12 miles north of Monticello in Woodbourne, the yoga center occupies 77 acres of secluded countryside. Wooded areas surround open lawns and a pond. Guests can participate in a single class, a weekend retreat, or a monthlong teacher-training program. The day begins with breathing and meditation exercises. Asana sessions take place at 8am and 4pm daily. After yoga practice, guests can walk the nature trails or enjoy the wood-fired sauna. Volunteers prepare meals from a large organic garden and greenhouse. Accommodations are shared rooms in either a turn-of-the-20th-century farmhouse or a 1920s-era hotel. Camping is also allowed. Call ahead for transportation from the bus terminal in Woodbourne. Rates are $70-130 per person per night depending on type of accommodations, and $50 for a full day of classes, $25 half day, and $12 for one class.

Hurleyville

Route 104 out of Monticello leads to Hurleyville, where you can take a walk through history at the **Sullivan County Historical Society Museum** (265 Main St., Hurleyville, 845/434-8044, www.sullivancountyhistory.org, 10am-4:30pm Tue.-Sat., 1pm-4:30pm Sun.). The building, built in 1912, housed the Hurleyville Schoolhouse until 1945. Exhibits include a vintage general store and post office, as well as a collection of textiles from the turn of the 20th century.

★ Bethel Woods Center for the Arts

Dairy farmer Max Yasgur put the unassuming town of Bethel in the global spotlight when he agreed to host the 1969 Woodstock Music Festival—a soggy, three-day extravaganza that turned green pastures to slop, private homes into soup kitchens, and schools into makeshift hospitals.

The idea for a rock concert near Bob Dylan's home in Woodstock began as a late-night conversation in a Manhattan apartment and became within a few short months the most notable music event in history. Hundreds of thousands attended, among them Ken Kesey and the Merry Pranksters. They grooved to the hottest sounds of the day, including Jefferson Airplane, Creedence Clearwater Revival, The Who, The Grateful Dead, and the closing act, Jimi Hendrix. Cars en route to Bethel jammed the New York State Thruway and created a 10-mile backup a full day before the event began.

Cable TV executive Alan Gerry purchased the former Yasgur Farm in the late 1990s and announced plans to invest $46 million to create the **Bethel Woods Center for the Arts** (200 Hurd Rd., Bethel, 866/781-2922, www.bethelwoodscenter.org). After a long legal battle, the Gerry Foundation broke ground in the summer of 2004 and produced its first season in 2006. Today, the center has a 4,800-seat copper-roofed pavilion, 7,500-square-foot stage, and lawn seating for 12,000. Performances span a range of genres, from rock and pop to classical, jazz, opera, and country music.

Over the years, Bethel Woods has expanded to include an interactive museum and arts education program. The museum's main exhibit, *Woodstock and the Sixties,* uses film, photos, articles, music, and personal narratives to show how the ideals of the era are relevant today. Special exhibits have honored the 50th anniversary of the Civil Rights Act of 1964 and the 50th anniversary of the Beatles' arrival in the United States. Students can get involved too, through creative writing workshops on Saturdays in the fall, or summer musical theater, jazz, or opera classes. Bethel Woods manages to serve as both a reminder of a key moment in history and a community-building engine today.

If you're headed to Bethel Woods for a concert, save time for a tasting at the **Catskill Distilling Company** (2037 Rte. 17B, Bethel, 845/583-8569, www.catskilldistillingcompany.com, 2pm-6pm Tues.-Sun. Memorial Day to Labor Day, off-season 2pm-6pm Fri.-Sun., or call for an appointment). Owner and distiller Monte Sachs blends Catskill Mountain water and locally grown grains, fruit, and botanicals in a creative mix of craft spirits. Aside from tours and tastings, the distillery hosts live music on Saturday nights.

Liberty to Livingston Manor

Back on the Quickway, Liberty's town center has a few antiques shops and a Greek Revival Methodist church. To the east, the **Neversink Reservoir** (Rte. 16, Neversink, open daily), completed in 1953, holds 34.9 billion gallons of water and covers 93 square miles in the northeastern corner of Sullivan County. Its northern section lies within the Catskill Park. The reservoir is open to fishing for brown trout, smallmouth bass, pickerel, panfish, and landlocked salmon. Follow Route 16 east from the Quickway.

Beyond Neversink, the privately owned

aerial view of Bethel Woods Center for the Arts

The New York City Watershed

New York City consumes 1.3 billion gallons of water a day, and most of it comes from reservoirs in the Catskill region. The massive watershed is the largest unfiltered surface water supply anywhere in the world.

Reservoir	Capacity *(billion gallons)*
Ashokan Reservoir (1915)	22.9
Cannonsville Reservoir (1964)	95.7
Croton System (1842)	86.6
Neversink Reservoir (1954)	34.9
Pepacton Reservoir (1955)	140.2
Rondout Reservoir (1950)	9.6
Schoharie Reservoir (1928)	17.6

Reservoir permits are free but required in order to fish. Rowboats are allowed, but motorboats are not. Camping is also not allowed.

Grahamsville Historic District (Rte. 55, Grahamsville) on State Route 55 consists of six Gothic Revival, Italianate, and Greek Revival structures on 200 acres. Outside of town, the **Kalonymus Escarpment,** a National Natural Landmark created by glacial activity, may pique the interest of amateur geologists. The **Rondout Reservoir** in Grahamsville is an observation point for bald eagles.

East of the Quickway along Route 82 lies the hamlet of DeBruce, where New York State operates one of its 12 fish hatcheries. The **Catskill Hatchery** (Mongaup Rd., Livingston Manor, 845/439-4328, www.dec.ny.gov, 8am-4pm Mon.-Fri., 8am-noon Sat.-Sun.) specializes in raising brown trout. Some 115,000 pounds of fingerlings and yearlings leave the hatchery each year, from a base of two million eggs. The state places the trout in rivers, streams, lakes, and ponds to support recreational fishing and to restore native species to damaged environments.

Livingston Manor might still be the kind of place where the milk arrives daily at your doorstep. During the railroad era, the town once known as Purvis had the only Y-shaped track in the area for turning trains around. The town became a transportation hub as a result. A pair of wagon wheels marks the beginning of Main Street, and the swift-flowing Willowemoc Creek runs parallel to it, with an attractive schoolhouse on the opposite shore. Fly-fishing conditions are just about ideal here, and every other storefront sells fishing gear.

These days, Livingston Manor seems to be waiting for something to lift the town out of the doldrums. A few years ago, a group of investors out of New York City purchased several buildings in an effort to turn the town into a vibrant community for the arts. But to date, little has changed.

★ Catskill Fly Fishing Center and Museum

A few miles farther up the Willowemoc is the **Catskill Fly Fishing Center and Museum** (1031 Old Rte. 17, Livingston Manor, 845/439-4810, www.catskillflyfishing.org, 10am-4pm daily Apr.-Oct., 10am-4pm Tues.-Sat. Nov.-Mar.), a beautiful facility on 55 acres. A one-lane wooden bridge leads to the parking lot, and you can often see fly-fishers casting right in front of the museum.

These waters were the stomping ground of the late Lee Wulff, celebrated angler, conservationist, and writer. His words appear on a plaque inside the museum: "Over my many years of fishing, I have learned that angling's problems are never solved. They rise anew with each new pool and each new day. Fishing, especially fly fishing, has problems, solutions, challenges and rewards, which have always captured my imagination and stimulated my creativity." His wife, Joan Wulff, continues to run the **Wulff School of Fly Fishing** (7 Main St., Livingston

Manor, 800/328-3638, www.royalwulff.com) nearby in Roscoe.

The exhibits in this well-funded museum will interest most outdoors enthusiasts, whether or not they care to learn how to tie a fly. Vintage rods and reels depict the sport in its early days. A wall of materials used in tying flies includes fox hair and a rare feather that comes from specially bred chickens. An old-fashioned Cortland line-braiding machine in the back corner still works.

Watch the pros tie their delicate flies on Saturdays April-October. The center offers courses on stream ecology and angling, fly tying, and rod building. A blue sign on the west side of Old Route 17 marks the entrance to the center.

Covered Bridges

Most visitors enjoy crossing Sullivan County's rivers, even if they don't want to catch the fish that live in them. Early settlers in the area constructed bridges over the Beaver Kill and Willowemoc using native hemlock trees, and three historic covered bridges have survived to the present day: **Covered Bridge State Park** (Livingston Manor) outside of Livingston Manor, **Beaverkill Campground** (792 Berrybrook Road Spur, Roscoe, 845/439-4281, www.dec.ny.gov/outdoor/24455.html) in Lewbeach (Rte. 154), and Willowemoc (Rte. 84).

★ Roscoe

The land around Roscoe, at the western edge of Sullivan County, once marked the disputed border between the Iroquois and Algonquin nations. Today the town is better known as a haven for anglers and outdoors enthusiasts, and store owners kindly ask patrons to leave their studded wading shoes at the door. The Beaver Kill and Willowemoc Creek meet in Roscoe, a.k.a. Trout Town USA, at a place called Junction Pool, which is recognized as the birthplace of dry fly casting. Opening day of trout season (Apr. 1) draws a crowd of fishing enthusiasts each year, from distinguished instructors and flytiers to renowned New York City chefs.

More developed than the surrounding hamlets, Roscoe has a number of reputable tackle shops, inns, and restaurants, most of them in a row along Stewart Street. Shortline Bus (800/631-8405, www.coachusa.com, $125 adult round-trip) offers weekend packages to Roscoe from Port Authority in New York City.

ALONG THE DELAWARE: ROUTE 97

★ Upper Delaware Scenic and Recreational River

Exit 53 off I-84 puts you at the intersection of Route 97 and the start of the **Upper Delaware Scenic and Recreational River** (Rte. 97, 845/252-7414, www.upperdelaware.com or www.nps.gov), a national park that extends 73 miles from the New York-New Jersey state line through Sullivan County and into the southern part of Delaware County. It takes about three hours to drive the length of the park.

Conceived in the early 1930s as a scenic and commercial route, Route 97 connects Port Jervis in Orange County to Hancock in Delaware County, with the majority of the highway running through Sullivan County. This winding road is New York's equivalent to the West Coast's Highway 1. It climbs over hills and crosses ravines, featuring many turnouts and picnic areas along the way. Route 97 enters Sullivan County at Mongaup, just after the Hawk's Nest section of the road in Orange County. Brown Scenic Byway signs depict a river and road with green on both sides.

At 410 miles in length, the Delaware is the longest free-flowing river in the northeast. Its East Branch originates in the natural springs of the Catskills, while the West Branch begins in Schoharie County, near Pennsylvania. The rocky terrain of the western Catskills forms Class I and Class II rapids along some stretches. Before the era of rail travel, the Delaware and Hudson Canal served as a vital connection between the two commercial rivers. For anglers, the Delaware is home to scores of trout, bass, walleye, eel, and shad.

Take a detour from Route 97 at the town of Pond Eddy (Rte. 41), about five miles past the Hawk's Nest, to head north to Glen Spey and the **St. Volodymyr Ukrainian Orthodox Cathedral** (Glen Spey, 845/856-5500). Like its counterpart in Greene County, this architectural wonder was built without a single nail.

Mongaup Valley Wildlife Management Area

An 11,000-acre expanse of forested hills, streams, and rivers connects the towns of Bethel, Lumberland, Forestburgh, and Highland in Sullivan County and extends to Deer Park in Orange County. The intersection of the Mongaup and Delaware Rivers is prime bald eagle habitat, but you may also see white-tailed deer, wild turkeys, grouse, coyotes, fox, porcupines, and black bear. Keep an eye out for other migrating raptors, owls, and wetland birds. The water supports many different kinds of fish, including smallmouth bass, largemouth bass, crappie, panfish, and stocked and wild trout. There are two blinds for viewing eagles—one on Route 43 and the other on Plank Road. Hiking, biking, snowshoeing, cross-country skiing, fishing, and hunting all are permitted.

The Eagle Institute

Although winter is not the most popular season to visit the Delaware River, it is the best time to catch once-endangered bald eagles in action. A small group of eagles are year-round residents along the Delaware, while a larger population migrates from Canada, spending mid-December through mid-March in the warmer climate.

The nonprofit **Eagle Institute** (Rte. 97, Barryville, 845/557-6162, www.eagleinstitute.org), based in Barryville, runs guided field trips and other educational programs. Popular observation points include: **Mongaup Falls Reservoir** (Forestburgh), off Route 42 (not to be confused with Mongaup Pond in northeastern Sullivan County) and **Rio Reservoir** in Forestburgh. The institute has a winter field office just across the Roebling Bridge from Minisink Ford (176 Scenic Dr., Lackawaxen, PA, 570/685-5960).

Novelist Stephen Crane reportedly penned *The Red Badge of Courage* from his cabin in nearby Forestburgh.

Minisink Ford

Sullivan County's only Revolutionary War skirmish took place at Minisink Ford in July 1779, when a group of 120 colonists were defeated by a combined force of Native American and Tory soldiers. Today, the site is listed on the National Register of Historic Places. **Minisink Battleground Park** (County Road 168, Minisink Ford, 845/807-0261, opens 8am daily) encompasses 57 acres of woodlands, with walking trails and an interpretive center that recounts both the political and the natural history of the site.

Also at Minisink Ford is the oldest suspension bridge in the country, the Delaware Aqueduct or **Roebling Bridge.** Built by John A. Roebling, the same engineer who designed the Brooklyn Bridge, this historic bridge dates back to 1848, when it was constructed to support the Delaware and Hudson Canal. Though the bridge has been converted to carry cars instead of coal, the original cables still hold it in place.

Narrowsburg

The Delaware River reaches its deepest point, 113 feet, at Narrowsburg, where the earliest colonial settlers arrived in the 1770s, during the French and Indian War. The **Fort Delaware Museum** (6615 Rte. 97, Narrowsburg, 845/807-0261 Sept.-Apr. or 845/252-6660 May-Aug., co.sullivan.ny.us, 10am-5pm Fri.-Mon., noon-5pm Sun. Memorial Day-Labor Day), run by the New York State Department of Education, recreates the pioneers' way of life and is a popular destination for local schoolchildren. Over the years, Narrowsburg has developed a vibrant community of artists and a number of cultural attractions. Several art galleries and theaters draw year-round visitors.

From Narrowsburg, Route 52 leads away from the river toward Cochecton Center, Kenoza Lake, Jeffersonville, and eventually Liberty. Along the way is a historical bridge made of stone instead of timber. While many covered bridges have been preserved, the only original stone bridge with three arches remaining in the United States crosses the Callicoon Creek in the town of Kenoza Lake. It was built in 1872 and is now known as **Stone Arch Bridge Historical Park** (Rtes. 52 & 52A, Kenoza Lake, 845/807-0261, co.sullivan.ny.us).

★ Callicoon

If you stay on Route 97 and continue north toward Delaware County, you'll reach the hamlet of Callicoon (Wild Turkey), where the only remaining single-screen movie theater in Sullivan County is still open for business. Built in 1948, the 380-seat **Callicoon Theater** (30 Upper Main St., Callicoon, 845/887-4460, www.callicoontheater.com) screens current releases year-round as well as alternative and foreign films from September through June. Although it was first settled in the 1600s, no building in Callicoon predates 1888 because of a fire that leveled the town.

SPORTS AND RECREATION

Winter Sports

Sullivan County has one small downhill ski area that's ideal for youngsters, or anyone who's just starting to get the hang of the sport. **Holiday Mountain** (99 Holiday Mountain Rd., Monticello, 845/796-3161, www.holidaymtn.com, trails open Dec.-Feb. 3pm-9pm Tues.-Thurs., noon-9pm Fri., 9am-9pm Sat., 9am-5pm Sun.) in Monticello has snowmaking facilities to cover all 14 of its trails.

For Nordic skiers, many of Sullivan County's hotels and inns maintain their own trails. The towns of Fallsburg and Thompson open trails to the public. **Morningside Park** (11 Morningside Park Rd., Fallsburg, 845/434-5877, www.townoffallsburg.com) is open dawn to dusk daily and skiers can enjoy 2.5 miles of parkland. **Thompson Park** (179 Town Park Rd., Monticello, 845/794-5280) features 150 acres of parkland for cross-country skiers, and is open from dawn to dusk.

Hiking

For many years, the 108-mile-long Delaware and Hudson Canal carried coal, cement, bluestone, and other industrial materials from Honesdale, Pennsylvania, to Kingston, New York, for the Albany and New York City markets. Built by Irish and German immigrants over the course of three years, the canal played an instrumental role in the growth and development of the Atlantic Seaboard. It had 108 locks and 22 aqueducts, and 136 bridges, 22 reservoirs, and 16 dams along its length. The advent of the steam train retired the canal from service, but today you can walk, bike, or ski some 20 miles of it. The restored sections, however, are not yet all connected. The canal runs mainly through Orange and Ulster Counties, but in Sullivan County, a 3.5-mile segment connects the towns of Wurtsboro with the hamlet of Phillipsport. Canoeing and fishing are also permitted along this stretch.

Willowemoc Wild Forest, in the southwest corner of the Catskill Forest Preserve, is another good place to get away from it all. Located 18 miles north of Liberty and nine miles northeast of Livingston Manor, its 14,800 "forever wild" acres include trails maintained for hiking, skiing, biking, and snowmobiling. About 15 miles of paths are reserved for hikers only. The terrain is gentle, with rolling hills instead of tall peaks. Four trailheads departing from Neversink and Rockland have parking nearby. Campfires and primitive camping are allowed, but there are no facilities.

Privately run **Eldred Preserve** (1040 Rte. 55, Eldred, 845/557-8316, www.eldredpreserve.com, 8am-4pm Wed.-Sun.) is a year-round fishing and hunting resort on 3,000 acres off Route 55. Facilities include three stocked fishing ponds and a sporting-clay range, and the resort runs fishing tournaments in summer. Services include guided trips, corporate events, a pro shop, and motel-style accommodations in log-cabin buildings.

The National Park Service maintains the challenging three-mile **Tusten Mountain Trail** (Rte. 97, www.tusten.org, 8:30am-6pm daily), between Barryville and Narrowsburg near the Ten Mile River. The route reaches 1,100 feet at its highest point.

Stock up on hiking gear and supplies at **Morgan Outdoors** (46 Main St., Livingston Manor, 845/439-5507, www.morgan-outdoors.com, 10am-6pm Mon. and Wed.-Sat., 10am-4pm Sun.). Rent gear for camping or snowshoeing, or pick up hand-drawn maps of the area. This store also functions as an information center for visitors who want to explore the nearby Catskill Park. Inquire about guided hikes on the calendar.

Cycling

Internationally recognized **Mike Fraysee Sports** (573 High Rd., Glen Spey, 845/856-3335, www.mikefrayssesports.com) trains elite athletes from the United States and beyond but also offers recreational tours for the rest of us. Guests ride to local destinations in groups of up to eight, accompanied by professional cyclists. Weekend tours cost $395 per person, weeklong tours are $995.

Pearson Park (Walnut Mtn., Liberty, 845/292-7690, 8am-dusk daily May-Sept.), on Walnut Mountain, has 265 acres of novice to expert terrain, including challenging singletrack riding.

At **Ridgeback Sports** (34 Audley Dorrer Dr., Callicoon, 845/887-3048, www.ridgebacksports.com, noon-5pm Tues., 10am-5pm Wed.-Sun.) personal trainer TJ Johnson and his wife, Stephanie, are avid athletes who offer bike rentals and guided bike tours along the Delaware River. The store sells running shoes and apparel, bikes and cycling accessories, and other fitness essentials. The owners also organized the first annual Bald Eagle Half Marathon in 2014.

Golf

Sullivan County offers several championship golf courses with moderate greens fees and inspiring views of the Catskills. The 7,650-yard, world-class course at the **Concord Golf Resort** ranks among the best courses in the country, according to *Golf Digest* (Concord Rd., Kiamesha Lake, 888/448-9686, www.concordresort.com, weekends $45-95, weekdays $35-65). **Tennanah Lake Golf and Tennis Club** (100 Fairway View Dr., Roscoe, 888/561-3935 or 607/498-5502, www.tennanah.com, weekends and holidays $37-45, weekdays $25-32) bills itself as "Sullivan County's Oldest Golf Course" and features daily specials that include meals at The Grille restaurant or discount rates for twosomes and foursomes. Serious golfers can stay at the club's Inn at Tennanah or Wood Lake Country Estates.

Swimming and Boating

Mongaup Pond is actually a 12-acre lake, the largest body of water inside the Catskill Park that is not a New York City reservoir. A variety of fish live in the lake, and visitors can swim, fish, and paddle in its refreshing waters. Boat rentals are available through the **Mongaup Pond Campground** (231 Mongaup Pond Rd., Livingston Manor, 845/439-4233, www.dec.ny.gov, daily fee $22). Camping is permitted mid-May through Columbus Day.

For a day at the beach, head to 1,400-acre **Lake Superior State Park** (Rte. 55, Bethel, 845/794-3000, www.nysparks.com, 9am-dusk mid-May-Sept.).

Several outfitters run trips along the Delaware: **Kittatinny Canoes** (3854 Rte. 97, Barryville, 800/356-2852, www.kittatinny.com, 8am-8pm daily May-Sept., 9am-5pm daily Oct.-Apr.) has canoes, rafts, kayaks, and tubes for trips ranging from calm to white water. **Whitewater Willie's** (37 S. Maple Ave., Port Jervis, 845/856-7055 or 800/724-8342, www.silvercanoe.com, Apr.-Sept.) has joined forces with Silver Canoe, and is another reputable operation with reasonable prices.

Mongaup Pond has a swimming beach with lifeguard supervision. Rowboats and canoes

American Ginseng

The Chinese weren't the only ones to discover the healthful effects of wild ginseng. Native Americans discovered the plant in the Catskills long before the Dutch settlers arrived, and local residents have been consuming it in teas, lotions, and tonics ever since.

In Chinese medicine, ginseng root is believed to energize and rejuvenate the body and enhance immunity. Although most of the world's supply is now cultivated in China and Korea, the highest-quality ginseng grows wild under the shade of deciduous trees like the sugar maple.

In the mid-1990s, Bob Beyfuss at the Cornell Cooperative Extension of Green County began an experiment—to teach local farmers how to simulate the wild growth of ginseng in their own backyards, the Catskill Mountains. Earning a price of $500 or more per pound, the root offered struggling farmers a way to supplement their meager income.

Wild ginseng is difficult to find and identify. Few who know it well are willing to share their secrets. But those who care to sustain its presence in the Catskills spread the seeds of a plant before they harvest its root. The plant is protected by law in New York State and may only be picked September 1-November 30.

are allowed on the lake (rentals available), but not motorboats.

Lander's River Trips (5961 Rte. 97, Narrowsburg, 800/252-3925, www.landersrivertrips.com, rentals $39-47), family-run since 1954, runs 10 bases along the Upper Delaware River, with rafts, canoes, and kayaks for rent. Camping and packages are available.

Fishing and Hunting

Fly-fishing was first introduced to the United States in Sullivan County, and the tradition draws a majority of Sullivan County visitors today. You can learn to tie flies at one of several area schools, such as the renowned **Wulff School of Fly Fishing** (7 Main St., Livingston Manor, 800/328-3638, www.royalwulff.com). Or drop in for a workshop at the **Catskill Museum of Fly Fishing** (1031 Old Rte. 17, Livingston Manor, 845/439-4810, www.catskillflyfishing.org, 10am-4pm daily Apr.-Oct., 10am-4pm Tues.-Sat. Nov.-Mar.). Trout season opens April 1, and the shad run peaks in May on the Delaware River. In addition, the county and state stock hundreds of lakes and streams. The **Beaverkill Angler** (52 Stewart Ave., Roscoe, 607/498-5194, www.beaverkillangler.com, 9am-5pm daily) has everything you need for a day of casting in the river. Leave your studded shoes at the door.

Guides and gear are available at a number of additional operations in Trout Town USA. **Catskill Flies Fly Shop & Fishing Adventures** (6 Stewart Ave., Roscoe, 607/498-6146, www.catskillflies.com, 8am-5pm daily) leads trips and rents equipment. You can sleep and fish with **Baxter House B&B and River Outfitters** (Old Rte. 17, Roscoe, 607/290-4022 or 607/348-7497, www.baxterhouse.net). A half day of wade fishing runs $325 for one or two people, full day $425. Drift boat trips are $425 full day and $300 evening hatch float. Modest accommodations are available in six recently renovated rooms ($65-125).

Local fisherman Anthony Ritter runs drift boat trips along the Upper Delaware River through **Gone Fishing Guide Service** (20 Lake St., Narrowsburg, 845/252-3657, www.gonefishingguideservice.com, daily Apr.-Nov.). Catches include shad, trout, smallmouth bass, and walleye. Half-day trips for one or two people run $250, and full-day trips run $350.

Other local guides include Stefan Spoerri out of Narrowsburg (845/252-7309). Stop in at the **Catskill Delaware Outdoor Store** for fishing and hunting supplies and licenses, as well as current river conditions (34A Dorrer Dr., Callicoon, 845/887-4800, daily 8am-6pm).

Aviation

Learn to fly (with or without an engine), or just take an aerial tour at the private **Wurtsboro Airport** (Rte. 209, Wurtsboro, 845/888-2791, www.wurtsboroairport.net, 9am-5pm Thurs.-Mon.). There are grass and paved runways. Taxi service is available for rides into town ($5-6). Other local facilities include **Sullivan County International Airport** (Bethel, 845/807-0273).

Yoga

Sat Nam Yoga Spa (333 Mount Cliff Rd., Hurleyville, 845/866-3063, www.satnamyogaspa.com) offers walk-in kundalini yoga and meditation classes, flotation therapy, massage treatments, and wellness packages. The studio is also a bed-and-breakfast inn with rooms in a converted barn.

ACCOMMODATIONS

Sullivan County lodging consists mainly of rustic country inns with a few B&B gems in the mix. Middletown has a handful of chain hotels, including a Courtyard by Marriot, Hampton Inn, and Best Western. Plan ahead in summer, as any of these places sell out on summer camp parent weekends and when there's a big concert playing at Bethel Woods.

Under $100

★ **The Reynolds House** (1934 Old Rte. 17, Roscoe, 607/498-4422, www.reynoldshouseinn.com, $80) is an excellent value option for cozy accommodations in a central location. Each room in this three-story inn has a private bath with a very small shower. Dark wood and floral prints define the look and feel. The breakfast room has a fireplace and kitchenette. The inn caters to hunters and fishers, as well as parents of children at local summer camps.

$100-150

The first building you notice when you roll into Callicoon is the Victorian **Western Hotel** (22 Upper Main St., Callicoon, 845/887-9871, $125), a pale yellow building with white trim. Built in 1852, the inn offers six guest rooms upstairs and a cozy downstairs taproom, with antique furnishings throughout. Carpeted rooms have air-conditioning, private baths, and king-size beds. The restaurant serves American Continental fare for dinner Thursday through Tuesday starting at 5:30pm.

As a hundred-year-old boarding house, **Sunrise House B&B** (193 N. Branch Rd., Jeffersonville, 845/482-3778, Apr.-Dec., $110-175) has five clean rooms on a 45-acre property. Owners Anita and Gene provide attentive service and a memorable breakfast spread.

Popular with the fly-fishing crowd, **The DeBruce Country Inn** (982 DeBruce Rd., 845/439-3900, www.debrucecountryinn.com, $110-130 pp) has 14 rooms and 2 suites in a hundred-year-old building on the bank of the Willowemoc inside the Catskill Forest Preserve. Rooms have not been updated in many years and are showing signs of wear and tear. Rates include a full breakfast and choice of dinner.

$150-200

Villa Roma (356 Villa Roma Rd., Callicoon, 877/256-7506, www.villaroma.com, Apr. 1-Jan. 1, $225), a resort and conference center, manages to blend some of the old-fashioned Catskill resort flavor with a host of modern amenities. A variety of vacation packages include meals and entertainment as well as accommodations.

The **Sat Nam Inn** (333 Mount Cliff Rd., Hurleyville, 845/866-3063, www.satnamyogaspa.com, $175) is part of a yoga center and wellness retreat located near the Sivananda ashram. Rates include accommodations in a renovated barn and breakfast. Visitors are welcome to take yoga classes, schedule flotation therapy sessions, and book massage treatments. Vacation rentals are also available for longer stays.

Bass' Hancock House Hotel (137 E. Front St., Hancock, 607/637-7100, www.hancockhousehotel.com, $125-175) is a modern building that's intended to keep the past alive. The site of the original Hancock Hotel, located two blocks away, hosted celebrities and world leaders in the first half of the 20th century. The new hotel, run by Lynn and Russell Bass, has 32 clean rooms with two queen beds in each. The hotel also has a taproom and restaurant on the main floor. Rooms fill up during summer camp parent weekends.

Over $200

★ The **Bradstan Country Hotel** (1561 Rte. 17B, White Lake, 845/583-4114, www.bradstancountryhotel.com, closed Dec.-Apr., $225-250) has the best accommodations close to the Bethel Woods Center for the Arts. The main house, a white building with three gables and a wide front porch, has two large rooms, a small suite, and two large suites. Several rooms have views of the lake across the street. Two separate cottages each have a large bedroom with a queen bed and additional twin bed, as well as a full galley kitchen. All rooms have air-conditioning and ceiling fans. Owners Scott and Eddie attend to guests and serve a tasty hot breakfast, included in the room rates. There is a two-night minimum on summer weekends.

Enjoy a peaceful retreat beside a 250-acre private lake at the ★ **Inn at Lake Joseph** (162 St. Joseph Rd., Forestburgh, 845/791-9506, www.lakejoseph.com, $185-410). Its gorgeous Redwood room has 18-foot ceilings, and the Tudor room has high ceilings and a deck with over 700 square feet of living space. There is a full-service fitness center and spa nearby, but chances are you won't want to leave the property.

★ **Ecce Bed and Breakfast** (19 Silverfish Rd., Barryville, 845/557-8562 or 888/557-8562, www.eccebedandbreakfast.com, $200-285) opened in 2004 in a former private home perched on a bluff above the Delaware River. The B&B is located 15 miles from the Bethel Woods Center for the Arts. Its five rooms have private baths (some with whirlpool tubs). Decks offer views of the surrounding mountains. From the artwork to the breakfast menu, hosts Alan and Kurt have an eye for detail, and they have built a loyal following of repeat guests.

In Liberty, **Lazy Pond Bed and Breakfast** (79 Old Loomis Rd., Liberty, 845/988-7061, www.lazypond.com, $225-300) caters to families and parents of summer camp kids with 25 guest rooms on a 12-acre property. Rooms are basic, but very clean.

Campgrounds

Beaverkill Campground (792 Berrybrook Rd. Spur, Roscoe, 845/439-4281 or 845/256-3099, www.dec.ny.gov, mid-May-Labor Day, $20) has 108 sites along the Beaver Kill with hot showers. On the Delaware, **Indianhead Campground** (Barryville, 800/874-2628, www.indianheadcanoes.com, $10-15 per person) has wooded campsites with fire rings, right next to the river. **Berentsen's Campground** (266 Roose Gap Rd., Bloomingburg, 845/733-4984, www.berentsencampground.com, tent sites $30 per day) has a stream winding through the property and a swimming pool that's popular with families. Full hookups are available and pets are welcome.

FOOD

While not as sophisticated as the cuisine found closer to the Hudson, Sullivan County has a few good standbys for hearty country cooking.

Along the Quickway

Catch a Willowemoc trout and have it prepared at **Ianine's** (982 DeBruce Rd., DeBruce, 845/439-3900, www.debrucecountryinn.com, 8am-10am and 7pm-10pm daily) inside the DeBruce Country Inn. Its Dry Fly Lounge is open 5pm-10pm daily.

Along the Delaware: Route 97

Order breakfast all day at the **Whistle Stop Café** (119 Kirk Rd., Narrowsburg, 845/252-3355, 6:30am-8pm Sun.-Thurs., 6:30am-9pm Fri.-Sat., $3-6). The dining room at family-oriented **Lander's River Café** (20A Dorrer

Dr., Callicoon, 845/887-6800, 7am-3pm daily, $3-7) overlooks the Delaware River.

The **Narrowsburg Inn Grille** (176 Bridge St., Narrowsburg, 845/252-3998, www.narrowsburginn.us, Thurs.-Sun. summer, Sat.-Sun. spring and fall, $6-15) offers a menu of North American favorites.

Callicoon boasts the best dining in Sullivan County. Filet mignon with bourbon sauce and blackened yellowfin tuna anchor a menu of country-style entrées at **The 1906 Restaurant** (41 Lower Main St., Callicoon, 845/887-1906, www.1906restaurant.com, 5pm-10pm Mon.-Sat., $15-30). Booth seating and a notable wine list complete the dining experience. ★ **Matthew's on Main** (19 Lower Main St., Callicoon, 845/887-5636, www.matthewsonmain.com, 11am-9pm Sun.-Thurs., 11am-10pm Fri., 10am-10pm Sat., $8-13) is an inviting country bistro with outdoor tables that offer a view of the Delaware River. The menu ranges from half-pound burgers and lamb moussaka to seafood linguini.

Villa Roma (356 Villa Roma Rd., Callicoon, 845/887-4880 or 800/533-6767, www.villaroma.com, Apr. 1-Jan. 1, $10-20) has several dining options that are open to the public, as well as resort guests. In the main dining room, a CIA graduate prepares Italian American cuisine, including rich pasta dishes and hearty meat entrées such as prime rib and roasted duck. The seasonal Beechwoods Restaurant & Grill offers a more varied menu.

Benji and Jakes (5 Horsehoe Lake Rd., White Lake, 845/583-4031, www.benjiandjakes.com, $13-26) tosses a reliable thin-crust pizza. Special pies include an eggplant parm and super spicy "Death by Pizza."

Concertgoers have several food options at Bethel Woods. **The Muse Café** (200 Hurd Rd., Bethel, 866/781-2922, www.bethelwoodscenter.org) has a menu of hot sandwiches, burgers, wraps, and panini. It also serves Ben & Jerry's ice cream. A preconcert buffet dinner is offered before select shows at **The Market Shed,** also on the concert grounds.

ENTERTAINMENT AND EVENTS

Performing Arts

The **Bethel Woods Center for the Arts** (200 Hurd Rd., Bethel, 866/781-2922, www.bethelwoodscenter.org) produces first-rate concerts that draw crowds from all over the Hudson River Valley area. John Mayer, Natalie Merchant, and the Dave Matthews Band all have performed here in recent years, as have Tim McGraw, Rosanne Cash, and Arlo Guthrie.

The **Forestburgh Playhouse** (39 Forestburgh Rd., Forestburgh, 845/794-1194, www.fbplayhouse.org) is the oldest professional summer theater in New York State. Productions include Broadway musicals, comedies, and cabarets before and after the shows. The playhouse also has a tavern and children's theater on-site.

Bars and Nightlife

Before or after the show at Bethel Woods, pop into the **Dancing Cat Saloon** (2037 Co. Rd. 17B, Bethel, 845/583-3141, www.dancingcatsaloon.com) for more live music, cocktails, or a bite to eat. Notice the art deco bar, which comes from the 1939 World's Fair in Flushing, and the custom-made copper stills behind it. Aptly named spirits like Peace Vodka and Most Righteous Bourbon are made at the adjoining Catskill Distilling Company, a microdistillery that applies the farm-to-table concept to its creative menu of spirits. In summer, the Curious Gin, made with locally grown juniper berries, makes a top-notch G&T. Or try it with house-made honey syrup and lemon.

Otherwise, the biggest entertainment venue in Sullivan County is the **Monticello Gaming & Raceway** (204 Rte. 17B, Monticello, 866/777-4263, www.monticellocasinoandraceway.com), which opened in 2004 at the Monticello Raceway.

Festivals and Events

The ultimate place to celebrate opening day of the trout season is the Junction Pool in

Roscoe. Crowds of locals and fly-fishing enthusiasts gather on the often icy rocks to watch celebrity "first casters" kick off the season. The annual **Two-Headed Trout Dinner** is held Saturday night at the Rockland House (www.roscoeny.com). Another annual outdoor event is **Eaglefest** (School Auditorium, Narrowsburg, 845/252-7234, www.narrowsburg.org), timed to coincide with the bald eagle migration from Canada in January.

Morgan Outdoors (46 Main St., Livingston Manor, 845/439-5507, www.morgan-outdoors.com, 10am-6pm Mon. and Wed.-Sat., 10am-4pm Sun.) hosts occasional events for outdoor enthusiasts. Recent talks have focused on Exploring the Catskill Forest, Geocaching, and Native Plants.

SHOPPING

Sullivan County shops carry antiques and a wide variety of handmade country goods, from marmalade to greeting cards. **Canal Towne Emporium** (169 Sullivan St., Wurtsboro, 845/888-2100, www.canaltowne.com, 10am-5pm daily) is a cavernous gift shop filled with gourmet foods (some locally produced and some from afar), as well as candles, bath products, and other country accents for the home.

Antiques

Turning the old into something new is a popular pastime in Sullivan County, and at least a dozen towns hold an antiques shop or two. Here are some of the best:

Browse collections of clothing, pottery, Depression-era glass, prints, mirrors, and more at the **Antique Center of Callicoon** (26 Upper Main St., Callicoon, 845/887-5918, 11am-4pm Mon. and Thurs.-Sat., 11am-3pm Sun. July-Aug., Sept.-June hours vary, so call ahead). Look for a three-story building across from the train station. Another find for collectible glassware is **In 2 Collecting Glass & More** (511 Hazel Rd., Livingston Manor, 845/665-9538, 9am-4pm summer weekends, weekdays by appointment).

The **Ferndale Antiques Marketplace** (52 Ferndale Rd., Ferndale, 845/292, 8701, www.ferndaleantiques.net, hours vary, call ahead) sells vintage furniture, as well as home decorations, lighting, and paintings. Browse for costume jewelry and accessories in The Boutique.

In business for more than 25 years, **Antique Palace Emporium** (300 Chestnut St., Liberty, 845/292-2270, www.antiquepalaceemporium.com) restores and reupholsters vintage American furniture, from the late 1800s to the early 1900s. The store is open year-round, but hours vary. Call ahead.

One of Wurtsboro's oldest homes—an 1825 canal house—is the storefront for **Hamill's Antiques** (81 Sullivan St., Wurtsboro, 845/888-5356, call ahead as hours vary). Shop for antique paintings, sculptures, jewelry, and chandeliers. On summer weekends, cars jam the roadside parking lot of **Memories** (Rte. 17, Parksville, 845/292-4270 or 800/222-8463, 10am-5pm daily), between Exits 97 and 98 on Route 17. Six showrooms with thousands of home furnishings, lighting, and other antiques are the draw.

Across from the Catskill Distilling Company, owners Monte Sachs and Stacy Cohen also run the **Stray Cat Gallery & The Next Door Store** (2032 Rte. 17B, Bethel, 845/423-8850, www.straycatgallery.com, 11am-6pm Fri.-Sun. or by appointment) in a restored Victorian home. A permanent exhibit of nature photographs by Jerry Cohen is displayed upstairs, with rotating works by other local artists on the lower level. The annex sells jewelry, crafts, antiques, and other collectibles.

Farm Stands and Farmers Markets

In this land of dairy farms and boutique growers, it's difficult to narrow the list of farm stands to manageable length. Callicoon's **Apple Pond Farm** (80 Hahn Rd., Callicoon Center, 845/482-4764, www.applepondfarm.com) is one of the standouts. **Silver Heights Farm** (216 Eggler Rd., Jeffersonville, 845/482-3608, www.silverheightsfarm.com) grows

Sullivan County Farmers Markets

The mid-summer harvest includes onions, beets, potatoes, carrots, and parsnips.

Farmers markets are a way of life in the Western Catskills. More than a place to stock up on fresh produce, they bring communities together to celebrate the season's harvest with heirloom fruits and vegetables, heritage meats, gourmet foods, and unique crafts. In three locations across the county, you'll find fresh-picked produce, as well as a variety of plants, flowers, soaps, pottery, candles, jewelry, and other crafts—all made by local artisans. Local farmers also bring their cheese, yogurt, jam, wine, maple syrup, eggs, fish, and meat to sell. You can easily consume a meal at the market, and leave with ingredients for another feast at home. To learn more about Sullivan County's three markets, visit www.sullivancountyfarmersmarkets.org.

CALLICOON

11am-2pm Sundays, May through December
Holiday Market: early December
Callicoon Creek Park, Audley Dorrer Drive near the bridge over Delaware River to Pennsylvania

LIBERTY

3pm-6pm Fridays, May through November
Holiday Market: early December
In the Municipal Lot on Darbee Lane near The First National Bank of Jeffersonville

heirloom vegetables, herbs, and flowering plants. The **Sullivan County Area Farmers Market** (845/292-6180, www.sullivancounty-farmersmarkets.org) takes place in multiple locations, primarily Callicoon. Hours vary by location.

Knaub's Farm Antiques & Gifts (1168 County Rte. 23, Narrowsburg, 845/252-3781, 9:30am-7pm Sat., 10am-4pm Sun. May-Dec.) is a combination antiques shop, gift shop, and roadside farm stand.

INFORMATION AND SERVICES

The Sullivan County Visitors Association (100 North St., Monticello, 845/794-3000, www.scva.net) operates information booths at Rock Hill, Livingston Manor, and Roscoe during the busy fishing season. Look for the red caboose off Route 17 at DeBruce Road.

GETTING THERE AND AROUND

Sullivan County is easily accessible from **Stewart International Airport** (1180 1st St., New Windsor, 845/564-7200, www.panynj.gov) and New York City transportation hubs. **Shortline Bus** (800/631-8405, www.coachusa.com, adult fare $110 round-trip with discounts for seniors, students, and children) provides service from Port Authority in New York City to Monticello, with frequent express service and connections to smaller towns like Roscoe. Many resorts provide shuttle transportation from Monticello. Car rentals are available through independent companies (no major chains) in Fosterdale and Monticello: **Fosterdale Rent-a-Car** (1166 County Road 114, Fosterdale, 845/932-8538, www.17brentals.com, 8:30am-8:30pm Mon.-Sat., until 2pm Sun., $39-52 per day) and **Marty's** (4461 Rte. 42, Monticello, 845/794-5025, 8am-5pm daily).

Taxi services in Monticello and Bloomingburg serve all major airports. Note that Route 17 is becoming an interstate, I-86.

Delaware County

It's hard to imagine two worlds more opposed than the exclusive Hamptons of Long Island and the fertile hills of rural Delaware County. And yet, scores of former beachgoers are trading their ocean view for a fixer-upper and a pair of cross-country skis.

The reason? Property that's beautiful, affordable, and within a three-hour drive of New York City. Roughly the size of Rhode Island, Delaware County is the third-largest county in New York State and has the lowest population density (33.2 persons per square mile) of any county in the Hudson River Valley and Catskill region—a figure that almost triples in summer. Encompassing the headwaters of the Delaware River, the area is known for an abundance of freshwater and unparalleled hunting and fishing. Lately, heirloom vegetables and heritage livestock farming are on the rise as well.

Early European settlers arrived in present-day Delaware County in the 1780s by traveling the Catskill Turnpike. This first route to the western frontier was a dirt road with periodic tollgates that connected the Village of Catskill in Greene County to the Susquehanna River in Unadilla.

New York State recognized Delaware County as a separate county in 1797. Lumbering and stone cutting sustained the local economy at first, followed by agriculture. In the 1840s, Delaware County became a focal point of the Anti-Rent Wars, during which poor farmers across the country began to protest the feudal system that prevented them from owning the land they farmed.

Holstein and Jersey cows still graze the hillsides here, and you'll find a sampling of barns in every shape, style, and condition—from those that are barely still standing to others that have been restored as inviting markets, homes, and bookstores.

ALONG ROUTE 28

Fleischmanns

A 40-mile drive from Kingston along Route 28 leads to Fleischmanns, at the eastern edge of Delaware County. Initially known as Griffin Corners in the early 19th century, the town is named for Charles F. Fleischmann (think yeast and whiskey). Fleishmann had emigrated from Austria-Hungary to Cincinnati in the 1860s and started the Vienna Bakery that would make him world famous. Already a successful businessman, he bought property in Delaware County in 1883 and began spending summers in the mountain air.

Soon an entire community of summer

residents, mostly well-to-do families, was building lavish Victorian homes along Wagner Avenue, many of which are standing today. Dozens of resorts opened in the surrounding area, but only a handful remains in business.

At the center of Main Street stands the handsome **Skene Memorial Library** (1017 Main St., Fleischmanns, 845/254-4581, www.skenelib.org, 1pm-5pm Tues.-Fri., 10am-2pm Sat.), founded with a $5,000 grant from Andrew Carnegie and completed in 1901. An old carriage barn behind the library houses the **Fleischmanns Museum of Memories** (1017 Main St., Fleischmanns, 845/254-5514, 11am-3pm Thurs.-Sat. July-Aug. and 11am-3pm Sat. Memorial Day weekend-Columbus Day weekend) with exhibits that document the town's history as a thriving summer resort.

Arkville

One of the most scenic railroad lines in the east connected Kingston on the Hudson to Oneonta at the western boundary of Delaware County. Over the course of its hundred-year history, the Delaware & Ulster Railroad transported lumber, bluestone, livestock, produce, coal, and tourists across 107 miles of mountains and valleys. To date, three stretches of the original route have been restored for visitor enjoyment: the Trolley Museum of New York in Kingston, the Catskill Mountain Railroad in Phoenicia, and the **Delaware & Ulster Railroad** (43510 Rte. 28, 800/225-4132 or 845/586-3877, www.durr.org, call for schedule, adults $12, seniors $9, children $7) in Arkville.

The depot is the most visible attraction around as you enter Arkville on Route 28 (south side of the street). Tours leave twice daily on weekends, May-October, and also Thursday-Friday in July and August. A round-trip tour to Roxbury takes less than two hours (one hour round-trip to Halcottsville). Dogs are welcome aboard the D&U.

Next to the Arkville Fire House, on the north side of Route 28, is the **Erpf House Gallery** (Rte. 28, 845/586-2611, 9am-5pm Mon.-Fri.), featuring artwork that explores themes of nature and captures the history of the Catskill region. Rotating exhibits include paintings, photography, sculpture, installation art, and crafts. The gallery also hosts periodic lectures, workshops, and an artist-in-residence program.

Margaretville and the Pepacton Reservoir

Delaware County sustained $20 million in flood damage when the "Blizzard of 1996" was followed by unseasonably warm temperatures and heavy rains. Margaretville's Bridge Street, along the banks of the East Branch of the Delaware, suffered some of the most severe damage from the disaster, and nine buildings were ultimately condemned.

In the years since, town officials have succeeded in turning the natural disaster into an economic opportunity. With a sizable disaster-relief grant from New York State, Margaretville constructed a new waterfront park and river walk, along with new sidewalks and landscaping along Main Street. The result is an attractive downtown, with several restaurants, shops, and inns—all of which are close to boundless areas for fishing, hiking, and cycling.

A scenic detour from Route 28 leads to the Pepacton Reservoir, formed by a dam at the beginning of the East Branch of the Delaware River. The reservoir is named for one of the four towns it flooded when construction was completed in 1955, and one gets the feeling that more than a few locals are still bitter over the loss.

With a capacity of 140.2 billion gallons of water, the Pepacton is the largest reservoir in the New York City Watershed and provides about 25 percent of the total supply. The artificially constructed lake covers 15 miles and 7,500 acres, supporting a healthy population of brown trout. Fish taken from these waters average about five pounds, with record-setters exceeding 20 pounds. Fishing and rowboats are allowed with a free permit. Several outfitters supply gear and lead trips on the reservoir. No swimming or motorboats are allowed.

At the western end of the reservoir on Route 30 is the village of Downsville and the **Downsville Covered Bridge,** at the intersection of Route 206. This 174-foot bridge still carries one lane of traffic at a time (maximum height six feet) across the East Branch of the Delaware River.

★ Andes

Northeast of the Peptacon Reservoir lies the upland village of Andes, where in 1845 Moses Earle and a group of local farmers refused to pay overdue rents to protest the feudal system of land ownership. Sheriff Osman Steele intervened in the dispute and was killed by the protesters, drawing national attention to the issue. President Abraham Lincoln signed the National Homestead Act into law 15 years later, in 1862, distributing hundreds of millions of acres of land into private hands.

One of the oldest buildings in town is the 1840s **Hunting Tavern Museum** (Rte. 28, 845/676-3775, call before visiting), named for its first proprietor, Ephraim Hunting. Sheriff Steele reportedly downed his last drink here and uttered the now-famous words, "Lead cannot penetrate Steele," shortly before he was shot. Today, the tavern hosts local art exhibits, dance performances, and period dinners.

Proximity to the reservoir and a handful of businesses make Andes a popular stop on the Delaware County loop. The **Andes Hotel and Restaurant** kicks off the visitor experience, with lodging, live music, a cozy tavern, and a menu that features locally caught wild trout, along with seasonal produce. Galleries and antiques shops invite exploration along Main Street. Admire rare 19th-century furniture, photography, and taxidermy at **Kabinett & Kammer** (7 Main St., Andes, 845/676-4242, www.kabinettandkammer.com, hour vary seasonally). Owner Sean Scherer personally finds and curates every item in the store. The aesthetic is unabashedly masculine.

In winter, snowmobilers gather at **Hogan's General Store** on Main Street (103 Main St., Andes, 845/676-3470) to refuel. The Trailways Bus Line (703/691-3052, www.trailways.com) passes through town.

Bovina

Scenic Route 6 connects Margaretville to Bovina, where actors Brad Pitt and Jennifer Aniston were residents until their split in 2005. Bovina Center is a blink-and-you'll-miss-it kind of place with a general store and some pockets of farm-to-table activity. For example, **Brushland Eating House** (1927 County Hwy. 6, Bovina, 607/832-4861, www.brushlandeatinghouse.com, $10-26) keeps it simple, with classics like pork schnitzel, hand-rolled pasta, and a "one flip burger." And **Russell's** (2099 Main St., Bovina, 607/832-4242, www.russellsstore.com, 7am-6pm Mon. and Wed.-Fri., 9am-4pm Sat.-Sun.), a general store run from a building that's been a store since 1823 and is now owned by the Bovina Historical Society. Pop in to refuel your car or yourself.

Roxbury

In an unlikely pairing, financier Jay Gould and naturalist John Burroughs share the town of Roxbury as their birthplace and family homesteads. When Gould left home to invest in railroads, Burroughs remained in the Catskills writing volumes about the natural wonders around him.

A line from "The Heart of the Southern Catskills" captures Burroughs' worldview: "Only the sea and the mountain forest brook are pure, all between is contaminated more or less by the work of man." **Woodchuck Lodge** (www.roxburyny.com), the Burroughs family farmhouse, is now a National Historic Landmark. It's located on Burroughs Memorial Road, off Hardscrabble Road, three miles north of Roxbury.

The Gould family left behind a legacy of architectural splendor. St. Lawrence marble and Tiffany stained glass windows adorn the **Jay Gould Reformed Church** (53873 Rte.

30, Roxbury, 607/326-7101, churches.rca.org/gouldchurch). Helen Gould Shephard, daughter of Jay Gould, built the 1911 classic Greek Revival building that has housed the **Roxbury Arts Group** (5025 Vega Mountain Rd., Roxbury, 607/326-7610, www.roxbury-artsgroup.org) since 1988. Recently restored **Kirkside Park** (Rte. 30, Main St., Roxbury, 607/326-3722, www.roxburyny.com) and the **Shephard Hills Golf Course** (Golf Course Rd. off Bridge St., Roxbury, 607/326-7121, www.shephardhills.com, greens fees $30-35, golf cart rental included) were also part of her original estate. Today, Roxbury is an attractive town of 2,300 residents, many of them retirees and second-home owners who enjoy the variety of outdoor activities within reach.

Delhi

In the center of Delaware County, where Route 10 meets Route 28, is Delhi (DEL-high), the largest and most commercially developed municipality in the region. As the county seat, this town of 50,000 centers on the historic **Delaware County Courthouse Square** (3 Court St.), now an open green space bounded by 2nd, Church, Main, and Court Streets. The striking 19th-century brick facade on the courthouse is now home to county offices.

The State University of New York (SUNY) College of Technology at Delhi opened in 1913 as the State School of Agriculture and Domestic Science and currently enrolls about 2,000 students per year.

Also in town are headquarters for several regional newspapers and radio stations, a few restaurants, and a couple of banks.

The **Delaware County Historical Association** (46549 Rte. 10, Delhi, 607/746-3849, www.dcha-ny.org, 11am-4pm Tues.-Sun. Memorial Day-Oct. 15, adults $4) maintains seven historic buildings on a property located 2.5 miles north of Delhi on Route 10. Among the restored buildings are a toll-gate house from the Catskill Turnpike and the 1797 Frisbee House and barn. The museum displays rotating exhibits in its two galleries, from war memorabilia to quilt shows.

Hamden Covered Bridge

The Hamden Covered Bridge spans the West Branch of the Delaware River, along Route 10 between Delhi and Walton. Built in 1859 in the long truss style, the 125-foot bridge was refurbished in 2000. Look for a dirt pullout with a visitor sign just north of the bridge, on the west side of Route 10. On a sunny day, bring lunch to the picnic table on the west side of the bridge and watch the tractors roll by.

Route 10 heads south from Delhi along the West Branch of the Delaware River, passing through the quiet towns of Hamden, Walton, and Deposit along the way.

ALONG ROUTE 23

Catskill Scenic Trail

If you follow Route 23 west from Greene County, you'll reach the town of Grand Gorge just over the Delaware County line. The East Branch of the Delaware River begins here, and you can pick up the **Catskill Scenic Trail** (Rte. 23, Grand Gorge, 845/586-2929, www.catskillscenictrail.org), which sits on top of the old railroad tracks of the Ulster & Delaware Railroad and runs 19 miles to Bloomville. The hard-packed trail is well suited for biking, jogging, horseback riding, and cross-country skiing, and it offers access to several fishing spots along the river. The railroad track foundation keeps the trail at a gentle grade, so visitors of all ages and physical conditioning can enjoy the hike. The trail may be accessed from many towns along the way; parking lots are available in Bloomville at Route 10 and Route 33. No overnight camping is available.

At the intersection of Routes 23 and 10 lies Stamford and Mount Utsayantha (Beautiful Spring). The West Branch of the Delaware originates at this 3,214-foot peak, and it's one of the few Catskill summits that you can reach by car. A one-mile gravel road leads to the top and a view of four states on clear days. On the way to the summit is the recognized gravesite of a Mohawk woman who drowned herself in a nearby lake in grief over the loss of her son.

Stamford evolved from a distribution

center for butter to a thriving resort town at the turn of the 20th century, and its 20-acre mountaintop park lured visitors from across the country. Today, the walking paths are overgrown and the abandoned observation tower shows signs of neglect. The Utsayantha Flyers Organization has built several launch ramps for hang gliders and keeps a watchful eye on the property.

a walk in the woods

★ Hanford Mills Museum

Turn off Route 23 onto Route 12 to reach East Meredith and the working saw and gristmill at the **Hanford Mills Museum** (73 County Hwy. 12, East Meredith, 607/278-5744 or 800/295-4992, www.hanfordmills.org, 10am-5pm Wed.-Sun. and holiday Mondays May 15-Oct. 15, adults $9, seniors $7, children under 12 free). Listed on the National Register of Historic Places, the museum offers a chance to see how a water-powered sawmill worked in the 19th century. Vintage woodworking equipment gives young and old a glimpse into the past. Seasonal demonstrations, such as the February ice harvest, are especially interesting.

Stone & Thistle Farm

Learn how a sustainable farm works and help get the day's chores done at **Stone & Thistle Farm** (1211 Kelso Rd., East Meredith, 607/278-5800, www.stoneandthistlefarm.com). Take a tour of the pastures and Kortright Creek Creamery operations, meet the grass-fed animals, or stop to pick up meat, eggs, dairy, maple syrup, jam, and homemade goodies at the farm store, open daily 9am-6pm. For a longer visit, sleep over in the creekside farm cabin or enjoy a bed-and-breakfast stay in the guest suite. Call ahead to join a Saturday evening dinner or Sunday brunch.

SPORTS AND RECREATION

Winter Sports

You have to be one of the first 2,000 skiers to get fresh tracks at **Plattekill Mountain** (Plattekill Mountain Rd., Roxbury, 607/326-3500, www.plattekill.com, 8:45am-4:15pm Fri.-Sun., adults $58, seniors and children $50, under 8 free) on a powder day. Normally open three days a week, the mom-and-pop mountain sells $25 tickets and runs the T-bar to expert terrain on days of 12 inches or more. But the owners stop selling tickets when they reach the 2,000 mark. Plattekill gets upwards of 200 inches of snow a year—more natural snow than even the Catskill High Peaks typically get.

The **Delhi College Golf Course** (Rte. 28, Delhi, 607/746-4653, www.delhi.edu) is open to the public all winter long for cross-country skiing and snowshoeing. Snowmobilers congregate in the town of Andes, often to refuel at **Hogan's General Store** (103 Main St., Andes, 845/676-3470 6am-6pm Sun.-Thurs. 6am-9pm Fri.-Sat.) and lunch at the **Andes Hotel** (110 Main St., Andes, 845/676-3980, www.andeshotel.com, lunch and dinner daily, Sun. brunch).

Hiking

The Catskill Forest Preserve and **Utsayantha**

Plattekill Mountain Statistics

- Base: 2,150 feet
- Summit: 3,500 feet
- Vertical: 1,100 feet
- Trails: 35
- Lifts: 4
- Skiable acres: 75
- Snowmaking: 75 percent
- Snow report: 607/326-3500

Trail System (Stamford, 607/652-7581) offer miles of wilderness for day hikes or overnight trips. A stretch of the 552-mile Finger Lakes Trail System crosses Delaware County with several good places to camp overnight, including Beale Pond at **Oquaga Creek State Park** (Rte. 20, Masonville, 607/467-4160, www.nysparks.com). Contact Finger Lakes Trail Conference Service Center (www.fltconference.org) for a current trail map and information about access points and routes.

Cycling

Whether you want to log 15 miles or 100, Delaware County has some of the best terrain around for cycling. Plan a route to tour the county's covered bridges. Avid cyclists won't want to miss the annual **Tour of the Catskills,** which bills itself as "America's Largest Pro-Am Stage Race" (www.tourofthecatskills.com).

In summer, the **Plattekill Bike Park** (Plattekill Mountain Rd., Roxbury, 607/326-3500, www.plattekill.com) opens its lifts to serve 60 miles of trails. Lift service is available Saturdays and Sundays from 10am until 5pm from early May through early November. Wednesday through Friday you can access the trails, but the lifts won't be running. Bike rentals are available. Rental rates are $50 for two hours, $110-150 for two days. Tickets for all-day lift and trail access cost $35; the trails-only rate is $15 per day. A single lift ride with your bike is $10. A SkyRide, sans bike, is $7. Shuttle service is offered to the Catskill Scenic Rail Trail in nearby Roxbury. RV and tent camping is permitted at the base of the mountain for $10 per night.

Golf

Hanah Mountain Resort and Country Club (576 W. Hubbell Hill Rd., Margaretville, 800/752-6494, www.hanahcountryresort.com, greens fees $32-63) has a U.S.G.A.-rated course that's known as the Terminator. Inquire about combined room and greens fee packages.

Swimming and Boating

Paddlers head for the Delaware and Susquehanna Rivers or the Pepacton Reservoir for adventure.

Located near the Pepacton Reservoir, **Al's Sport Store** (Rtes. 30 & 206, Downsville, 607/363-7740, www.alssportstore.com, 6am-6pm daily) offers day or overnight camping trips on the Delaware River. Shuttle service is available.

Fishing and Hunting

Delaware County offers hundreds of miles of some of the top fishing streams, rivers, and reservoirs in the country. The season begins each April with the hatching of the blue-winged olive fly. For freestone stream fishing, the Willowemoc and Beaver Kill are legendary. The Pepacton Reservoir offers stillwater anglers plentiful opportunities for catching bass and occasionally huge brown trouts.

ACCOMMODATIONS

Accommodations are hit or miss in rural Delaware County. Small country inns range from musty and neglected to positively charming. The good news is that even the best are relatively affordable. Plattekill ski and mountain biking area (www.plattekill.com) has listings of local house rentals, as an alternative to the standard B&B or motel lodging. Based in Margaretville, **Pine Hollow Lodging** also manages a number of vacation rentals (845/586-1433, www.pinehollowlodging.com).

$100-150

For a motel with a pop culture twist, try ★ **The Roxbury** (2258 County Hwy. 41, Roxbury, 607/326-7200, www.theroxburymotel.com, $140-175). Its rooms combine technology, style, and simplicity to redefine the motel experience around the concept of creativity. A few of its signature rooms take bold use of color to the extreme, with mosaic quilts, zebra stripes, and psychedelic swirls. Some have kitchenettes as well. The Digs, the owners' latest creative endeavor, made TV history in 2013 when a crew from Animal Planet's Tanked came to film the installation of a 400-gallon saltwater aquarium inside the cottage. Amenities include Wi-Fi and flat-screen TVs, as well as high-end linens and bath products. Service is exceptionally attentive. Best of all, access to the on-site spa facilities (for guests only) costs just $20 per person per *stay*.

Set in a Victorian home on a hill above the town, the **Margaretville Mountain Inn** (1478 Margaretville Mountain Rd., Margaretville, 845/586-3933, www.margaretvilleinn.com, $125-150) has several floral rooms with brass bed frames. Some rooms share a bath. Views from the porch are a highlight, and breakfast is included with an overnight stay. For modern accommodations and a more convenient location, request a room in the newer building in town.

Just outside of Hancock, **Smith's Colonial Motel** (23085 State Hwy. 97, Hancock, 607/637-2989, www.smithscolonialmotel.com, $65-125) is a well-kept property with an impressive list of amenities for the price, including cable TV with HBO and high-speed Internet. Guest room walls are paneled in knotty pine, and minimal furnishings accent scenic views of the Delaware River below.

Want to help out on a family farm, or simply enjoy the scenery and the food? **Stone & Thistle Farm** (1211 Kelso Rd., East Meredith, 607/278-5800, www.stoneandthistlefarm.com, $100-150) has a private suite in the main farmhouse and a rustic cabin by the creek. The cabin has electricity and a refrigerator, hot plate, microwave, and outdoor grill. There are a solar shower, sink, and compost toilet outside. Guests can participate in farm chores through a Farm Stay program, or

canoeing down the Delaware River

relax on the stone patio with a book. Horses are welcome to stay in the horse barn for $25 per night.

Brushland Eating House (1927 County Hwy. 6, Bovina, 607/832-4861, www.brushlandeatinghouse.com, $110) is primarily a restaurant, but it has a two-bedroom apartment upstairs that appeals to artists, writers, and anyone in search of a quiet retreat. It has good natural light, hardwood floors, pine cabinets, exposed beams, and white walls. Furnishings are simple, like the menu. Best of all, a good meal is just a flight of stairs away. Book at airbnb.com.

$150-200

Hanah Mountain Resort and Country Club (576 W. Hubbell Hill Rd., Margaretville, 800/752-6494, www.hanahcountryresort.com, $160-250) provides standard chain hotel-style accommodations, but the resort offers enough activities to keep you out and about the entire day. Take the free shuttle to Plattekill Mountain for some downhill mountain biking, or head out to face the Terminator golf course. A golf school on-site will help tune up your game. The resort offers numerous golf, ski, and mountain biking packages.

Nearby, at **Harmony Hill Lodging and Retreat Center** (694 McKee Hill Rd., East Meredith, 607/278-6609, www.harmonyhillretreat.com) a stay begins with a walk around the fieldstone labyrinth. Two treehouse yurts are available May-October for $125 on weekdays, $145 weekends. Or for a small group, choose the Mountain Chalet, a 1,200-square-foot cabin that sleeps up to six adults ($195-225). Set on 70 acres of meadow and woods, the property has its own trails and a creek. Guided meditation and yoga instruction can be scheduled during your stay.

Campgrounds

Peaceful Valley Campsite (485 Banker Rd., Downsville, 607/363-2211, www.nypeacefulvalley.com, $10 per person) is the place to pitch your tent. You can also rent a room in a cottage or cabin ($45-120). Canoe rentals are available by the day or by the week. An alternative is the **Little Pond Campground** (549 Little Pond State Campground Rd., Andes, 845/439-5480, www.dec.ny.gov, $22). From Route 30 in Margaretville, go south about six miles to New York City Road and then to Barkaboom Road, and the campground will be on the right.

the farmhouse at Stone & Thistle Farm

FOOD

Along Route 28

The **Arkville Bed and Breakfast** (43285 State Hwy. 28, Arkville, 845/586-1122, 7am-1:45pm Mon.-Sat., 7am-1pm Sun.) serves omelets, home fries, bacon, and a long list of specialty pancakes in a casual setting. Real maple syrup is available for extra charge. Lunch fare includes burgers and a croque monsieur on grilled challah bread.

Thursday and Sunday schnitzel nights draw a crowd at **Binnekill Square** (746 Main St., Margaretville, 845/586-4884). The rest of the week, the Swiss/American menu includes fresh fish, steaks, and pasta dishes. Kid-friendly American fare comes out of the kitchen at the **Inn Between Steak & Seafood Restaurant** (42377 State Hwy. 28, Margaretville, 845/586-4265), making it a good choice after a day on the ski hill. **The Cheese Barrel** (799 Main St., Margaretville, 845/586-4666, www.cheesebarrel.com, 8am-5pm Mon.-Sat., 8am-4pm Sun.) is a deli, coffee shop, and gourmet food store all in one. Stop in for a bowl of hot soup, ice cream cone, or jelly beans by the pound.

Downsville has the **Old Schoolhouse Inn** (Upper Main St., Downsville, 607/363-7814, www.oldschoolhouseinn.com, 11:30am-9pm Wed.-Thurs. and Sun., 11:30am-9pm Fri.-Sat., $6-31). The menu includes lobster, prime rib, and trout dishes, and you'll dine under a large collection of stuffed hunting trophies.

Blueberry pancakes are the way to go at **Woody's Kitchen** (85 Main St., Andes, 845/676-4500, 7am-2pm Thurs.-Tues., 7am-8pm Wed.). **The Restaurant at the Andes Hotel** (110 Main St., Andes, 845/676-3980, www.andeshotel.com, lunch and dinner daily, brunch Sun., $16-24) uses farm-fresh ingredients to make its wild mushroom bisque, smoked trout platter, and fried chicken BLT. Dinner specialties range from a wild boar ragout to the shrimp Veracruz.

The owners of **Two Old Tarts** (22 Lee Ln., Andes, 845/676-3300, www.twooldtarts.com, 5pm-9pm Sun., Mon., Thurs., 5pm-10pm Fri.-Sat., $5-22) started their businesses as a bakery stand at the Pakatakan Farmers Market before opening a full-fledged restaurant in 2012. The menu covers a lot of ground, from Texas beef chili to a veggie burger.

Table on Ten (52030 Main St., Bloomville, 607/643-6509, www.tableonten.com, $9-15) has captured a slice of the farm-to-table movement with a café menu that gives credit to Hudson River Valley farms including Irving Farm (coffee), Cowbella (butter and yogurt), and Last Harvest (eggs). Don't overlook the house-made ice cream and sodas. Try the fresh turmeric tonic for a twist.

A couple from Brooklyn opened **Brushland Eating House** (1927 County Hwy. 6, Bovina, 607/832-4861, www.brushlandeatinghouse.com, 5:30pm-10pm Wed.-Thurs. and Sun., 5:30pm-11pm Fri.-Sat., $10-26) in 2014 to focus on simple foods for supper. In summer, they also serve breakfast and lunch. Seasonal ingredients such as carrots and beets and cuts of meat from locally raised livestock define the menu. Try whatever cheese they are serving that night. Aside from one Long Island white, wines by the glass come from the Continent. A two-bedroom apartment above the restaurant can be home for the weekend or longer. It has hardwood floors, pine cabinets, exposed beams, and white walls. Furnishings are simple, like the menu. Book at airbnb.com.

Roxbury has a handful of decent places for a bite to eat. Situated between a lake and a golf course, **Petra Taverna** (62 Shephard Hills Rd., Roxbury, 607/326-6030, $13-25) specializes in Greek dishes including lamb chops, moussaka, and chicken souvlaki. At **Cassie's Café** (53535 State Rte. 28, Roxbury, 607/326-7020, 7am-3pm Mon.-Tues. and Thurs.-Sun., $5-8), you can order breakfast all day. Buttermilk or blueberry pancakes, a three-egg omelet, and the corned beef hash are a treat when you order them late in the afternoon. Aside from the morning fare, the lunch menu features a long list of sandwiches, wraps, soups, and salads. **Public Restaurant & Lounge** (2318 County Road 41, Roxbury, 607/326-4026, www.publicnewsaunts.com,

5pm-9pm Sun. and Wed., 5pm-10pm Thurs., 5pm-midnight Fri.-Sat.) makes a rotating menu of stews and chowders, pizzas and quesadillas, and dinner specials like flat iron steaks, tilapia filets, and pork chops. Save room for the cheesecake at the end.

Roxbury also has a gourmet food truck called **Ate O Ate** (607/326-3392, www.ateoatecatering.com). Check the website for the truck's whereabouts, and then you can order and pay online before you go. The menu rotates among dishes such as marinated duck breast and pineapple wrapped in bacon, pulled pork sliders, and butternut squash soup.

Along Route 23

In South Kortright, the **Hidden Inn** (Main St., South Kortright, 607/538-9191, www.hiddeninn.com, 5pm-9pm daily, lunch served noon-4pm Sat.-Sun., $12-18) prepares a long menu of surf-and-turf entrées alongside more exotic offerings such as frog legs and escargot. The prime rib is a popular order, and the restaurant is well known for its duck à l'orange.

If you want to escape the crowds at Windham Mountain, take a short drive to Stamford and try **Gabrielle's** (60 Main St., Stamford, 607/652-2535, www.gabriellesrestaurant.net, 3pm-9pm Mon.-Thurs., 3pm-10pm Fri.-Sat.). New owners Jim and Jill Mullen took over in early 2014, and the menu now covers a wide range of comfort foods. Start with deep-fried zucchini sticks or a plate of wings, and then move on to the cream of broccoli soup, chicken marsala, or Jack Daniels flat iron steak.

A dinner at ★ **Stone & Thistle Farm** (1211 Kelso Rd., East Meredith, 607/278-5800, www.stoneandthistlefarm.com, $35-50 per person) will change how fresh you thought farm-to-table food could be. On select Saturdays June through October, this sustainable farm offers a tour at 6:30pm followed by dinner at 7pm in an 1863 Greek Revival farmhouse. The menu is prix fixe and features the farm's own meats, dairy, and produce, plus locally grown fruits and artisan cheeses. On Sundays, the farm prepares brunch for $20 per person. Tours start at 11am, and the meal is served at noon. Families are welcome, and children may be allowed to pet the animals and help collect eggs. Stone & Thistle's cattle, sheep, and goats are exclusively grass-fed; pigs, poultry, and rabbits eat a small amount of local grains as a supplement. Reservations are required for brunch or dinner. A separate cabin by the creek and private suite in the farmhouse are available for overnight accommodations.

ENTERTAINMENT AND EVENTS

Performing Arts

The **West Kortright Centre** (49 W. Kortright Church Rd., East Meredith, 607/278-5454, www.westkc.org) is one of the premier performance venues in Delaware County. Housed in a restored Greek Revival church on Turnpike Road in West Kortright, it has hosted world-famous composers, poets, musicians and other artists since the 1970s. A series of musical performances takes place throughout the summer season, as well as gallery exhibits.

Set in a historic building in downtown Franklin, the **Franklin Stage Company at Chapel Hall** (25 Institute St., Franklin, 607/829-3700, www.franklinstagecompany.org) produces a mix of modern and classical theater. The company's free admission policy sets a fun and irreverent tone.

Bars and Nightlife

In Roxbury, the **Public Lounge** (2318 County Road 41, Roxbury, 607/326-4026, www.publicnewsaunts.com, 5pm-9pm Sun. and Wed., 5pm-10pm Thurs., 5pm-midnight Fri.-Sat.) is located across the street from The Roxbury motel. A full dinner menu is available Wednesday through Sunday. Signature cocktails include a Flamingo Cosmo that is "unabashedly pink."

Festivals

Set on a 500-acre farm and year-round campground, the **Peaceful Valley Bluegrass Festival** (Downsville) takes place in July. RV hookups and a swimming pool help beat the heat during the day, but nights can be chilly.

Listen to classical music performances at the **Honest Brook Music Festival** (off Rte. 28 between Downsville and Meridale, 607/746-3770, www.hbmf.org, $30).

SHOPPING

If you love to buy and sell goods on eBay, try the offline equivalent at one of Delaware County's professional auction houses. At **McIntosh Auction Service** (Bovina Center, 607/832-4829 or 607/832-4241, www.mcintoshauction.com), Chuck McIntosh has been in the business for 30 years. After you've won the farm, you can sample the local bounty at the **Pakatakan Farmers Market** (Kelly Round Barn, Rte. 30, Halcottsville, 845/586-3326, www.roundbarnmarket.org, 9am-2pm Sat.). A restored carriage house holds a collection of rare and used books at **Bibliobarn** (627 Roses Brook Rd., South Kortright, 607/538-1555, 10am-6pm daily).

Lucky Dog Organic Farm Store (35796 State Hwy. 10, Hamden, 607/746-8383, www.luckydogorganic.com, 10am-5pm Tues.-Fri., 8:30am-5pm Sat., 11am-4pm Sun.) is a combination farm stand/eatery/inn that grows much of its own produce on a 160-acre farm. It also carries meat, dairy, eggs, and prepared foods from other local farms, as well as candles, soaps, and other gifts.

Maple Shade Farm (www.mapleshadefarmny.com) runs two markets in Delhi (2066 County Hwy. 18, 607/746-8866) and Margaretville (213 Fair St., 607/435-5508), where you can pick up fresh berries in summer, stock up on apple cider in the fall, and buy gift baskets in December.

Blink Gallery (454 Lower Main St., Andes, www.blinkgallery.net, 11am-6pm Sat., 11am-3pm Sun. and holiday Mondays) features contemporary artists in a wide variety of media including ceramics, pastels, art glass, and hand-crafted pieces of jewelry. At the other end of Main, **Paisley's Country Gallery** (75 Main St., Andes, 845/676-3533, 10am-5pm Thurs.-Sun. Apr.-Feb.) is also worth a look for decorative dishes, kilim rugs, and sterling silver jewelry at reasonable prices.

INFORMATION AND SERVICES

The **Delaware County Chamber of Commerce** (5½ Main St., Delhi, 607/746-2281, www.delawarecounty.org) is located in Delhi and maintains an informative website.

GETTING THERE AND AROUND

It's easier to rent a canoe than a car in outdoor-oriented Delaware County, but you'll need wheels to get around this rural county, as public transportation is virtually nonexistent. **Albany International Airport** (518/242-2200, www.albanyairport.com) is your best bet for a rental. Some of the national rental companies also have outposts in Kingston.

Upper Hudson Valley and the Northern Catskills

Look for ★ to find recommended sights, activities, dining, and lodging.

Highlights

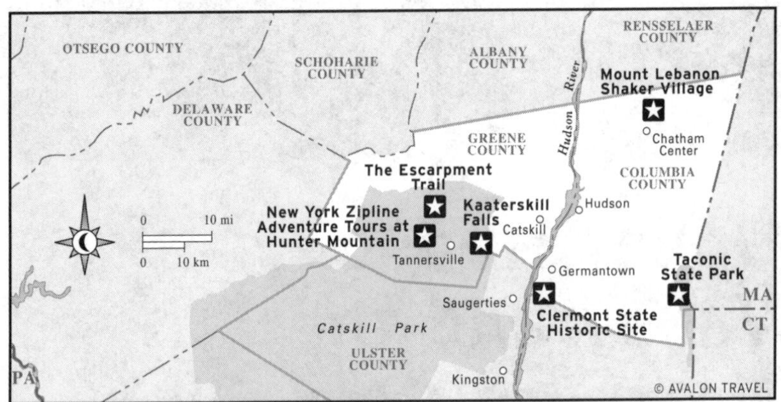

★ **Kaaterskill Falls:** An hour-long walk on a well-marked but strenuous trail leads to the base of the 180-foot falls that inspired many a Hudson River School painter. With the old tanneries and hotels long gone, the falls are actually more pristine today than they were 100 years ago (page 193).

★ **The Escarpment Trail:** Near the town of Haines Falls, a 1,500-foot plateau marks the site of the old Catskill Mountain House, one of America's first resort hotels. The five-state view from the edge of the escarpment makes the park one of the most popular in the Catskill region today (page 193).

★ **New York Zipline Adventure Tours at Hunter Mountain:** Soar above the treetops on the longest and highest zipline in North America (page 195).

★ **Clermont State Historic Site:** The classical Clermont Estate on the Hudson River north of Germantown belonged to the high-society Livingston family (page 211).

★ **Taconic State Park:** This expansive green space encompasses 5,000 acres at the base of the Taconic Range, near the Massachusetts and Connecticut state lines (page 215).

★ **Mount Lebanon Shaker Village:** This remarkable collection of artifacts offers an informative introduction to the Shaker way of life (page 216).

The Catskill and Berkshire Mountains frame the upper—and most rugged—section of the Hudson River Valley. In between, small lakes and dense hardwood forests alternate with rolling hills and cultivated fields. Rural communities dot the landscape, welcoming visitors with historic sights, heirloom vegetables, antiques shops, and the promise of outdoor adventure.

Striking in any season, the Upper Hudson Valley makes an exceptionally enjoyable winter getaway, when every inn has a wood fire burning and hearty meals warm you from the inside out. Greene and Columbia Counties' many lodges, bed-and-breakfasts, and country inns create that cozy feeling the Austrians call *gemütlichkeit*. Cross-country skiers can explore varied terrain on private and public lands, while downhill skiers and riders can find steeps and parks for all levels at the Windham, Hunter, Belleayre, and Catamount resorts. And for those who don't measure fun in vertical feet, snowmobiles, snowshoes, and ice skates provide a few more alternatives.

In August 2011, Tropical Storm Irene struck the Catskills with heavy rainfall, high winds, and severe flooding. It was the most severe storm in the area in at least a century. The Windham and Hunter ski areas sustained the greatest damage. Although some businesses were able to reopen within days, many were forced to close at least temporarily and some never recovered. The aftermath is still visible in the form of slides along Route 23A near Haines Falls and on Twin Mountain. Many of the creeks have been permanently widened and filled with debris.

If you're the kind of person who travels to eat, the Upper Hudson Valley also holds a few surprises. Bistro Brie & Bordeaux in Windham, Local 111 in Philmont, and Fish & Game in Hudson should top any gourmet's must-try list.

And there's another way to sample the fruits of the land: by rolling up your sleeves and picking what's in season. There is at least one farmers market, roadside stand, or pick-your-own orchard in just about every town in Columbia and Greene Counties.

Previous: view of North-South Lake and the Hudson River Valley in the Catskill Mountains; Kaaterskill Falls in autumn. **Above:** the canning station in a family sugarhouse.

Upper Hudson Valley and the Northern Catskills

PLANNING YOUR TIME

With a selective itinerary, you can easily tour Greene or Columbia in a day of scenic driving. (It takes less than an hour to drive the length of either one.) But you'll need a long weekend to take in a few of the historic sights and outdoor activities these counties offer. Allow an hour for the round-trip hike to Kaaterskill Falls or a day to summit one of the High Peaks. Tours of Clermont and Olana last about an hour, plus time to walk the grounds and contemplate the views. Serious antiques shoppers can spend a full day or more in downtown Hudson.

Many visitors to the Upper Hudson Valley plan weekend getaways around a farm visit, local festival, or bed-and-breakfast inn. Others choose to take in a history tour or special meal en route between New York City and New England or western New York State.

In Greene County, the loop along Routes 23 and 23A covers about 40 miles and takes less than an hour to complete by car with no stops. An out-and-back excursion to Coxsackie along Route 385 and the Hudson River adds another hour round-trip. Columbia County has three parallel routes running north to south: Route 9G follows the river's edge, the Taconic State Parkway is the fastest, and Route 22 runs along the foot of the Taconic Hills in the eastern part of the county.

Starting at the southern border with Dutchess County, take a favorite scenic drive that follows Route 9G about a half hour north to the city of Hudson, then meander on local roads up to Kinderhook and Chatham. From there, you can zip back to your starting point along the Taconic, or continue east and take Route 22 south through Hillsdale and Copake. The entire loop should take 2-3 hours with no stops.

Greene County

In the days before New York City residents could hop a flight to Bermuda for the weekend, they vacationed in the Catskills. If you had the means to vacation in remote Greene County during the early to mid-19th century, you might have stayed at the world-famous Catskill Mountain House—along with Alexander Graham Bell, Henry James, Oscar Wilde, Ulysses S. Grant, Mark Twain, and their contemporaries. A one-day journey from New York City began with a steamboat ride to Catskill Landing and concluded with a harrowing 12-mile, four-hour stagecoach ride to the eastern edge of the High Peaks region.

Between the Kaaterskill Creek and Sleepy Hollow, a steep and narrow road climbed to the top of a rocky plateau called Pine Orchard. Here, the classical Mountain House stood with its 13 Corinthian columns, painted stark white against a backdrop of hemlock and white pines and surrounded by hundreds of square miles of untamed forest. In the words of author Roland Van Zandt, the hotel offered the "ideal combination of wilderness and luxury" and symbolized "a nation's young wealth, leisure, and cultural attainments."

Modern rail and jet travel changed Greene County forever, sending would-be visitors to more exotic destinations. In 1963, the New York State Department of Conservation declared the long-abandoned hotel a danger to hikers and burned what remained of the building to the ground one winter morning. Visitors today can only imagine the imposing white structure and the famous people who stayed in it, but the setting remains as enchanting as two centuries ago.

Located on the west side of the Hudson, with Albany County to the north and Ulster County to the south, Greene County has 20 miles of riverfront, several bustling valley and mountain towns, and Kaaterskill Falls—at 260 feet, the highest waterfall in the east. The magical surroundings inspired American literary master Washington Irving to write the tale of Rip Van Winkle, the hen-pecked husband who wandered into the mountains and fell into a 20-year sleep.

Named after Revolutionary War General Nathanael Greene of Rhode Island, the original Greene County consisted of four towns: Catskill and Coxsackie on the river, Freehold in the valley, and Windham on the mountaintop. Agriculture, forestry, and a few dozen tanneries drove the local economy in the early days. But the opening of the Erie Canal in 1825 diverted ships and manufactured goods from Catskill to Troy, sending the once-prosperous county into a tailspin—until a group of Romantic Era writers and painters, including Thomas Cole, popularized the region for its natural beauty.

Dairy farms and orchards came next, along with German and Irish immigrants and summer residents. From the polka dancers at the Mountain Brauhaus to the International Celtic Festival at Hunter Mountain, the county retains much of its immigrant influence today.

After a steady decline during the mid-20th century, Greene County is quietly capturing the imagination of travelers, writers, and outdoor enthusiasts again. Author Allegra Goodman chose the valley as the setting for her first novel, *Kaaterskill Falls* (Delta, 1999), which intertwines the stories of three Orthodox Jewish families from New York City who spend summers in the area. On the mountaintop, an effort is under way to revive Hunter Village with a focus on art and cultural events.

Members of the Catskill 3500 Club visit Greene County to climb many of the highest peaks in the range, including Blackhead, Black Dome, and Thomas Cole mountains. The county also supports three winter ski resorts—Hunter Mountain, Cortina Mountain, and Windham Mountain—which offer city dwellers a convenient alternative to driving four hours to New England resorts or traveling by plane to the Rockies.

Note that the weather is often cooler, windier, and wetter on the mountaintop than at the river's edge. Bring layers, regardless of the season.

ALONG THE RIVER: ROUTE 385

Rip Van Winkle Bridge

The Rip Van Winkle Bridge spans the Hudson at mile 112, counting from the south. If you approach the crossing from Routes 9G or 82, both in Columbia County, the first sight of the Catskills' purple-gray peaks may catch you off guard. For generations, the bridge has stood as a divider between civilization and wilderness, or what many locals call "up country." The range's cluster of High Peaks rises to 4,000 feet, just 12 miles west of the sea-level river.

Begin your tour of Greene County with a walk across the mile-long span of the bridge. Built during the Great Depression at a cost of $2.4 million and opened in 1935, the bridge connects the small cities of Catskill and Hudson, ushering visitors into the forever-wild lands of the Catskill Preserve. (Car toll $1, eastbound only.) The New York State Bridge Authority has preserved the look of the original Dutch colonial toll plaza so as not to alter the view from the Olana State Historic Site directly across the river.

Park in a lot near the toll plaza on the Catskill side of the bridge. (Pedestrians only on the sidewalk. Bikes must use the narrow traffic lanes.) Pause at the middle of the span to take in the 360-degree views. The river below is tidal freshwater. To the north, Stockport Middle Ground Island is one of four sites belonging to the National Estuarine Research Reserve System. The Hudson-Athens Lighthouse, on a smaller island to the northwest, was established in 1874 and had a live-in keeper until 1949. The gentle hills of Columbia County rise in the east behind the waterfront city of Hudson. And the clay-tiled rooftop of Olana, the Persian-style castle of painter Frederic Church, stands above the trees to the southeast. Turn back west, and the Catskill Mountains beckon.

Catskill

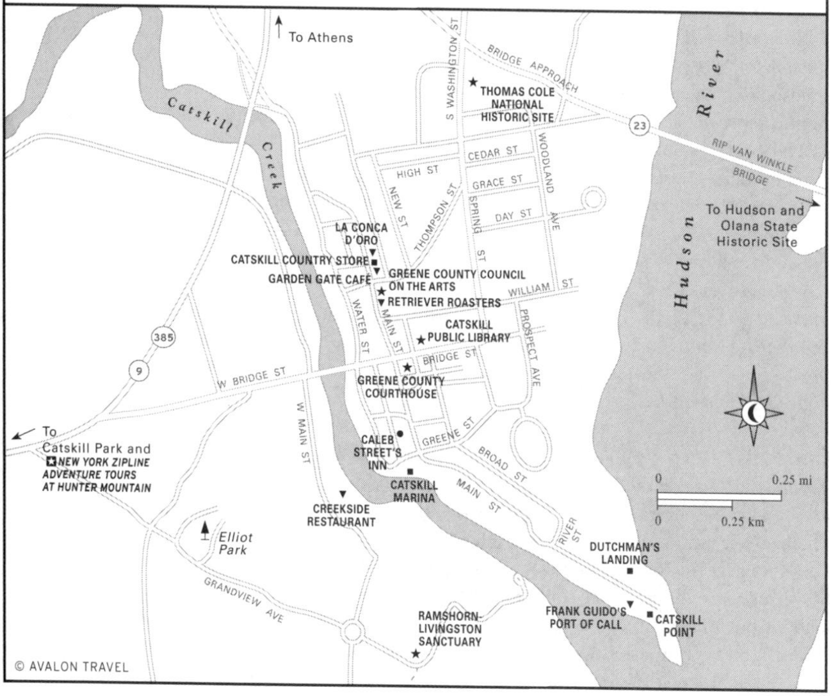

Catskill

Historian Henry Brace wrote in 1876 that early Dutch settlers purchased the village of Catskill in 1684 for "a gun, two shirts, a kettle, two kegs of beer, and, as usual, a little rum." For more than two centuries, the village thrived as an agricultural crossroads and a gateway to the mountains. But the building of the Rip Van Winkle Bridge marked the beginning of a long decline. These days, the town is dreadfully quiet in winter; come summer, however, the waterfront awakens with boating, outdoor dining, and an open-air market.

The flurry of development taking place across the river in Hudson has spread to Main Street in Catskill as well. The crowds are yet to come, but optimistic entrepreneurs have opened new restaurants, cafés, and gift shops, giving the village an up-and-coming feel.

Catskill's Main Street runs parallel to Catskill Creek, which widens and empties into the Hudson just past the center of town. (There is a municipal parking lot off Main.) Two-story row houses line both sides of the street, many of them housing attorneys' offices, as Catskill is the county seat. The **Greene County Courthouse,** at the intersection of Main and Bridge (also Rte. 385), is a white, neoclassical structure that towers over its neighbors. Behind it is the **Catskill Public Library** (1 Franklin St., 518/943-4230, www.catskillpubliclibrary.org, noon-8pm Mon. and Wed., 10am-8pm Tues., 10am-5pm Thurs.-Fri., 10am-2pm Sat.), in another neoclassical building. The library has a local history collection with many books about the steamboats of the Hudson.

Main Street takes a sharp turn to the left as you approach the mouth of the Catskill Creek. Follow West Main to its end to reach Catskill

Point, Dutchman's Landing, and Mariner's Point Restaurant. Many community activities take place here during the summer months.

RamsHorn-Livingston Sanctuary (Grandview Ave., 518/678-3248, www.scenichudson.org, dawn-dusk) is the largest tidal swamp forest along the Hudson. Paddlers can rent boats and explore some 480 acres via 3.5 miles of waterways that lead out to the river itself. Heron, waterfowl, and other birds feed here, and American shad and bass come in spring to spawn. Open dawn to dusk year-round, the sanctuary is jointly owned and operated by the Scenic Hudson Land Trust and the **National Audubon Society** (P.O. Box 1, Craryville, 518/325-5203, ny.audubon.org/rheinstrom-hill).

Cedar Grove

Around the time that the Romantic Era began to take hold in America, a young artist named Thomas Cole ventured up the river from New York City in search of inspiration for a series of sketches. The canvases and exhibition that followed put him in the national spotlight and helped to make the Catskills world-famous.

Cole spent most of his adult years at Cedar Grove in the town of Catskill, now the **Thomas Cole National Historic Site** (218 Spring St., Catskill, 518/943-7465, www.thomascole.org, 10am-4pm Thurs.-Sun. May-Oct., adults $10, seniors and students $9, children 12 and under free). He painted landscapes and taught students including Frederic Church, who later established his own residence on a hillside across the river. With a shared interest in painting mountain peaks and waterfalls instead of portraits, Cole and his students became known collectively as the Hudson River School of painting.

Today, the pale yellow house sits on the outskirts of town, close to a busy traffic light and a Mobil gas station. Despite the encroaching surroundings, the views continue to inspire awe. On display inside the house and studios are a few of Cole's paintings, as well as furniture and family memorabilia. A $1 million restoration of the main house was completed in 2003. A restoration of Cole's studio was unveiled in 2004.

Athens

Head north on County Route 385 (Spring St.) from Catskill about four miles, and you'll come to the much smaller village of Athens. The Dutch arrived here in 1686, and the town was a landing point for the Athens-Hudson ferry service, which dates back to the late 1770s. Built into a hillside, with a splash of color on some of its old Victorian homes, the town hints of San Francisco, except for the two industrial plants that frame its borders.

It's rare to find many cars in the **Cohotate Preserve** (Rte. 385, www.gcswcd.com/env-ed/cohotate), south of town, but the site is worth a visit for its river views and environmental information. The parking lot is well marked with a large sign on Route 385. A gravel road leads to the river, and from there, an interpretive trail describes the habitats of local plants, animals, and fish, leading to spectacular river views. The Greene County Environmental Education Center recently added a pond to attract and support a greater variety of wildlife for nature walkers. Students of Columbia-Greene Community College take environmental classes in a new lab on the premises. For those who want to get on the water, there is a well-maintained boat ramp with parking for 25 cars just north of town.

Coxsackie

Continuing north along Route 385 brings you to Coxsackie (cook-SAK-ee), borrowed from an Algonquin Indian expression meaning "owl hoot" or "place of wild geese." Reed's Landing was once a busy center for shipbuilding and transportation, and today the town retains an industrial feel. The remains of a Hudson River freighter called the *Storm King* rest in shallow water near the town's River Park.

When the icehouses of the Hudson became irrelevant, creative entrepreneurs discovered they were ideal for growing mushrooms. The Greene County Historical Society has estimated that by the late 1930s, Coxsackie-based Knaust Brothers controlled about 85 percent of the country's mushroom business as a supplier to companies like Heinz and Campbell's.

One mile south of the Coxsackie boat launch is the **Hudson River Islands State Park** (1 Hailes Cave Rd., Rte. 157, Voorheesville, 518/732-0187, www.nysparks.com), on the islands of Gay's Point and Stockport Middle Ground. Accessible only by boat, the park protects many rare and endangered species and allows picnics, fishing, and camping Memorial Day-Columbus Day.

Moving away from the river, the main attraction in Coxsackie is the oldest surviving dwelling in upstate New York, a 1663 stone house now known as the **Bronck Museum** (90 County Rte. 42, 518/731-6490, www.gchistory.org, noon-4pm Wed.-Fri., 10am-4pm Sat. and holiday Mondays, 1pm-4pm Sun., Memorial Day weekend-Oct. 15, adults $5, youth 12-15 $3, children 5-11 $2, under 5 free). In 1662, Pieter Bronck, a Dutchman who lived in Albany, received a land patent from the British government to settle in modern-day Coxsackie. He built a one-room structure in 1663 and expanded it 20 years later to include a loft with an Indian lookout. In 1738, Bronck's grandson added a new brick house to the property.

The museum consists of these two homes—furnished with period art, linens, ceramics, and silver—and several Dutch colonial barns. The Victorian Horse Barn contains a model of the famous Catskill Mountain House and other Greene County memorabilia. A single, center pole supports the roof of the Thirteen-Sided Barn. And the Dutch Barn has its original wood floor, made of pegged oak planks three inches thick. The Greene County Historical Society runs the museum and holds special events throughout the year. Check www.gchistory.org for a current calendar.

Unless you are continuing on to Albany via Route 9W or the New York State Thruway, now is a good time to retrace your steps to Catskill and head west on Routes 23 or 23A toward the mountaintop.

ALONG ROUTE 23A

★ Kaaterskill Falls

Asher B. Durand, another of the Hudson River painters, spent many summers in Palenville and established one of America's first artist colonies here in the 1840s. This quiet town sits at the base of the High Peaks and the edge of the Catskill Park. Washington Irving's Rip Van Winkle fell into his 20-year slumber above Palenville in the Kaaterskill Clove.

Leaving town, you enter the Catskill Park, and the road becomes narrow and steep with retaining walls and hairpin turns. Ice-climbers scale the frozen waterfalls in winter, while hikers take to the trails in spring, summer, and fall. Look for the trailhead to Kaaterskill Falls about a mile into the ascent. Thomas Cole wrote of the falls:

> There is a deep gorge at the midst of the loftiest Catskills, which, at its upper end, is terminated by a mighty wall of rock; as the spectator approaches from below, he sees its craggy and impending front rising to the height of three hundred feet. This huge rampart is semi-circular. From the centre of the more distant or central part of the semi-circle, like a gush of living light from Heaven, the cataract leaps, and foaming into feathery spray, descends into a rocky basin one hundred and eight feet below.
>
> "The Falls of Kaaterskill in Winter," from the *New York Evening Post,* March 29, 1843

With the old tanneries and hotels long gone, the falls are actually more pristine today than they were a hundred years ago. An hour-long walk (2.7 miles) on a well-marked but strenuous trail brings you to the base of the falls and back. (It is also possible to reach the top from the North Lake Public Campground; however, the descent along the waterfall is extremely dangerous and not advised.)

★ The Escarpment Trail

The first town you reach on the mountaintop,

driving west on Route 23A, is Haines Falls, at 2,200 feet elevation. A small green hut before the turnoff to North Lake has visitors information. Gas, groceries, and banking services are all located along Main Street (Rte. 23A), and several places in town rent snowmobiles and mountain bikes. Turn right on County Route 18 (North Lake Rd.) to reach North Lake Public Campground and trails leading to the escarpment, a 1,500-foot plateau upon which the sprawling Catskill Mountain House once rested. Poet and journalist William Cullen Bryant described the site like this:

> On that point, scarce visible on the breast of the mountain, the beautiful and the gay are met, and the sounds of mirth and music arise, while for leagues around the mountain torrents are dashing, and the eagle is uttering his shriek, unheard by human ear.
>
> As quoted in *The Catskill Mountain House,* by Roland Van Zandt

By virtue of its remote setting within a day's journey from thriving New York City, the antebellum Catskill Mountain House became one of America's first luxury resorts. Under the direction of Charles L. Beach, son of a stagecoach operator, the inn drew influential artists, designers, businessmen, and politicians from the entire Atlantic corridor for a period of more than 50 years. Some guests stayed a week, while others spent the full summer in the cool mountain air. Beach expanded the original Greek-style building rapidly to keep up with demand, growing from 10 rooms in 1824 to more than 300 by the 1880s.

The Catskill Mountain House remained a focal point of the American Romantic Movement until the advent of modern rail and auto transportation diverted visitors away from the region. By 1950, the building stood in ruins. Today, it is lost to history. The view, however, continues to astound first-time visitors. On a clear day, you can see five states from the edge of the escarpment, making the park one of the most popular in the Catskills.

Tannersville

Tannersville bears the responsibility of reminding locals and visitors of an unfortunate episode in Catskill history. Around the turn of the 19th century, the business of manufacturing leather became lucrative for those who were willing to endure the labor-intensive process. When mountaintop tanners discovered that hemlock bark served as an effective tanning agent, they began to strip the virgin forest of its trees, peeling the bark away and leaving the trunks to rot on the forest floor. By 1855, the forest had been stripped of almost every hemlock tree, and the mountaintop had to reinvent itself.

Tannersville didn't actually incorporate until after the tannery boom had passed, but the centrally located **Mountain Top Arboretum** (Rte. 23C, 518/589-3903, www.mtarboretum.org, open year-round) seems to make amends for the past. Stop by for a lesson in native and exotic trees and shrubs. You can wander across seven acres in a guided or self-led tour, or join one of many horticultural education programs.

Extending in both directions from the arboretum, Main Street is sporting a new look: Charming Victorians freshly painted in purples, reds, and yellows give the place an updated yet old western feel.

Hunter Mountain

As soon as temperatures dip below freezing, the 1,100 snow guns at **Hunter Mountain** (Rte. 23A, 518/263-4223, www.huntermtn.com, 8:30am-4pm daily) begin to paint the mountain white. A winter destination since 1960, Hunter still attracts diehard skiers from the Tri-State Area.

You can walk to the sleepy town of Hunter from the parking lot, as long as you aren't wearing ski boots. Many of the buildings on Main Street flooded during Hurricane Irene in 2011; those who could afford to rebuilt over the next few years. The Catskill Mountain Foundation (CMF) has set up shop in Hunter Village. It is a nonprofit organization dedicated to revitalizing the mountaintop with

the ski lift at Hunter Mountain

cultural events and programs. Look for its free *Catskill Mountain Guide,* which has a detailed calendar of events.

★ New York Zipline Adventure Tours at Hunter Mountain

The most exciting summer attraction at Hunter Mountain is a 4.6-mile zipline that opened in 2010 as the longest and highest course in North America (Hunter Mountain, Rte. 23A, 518/263-4388, www.ziplinenewyork.com, year-round morning and afternoon tours). The family-friendly Mid-Mountain ($89) canopy tour is designed for all levels, while the Skyrider tour ($119 Mon.-Fri., $129 Sat.-Sun.) sends the adrenaline rushing as you reach a height of 600 feet and have to complete segments up to 3,200 feet long. This is an extreme sport, and you may reach speeds of 50 miles per hour on the first line. Allow three hours to complete the entire course.

Leaving Hunter on Route 23A, you pass Route 296, a shortcut to Windham. An alternative and more scenic route, however, is to continue west until County Route 17, the turnoff to Jewett, which winds its way through orchards and historical homes up to Maplecrest, just outside of Windham.

If you skip the scenic drive and head toward Lexington, you'll soon pass the Baroque-style lanterns of the **St. John the Baptist Ukrainian Catholic Church** (518/263-3862, www.brama.com/stjohn/shop.html, 9am Mass daily, additional service 10am Sun., store hours noon-4pm Tues.-Fri., 10am-2pm and 6pm-8pm Sat., 11:30am-2pm Sun.). Built of cedar logs imported from British Columbia, the church serves as a spiritual and cultural center for Ukrainians living in the United States and represents the traditional architecture and wood carvings of the Carpathian highland people. The church hosts art exhibits and a folk art store in a separate community center.

Prattsville

Route 23A meets up with Route 23 out of Windham in an open field at the Batavia Kill crossing. From there, it is a mile into Prattsville, another mountaintop village. You can't drive through Prattsville without learning a thing or two about its founder, the eccentric Colonel Zadock Pratt. For some 13 years in the early 19th century, Pratt ran one of the world's largest and most successful tanneries, and he used the profits to build present-day Prattsville. According to local lore, he completed the building of a new tannery dam in November 1824, as the first layer of ice was forming on the Schoharie Creek, and then celebrated by swimming the length of the dam.

Despite his role in destroying a large chunk of the Catskill forest, Zadock was well liked by his community, as his generosity far outweighed his shameless self-promotion. His life's achievements are depicted in a bas-relief sculpture on a large, flat rock at the outskirts of town. Called Pratt Rock, the stone carving includes the tannery, a hemlock tree, and many of Pratt's family members.

In the center of town, Pratt's former residence is now the **Zadock Pratt Museum**

(Main St., Prattsville, 518/299-3258, www.prattmuseum.com, 10am-5pm Fri.-Mon.). It contains period furnishings, a Steinway piano, photographs of Pratt, and a model of his tannery.

ALONG ROUTE 23

Windham Mountain

From the intersection of Routes 23 and 23A, it is a nine-mile drive along the Batavia Kill to **Windham Mountain** (Rte. 23, Windham, 518/734-4300, www.windhammountain.com). With a base elevation of 1,500 feet and a summit of 3,100 feet, Windham attracts New York City day-trippers by the busload. Mogul experts head for the bumps on Wheelchair and Wedel, while speed demons let loose on Wolverine. Intermediate skiers enjoy the two-mile-long Wrap Around trail, and a run through the terrain park ends with an enormous gap jump at the bottom.

Windham Village is about a mile from the ski resort parking lot, too far to walk in winter weather. Along Main Street, contemporary art galleries alternate with skier-friendly eateries. A few of the ski shops rent mountain bikes in summer.

From Windham, the Mohican Trail (Route 23) begins to descend back down to the valley floor, and the peaks of Blackhead and Black Dome come into view. Local artist **Alec Alberti** (4924 Rte. 23, Windham, 518/734-4689, www.albertiwoodcarving.com) runs a creative firewood stand by sculpting split wood into a new design each winter—for example, a barn or a railroad train. The western trailhead for the Escarpment Trail begins here as well.

East Durham

Irish immigrants were among the first settlers on the north side of Route 23. Stonewalls mark old boundaries along County Route 31, and every sign in Durham and East Durham has a shamrock, or at least green lettering. A visit to **Guaranteed Irish** (2220 Rte. 145, East Durham, 518/634-2392, 9am-5pm daily), at the corner of County Routes 31 and 145, will put you in the proper frame of mind to enjoy this town. An enormous retail space has an overwhelming selection of Irish-made goods.

Next door is Darby's Irish Pub and Restaurant, the local watering hole. The **Zoom Flume Water Park** (Shady Glen Rd. off Rte. 145, East Durham, 800/888-3586, www.zoomflume.com, 10am-6pm June-Sept., some weekends until 7pm, adults $27.99, kids 7 and under $20.99, infants 2 and under

the trail map at Windham Mountain

free) is a popular attraction for families on hot summer days. Lazy River is a gentle tube ride, while Black Vortex shoots you through a completely dark tunnel and the Canyon Plunge is just about vertical. There is a short open tube run for the littlest thrill seekers and a zipline for the older set. Stay-and-play packages are available at **The Country Place Resort** (www.thecountryplace.com) adjacent to the park.

On the same road, **Hull-O Farms** (10 Cochrane Rd., Durham, 518/239-6950, www.hull-o.com), founded in 1779, is a working dairy farm that allows overnight guests to participate in everyday farm activities.

Freehold and Greenville

There are two reasons to divert to Freehold when traveling along Route 23: to take an aerial tour in a classic J-3 Cub or to savor the French-inspired menu at **Ruby's Hotel** (3689 Rte. 67, Freehold, 518/634-7790, www.rubyshotel.com). The **Freehold Airport** (4000 Rte. 67, Freehold, www.freeholdaviation.com, 9am-6:30pm daily Apr.-Dec.) offers daily scenic rides (weather permitting), a ground and flight school, and general aviation services. The restaurant is about a 10-minute walk from the runway.

A few miles up the road from Freehold on Route 32, William Vanderbilt constructed a Queen Anne-style home in 1889. Today, the white, two-story building is a county inn set on six acres of manicured lawns and decorated in Victorian and country accents. In summer, the **Greenville Arms 1889 Inn** (11135 Rte. 32, Greenville, 888/665-0044, www.greenvillearms.com, $118-235) hosts a series of Hudson River Valley Art Workshops in its Carriage House Studio.

Cairo

Once the center of a booming Greene County poultry business and a major producer of fresh fruits, Cairo (CARE-o) is a good place to stop for services. You'll find groceries at Hannaford supermarket, gas at Cumberland Farm, a liquor store, and a True Value hardware. A new set of decorative streetlights and real concrete sidewalks line Main Street, but the town is still lacking in restaurants.

The primary colors of the **Mahayana Buddhist Temple** (700 Ira Vail Rd., 518/622-3619, 7am-7pm daily, donations accepted) look oddly out of place in South Cairo, 2.5 miles from Route 23B. Members of the New York City-based Eastern States Buddhist Temple of America retreat to the woods here

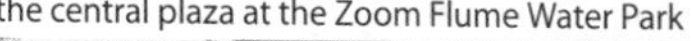
the central plaza at the Zoom Flume Water Park

The Most Interesting River in America

At the conclusion of an 1859 journey from the river's source to its end, Poughkeepsie resident Benson John Lossing wrote of the Hudson:

> It is by far the most interesting river in America, considering the beauty and magnificence of its scenery, its natural, political, and social history, the agricultural and mineral treasures of its vicinage, the commercial wealth hourly floating upon its bosom, and the relations of its geography and topography to some of the most important events in the history of the Western hemisphere.
>
> *The Hudson: From the Wilderness to the Sea,* originally published by H. B. Nims & Co., 1866

for quiet contemplation. A red-and-yellow arch leads the way down a steep driveway to the temple, set on two small ponds. Visitors are welcome to explore the site.

Don't leave Cairo without wandering through the hamlets of Purling and Round Top. Newly built log cabins alternate here with 150-year-old farmhouses, and fields have grown up around abandoned farm equipment. Leaving Cairo on Mountain Avenue (County Rte. 24), you'll pass the Purling post office, Shinglekill Falls, and a roller rink that has been open more or less continuously since the 1950s.

SPORTS AND RECREATION

Downhill Skiing

You haven't skied the Northeast until you've endured subzero temperatures, frostbite warnings, and the wet blast of artificial snow in your face. The après-ski whirlpool tub (there are many options) becomes an all-important finish to the day. **Hunter Mountain** (Rte. 23A, Hunter, 800/367-7669, www.huntermtn.com, 8:30am-4pm weekends and holidays and 9am-4pm weekdays mid-Nov.-Apr., $72 weekend/holiday, $62 weekdays) has three mountains that can handle 15,000 skiers per hour, but lift lines can still run up to an hour on busy weekends. The addition of a new quad at Hunter West helps manage the crowds.

Windham Mountain (33 Clarence D. Lane Rd., Windham, 800/754-9463, www.windhammountain.com, $75 weekend/holiday, $58 weekdays) is open 8am-4pm weekends and 9am-4pm weekdays mid-November through mid-April, as long as the weather cooperates. You can also ski at night Fridays, Saturdays, and some holidays 4pm-10pm from December until March. Pick up Route 23 West at New York State Thruway Exit 21. Book lift tickets and rental equipment, or listen to the snow report updated daily, at www.windhammountain.com.

A left turn off Route 23A before Selena's Diner in Tannersville leads to a hemlock-lined road and the entrance to **Cortina Mountain** (227 Clum Hill Rd., Hunter, 518/589-6378 or 866/926-7846, www.cortinamountain.com, weekends $20, weekdays $15). Cortina maintains a tubing run, terrain park, and paintball facility. The owners modeled their recent renovation plans on the upscale Hotel Scribner Hollow. When the lifts start running, the tiny hill may once again become a fine place for kids to learn to ski or snowboard. With a base elevation of 2,200 feet, Cortina has the highest base of any ski area in the Catskills; however, lifts have not been running for several years.

Nordic Skiing

Several areas on the mountaintop offer varied terrain for Nordic skiers: The **Mountain Trails Cross Country Ski Center** (Rte. 23A, Tannersville, 518/589-5361, www.mtntrails.com, adult full-day $20, $18 after 2pm, teens $18, juniors $10, full-day rental $20) has 35 kilometers of groomed, patrolled trails with rentals, sales, a lodge, lessons, and a snack bar on-site. Daily hours vary according to snow conditions. Note: The summer Escarpment Trail is not safe for cross-country skiing.

In the valley, the **Winter Clove Inn Nordic Skiing Area** (Winter Clove Rd., Round Top, 518/622-3267, www.winterclove.com) opens 400 acres to the public, with rentals available. Expert trails climb into the hills, while the easier trails follow a streambed.

Snowshoeing, Tubing, and Snowmobiles

Snowshoeing is one of the fastest-growing sports in America, and Greene County offers plenty of great trails. **Mountain Trails Cross Country Ski Center** (Rte. 23A, Tannersville, 518/589-5361, www.mtntrails.com) offers trails of varying grades that traverse bridges and wind through conifers. Ski patrol monitors the trails for safety. **North Lake Public Campground** (County Rte. 18, Haines Falls, 518/589-5058, www.dec.ny.gov) has trails along wooded areas and up to the site of the Catskill Mountain House with stunning views of the Hudson River Valley. Rent equipment in nearby Hunter. The trails at **Colgate Lake** (off Rte. 78, East Jewett) run through an open meadow with great views of the Blackhead Mountain Range. Take Route 23A to Tannersville, and turn onto Route 23C, and then right onto Route 78 by the post office.

Cortina, Hunter, and Windham all have 4- to 12-lane snow tubing runs with lift access. Tickets range from $20 all day at Cortina to $25 at Windham and Hunter.

Several outfitters run guided snowmobile trips: **Rip Van Winkle Ranch** (Rte. 23A, Haines Falls, 518/589-6215, www.ripvanwinkleranch.com) has snowmobile and ATV rentals for use on mountain trails.

Hiking

Hikers can't get enough of the northern Catskills in summer and fall. They hit the trails in search of tasty wild blueberries, geological wonders, or simply a view and a breath of fresh air. Trailhead parking lots fill early on sunny weekends, but with a little determination, it's still possible to escape the crowds. Although the most popular trails are well maintained, it's not uncommon to encounter some bushwhacking on many hikes. It's a good idea to carry water, topographical maps, and a compass or GPS, no matter how far you plan to go. *Catskill Trails: A Ranger's Guide to the High Peaks, Book One,* by Edward G. Henry (Black Dome Press, 2000), covers more than 20 hikes in the area, including the trails to Kaaterskill Falls and the escarpment.

Major trailheads are clustered around the towns of Hunter, Jewett, and Prattsville. From Route 23A in Hunter, you can access the escarpment and the vista from the site of the old Catskill Mountain House, as well as Roundtop and Twin Mountains. The Big Hollow Road in Jewett leads to trails that summit the High Peaks of Blackhead, Black Dome, and Thomas Cole. Farther west, near Prattsville, you can reach trails to West Kill, Huntersfield, and Bearpen Mountains.

To see what inspired the romantic landscapes of the Hudson River School painters, hike a portion of the 23-mile-long Escarpment Trail, which connects Route 23 in East Windham with the North Lake Public Campground to the south. A three-day out-and-back hike with loops at each end traverses 30 miles of thick hardwood forests and hemlock groves, allowing time for diversions to the summits of Windham High Peak, Acra Point, and Blackhead Mountain along the way.

Dramatic elevation changes make for challenging terrain, so plan to take it slow. Camping is not restricted below 3,500 feet, but it's best to set up camp in designated areas to minimize the impact on the forest. You can fill water bottles at numerous natural springs along the trail.

For a guided hike, the **Mountain Top Historical Society** (Haines Falls, 518/589-6657, www.mths.org) leads summer and fall trips. There is no charge to join, but the organization asks participants to complete a registration form in advance. The site links to online versions of area topographical maps on maptech.com.

Back at the river's edge, the Scenic Hudson Land Trust has rescued a seven-acre stretch of shoreline from development and created **Four-Mile Point Preserve** (Four-Mile Point Rd., Coxsackie, 845/473-4440, www.scenichudson.org, dawn-dusk daily), which features a nature trail that leads to an overlook 60 feet above the river. From the Rip Van Winkle Bridge, follow Route 385 almost eight miles north to Four-Mile Point Road.

Cycling

Cyclists in Greene County can find miles of traffic-free roads to pedal, but be prepared to climb. The Tour of the Catskills (www.tourofthecatskills.com) is a three-day cycling race that takes place in August each year. Part of the event is a 77-mile gran fondo ride around the Route 23A-Route 23-Route 32 loop. Along the way, you'll gain 5,538 feet of elevation. The course map is posted on the tour's website.

Many old logging roads offer scenic and challenging mountain biking terrain. And when the snow melts away, Hunter opens part of its trail system to mountain bikers who want to start at the top. Hikers may try to tell you otherwise, but nonmotorized bikes are allowed on most of the trails in the area; take caution, however, when considering a loop on the ridge trail. The terrain is steep and rocky, making much of it unsuitable for riding.

Several shops on the mountaintop offer rentals and trail maps: **Hunter Mountain Biking** (Rte. 23A, Hunter, 888/486-8376, www.huntermtn.com, weekends July-Oct.) has trails at the base and summit of the mountain, with lift access. **The Bike Shop at Windham Mountain Outfitters** (Rte. 296 & South St., Windham, 518/734-4700, www.windhamoutfitters.com) rents bikes and leads trips for all levels.

Golf

Greene County has 10 golf courses with scenic views of the surrounding countryside. Most are open April through November. The **Blackhead Mountain Lodge & Country Club** (Blackhead Mountain Rd., 518/622-3157, www.blackheadmtn.com, weekend 18 holes with cart $50, midweek $37) maintains a challenging 18-hole par 72 course with stunning views of the High Peaks. **Christman's Windham House Country Inn and Golf Resort** (5742 Rte. 23, Windham, 518/734-4230, www.windhamhouse.com, $45 weekdays, $60 weekends) operates two courses—an 18-hole and a 9-hole—with four sets of tees. Tannersville has two nine-hole par 35 courses that are open to the public: **Colonial Country Club** (Main St., Tannersville, 518/589-9807, $45) and the **Rip Van Winkle Country Club** (3200 Rte. 23A, Tannersville, 518/678-9779, www.rvwcc.com, weekends and holidays 9 holes $18, 18 holes $22, weekdays 9 holes $15, 18 holes $18, after 4pm $12, cart extra). The **Windham Country Club** (Rte. 296, Windham, 518/734-9910, www.windhamcountryclub.com, $25/47 weekday/weekend) is a challenging 18-hole public course with a five-acre driving range and pro shop on-site.

Swimming and Boating

A dip in a mountain lake or a paddle along the river are the watersports of choice in Greene County. **North Lake** (County Rte. 18, Haines Falls, 518/589-5058, www.dec.ny.gov) offers swimming and nonmotorized boating, and lifeguards are on duty Memorial Day through Labor Day. Farther west, **Dolan's Lake** (Ski Bowl Rd., Hunter, 518/263-4020) has a picnic area and lifeguard on duty in summer months.

Several marinas offer boaters convenient access to the Hudson. Part of the New York State Parks system, the **Athens Boat Launch** (Rte. 385, Athens, 518/732-0187) has a hard surface ramp and parking for 25 cars. The **Coxsackie Boat Launch** (Reed St., Coxsackie, 518/731-2718), also a state facility, has a hard surface ramp and parking for 36 cars and trailers.

In Catskill, turn right at the bend in Main

Street onto Greene Street to get to the full-service **Catskill Marina** (Greene St., 518/943-4170, www.catskillmarina.com), which has gasoline, 20 boat slips (150 feet maximum), showers, restrooms, laundry, and even a heated pool. Two other marinas, Hop-O-Nose and Riverview Marine Services, are located farther out on West Main. **Riverview** (103 Main St., Catskill, 518/943-5311, www.riverviewmarineservices.com) rents kayaks, rowboats, and canoes. **Dutchman's Landing** (Lower Main St., 518/943-3830) has four boat ramps, picnic tables, and barbecues.

The **Hudson River Watertrail Association** (www.hrwa.org) sponsors numerous outings and operates facilities for river-goers. The group is lobbying to develop a water trail from the mouth of the Hudson to the Great Lakes.

Fishing and Hunting

Whether you want to catch shad, bass, or trout, **River Basin Sport Shop** (66 W. Bridge St., Catskill, 518/943-2111, www.riverbasinsports.com) will provide all the tackle and advice you need for fishing in the area. Around the same time, the Batavia Kill near Prattsville becomes a mecca for fly fishers. Bass season begins on the third Saturday in June and runs through October.

Licensed hunters may take grouse, pheasant, turkey, deer, black bear, and small game from public wilderness areas or private clubs during specified seasons. For regulations and information, contact the **New York State Department of Environmental Conservation** (866/933-2257, www.dec.ny.gov).

Spas

The Mountain Club Spa inside the Kaatskill Mountain Club at Hunter Mountain (62 Liftside Dr., Hunter, 800/486-8376, ext. 3017, www.mountainclubspa.genbook.com) sets the mood for a relaxing and rejuvenating weekend. Massage therapy services including aromatherapy, reflexology, and hot stones run $100-125 for a 50-minute treatment. Facials, body wraps, and nail services are also available.

ACCOMMODATIONS

Country inns with a colonial ambience are the theme for places to stay in Greene County. You can find a few modern hotels near the ski resorts and budget motels along the highways, but the accommodations with the most character include a hearty breakfast and a friendly chat with the innkeeper.

$100-150

Just above the Catskill Marina, **Caleb Street's Inn** (251 Main St., Catskill, 518/943-0246, www.calebstreetsinn.com, $100-160), at the corner of Greene and Main, occupies a white 1790s house with black shutters and a veranda that overlooks Catskill Creek. Its bright guest rooms feature hardwood floors, large windows, and antique beds and dressers.

Linda and Hugh are your friendly hosts at the creekside **Tumblin' Falls House** (Rte. 24, Purling, 518/965-0536, www.tumblinfalls.com, $100-175). The inn accommodates 8-10 guests in a pale yellow Victorian that's set back from the road by the falls and across from the retro roller rink. All four rooms have mountain views, and a large, terraced deck and hot tub overlook the 30-foot falls. The Falls View Suite has the best view.

★ **The Thompson House** (19 Rt. 296, Windham, 518/734-4510, www.thompsonhouse.com, $72-144 per person including meals) has a loyal clientele of families who return year after year—and generation after generation—for reunions and other group events. This is one of the few old-time Catskill resorts that have managed to adapt to the changing needs of modern travelers. There are 80 rooms in six buildings, each a bit different from the next. Some have air-conditioning, balconies, and refrigerators and/or mountain views. All have private baths, basic cable, and phones. There is Wi-Fi, a library, fitness center, heated pool, and laundry room. Also on the 12-acre property are tennis courts, boccie ball, horseshoes, a putting green, and nature trail. Children under 4 stay for free, and the youngest paying child, aged 4-14, stays free when sharing the room with two adults. There is a onetime charge of $15 to have a crib or rollaway bed set up in the room. Minimum stay is seven nights, usually Saturday to Saturday. Breakfast and dinner, included in the per-person rates, are served in a family-style dining room. The food is hearty country fare, and there's plenty of it. Inquire about golf packages with the Windham Country Club.

In winter, the same owners open **Evergreen at the Thompson House** (20 Rte. 296, Windham, 518/734-4510, www.thompsonhouse.com, weekends $175-260, midweek $80-150) with free shuttle service to/from the ski area, which is one mile away.

A mile from the slopes, on the road that connects Windham to Hunter, is the modern ★ **Hotel Vienna** (107 Rte. 296, Windham, 518/734-5300, www.thehotelvienna.com, $100-200). Straight out of the Austrian Alps, rooms have beamed ceilings, cherry furniture, lace curtains, and tiled balconies. Amenities include cable TV, phones, and air-conditioning, as well as an indoor pool and whirlpool tub. For those returning from the slopes, the innkeeper serves afternoon cookies and tea by the breakfast room fireplace. Midweek specials and ski packages are available.

Sunny Hill Resort & Golf Course (352 Sunny Hill Rd., Greenville, 518/634-7642, www.sunnyhill.com, $805-980 pp per week, including all meals) is popular with golfers and families. The resort has 100 basic motel-style rooms in seven different buildings gathered around the 18-hole golf course. Some rooms have balconies and mountain views.

Many repeat visitors at the **Greene Mountain View Inn** (132 S. Main St., Tannersville, 518/589-9886, www.greenemountainviewinn.net, $100-125 weekends) come to attend services at the 100-year-old synagogue located four doors down the street. A 1981 Ms. Pac-Man machine and big-screen TV in the lounge area complement the antique jukebox and mirror in the breakfast room. Rooms are small but clean, with natural wood accents and sloping roofs on the top floor; some have more recently updated bathrooms than others. No. 19, the newest guest room, is a mini-loft with four steps leading from the bed area up to a small sink and shower. The room has mountain views on two sides, and many guests request it in advance, despite its small size.

$150-200

The ★ **Winter Clove Inn** (Winter Clove Rd., Round Top, 518/622-3267, www.winterclove.com, $95-140 per person per night, including all meals) is a great choice for value and hospitality in a historical setting. It rests on 400 acres at the base of North Mountain, bordering the Catskill Forest Preserve. A creek meanders through the property, and when the winter storms roll in, guests can ski on 15 kilometers of marked cross-country trails. Inside, guest rooms feature a colonial decor, with hardwood floors, four-poster beds, and lacy white linens. The hotel attracts more suburban families than city folk. Its amenities include heated indoor and outdoor swimming pools and a nine-hole golf course. The old carriage house was converted into a bowling alley and soda fountain in the 1950s. Repeat visitors to the bowling alley quickly learn to use the warp in the floor to their advantage.

Winwood Inn (Main St., Windham, 518/734-3000, www.winwoodinn.com, $129-259), previously the Windham Arms, offers free transportation to Windham from the train station in Hudson, 40 minutes away. Its 55 modern rooms are painted in earthy tones and are minimally furnished. Ask for a mountain view, or you may end up facing the courtyard instead. Amenities include an indoor fitness center and movie theater.

The combination of antique furnishings and original, contemporary art at the **Greenville Arms 1889 Inn** (11135 Rte. 32, Greenville, 888/665-0044, www.greenvillearms.com, $118-235) gives the place a unique feel. Some rooms in the main house of this country inn feature canopied or four-poster beds and private porches or balconies. Owners Eliot and Letitia Dalton also offer two rooms in a Victorian cottage on the grounds.

Family-run **Albergo Allegria** (43 State Rte. 296, Windham, 518/734-5560, www.albergousa.com, $150-250) operates a bed-and-breakfast inn in an 1892 Victorian, as well as a separate cottage on Main Street and a farmhouse on Maplecrest Road. Rooms in the inn range from small and cozy to spacious and private. Guests rave about the frittatas, and best of all, the kitchen stays open 24/7.

The Kaatskill Mountain Club at Hunter Mountain ($250 and up) has everything you need for an indulgent winter getaway: lodging in suites, its own bar/restaurant, a swimming pool, spa, and massage services. Accommodations are studios or suites with up to three bedrooms. Packages are offered for the zipline in summer and ski lift tickets in winter.

Over $200

The expansive **Scribner Hollow Lodge** (13 Scribner Hollow Rd., Hunter, 518/263-4211 or 800/395-4683, www.scribnerhollow.com, $230-300) is a rustic mountain chalet with modern amenities, including an underground pool and spa called the Grotto. Deluxe rooms are decorated in a southwestern, hunting lodge, or country motif. The Prospect Restaurant on the premises stocks an impressive wine cellar to accompany entrées such as locally smoked Catskill rainbow trout, pheasant sausage, and various wild game dishes. Mains are $23-34.

Built in the 1940s and renovated in 2008, the ★ **Mountain Brook Inn** (57 Rte. 23C/Hill St., Tannersville, 518/589-6740, www.hotelmountainbrook.com, $250-375) suits travelers in search of modern comforts and country quiet in a classic Adirondack lodge setting. You'll have three choices for accommodations. Rooms in the main lodge have queen beds and mountain views. The east lodge is a separate building with some larger rooms and more mountain views. Pets are allowed in this building, but not in the main lodge. Private cabins have king-size beds, fireplaces, and private porches. All rates include a full breakfast with choices such as eggs any style, buttermilk pancakes, bread pudding French toast, or a breakfast skillet. The innkeepers help make any stay here special and memorable.

Campgrounds

Greene County has two state campgrounds and more than a dozen private campgrounds to choose from. **North Lake Public Campground** (North Lake Rd., Haines Falls, 518/589-5058, www.dec.ny.gov, early May-Oct.) has 200 tent and RV sites, plus picnic areas, hot showers, flush toilets, and a boat launch. **Devil's Tombstone State Campground** (Rte. 214, Hunter, 845/688-7160, www.dec.ny.gov, May 16-Sept. 1) has 24 sites, picnic tables, and a playground.

Catskill Campground (79 Castle Rd., Catskill, 518/678-5873, www.dec.ny.gov, May 15-Columbus Day) has 50 sites for tents and RVs. You can also set up camp at the long-standing **Whip-O-Will** (3835 County Rte. 31, Purling, 518/622-3277 or 800/969-2267, www.whip-o-will.com, Apr.-Oct. 15).

FOOD

Along the River: Route 385

The **Garden Gate Café** (424 Main St., Catskill, 518/943-1994, www.welcometocatskill.com/GardenGate, 6:30am-3pm Mon.-Fri., $5) serves breakfast and lunch with a menu covering everything from omelets to burgers. A couple of tables are set up on the sidewalk for al fresco dining. Up the street a bit, **La Conca D'Oro** (440 Main St., Catskill, 518/943-3549, 11:30am-9pm, $7-11), a small brick building with green awnings, serves dependable Italian fare to a local clientele. Gnocci with cream sauce, osso buco, and rotating appetizer specials won't disappoint. Reservations recommended. **Retriever Roasters** (394 Main St., Catskill, 518/943-5858, www.retrieverroasters.com, 8am-2:30pm Mon.-Fri., 8am-noon Sat., $4-8) is a Catskill mainstay for caffeine and café fare.

River views are the main reason to go to **Frank Guido's Port of Call** (7 Main St., Catskill, 518/943-5088, $10-30) at Catskill Point. The menu puts seafood in the spotlight with steamed littleneck clams, lobster salad, ahi tuna, and the like. The owners also operate a popular restaurant in Kingston, Mariner's Harbor. At the Hop-O-Nose marina, **Creekside Restaurant** (160 W. Main St., Catskill, 518/943-6522, 11:30am-9pm daily, $11-30) is an unexpected delight with memorable crab cakes, scallops, oysters, and fish-and-chips.

One of the Hudson River Valley's culinary destinations is found on a country road a few miles west of Coxsackie. Named after its owner and chef, **Damon Baehrel** (776 Rte. 45, Earlton, office voicemail 518/634-2338, information line 518/269-1009, reservations by email only reservationrequests@damonbaehrel.com, www.damonbaehrel.com, seating times change seasonally) began in 1990 as a showcase for the chef's former catering business, Sagecrest Catering. He built and landscaped the property by hand to create a warm and elegant restaurant setting. A 2002 renovation added more elbow room and a wine cellar. Baehrel has mastered the element of surprise in fine dining. His prix fixe menu ($168 per person) features 9-12 courses—many of which arrive at the table unannounced. He works alone in the restaurant, cooking and serving, and on the surrounding 12-acre property that sustains the restaurant year-round with native and cultivated ingredients. The restaurant currently has a three-year waiting list, with guests from around the world waiting to take in the four-hour-plus experience.

Along Route 23A

Whatever time of day you pass through town, chances are you'll find something to eat in Tannersville, where new restaurants and cafés seem to be opening all the time. Just outside of town, the **Deer Mountain Inn** (790 County Rte. 25, Tannersville, 518/589-6268, www.deermountaininn.com, 5pm-9pm Sun., Mon., Thurs. and 5pm-10pm Fri.-Sat., $16-29) has been renovated and reopened with a new chef at the helm. For small plates, there's a smoked trout toast with deviled eggs and house pickles. Monkfish cheeks is among the more interesting main dishes, served with braised escarole, sausage, potatoes, and brown butter bread crumbs.

The Astor House (5980 Main St., Tannersville, 518/589-9500, 10am-6pm Thurs.-Mon.) draws a crowd for chocolate croissants, cranberry oat bread, and raspberry coconut pecan bars. The adjoining Mountain Market stocks produce from nearby RSK Farm in Prattsville.

The **Last Chance Antiques and Cheese Café** (6009 Main St., Tannersville, 518/589-6424, www.lastchanceonline.com, 11am-8:30pm daily, and until 9pm Fri.-Sun., $10-20) is known as much for its comfort food as its antiques. French dip, meatloaf, a tuna melt, or the chicken potpie won't disappoint.

★ **Maggie's Krooked Café & Juice Bar** (Main St., Tannersville, 518/589-6101, www.krookedcafe.com, 7am-7pm daily, $12-15) is known for a reliable cup of coffee, delicious homemade muffins, and hearty breakfast fare. Locals say the prices are high, but where else are you going to get an icy fruit smoothie?

Pancho Villa's Mexican Restaurant (3087 Main St., Tannersville, 518/589-5134, www.panchovillasmex.com, 4pm-9:30pm Mon. and Wed.-Thurs., 4pm-10pm Fri., noon-10pm Sat., noon-9pm Sun., average main dish $13) will satisfy a craving for south-of-the-border cuisine.

Aside from fast food in the lodge, dining options at Hunter Mountain include **Van Winkles** at the Kaatskill Mountain Club (62 Liftside Dr., Hunter, 518/263-5580, www.kaatskillmountainclub.com, $10-25) where Chef Tim Lang is a Catskill native and CIA graduate. In addition to hearty pub fare, he offers vegetarian and gluten-free dishes, such as a strawberry and fig salad and a Thai vegetable stir-fry. The restaurant opens at noon Friday-Sunday and at 3pm Monday-Thursday.

Along Route 23

After an eight-year run with the popular Freehold Country Inn, the Buel and Suhner families sold the business and moved to the next town over. Their newly renovated ★ **Mountain View Brasserie** (10697 Rte. 32, Greenville, 518/966-5522, www.mountainviewbrasserie.com, noon-3pm and 4pm-9pm Mon. and Wed.-Sat., noon-9pm Sun.) opened in 2007 to widespread applause. Its large, U-shaped dining room maintains a cozy feel. Menu highlights include a classic French onion soup, an outstanding cut of prime rib, traditional seafood bouillabaisse, and some unusual wines, including a pinot noir from Switzerland.

A 10-minute walk from the Freehold airstrip is **Ruby's Hotel** (3689 Rte. 67, Freehold, 518/634-7790, www.rubyshotel.com, 5pm-9pm Thurs. (summer only), 5pm-10pm Fri., 5pm-10pm Sat., $18-29), in a restored art deco building that dates back to the 1800s. New York City chef Ana Sporer serves French-influenced cuisine, including duck confit and coq au vin, as well as steaks and seafood. The restaurant has a bar and soda fountain in the front and a formal dining room in the back. Outdoor seating is available in the summer.

The stately ★ **Bavarian Manor** (866 Mountain Ave., Purling, 518/622-3261, www.bavarianmanor.com, 5pm-9pm Thurs.-Sat., 1pm-8pm Sun., $18-25) sits on 100 acres of prime Catskill forest in Purling. The business has hosted German Americans (and those who wish they were) since 1865. A decidedly old-world German restaurant serves all the requisite dishes—schnitzel, sauerbraten, spaetzle, rouladen, and bratwurst—as well as seafood and wild game. Upstairs, each of 19 guest rooms has a private bath, TV, fireplace, whirlpool tub, and air-conditioning.

Maassmann's Restaurant (Blackhead Mountain Rd., Round Top, 518/622-3157, www.blackheadmountaingolf.com, 5:30pm-9pm Wed.-Sun. May-Oct., 5:30pm-9pm Fri.-Sat., 5:30pm-8:30pm Sun. Nov.-Apr., $12-26), at the Blackhead Mountain Golf Course, is popular with locals for special occasions like Easter dinner. On the menu are American and German dishes. Call ahead to reserve the Stammtisch Corner, which seats 5-7 people.

Hartmann's Kaffeehaus (1507 Hearts Content Rd., Round Top, 518/622-3820, www.hartmannskaffeehaus.com, 9am-5pm Wed.-Sun.) has been in business since 1959 and is well known among locals for its traditional homemade pastries and cakes. It is also a small café serving breakfast and lunch. Fare

making maple snow cones

is standard sweet stuff, but tasty and prepared with care. Breakfast mains are omelets and French toast, and lunch offers sandwiches, wraps, chicken, fish-and-chips, and house specialty bratwurst and German potato salad.

The Alpine Pork Store (Rte. 23B, South Cairo, 518/622-3056, www.alpineporkstore.com, 9am-5pm Thurs.-Fri., 9am-3pm Sat.), in South Cairo, sells German-style sausages or wursts, as well as a full menu of fresh meats cut to order. This is a good place to stop on the way to a ski condo at Windham Mountain.

The smell of fresh-baked bread wafts out of ★ **Bistro Brie & Bordeaux** (5386 State Rte. 23, Windham, 518/734-4911, www.bistrobrieandbordeaux.com, 5pm-9pm Thurs.-Sun.) in the afternoon as the kitchen prepares for the evening meal. This is an unusual find on the mountaintop—real country French food, from an endive Roquefort salad and classic French onion soup to bouillabaisse and a duck breast with poached pears and port sauce. Dine on the heated front porch or choose a table inside.

The Catskill Mountain Country Store & Restaurant (5504 Rte. 23, Windham, 518/734-3387, www.catskillmtncountrystore.com, 9am-3pm Mon.-Fri., 8am-4pm Sat., 8am-3pm Sun.) serves breakfast all day with entrées made from organic eggs and milk. An adjoining gift shop has a wide selection of house-made preserves, pickles, and mustards, as well as New York maple syrup. The refrigerator has smoked trout, Cowbella milk and yogurt, and hard salami. Pies are baked following the owner's grandfather's recipes. The maple pecan fudge is a sinful treat. A second location opened in Tannersville in 2014 (6014 Main St., Tannersville, 518/589-6777).

Messina's Restaurant (5658 Rte. 23, Windham, 518/734-4499, www.messinasitalianrestaurant.com, opens at 4:30pm Mon. and Wed.-Sun., brunch noon-4pm Sun., $16-28) has been in business for a quarter century making Italian standards with a local flare. The casual setting features views of the ski slopes. Rainbow trout almondine is sautéed in a lemon butter and white wine sauce. Chicken cutlets can be prepared four ways: Francese, marsala, classic, or parmigiana. Orecchiette pasta comes with a sauce made of chopped broccoli and sweet Italian sausage. Main dishes come with warm bread.

ENTERTAINMENT AND EVENTS

Bars and Nightlife

The German theme continues all year

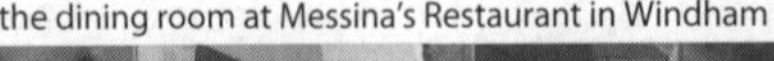

the dining room at Messina's Restaurant in Windham

long in Round Top, where the **Mountain Brauhaus** (430 Winter Clove Rd., Round Top, 800/999-7376, www.crystalbrook.com) pours Dinkelacker beer by the stein. Polka dancers take the floor on weekend nights. A much younger crowd gathers at **Dublin Slopes Bar** (6002 Main St., Tannersville, 518/589-5006, www.dublinslopes.com, 5pm-4am Fri.-Sat.) in Tannersville for après-ski refreshments and late-night entertainment. Also in Tannersville, **The Spinning Room** (5975 Main St., Tannersville, 518/589-7746, www.thespinningroombar.com) is a divvy place that plays DJ music seven days a week year-round.

Van Winkles at the Kaatskill Mountain Club (62 Liftside Dr., Hunter, 518/263-5580, www.kaatskillmountainclub.com) is a quieter alternative to the main **Hunter Mountain Bar** (518/263-4223). Take advantage of happy hour drink prices 4pm-6pm daily.

Après-ski options at Windham include the **Cave Mountain Brewing Company** (5359 Rte. 23/Main St., Windham, 518/734-9222, www.cavemountainbrewing.com) for a round of microbrews and OK pub fare. Seasonal brews include a chai milk stout and blueberry stout. There is also a gluten-free pale ale. The bar opens at 5pm Monday, Thursday, and Friday and at noon Saturday and Sunday. Windham also has the lively **Rock'n Mexicana Cantina and Grill** at the Winwood Inn (5220 Main St., Windham, 518/534-3000, www.winwoodinn.com). Margaritas are the way to go, of course.

Festivals

Bass tournaments draw large crowds to Catskill in spring, when the striped bass are running. Anglers should head to **River Basin Sports** (66 W. Bridge St., Catskill, 518/943-2111, www.riverbasinsports.com, 8:30am-5pm Tues.-Sat.) for dates and details. For longtime Catskill residents, the run of the American shad heralds the arrival of summer.

For 27 years, the **Michael J. Quill Irish Cultural & Sports Centre** (2267 Rte. 145, 518/634-2286, www.mjqirishculturalcenter.com) has hosted the **East Durham Irish Festival,** drawing participants from across the Hudson River Valley with Irish music performances and a one-acre "map" of Ireland, decorated with flags of the country's provinces and counties.

The Catskill Mountain Foundation theater shows a mix of independent and Hollywood films. In summer, a series of Hunter Mountain Festivals draws large crowds, with the **International Celtic Festival** and **Oktoberfest** (Belleayre Ski Center, Lower Lodge, State Rte. 28, Highmount, 845/586-3175 or 845/586-2246, www.gacnc.org/oktoberfest.htm, $8, children under 12 free) among the most popular events. A calendar is available at www.huntermtn.com.

In summer, beginner and experienced artists can enroll in a series of **Hudson River Valley Art Workshops** (South St., Greenville, 518/966-5219 or 888/665-0044, www.artworkshops.com) at the Greenville Arms 1889 Inn. Weekend and weeklong programs cover watercolor, oil, acrylic, pastel, drawing, or collage. Tuition costs $405 for a weekend course and $610 for a weeklong course. A package with accommodations and dinners is $804 for three nights and $1,342 for six nights.

Mudfest (14527 Main St., Prattsville) is an August tradition that began in the aftermath of Hurricane Irene. Prattsville residents now take the opportunity to celebrate their recovery from the flooding with a mud-filled weekend. Local businesses get in on the action with mud-like food and drinks, mud games, sculptures, and more. Games, a craft fair, exhibits, and live music all accompany the festivities, and proceeds go back to the community for improvements.

SHOPPING

Antiques, crafts, and locally made foods are among the best finds in Greene County.

Farm Stands

Local farmers bring produce to the **Riverside Market** (Dutchman's Landing, Catskill,

518/622-9820) on Saturday mornings June through October.

In summer, stop by **Black Horse Farms** (10094 Rte. 9W, Athens, 518/943-9324, www.blackhorsefarms.com, 9am-6pm daily) for fresh-picked corn on the cob and other seasonal produce. The family-run store also sells baked goods, plants, maple syrup, and honey.

Catskill Country Store (430 Main St., Catskill, www.catskillcountrystore.com, 11am-6pm daily) stocks a limited selection of Hudson River Valley cheeses and produce, as well as picnic basket essentials in a small storefront on Main Street in downtown Catskill. The oatmeal cookies from Bread Alone are irresistible.

At the corner of Routes 23A and 32 outside of Catskill, **Story Farms** (4640 Rte. 32, Catskill, 518/678-9716, 9am-5pm daily) is one of the most popular stands in the area. Locals stop for corn, tomatoes, peppers, onions, squash, apples, pears, plums, peaches, and whatever else has been picked that day.

On the mountaintop, **The Catskill Mountain Country Store & Restaurant** (5504 Rte. 23, Windham, 518/734-3387, www.catskillmtncountrystore.com, 9am-3pm Mon.-Fri., 8am-4pm Sat., 8am-3pm Sun.) has a great selection of house-made preserves you can bring home. Pickled beets, relish, and jams all are made using locally grown produce. The back of the store has home goods, candles, and a few books and games for children. (This is a different business from the store in downtown Catskill.)

Pop into **Traphagen's Honey and Gourmet Shop** (Rte. 23A, Hunter, 518/263-4150, 9am-5pm Fri.-Mon.) on the way out of Hunter to satisfy a craving for sugar.

Antiques and Eclectic

At the offbeat **Last Chance Antiques and Cheese Café** (6009 Main St., Tannersville, 518/589-6424, www.lastchanceonline.com, 11am-8:30pm daily, and until 9pm Fri.-Sun.), what began as a way of luring antiques shoppers in the door has evolved into a full-fledged gourmet food store and restaurant. The store is covered floor to ceiling in antique instruments and Victorian-era accessories. Enjoy an unusual brew (there are 300 to choose from), a cheese platter, or a rich chocolate fondue.

With support from the Hunter Foundation, **Tannersville Antique & Artisan Center** (6045 Main St., Tannersville, 518/589-5600, www.tannersvilleantiques.com, 10am-6pm

the Catskill Mountain Country Store in downtown Catskill

Thurs.-Mon.) represents 20 different artists and vendors including photographer Francis X. Driscoll, whose work captures striking images of the Catskill Forest Preserve.

Guaranteed Irish (2220 Rte. 145, East Durham, 518/634-2392, 9am-5pm daily), at the corner of County Routes 31 and 145, contains a wide variety of Irish-made goods, including handcrafted jewelry, tweed jackets, and Celtic music. With 5,000 square feet of space, Guaranteed Irish bills itself as America's largest Irish import store.

Magpie Bookshop (392 Main St., Catskill, 518/303-6035, www.magpiebookshop.com, 10am-6pm Mon. and Wed.-Sat., noon-5pm Sun.) is the place to browse nature books and other good reads on a rainy day. If you forgot to bring a book for a stormy ski weekend, head over to **Kaaterskill Fine Arts and the Village Square Bookstore** (Hunter Village Square, Hunter, 518/263-2001, 10am-5pm Fri.-Sat., 10am-3:30pm Sun.).

Play in Catskill (362 Main St., Catskill, 518/291-6476, www.playcatskill.storenvy.com, 1pm-6pm Thurs., 1pm-7pm Fri.-Sat., 1pm-5pm Sun.) is an artist collective that sells handmade wooden and fabric toys online and in a storefront on Main Street. **Mahalo Gifts and Jewelry** (397 Main St., 518/943-7467, www.mahalocatskill.com, 10am-6pm Mon.-Sat.). sells a wider variety of gifts. Shop here for shawls, candles, jewelry, baby gifts, and kitschy signs that say things like "Bed-and Breakfast. Make both yourself."

Opportunities for shopping in Windham trend toward country kitsch. **Carole's Gift Emporium** (5335 Main St./Rte. 23, Windham, 518/734-3387) has Yankee Candles and Christmas decorations year-round.

INFORMATION AND SERVICES

Visitor information is available at Exit 21 off the New York State Thruway/I-87. The **Greene County Tourism office** (700 Rt. 23B, Leeds, 518/943-3223 or 800/355-2287, www.greatnortherncatskills.com, 9am-4pm daily year-round, longer hours in summer) will answer questions through its website; by email, phone, and fax; or in person. After hours, an outdoor kiosk provides information on local sights and accommodations.

The **Greene County Council on the Arts** (398 Main St., Catskill, 518/943-3400, www.greenearts.org, 10am-5pm Mon.-Sat.) keeps a calendar of countywide gallery exhibits, performances, lectures, and related events.

an antiques store outside of Windham Village

Apples to Apples

New York State produces some 28 million bushels of apples each year, and almost a quarter of those come from orchards in the Hudson River Valley. These are small operations that sell their harvest at farm stands, farmers markets, and as you-pick activities.

Growing conditions favor many varieties of the fruit, from best sellers like McIntosh, Empire, and Gala to heirlooms like the Esopus Spitzenburg and Cox's Orange Pippin. Flavors vary widely from sweet to tart.

Farming techniques have changed in recent years to dense plantings with built-in irrigation and trellises to support heavy branches. Dwarf trees make picking much more efficient.

In the late summer through fall, apples appear on many local menus. When no longer fresh and crisp, they can be baked into pies, mashed into sauce, dried, cooked down into apple butter, or distilled into cider and liquor. The possibilities are endless. Seek out an orchard or two as you roam about the farmland.

GETTING THERE AND AROUND

Bus

Adirondack Trailways (800/858-8555, www.escapemaker.com) offers daily service year-round from the Port Authority Terminal in New York City. Stops include Catskill, Palenville, Hunter, and Windham, and you can walk to town from the bus stops, or inquire about hotel and resort shuttles.

Train

Greene County does not have its own rail service, but **Amtrak** (800/872-7245, www.amtrak.com) stops in Hudson across the river, about eight miles from Catskill Village. You can get a taxi from the station, and some area hotels also run free shuttles.

Car

The New York State Thruway (I-87) and Route 9W are the primary north-south arteries through Greene County. Exit the Thruway at Exit 21 for the most direct approach to the mountaintop. Routes 23 and 23A traverse the county from the Rip Van Winkle Bridge to the border with Delaware County.

Enterprise Rent-a-Car (78 Green St., 518/828-5492, www.enterprise.com) has a location in Hudson.

Columbia County

Framed by the Hudson River to the west and the Berkshire Mountains to the east, the landscape of Columbia County features rolling hills, green pastures, and extensive woodlands. Many longtime farmers in Columbia County have converted their struggling dairy operations into niche organic businesses that cater to local restaurants and residents who join community-supported agriculture programs. The transition has allowed many local growers to keep their connection to the land while earning an almost satisfactory living. The historic city of Hudson got its start as a center for whaling and shipping in the early 19th century and later became a center for iron ore production. An industrial past continues to haunt the city.

Named after Christopher Columbus, Columbia County's history is closely tied to that of the powerful Livingston family. In the late 17th century, Scottish entrepreneur Robert Livingston began buying land along both sides of the Hudson from Native American tribes. In the early 1700s, King

George I deeded him a large tract of land covering most of present-day Columbia County. He became the first lord of Livingston Manor, which served as the county seat with its own representation in the New York State legislature. Six more generations of Livingstons held prominent political and economic positions in the area until the mid-20th century, when the family's riverside property, Clermont, was handed over to the state.

ALONG THE HUDSON: ROUTE 9G

★ Clermont State Historic Site

Wild turkeys roam the grounds at Clermont (Clear Mountain, in French), the former riverside estate of Robert Livingston Jr., who is also known as Robert of Clermont, or simply as the Chancellor. Robert Jr. served as New York State chancellor, signed the Declaration of Independence, and later became ambassador to France. In 1728, he inherited 13,000 acres of present-day Columbia County from his father, the first lord of Livingston Manor, and built a Georgian-style riverside home between 1730 and 1750. The house was designed to catch stunning views of the Catskill Mountains across the river.

The British burned this first home to the ground during the Revolutionary War, as punishment for Livingston's support of colonial independence. Margaret Beekman Livingston, who managed the estate during the war, escaped with a grandfather clock that remains in the foyer today. She promptly rebuilt the home in time to host George and Martha Washington in 1782.

When he wasn't involved in national affairs, Robert of Clermont turned his attention to entrepreneurial projects. For example, he introduced merino sheep from France and partnered with Robert Fulton to build the first steamship to cruise the Hudson.

Frozen in time since the start of the Great Depression, the manor reflects the tastes of the seven generations that lived in it. A crystal chandelier in the drawing room came from 19th-century France, and the library contains books from the 17th century. The dining room, which was restored in January 2004, has a marble fireplace mantel. And the original house telephone sits on a table outside the dining room. (The telephone number was 3.) A frieze over the fireplace in the study depicts Alice Livingston and her two daughters, the last residents of the estate. Oddly, an entire room upstairs is dedicated to pets of the family.

Today, the beautifully landscaped grounds of the 500-acre **Clermont State Historic Site** (1 Clermont Ave., Germantown, 518/537-4240, www.friendsofclermont.org, 11am-4pm Wed.-Sun. and Monday holidays Apr. 2-Oct. 31, 11am-3pm Sat.-Sun. Nov. 1-Dec. 20, adults $5, seniors/students $4, children under 12 free) are open to the public year-round. A popular time to visit is mid-May, when the lilacs are in bloom.

The visitors center, located in the old carriage house, stocks a good selection of local interest books. And a reference library in the house is open by appointment. Nearby Germantown has gas stations, ATMs, and the obligatory Stewart's Shop.

Olana State Historic Site

Ten miles north of Germantown stands another historic residence, in every way quite the opposite of Clermont. Landscape painter Frederic Edwin Church began his career in 1846 under the tutelage of Thomas Cole and went on to earn worldwide recognition. At age 24, he became the youngest artist ever elected to the National Academy of Design. As a painter who also grasped the power of marketing, Church learned how to generate hype and income for his paintings. He often showed a single painting at a time and charged admission for anyone who wished to view it.

Though he traveled extensively during his lifetime, Church held a strong connection to the Hudson River Valley and chose to settle on 126 acres just south of the present-day Rip Van Winkle Bridge. Following a trip to the

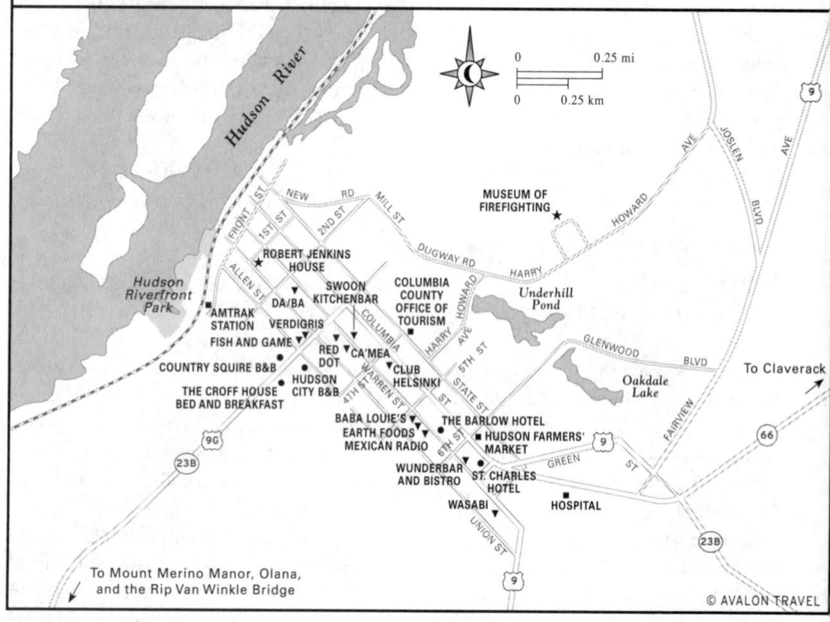

Middle East, he designed a sprawling Persian-style residence on top of a hill overlooking the Hudson and landscaped the grounds as if he were composing one of his romantic paintings. New York State rescued the home in 1966 from the nephew of Church's daughter-in-law, who intended to sell all of its furnishings in a Sotheby's auction. On display are a few of Church's own works, as well as many of the paintings, sculptures, and furnishings he collected from his travels to South America and the Middle East.

Olana (5720 Rte. 9G, Hudson, 518/828-0135, www.olana.org, 10am-5pm Tues.-Sun. May-Oct., 10am-5pm Fri.-Sun. Nov.-Apr.) is open with guided tours on the hour. Tours cost $9 for adults, $8 for seniors and students, and children under 12 are admitted free; there is a grounds fee of $5 per car 10am-7pm on weekends and holidays April through October. Visitors are welcome to walk the trails in summer or cross-country ski in winter.

Hudson

If you looked down Hudson's Warren Street for the first time and thought you had landed in an Atlantic Seaboard beach town, you wouldn't be far from the truth. The city still reflects its heritage as a whaling port in the early 19th century.

Fearing a British retaliation after the American Revolution, a group of Nantucket whalers moved inland to the Hudson River shoreline and incorporated a city in 1785. With a strategic location and carefully planned grid of streets, Claverack Landing, later renamed Hudson, became a center for shipbuilding and whale-oil production. By the mid-19th century, the city was firmly established as the economic and political center of Columbia County.

As the city declined in the early 20th century, it earned a reputation for its active red light district. Author Bruce Hall revisits this aspect of Hudson's history in a book called *Diamond Street: The Story of the Little Town*

downtown Hudson

with the Big Red Light District (Black Dome Press, 1994). Today, antiques shops have replaced the brothels and sparked an economic boom. Rows of restored Greek Revival and Federal townhouses line both sides of historic Warren Street for several blocks, extending from the town square to the river. New York City designers flock to more than 70 antiques shops, which carry everything from Tibetan tapestries to Russian furniture. Hudson today gives city escapees some of the comforts of home and rural residents a place to experience a blossoming arts and culture scene.

In the 100 block is the **Robert Jenkins House & Museum** (113 Warren St., 518/828-9764, 1pm-3pm Sun.-Mon. July-Aug., or by appointment), an 1811 Federal-style building with whaling and military exhibits that document the city's colorful past. A promenade at the end of Warren Street offers river views, and the city has developed the area surrounding the train station into a green space called the Henry Hudson Riverfront Park.

The Firemen's Association of the State of New York (FASNY) operates the **Museum of Firefighting** (117 Harry Howard Ave., Hudson, 518/822-1875, www.fasnyfiremuseum.com, 10am-5pm daily, closed holidays, adults $7, children $5, children under 3 free) in downtown Hudson. Two exhibit halls include paintings, photographs, and related memorabilia. The fire engines, pumps, and clothing on display date back to the 18th and 19th centuries. Residents of New York's Volunteer Fireman's Home, next door, staff the museum and happily answer questions about the history and current state of their profession.

Kinderhook

Kinderhook received its name, which is Dutch for "children's point," from Henry Hudson himself. The story goes that when he arrived in 1609, Hudson saw a group of Mohican children staring at the *Half Moon* and named the place Kinderhook Landing, now the town of Stuyvesant. Present-day Kinderhook lies several miles inland, on Kinderhook Creek. Numerous restored homes and historical sites make this town one of the most interesting destinations in northern Columbia County. The village hosted several notable guests during the Revolutionary War: Colonel Henry Knox passed though on his way to deliver a shipment of artillery from Fort Ticonderoga to Boston. And Colonel Benedict Arnold spent the night to recover after the victory of Bemis Heights.

Washington Irving reportedly wrote "Rip Van Winkle" during a stay in Kinderhook, and he based "The Legend of Sleepy Hollow" on local residents, though the story took place in Tarrytown. The town of Kinderhook has published a detailed guide to its many private and public historical homes at www.kinderhookconnection.com. The walking tour begins at the Village Green, formed by the intersection of several streets that date back to the early 19th century: Albany Avenue, Broad Street, Hudson Street, and Chatham Street.

The **Columbia County Museum** (5 Albany Ave., 518/758-9265, www.cchsny.org,

10am-4pm Thurs.-Sun.), run by the Columbia County Historical Society, has extensive collections of paintings and artifacts from around the county.

Take a tour of a Federal-style mansion at the **James Vanderpoel House** (16 Broad St., 518/758-9265, www.cchsny.org, by appointment only). This restored brick building is the former home of James Vanderpoel, a prominent lawyer and politician. Inside, an elegant, curved staircase rises from a grand entryway. The home is decorated throughout with furnishings from the 1820s.

The **Luykas Van Alen House** (Rte. 9H, 518/758-9625, www.cchsny.org, noon-4pm Fri. and Sun., 10am-4pm Sat. May-Oct.) is a 1737 Dutch farmhouse with mid-18th-century furnishings. The site appeared in Martin Scorsese's 1993 film *The Age of Innocence.* On the property is the white 1920 Ichabod Crane Schoolhouse, named after the teacher in Washington Irving's famous story "The Legend of Sleepy Hollow." An admission fee of $7 ($2 for seniors, students free) includes museum, houses, and schoolhouse.

Located two miles outside of Kinderhook, the former home of Martin Van Buren, the eighth president of the United States, is now a historic site. The surrounding land was a working farm of over 200 acres. Built in 1797, the **Martin Van Buren National Historic Site** (1013 Old Post Rd., 518/758-9689, www.nps.gov/mava, 9am-4pm daily mid-May-Oct. 31, admission $5) is a Federal-style home that was remodeled in 1849, and Van Buren spared no expense: Brussels carpets and 51 elaborate wallpaper panels that form a hunting mural are on display inside.

ALONG THE TACONIC STATE PARKWAY

Lake Taghkanic State Park

During sticky summer heat waves, **Lake Taghkanic State Park** (1528 Rte. 82, Taghkanic, 518/851-3631, www.nysparks.com) is a popular day trip for Mid-Hudson Valley residents. The clean and refreshing lake has two beaches with lifeguard supervision and a boat launch. Overnight accommodations include tent and RV campsites, as well as cabins and cottages (May-Oct. only, reserve online through www.reserveamerica.com). The park service maintains trails for hiking and biking. In winter, it allows cross-country skiing, snowmobiles, ice-skating, and ice fishing when the lake freezes. Hunters can take deer and turkey in season.

Claverack

Continuing north on the Taconic State Parkway, you arrive at the intersection of Route 23, an old canon route from the Revolutionary War that connects Hillsdale to Hudson. Equidistant between Hudson and the Taconic is the hamlet of Claverack, best known for its 1786 stone courthouse, where Alexander Hamilton tried a famous libel case involving a Hudson newspaper publisher and President Thomas Jefferson. Today, Claverack is the center of an ongoing controversy over a proposed cement plant.

The name Claverack derives from the Dutch for clover field. Historians believe Henry Hudson chose the name for the fields of white clover he saw when he first arrived. The 1727 Reformed Protestant Dutch Church stands as a testament to the town's first settlers, and Dutch architecture populates this stretch of Route 23.

Several pick-your-own berry farms and orchards are nearby, including **Philip Orchards** (270 Rte. 9H, Claverack, 518/851-6351, www.philiporchards.com, 8:30am-5:30pm daily Labor Day-Nov. 1) for apples and pears. Contemporary writer Leila Philip wrote a memoir of her family's long-standing connection to Claverack entitled *A Family Place: A Hudson Valley Farm, Three Centuries, Five Wars, One Family* (Viking, 2001).

Chatham and Ghent

Though it is technically part of Columbia County, Chatham marks the unofficial gateway to southern New England and the Berkshires. There are actually several Chathams: At the commercial center is the town of Chatham, Route 203 off the Taconic State Parkway. The Village of Chatham, founded in 1795, has dozens of historical markers and claims one of the country's last operational one-room schoolhouses, now home to the **Riders Mills Historical Association** (at the intersection of Riders Mills Rd. and Drowne Rd., 518/794-7146, www.ridersmillsschoolhouse.org). Quiet North Chatham lies on the Valatie Kill and the Rensselaer County line, while East Chatham offers a treasure trove for book lovers: a secondhand bookstore called **Librarium** (126 Black Bridge Rd. II, 518/392-5209, www.thelibrarium.com).

The **Old Chatham Sheepherding Company** (155 Shaker Museum Rd., 888/743-3760, www.blacksheepcheese.com) operates one of the largest sheep farms in the United States and makes a Camembert that aficionados claim rivals the best that France can produce. Many of the nation's top restaurants serve the award-winning cheese, including the French Laundry, in California's Napa Valley. Stop in to observe the morning or afternoon sheep-milking (especially popular with young kids), watch the cheese-making operation, or see the newborn lambs in early spring.

Omi International Arts Center (1405 County Rte. 22, Ghent, www.artomi.org) offers an artist-in-residence program on 300 acres of farmland. The Fields Sculpture Park is open to the public, with works by 80 artists. The Charles B. Benenson Visitors Center has an indoor gallery and a café for additional exhibitions.

ALONG ROUTE 22

★ Taconic State Park

Just east of Route 22, at the intersection of the New York, Massachusetts, and Connecticut state lines, lies a hidden outdoor gem: the 6,000-acre **Taconic State Park** (Rte. 344 off Rte. 22, Copake Falls, 518/329-3993, www.nysparks.com, open year-round). The park encompasses an 11-mile stretch of the Taconic Range—the vestiges of a mountain range that geologists believe stood taller than the Himalayas during the Ordovician time period, 450 million years ago.

The state has developed two areas for year-round use—Copake Falls and Rudd Pond—with extensive hiking, biking, and nature trails, as well as fishing, swimming, and camping. In winter, the trails belong to cross-country skiers and snowmobiles. The **Copake Falls Area** (518/329-3993, www.nysparks.com) is located on State Route 344 or Valley View Road. To find the **Rudd Pond Area** (59 Rudd Pond Rd., Millerton, 518/789-3059, www.nysparks.com, open year-round), turn off Route 22 at Route 62 in Millerton, and head two miles north.

The highlight of this wilderness area is **Bash Bish Falls,** at 80 feet, the tallest single-drop waterfall in Massachusetts. (The falls are located just over the state line.) Beginning about a mile upstream from the town of Copake Falls, a moderate one-mile hike through a hemlock and hardwood forest takes you to the base of the falls. The water cascades over a sheer granite cliff, landing in a pristine mountain pool. Cold temperature and strong currents discourage most hikers from taking a dip. The ecosystem supports a diverse population, including coyote, red fox, and brook trout. After the falls, the Bash Bish Brook winds its way through the Mid-Hudson Valley and empties into the Hudson River. Plan to get there before 10am to enjoy the view before the crowds.

South of the state park, Columbia and Dutchess Counties have teamed up to convert a 43-mile stretch of the old New York and Harlem Railroad into a pathway for walking, running, and cycling. A four-mile piece of the **Harlem Valley Rail Trail** (51 S. Center St., Millerton, 518/789-9591, www.hvrt.org) now connects Ancram to the Taconic State Park entrance in Copake Falls. Lined in spots with weathered split rail fencing, the paved trail traverses the base of the Taconic Mountains. In several clearings, you can see the Catskill Mountains to the west.

According to local residents, Mohican Indian arrowheads, spears, and axes can still occasionally be found in the vicinity of Copake. A tall clock and a Vietnam Veterans War Memorial at the intersection of Routes 22 and 7A mark the center of town, but there's not much reason to stop.

Hillsdale and Catamount

When Hillsdale residents speak of "the mountains," they mean the Berkshires, not the Catskills. Located at the Massachusetts state line, the town is part sleepy Hudson River Valley, part upscale New England.

Catamount Ski & Snowboarding Area (3290 State Hwy. 23, Hillsdale, 518/325-3200, www.catamountski.com, 9am-4pm weekdays, 8:30am-4pm weekends and holidays, $33 weekdays, $63 weekends and holidays), at the Massachusetts state line, is a great mountain to hit on a midweek snow day. With 33 trails, seven lifts, and a fun terrain park, the area draws families from across the Hudson River Valley. The minimal lodge has stacks of blue lockers and cafeteria-style lunch fare. A heated tent next to the lodge houses a small gift shop with winter wear. In spring, summer, and fall, the **Catamount Aerial Adventure Park** (3290 Rte. 23, Hillsdale, 518/325-3200, www.catamounttrees.com, 9am-5:30pm weekends only in fall, $51 adults, $44 juniors, $37 children) opens 11 zipline courses and 162 platforms above the trees to riders of all levels, ages 7 and up. Two of the runs are 2,000 feet long.

Catamount Statistics

- Base: 1,000 feet
- Summit: 2,000 feet
- Vertical drop: 1,000 feet
- Trails: 29
- Lifts: 7
- Skiable acres: 110
- Snowmaking: 100 percent of terrain
- Snow report: 800/342-1840

Austerlitz

The sale of abundant fresh blueberries helped early settlers pay their taxes in rural Austerlitz. Today, an annual Blueberry Festival commemorates the town's heritage. The **Austerlitz Historical Society** (518/392-0062, www.oldausterlitz.org) completed the creation of Old Austerlitz, a museum site at the intersection of Route 22 and Harvey Mountain Road that collects and restores buildings, artifacts, and related town memorabilia. To date, the site includes a blacksmith shop; the 1794 Morey-Devereaux House from Nassau, New York; the 1790 Harvey House from northeastern Connecticut; an 1840 granary from Stillwater, New York; a one-room schoolhouse from 1818; and an 1850s church. The society sponsors events and workshops year-round.

★ Mount Lebanon Shaker Village

In 1772, an Englishwoman named Ann Lee rose to the forefront of a radical dissident movement and led a small group of Shaking Quakers—so named for their tendency to break out in violent shakes during their worship services—to the New World to escape religious persecution. The United Society of Believers eventually established a leadership center in New Lebanon, New York, and grew to include some 6,000 members in 19 communities by the mid-19th century. The Shaker community evolved considerably over the years, but two ideals underpinned the religion: simplicity and celibacy. Above all, members strove to live a selfless and communal existence. Industrialization during the 19th century gradually eroded the once-thriving Shaker community (along with other utopian social experiments like it), and the few remaining followers withdrew from society, leaving only traces of the culture.

Mount Lebanon Shaker Village (202

Shaker Rd., New Lebanon, 518/794-9100, www.shakermuseumandlibrary.org) is a National Historic Landmark located in the northeast corner of Columbia County. Eight families once farmed and lived here on 6,000 acres of rolling hills, forests, and fields. More than two dozen of the original buildings have been preserved. The museum contains one of the largest collections of Shaker artifacts and offers an informative introduction to the Shaker way of life. Among other values, the culture emphasizes high quality, precision, hospitality, invention, and systematic thinking. As a result, the industrious Shakers made fine furniture, tools, farm produce, and clothes. The museum has Shaker stoves, a washing machine, chairs, and textiles for display.

Visitors are welcome June-October. Once on-site, you can view the original beams and chutes of the granary and the drying racks in the washhouse, as well as cemeteries, aqueducts, and the remains of several old mills. The site is a short drive from the Hancock Shaker Village across the Massachusetts state line, in the Berkshires.

SPORTS AND RECREATION

Winter Sports

Catamount Ski & Snowboarding Area (3290 State Hwy. 23, Hillsdale, 518/325-3200, www.catamountski.com) is open 8:30am-4pm weekends and holidays, 9am-4pm weekdays. Weekend and holiday adult lift tickets cost $62 during the 2014-2015 season, with $33 days Monday through Friday. A new resort hotel called the **Berkshire Mountain Club** (www.berkshiremtnclub.com) is under development at the base of the ski hill. Catamount also offers night skiing (3pm-9pm Wed., 3pm-10pm Fri.-Sat.).

Nordic skiers will find more than 15 wilderness areas with groomed and ungroomed trails across Columbia County. **Clermont** (1 Clermont Ave., Germantown, 518/537-4240, www.friendsofclermont.org) opens its trails and grounds free to cross-country skiers. Or explore the carriage roads and six miles of trails on the grounds of **Olana State Historic Site** (5720 Rte. 9G, Hudson, 518/828-0135, www.olana.org). **Lake Taghkanic State Park** (1528 Rte. 82, Taghkanic, 518/851-2060, www.nysparks.com) has trails around the lake. **Taconic State Park** (Rte. 344, off Rte. 22, Copake Falls, 518/329-3993) has extensive trails in both developed areas, Copake Falls and Rudd Pond. Two cottages for rent year-round each have a refrigerator, stove, microwave, dishes and utensils, a bathroom with shower, and oil heat.

Hiking

Hikers can explore state forests, historic sites, and wildlife preserves in Columbia County. Olana, Clermont, and Martin Van Buren National Historic Site have well-maintained trails for nature walks and scenic views. To get farther away from civilization, head to **Beebe Hill State Forest** (County Rte. 5, Austerlitz), Harvey Mountain State Forest (E. Hill Rd. off Rte. 22, Austerlitz), or the 5,000-acre Taconic State Park.

Swimming and Boating

Lake Taghkanic State Park (access from the Taconic State Parkway or Rte. 82, 518/851-2060) offers swimming and boating in a natural lake, while **Taconic State Park** allows swimming in the Rudd Pond Area (Rte. 62 in Millerton, off Rte. 22, 518/789-3059). Queechy Lake in Canaan is another popular venue for swimming and canoeing. For Hudson River access, head to the boat launches on Front Street in Hudson or on County Route 35A (Northern Blvd.) in Germantown.

Fishing and Hunting

The New York State Department of Environmental Conservation stocks Kinderhook Creek, Claverack Creek, Roeliff Jansen Creek, and the unfortunately named Ore Pit Pond in Taconic State Park with trout. Fly fishers head to the Taghkanic Creek or Bash Bish Falls. Queechy Lake and Kinderhook Lake allow fishing from car-top boats only. A New York State fishing license is required at all locations.

Several state forests allow hunting in season: New Forge on New Forge Road off Route 82 in Taghkanic, Beebe Hill on County Route 5 in Austerlitz, and Harvey Mountain on East Hill Road off Route 22. Call the local state ranger for information: 518/828-0236. Taconic State Park permits bow and rifle hunting for deer only. **Lido's Game Farm** is a private club in the town of Hillsdale (68 Berkshire Rd. off County Rte. 11, 518/329-1551).

Golf

A dozen golf courses are scattered among Columbia County's rolling hills. **Undermountain Golf Course** (274 Undermountain Rd., Copake, 518/329-4444, www.undermountaingolf.com, 7am-7pm Mon.-Fri., 7am-6:30pm Sat.-Sun., $21 weekdays, $24.25 weekend and holiday, $18 senior/junior) operates a public, 18-hole course with views of the Taconic Range, Berkshire Mountains, and Catskills.

Copake Country Club's (44 Golf Course Rd., off County Rte. 11, Copake Lake, 518/325-4338, www.copakecountryclub.com, 7am-7pm daily, Mar.-Nov., weekday 9 holes $22, 18 holes $30, weekend 9 holes $32, 18 holes $48) 18-hole par 72 course overlooks Copake Lake with distant views of the Catskills across the Hudson. The club offers cart rentals, a pro shop, lessons, and a restaurant.

Cycling

Cyclists have many options for touring country roads and trails in this part of the Hudson River Valley. An aggressive 83-mile road ride with a 60-mile option traverses nearly every major town in the county on back roads that meander by old homes, farms, rolling hills, and waterfalls (www.roberts-1.com/bikehudson/r/east/gt_columbia/map/index.htm). For an easier ride, the paved **Harlem Valley Rail Trail** (51 S. Center St., Millerton, 518/789-9591, www.hvrt.org) follows a set of old railroad tracks along the base of the Taconic Range. Access the path at Undermountain Road, off Route 22 in Ancram or at the Taconic State Park entrance in Copake Falls. The same rail trail continues into Dutchess County connecting the towns of Millerton, Amenia, and Wassaic. The section from Millerton to Undermountain Road is under development.

Mountain bikers will find challenging terrain in both Taconic State Park and Lake Taghkanic State Park.

Steiner Sports (301 Warren St., Hudson, 518/828-5063, www.steinersskibike.com, 10am-6pm Mon.-Fri., 9am-5pm Sat., 11am-4pm Sun.) carries high-end ski, bike, and kayak equipment in three locations: Hudson, Valatie, and Glenmont. Stop in for maps, supplies, and route advice. You can also rent bikes for a cruise around town.

Aviation

Private pilots and aviation enthusiasts should head to **Richmor Aviation** (1142 Rte. 9H, Hudson, 518/828-9461, www.richmor.com), at the Columbia County Airport, for training and scenic flights.

ACCOMMODATIONS

Aside from a couple of modern hotels that cater to business travelers, places to stay in Columbia County tend toward the upscale. An increasing number of bed-and-breakfast inns are opening throughout the county; more than a dozen of them are in Hudson alone.

Under $100

Wireless Internet in every room is a plus at the **St. Charles Hotel** (16-18 Park Pl., Hudson, 518/822-9900, www.stcharleshotel.com, $89-129). Rooms are basic but adequate, and the location is within walking distance of the antiques shops on Warren Street.

$100-150

The **Hudson City B&B** (326 Allen St., Hudson, 518/822-8044, www.hudsoncitybnb.com, $125-175) occupies the former residence of Joshua T. Waterman, four-term mayor of Hudson beginning in 1853. The house is painted green with cream trim and sits within walking distance of the Warren Street antiques shops. Its comfortable rooms are decorated in 19th-century furnishings.

The **Inn at the Shaker Mill Farm** (40 Cherry Ln., Canaan, 518/794-9345, www.shakermillfarminn.com, $100-120, dinner $25) puts you a short drive from Berkshire attractions, including summer performances at Tanglewood, 10 miles away. As the name implies, guest rooms occupy a converted 1834 mill, and owner Ingram Paperny has embraced the Shaker philosophy with zeal. Be prepared for bare-bones decor and a communal experience, including family-style meals.

Next door to the restaurant of the same name, ★ **Swiss Hütte** (Rte. 23, Hillsdale, 518/325-3333, www.swisshutte.com, $110-130 per person per night, including breakfast and dinner) offers immaculate, recently renovated rooms with tiled baths and mountain views.

$150-200

At the edge of the Berkshires, pine floors, antique trunks, and down comforters lend a cozy feel to guest rooms at ★ **The Inn at Silver Maple Farm** (1871 Rte. 295, Canaan, 518/781-3600, www.silvermaplefarm.com, $130-335). Breakfast includes homemade breads and muffins.

The Country Squire B&B (251 Allen St., Hudson, 518/822-9229, www.countrysquireny.come, $175-195) is a cozy and stylish home with five inviting guest rooms and beds of all sizes. In the morning, owner Paul Barrett sees to every detail and also makes a killer quiche. This B&B is within walking distance of all the action on Warren Street.

On a quiet cul-de-sac in Hudson, ★ **The Croff House Bed and Breakfast** (5 Willard Pl., Hudson, 518/828-1688, www.thecroffhouse.com, $170-280) has five guest rooms in a historical home with a garden and porches for relaxation between trips to the antiques shops on Warren Street. Afternoon tea, aromatherapy candles (yours to keep), and nightly turndown service add a special touch to your stay. The list of amenities is long: luxury linens, flat-screen TVs, iPod docking stations, spa showers. Mindful of its environmental impact, the owners have installed efficient lighting, use eco-friendly cleaners, and use high-efficiency appliances to reduce water usage.

Over $200

Close to Olana, the Rip Van Winkle Bridge, and the city of Hudson, ★ **Mount Merino Manor** (4317 Rte. 23, Hudson, 518/828-5583, www.mountmerinomanor.com, $175-395) has seven guest rooms and suites, all with king- or queen-size beds, air-conditioning, and high-quality bed linens. Some have fireplaces and soaking tubs and spa showers. Hosts Patrick and Rita reportedly make a mouthwatering breakfast, too.

The owners of The Croff House Bed and Breakfast opened **The Barlow Hotel** (542 Warren St., Hudson, 518/828-2100, www.thebarlowhotel.com, $165-270) in June 2013 in a central location on Warren Street near the intersection with Route 9. The hotel is small, with guest rooms and suites on three floors. The decor is contemporary, beds are firm in a good way, and showers are like a car wash with multiple faucets and sprays. Keurig coffee machines and electric fireplaces are a nice touch. The only challenge of a stay here for some may be figuring out how to use all the gadgets. Mexican Radio restaurant is right across the street, and you can walk to many other shops and eateries to take in more of the downtown Hudson scene.

Campgrounds

Woodland Hills Campground (386 Fog Hill Rd., Austerlitz, 518/392-3557, www.whcg.net, May 15-Columbus Day, $29 for tents, $38 for full hookups), near the intersection of the Taconic State Parkway and the Massachusetts Turnpike (I-90), has 200 sites for tents and RVs. Amenities include hot showers, laundry, and family activities.

Taconic State Park (Rte. 344, off Rte. 22, Copake Falls, 518/329-3993, year-round) offers two recreational areas—Copake Falls and Rudd Pond—with campsites, trailer sites, and cabins available from mid-May until November. (Deer hunting is allowed in season, and camping is extended for hunters.) Reserve online through www.reserveamerica.com. Tent sites cost $15, and cabins cost $116-175. The Rudd Pond Area is located off Route 22 on Route 62, two miles north of Millerton.

Camp Waubeeka Family Campground (133 Farm Rd., Copake, 518/329-4681 or 866/617-8464 for reservations, www.campwaubeeka.com $21-53 per day) has four rustic cabins, as well as campsites and trailer hookups. Cabins cost $109-127 per night; a basic tent site is $35.

ice cream on Warren Street in Hudson

FOOD

Along the Hudson: Route 9G

The list of trendsetting eateries in Hudson is growing, and many deliver dining experiences on par with what you'd find in New York City. Among them, **Swoon Kitchenbar** (340 Warren St., Hudson, 518/822-8938, www.swoonkitchenbar.com, lunch noon-3:30pm Sat.-Sun., dinner 5pm-10pm Mon., Thurs., and Sun. and 5pm-11pm Fri.-Sat., $23-27) quickly cornered the market for New American cuisine. You might start with a rhubarb sidecar cocktail and oysters on the half shell, then dive into the duck confit or pan-seared Maine scallops. Meanwhile, **Wasabi** (807 Warren St., Hudson, 518/822-1888, www.wasabiyummy.com, lunch 11:30am-2:30pm Mon.-Sat., dinner 4:30pm-9:30pm Mon.-Thurs. and until 10:30pm Fri.-Sat., 3pm-9:30pm Sun., mains $12-24) filled the void for Japanese with creative sushi rolls and some hot dishes as well. At the more casual end of the scale, **Earth Foods** (523 Warren St., Hudson, 518/822-1396, breakfast and lunch Wed.-Mon., mains $7-10) treats vegetarians right, with veggie burritos, seasonal soups, salads, and other lunch fare. Cash only.

Locals fill the ★ **Red Dot Restaurant & Bar** (321 Warren St., Hudson, 518/828-3657, www.reddotrestaurant.com, 5pm-10pm Mon. and Wed.-Sat., 5pm-9pm Sun., 11am-3pm Sat.-Sun., bar until 1am, mains $10-30) on weekend evenings, even in the dead of winter. Entrées range from basic steak frites to the more exotic Thai beef salad. **Mexican Radio** (537 Warren St., Hudson, 518/828-7770, www.mexrad.com, 11:30am-11pm daily, mains $12-19) serves fancy Mexican food and has sister restaurants in New York City and Schenectady.

Wunderbar & Bistro (744 Warren St., Hudson, 518/828-0555, www.wunderbarbistro.com, lunch mains $6-14, dinners $12-16) up the street serves dependable Austrian and Hungarian dishes at reasonable prices. The restaurant is open 11:30am-2am daily with trivia on Wednesday nights and live music on Saturdays. **Baba Louie's Pizza** (517 Warren St., Hudson, 518/751-2155, www.babalouiespizza.com, 11:30am-3pm and 5pm-9:30pm Thurs.-Tues., until 10pm Fri.-Sat., $15-20) makes its pies from a sourdough crust. Toppings are fresh and often appear in creative combinations. The menu includes soups and salads, and the casual atmosphere is perfect for families. The menu works for vegetarians, and house-made soups are vegan.

With locations in Hudson and Cortona, Italy, **Ca'Mea Restaurant** (333 Warren St., Hudson, 518/822-0005, www.camearestaurant.com, noon-3pm and 5pm-10pm Tues.-Sat., noon-3pm and 5pm-9pm Sun., $17-25) is wildly popular with pasta lovers. House-made ravioli are stuffed with spinach and ricotta. Gnocci come with a zucchini basil pesto and cherry tomatoes. Go for a half-portion so you have room for an entrée afterward. Try the apple martini or the apple gin fizz to start, and finish with the sorbet.

Scandinavian flavors and decor prevail at **DA|BA Restaurant** (225 Warren St., Hudson, 518/249-4631, www.dabahudson.com, 6pm-10pm Mon.-Sat., $21-28). After the *amuse-bouche,* you can order herring three ways, a lobster ravioli salad, Swedish meatballs, or dill-baked Arctic char.

Fish & Game (13 S. 3rd St., Hudson, 518//822-1500, www.fishandgamehudson.com, lunch noon-2pm Sat.-Sun. and dinner Thurs.-Sun. from 5pm) is a farm-to-table affair conceived by a New York City chef and his wife, who fell in love with the Hudson River Valley and decided to make a go of it with a farm and restaurant combo. The menu is set daily, and the kitchen grows or makes most of its own ingredients, from vermouth to vinegars.

★ **Verdigris Tea & Chocolate Bar** (135 Warren St., Hudson, 518/828-3139, www.hudsonchocolatebar.com, 10am-6pm Sun.-Tues., 10am-8pm Thurs.-Sat.) is paradise for those serious about tea. Choose a black, white, green, chai, or herbal tea and have a fresh pot brewed at the bar, or buy an ounce to go. Along with the tea itself, all manner of accessories are sold here including pots, infusers, mugs, and timers. The chocolate bar features chocolates from around the world and serves up homemade pastries and chocolate drinks that are pure indulgence. Try the classic hot chocolate, which is a rich ganache of melted dark chocolate blended with milk and topped with whipped cream and chocolate shavings. You won't be sorry.

For ribs and southern fare, head to **Carolina House** (59 Broad St./Rte. 9, Kinderhook, 518/758-1669, www.carolinahouserestaurant.com, 5pm-9:30pm Mon.-Thurs., 5pm-10pm Fri.-Sat., 4pm-9:30pm Sun., $18-31).

Along the Taconic State Parkway

Jackson's Old Chatham House (Village Square, Old Chatham, 518/794-7373, 11am-10pm daily, mains $15-25) serves reliable tavern-style food, including burgers, steaks, pork chops, and reportedly the best prime rib around. The wood-burning fireplace is a plus in winter months.

Nearby, **The Old Chatham Country Store** has homemade soups and sandwiches in a casual setting (Village Square, Old Chatham, 518/794-6227, www.oldchathamcountrystore.com).

Blue Plate (1 Kinderhook St., Chatham, 518/392-7711, www.chathamblueplate.net, 5:30pm-9pm Tues.-Sat., 5pm-9:30pm Sun., $10-22) is an American bistro where you can begin the meal with Maryland crab cakes, move on to "The Legendary Blue Plate Meatloaf," and finish with a hot fudge sundae.

Peint O Gwrw (36 Main St., Chatham, 518/392-2337, 4pm-midnight Tues.-Sun.) is one of only four Welsh pubs in the United States. Picture dark mood lighting, walls covered with hunting trophies, and a wide selection of scotches and beers. It's family-friendly with board games for the kids and a pool table upstairs. Rave reviews go to the one menu item that doesn't hail from Wales—the kimchi burger.

Along Route 22

A chalet straight out of the Swiss Alps, **Swiss Hütte** (Rte. 23, Hillsdale, 518/325-3333, www.swisshutte.com, noon-2pm and 5:30pm-9pm Tues.-Sat., noon-3pm and 5pm-9pm Sun., $28-34) is a restaurant and inn directly across the parking lot from the lifts at Catamount.

A friendly golden retriever named Beano will likely greet you at the door. Owned since 1986 by Swiss-born Gert Alper (who is also the chef) and his wife, Cindy, the restaurant serves cheese fondue, homemade European-style hard rolls, and a full menu of hearty entrées in a cozy, mountainside setting.

The popular **Four Brothers Pizza Inn** chain (2828 Rte. 23, Hillsdale, 518/325-7300, www.fourbrotherspizzainn.com, 10am-10pm daily, $10-15) is open late, serving Italian, Greek, and American dishes. The restaurant is one of nine pizzerias in the Hudson River Valley, which, as the name implies, were established by four Greek brothers who immigrated to the United States.

Eight miles from the town of Hudson and 10 miles from Catamount, ★ **Local 111** (111 Main St., Philmont, 518/672-7801, www.local111.com, 5:30pm-9pm Wed.-Thurs., 5:30-9:30pm Fri.-Sat., 10am-2pm and 5pm-9pm Sun.) is leading Columbia County's farm-to-table movement from a converted service station in a rather run-down mill town off Route 82. At least 18 local farmers contribute foods; some of them deliver their goods in the morning and return for dinner that night.

After a round of golf at the Copake Country Club, enjoy lunch or dinner at **The Greens** (Copake Country Club, 44 Golf Course Rd., Copake Lake, 518/325-0019, www.copakecountryclub.com, 11:30am-9pm Mon.-Thurs., 11:30am-10pm Fri.-Sat., 11am-8pm Sun., closed Tues.-Wed. in the off-season, $22-28), which serves a club menu of appetizers, salads, pizzas, and sandwiches and a dinner menu featuring seafood, beef, pork, and duck dishes. Many of the ingredients are harvested locally.

ENTERTAINMENT AND EVENTS

Performing Arts

With support from the Catskill Mountain Foundation, the **Pleshakov Music Center** (7967 Main St., Hunter, 518/263-3330) has moved from Hudson to the new Doctorow Center for the Arts in Hunter; Vladimir Pleshakov and his wife Elena Winther, both accomplished pianists, have realized a lifelong dream in the Pleshakov Piano Museum, which houses 16 antique but playable pianos collectively worth $2.5 million. The idea is for the space to function as a living museum in which Pleshakov and Winther will perform from time to time. The museum opened in August 2007.

After three decades of neglect, Hudson's 19th-century city hall building reopened in 1998 as a local performing arts center, **Hudson Opera House** (327 Warren St., Hudson, 518/822-1438, www.hudsonoperahouse.org, noon-5pm daily, tickets free-$20). Artist exhibitions and concerts are hosted throughout the year.

Set in an 1847 schoolhouse, the **Spencertown Academy Arts Center** (790 Rte. 203, Spencertown, 518/392-3693, www.spencertownacademy.org, 1pm-5pm Thurs.-Sun. Feb.-Dec.) has a 140-seat auditorium and four exhibit spaces. Events range from jazz and classical concerts to yoga classes.

The quaint **Mac-Haydn Theatre** (1925 Rte. 203, Chatham, 518/392-9292, www.machaydntheatre.org, tickets $28-30), on a hilltop overlooking the town of Chatham, specializes in musicals and runs a summer children's theater. The theater runs seven or eight shows per season.

Bars and Nightlife

Hudson residents congregate at the **Red Dot** (321 Warren St., Hudson, 518/828-3657, www.reddotrestaurant.com, 5pm-10pm Mon. and Wed.-Sat., 5pm-9pm Sun., 11am-3pm Sat.-Sun.) after work to drink Morland Old Speckled Hen by the pint.

For live music in a hip dinner-theater setting, **Club Helsinki** (405 Columbia St., Hudson, 518/828-4800, www.helsinkihudson.com) is a win. It's open for concerts and special events. The reservation process is a bit confusing at first. You can buy general admission tickets online, but in order to reserve a seat for the show, you must call ahead to reserve a table in the club. Tables are arranged in front of the small stage and on a mezzanine level above. You can also skip the table and watch from a seat at the bar. This is a popular venue for the local residents, and shows frequently sell out, even on rainy weekday nights. An adjoining restaurant (same building out of earshot of the club) serves dinner daily starting at 5pm. Recent performance have included Black Francis of the Pixies and Shawn Colvin. When the music of the evening plays the sounds of the south, Louisiana native Chef Hugh Horner plans a special menu of Creole dishes such as deep-friend okra and Savannah-style low-country boil.

For maritime entertainment, **Hudson Cruises** (518/822-1014, www.hudsoncruises.com) offers afternoon or evening cruises with dinner, dancing, and scenic river views. Boats depart from Waterfront Park on Front Street in Hudson at various days and times.

Chatham Brewing (59 Main St., Chatham, 518/392-1026, www.chathambrewing.com, 4pm-8pm Wed.-Fri., 11am-8pm Sat., noon-4pm Sun.) is a relatively new option for craft beers made on-site. The setting is small and somewhat quiet for a bar, so you'll be able to have a conversation with a friend. Stop in for a taste or a pint.

For a little nightlife during the day, plan a visit to **Hillrock Estate Distillery** (408 Pooles Hill Rd., Ancram, 518/329-1023, www.hillrockdistillery.com). On a 200-acre barley farm, the former head distiller of Maker's Mark is experimenting with the Solera system of aging whiskey—sort of blending a little old with a little new—to get the complex flavors that connoisseurs desire. The bourbon is then finished in 20-year-old Oloroso Sherry casks to add the final touch. Call to arrange a tour.

Festivals

Folk dancers and bluegrass music lovers attend the popular **Falcon Ridge Folk Festival** (Dodds Farm, 44 County Rte. 7D, Hillsdale, 860/364-0366, www.falconridgefolk.com) each July to watch up to 40 bands perform on three stages, with plenty of flat areas for camping.

Lebanon Valley Speedway (1746 Rte. 20, West Lebanon, 518/794-9606, www.lebanonvalley.com, Sat. mid-Apr.-Sept., admission $10) holds stock car races, monster truck rallies, and hot rod events.

The **Columbia County Fair** (Columbia County Fairgrounds, Rtes. 66 & 203, Chatham Village, 518/392-2121 or 518/758-1811, www.columbiafair.com) is an old-fashioned fair with live music, a rodeo, tractor

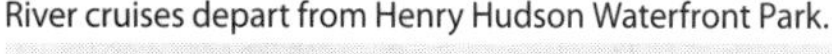
River cruises depart from Henry Hudson Waterfront Park.

pulls, and amusement rides. It takes place on Labor Day weekend. And the Clermont hosts various festivals and educational events throughout the year, including a sheep festival in April.

The **Tour of the Catskills** (www.tourofthecatskills.com) is a challenging multiday cycling event held in early August. Hundreds of amateur and professional cyclists compete in a Friday time trial and two stages Saturday and Sunday. The route follows some of the most scenic country roads through Greene and Ulster Counties. The town of Windham is a good place to watch the action.

SHOPPING

Antiques and Boutiques

The town of Hudson is chock-full of boutiques and galleries, where you can find everything from contemporary art and jewelry to vintage records, first-edition books, and loose-leaf tea. Start your tour of Hudson's antiques shops at **Hudson Supermarket** (310-312 Warren St., Hudson, 518/822-0028, www.hudsonsupermarket.com, 11am-5pm Mon.-Thurs. and Sun., 11am-6pm Fri.-Sat.), a collective of six dealers that occupies a former grocery store.

More a gallery than a store, **East Market Street Antiques** (25 E. Market St., Red Hook, 845/758-9000, www.eastmarketstreetantiques.com) shows its Americana, folk, primitive, industrial, decorative, and fine arts in museum-quality displays. You might find anything from barbed wire to train signs. For serious collectors, everything is for sale, and some items are also available for rent as professional props. **Five and Diamond Vintage Clothing** (502 Columbia St., Hudson, 518/828-4140, www.fiveanddiamond.blogspot.com, noon-5pm Thurs.-Sun. and by appointment) houses a well-curated selection of vintage men and women's clothing. Owner Lisa does all the buying and offers customers her personal expertise and knowledge of fashion history.

Away from the Warren Street bustle, **Copake Auction** (266 Rte. 7A, Copake, 518/329-1142, www.copakeauction.com, 8am-4pm Mon.-Fri.) has specialized in the sale of Americana items for the past 50 years. Its annual antique bicycle auction draws cycling enthusiasts from across the nation and overseas.

The Bees Knees (302 Warren St., Hudson, 518/697-0888, www.thebeeskneeshudson.com, 11am-5pm Mon., Wed., Thurs., 10am-5pm Fri.-Sat., noon-4pm Sun.) is a cute children's store and community center for parents—the perfect place to find an eco-friendly baby gift or a new toy for the rest of your travels.

If you are looking for homey gifts, step into **Classic Country** (2948 County Rte. 9, East Chatham, 518/392-2211, 10am-5pm Wed.-Sat., 11am-4pm Sun.) where you will find a wide selection of hand-picked furniture, linens, baby gifts, blankets, soaps, and other trinkets.

Books

Bookworms will want to spend an hour or two browsing the shelves at **Librarium** (126 Black Bridge Rd. II, East Chatham, 518/392-5209, www.thelibrarium.com) or **Rodgers Book Barn** (467 Rodman Rd., Hillsdale, 518/325-3610, www.rodgersbookbarn.com, 11am-5pm Fri.-Mon. Nov.-Mar., 11am-5pm Thurs.-Mon. Apr.-Oct.). Better yet, save time for both. Each shop houses tens of thousands of titles in a converted barn that sets the mood for reading.

Over 12,000 used and rare book titles are housed in **Hudson City Books** (553 Warren St., Hudson, 518/671-6020, 11am-5pm Sun.-Mon. and Thurs.-Fri., 11am-6:30pm Sun., by appointment Tues.-Wed.). Browsing the store could occupy serious readers for hours, and collectors are sure to find some new gems here. For current fiction and nonfiction, along with a pint of ale on tap, wander into **The Spotty Dog Books & Ale** (440 Warren St., 518/671-6006, www.thespottydog.com, 11am-8pm Mon.-Thurs., 11am-10pm Fri.-Sat., noon-6pm Sun.). There is a special section of books and toys for kids, and frequent author events.

What Grows When

Baskets of summer squash are a sign of summer in Columbia County.

Each season brings a new crop of fruits and vegetables to market. Harvest times change year to year depending on the weather, but here are some general guidelines for what to expect throughout the growing season.

SPRING

The first veggies to appear in local farmers markets are leafy greens that can handle the cold, such as spinach, chard, lettuce, and kale. Asparagus spears reach for the sky in April and May. Fiddleheads, wild mushrooms, garlic scapes, and edible pea pods come next, followed by strawberries in early June.

SUMMER

The longer days of summer ripen cherries, blueberries, raspberries, currants, and peaches. Sweet corn, summer squash, broccoli, beets, potatoes, peppers, beans, garlic, and tomatoes are abundant in August.

FALL

The first frost sweetens the flavor of brussels sprouts and cauliflower. Butternut squash and pumpkins grow large on the vine, while apples and pears reach their peak.

Farm Stands and Farmers Markets

There is at least one farm stand, farmers market, or pick-your-own orchard in every town in Columbia County. The **Hudson Farmers' Market** (518/851-7515, www.hudsonfarmersmarketny.com, 9am-1pm Sat. May-Nov.), at 6th Street and Columbia Street has meat, eggs, plants, flowers, cheese, wool, and fruits and veggies in season. To the east, near Claverack, you can pick apples and pears at **Philip Orchards** (518/851-6351).

Just north of Hudson on Route 9, **Van Wie Natural Foods** (6798 Rte. 9, Hudson, 518/828-0533, www.vanwienaturalmeats.com, 10am-5pm Tues.-Sat.) offers organic-standard meat, including pork, beef, free-range chicken and turkey, lamb, seafood, pheasant, duck, rabbit, goat, and buffalo. All animals are raised without the use of chemicals, hormones, or antibiotics.

Green Acres Farm (269 Schneider Rd., Hudson, 518/851-7460, www.greenacreshudson.com, 9am-6pm Fri.-Mon.) opens with the summer's first harvest of tomatoes, peaches, and corn. Stop in for a weekend's worth of fresh produce and irresistible pastries baked right on the premises. The stand closes precisely at noon on Thanksgiving Day, after the holiday's homemade pies are delivered to its loyal customers.

Fix Brothers Fruit Farm (215 White Birch Rd., Hudson, 518/828-7560, www.fixbrosfruitfarm.com) runs a popular you-pick apple farm just off Route 9G, between Bard College and Hudson. Grab a bag or two and for $1/pound, you can pick any mix of Honeycrisp, Fuji, Macoun, Golden Delicious, Mutsu, and Cortland apples.

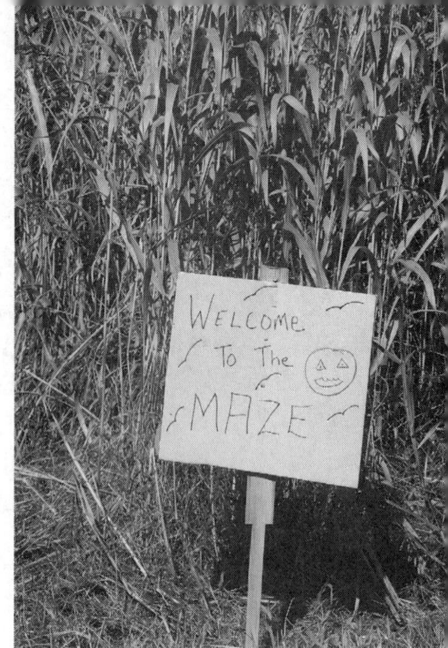

a corn maze at the Fix Brothers Fruit Farm

Verdigris Tea & Hudson Chocolate Bar (135 Warren St., Hudson, 518/828-3139, www.hudsonchocolatebar.com, 10am-6pm Sun.-Tues., 10am-8pm Thurs.-Sat.) is the place for hard-to-find loose-leaf tea, tea accessories, and gourmet chocolates to give to a friend.

Several organic farms set up shop near Germantown in summer. **V. R. Saulpaugh & Sons** (1960 Rte. 9, Germantown, 518/537-6494) grows unusual varieties of eggplant, peppers, and squash.

Deer, buffalo, elk, antelope, and llama are just some of the animals that share the pastures at **Highland Farm** (283 County Rte. 6, Germantown, 518/537-6397, www.eat-better-meat.com). The farm sells venison and smoked venison products, breeds animals for zoos, and shelters endangered species, all under one roof.

Otto's Market (215 Main St., Germantown, 518/537-7200, www.ottosmarket.com, 7am-7pm Mon.-Sat., 7am-5pm Sun.) stocks some standard food brands, but also maintains a wide selection of unique and local products. Owner Otto Leuschel makes an effort to cover the basics in a more personal setting. The beer selection is impressive. The market also has a deli serving baked goods made fresh daily, a breakfast selection including a variety of breakfast burritos, and specialty hot and cold sandwiches.

INFORMATION AND SERVICES

The **Columbia County Office of Tourism** (401 State St., Hudson, 518/828-3375 or 800/724-1846, www.columbiacountyny.org, 8:30am-4pm weekdays) has maps and brochures covering the county, as well as the greater Hudson River Valley. The **Columbia County Chamber of Commerce** (1 N. Front St., Hudson, 518/828-4417, www.columbiachamber-ny.com) can also provide visitor information.

GETTING THERE AND AROUND

Bus

Adirondack Trailways (800/858-8555, www.escapemaker.com) stops across the river in the village of Catskill, eight miles from downtown Hudson. Taxis are available, and some hotels offer free shuttle service.

Hudson's Waterfront Park is adjacent to the Amtrak Station.

Train

Hudson is a two-hour train ride away from New York City's Penn Station. The **Amtrak Rail Station** (69 S. Front St., Hudson 800/872-7245, www.amtrak.com) is located at the water's edge. A one-way ticket from Penn Station to Hudson costs $34-65. You can hop a cab from the train station or rent a car from **Enterprise Rent-a-Car** (78-80 Green St., 518/828-5492, www.enterprise.com).

Car

From New England, turn off I-90 at Exit B2 to reach the northern end of the Taconic State Parkway, the speediest north-south route through Columbia County. Route 23 crosses northern Columbia County, connecting Hillsdale to Hudson. Route 9 and its many spinoffs form a major commercial corridor along the river, while the more rural Route 22 runs along the base of the Taconic Range at the eastern edge of the county.

The Capital-Saratoga Region

The Capital-Saratoga Region of Albany, Rensselaer County, and Saratoga Springs marks the end of the tidal Hudson River and serves as a bookend to a journey through the Hudson River Valley. After Albany and Troy, the river becomes part of the Champlain Canal before veering west to its origin, high in the Adirondack Mountains.

Henry Hudson reached Albany in September of 1609 and had to turn the 122-ton *Half Moon* around when the river became too shallow. Word spread after that maiden voyage, and Fort Orange became one of the earliest and largest Dutch settlements along the river. Today's state capital is a destination in its own right, but with an international airport and modern train station, the city also serves as a gateway to surrounding towns and wilderness areas.

Across the Hudson River from Albany lies sleepy Rensselaer County, home of the nation's first engineering school, Rensselaer Polytechnic Institute (RPI), two attractive state parks, and a large concentration of Tiffany glass.

Although it's best known for its summer horse-racing scene, Saratoga Springs offers a much wider appeal. A Victorian-era village is packed with boutique shops selling treasures old and new. Wellness spas, historic homes, a world-class outdoor performing arts theater, and several chefs of Food Network television fame make for a rich and varied travel experience. Apple orchards and art shows also have their place. Ideally situated at the edge of the Adirondack Park, the largest publicly protected area in the contiguous United States, this small city of 26,000 residents offers hikers and backpackers convenient access to supplies and outfitters. Lake George is just 30 minutes farther up the Northway (I-87) for summer swimming and boating.

PLANNING YOUR TIME

One day allows plenty of time to explore most of downtown Albany, but you'll need extra time to schedule a tour of the capitol building or Executive Mansion. Popular Albany itineraries include dinner downtown followed by

Previous: Dutch Apple Cruises, Upper Hudson River; the New York State Capitol Building in Albany.
Above: Yaddo Rose Garden, Saratoga Springs.

Look for ★ to find recommended sights, activities, dining, and lodging.

Highlights

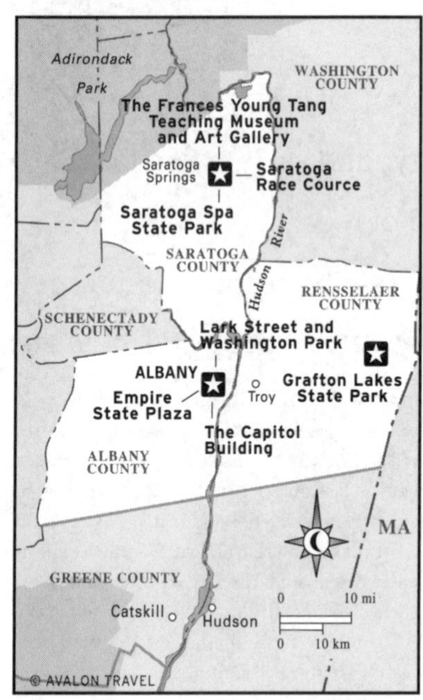

★ **Empire State Plaza:** The centerpiece of downtown Albany is a 98-acre plaza with an impressive collection of art displayed indoors and out (page 232).

★ **The Capitol Building:** Elaborate stone carvings line the imposing outdoor stairway that leads from the Empire State Plaza to the entrance of New York's state capitol building. Built by hand over a period of 30 years, the building defines the Albany skyline and serves as headquarters for the New York State Assembly (page 234).

★ **Lark Street and Washington Park:** Downtown Albany has a bohemian enclave at the east end of Washington Park, with several blocks of eclectic boutiques and trendy restaurants (page 235).

★ **Grafton Lakes State Park:** A pleasant sandy beach and rare peace pagoda draw visitors from near and far to this corner of Rensselaer County (page 249).

★ **Saratoga Spa State Park:** Natural hot springs, towering pine trees, and an outdoor concert venue are highlights in Saratoga's 2,300-acre park (page 252).

★ **Saratoga Race Course:** The Saratoga racetrack is the oldest continuously operating thoroughbred track in the United States, and the town's population triples during the summer racing season (page 254).

★ **The Frances Young Tang Teaching Museum and Art Gallery:** Skidmore College has a state-of-the-art museum dedicated to presenting and teaching contemporary works (page 255).

The Capital-Saratoga Region

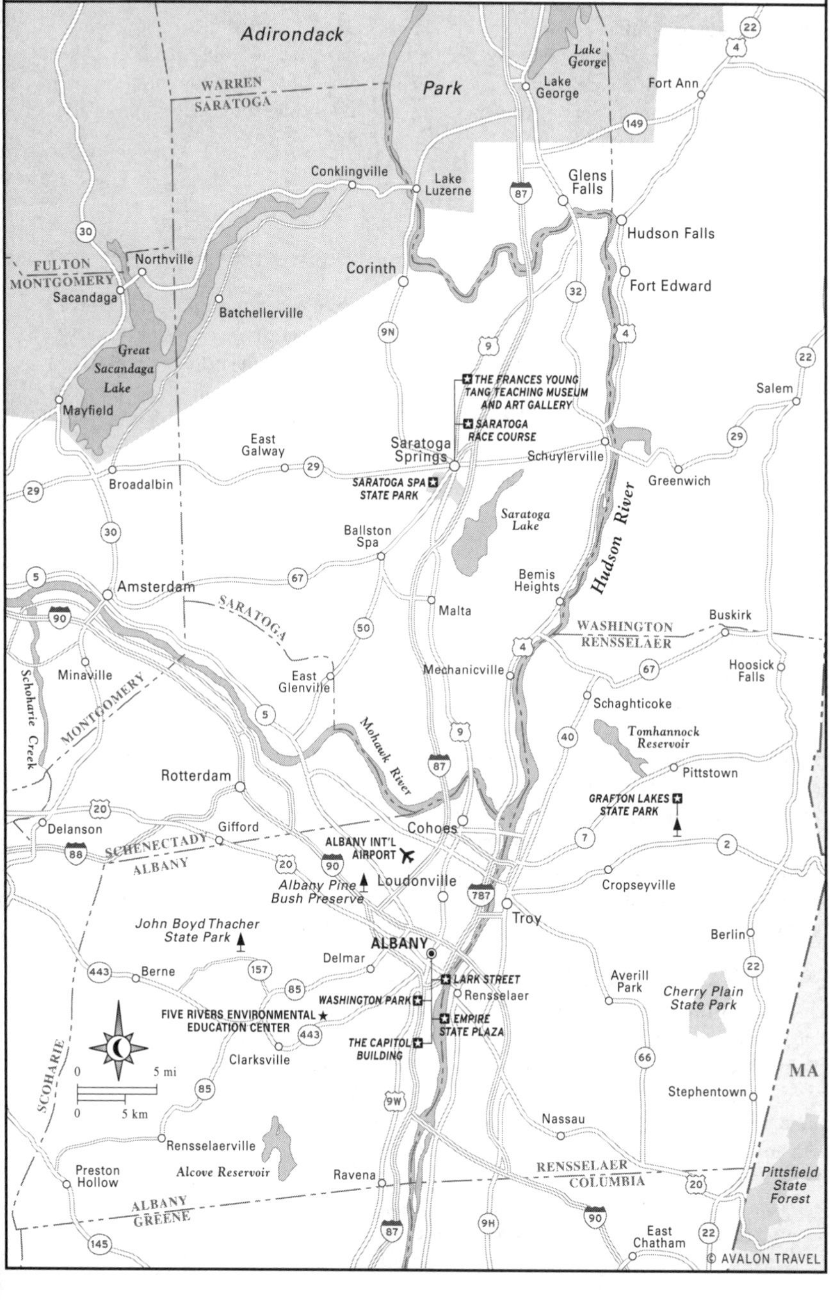

Adirondack Park
WARREN
SARATOGA
Lake George
Lake George
22
4
Fort Ann
149
Conklingville
Lake Luzerne
87
Glens Falls
Hudson Falls
30
FULTON
MONTGOMERY
Northville
Sacandaga
Corinth
Fort Edward
32
Batchellerville
9N
4
Great Sacandaga Lake
9
22
THE FRANCES YOUNG TANG TEACHING MUSEUM AND ART GALLERY
Salem
Mayfield
SARATOGA RACE COURSE
29
East Galway
Saratoga Springs
Schuylerville
29
29
Broadalbin
SARATOGA SPA STATE PARK
Greenwich
Saratoga Lake
Hudson River
30
Ballston Spa
5
67
Bemis Heights
Amsterdam
SARATOGA
Malta
Buskirk
90
50
WASHINGTON
RENSSELAER
4
Minaville
Mechanicville
67
Hoosick Falls
East Glenville
MONTGOMERY
Schaghticoke
Schoharie Creek
5
9
Tomhannock Reservoir
Mohawk River
40
87
Pittstown
Rotterdam
GRAFTON LAKES STATE PARK
20
Delanson
Gifford
Cohoes
SCHENECTADY
ALBANY
ALBANY INT'L AIRPORT
7
2
88
90
20
Albany Pine Bush Preserve
Loudonville
Cropseyville
787
Troy
John Boyd Thacher State Park
Berlin
ALBANY
443
Berne
157
Delmar
22
LARK STREET
Averill Park
85
WASHINGTON PARK
Rensselaer
Cherry Plain State Park
FIVE RIVERS ENVIRONMENTAL EDUCATION CENTER
EMPIRE STATE PLAZA
443
THE CAPITOL BUILDING
Clarksville
66
0 5 mi
0 5 km
MA
SCHOHARIE
85
Stephentown
9W
Nassau
Rensselaerville
Alcove Reservoir
Preston Hollow
Ravena
RENSSELAER
COLUMBIA
20
Pittsfield State Forest
ALBANY
GREENE
87
9H
90
East Chatham
22
145
© AVALON TRAVEL

an evening event at the **Times Union Center** (www.timesunioncenter-albany.com) a weekend of historic colonial sights, or a day of holiday shopping at the malls.

Rensselaer County is easily explored in a day or two of driving scenic back roads. The drive from Albany to Saratoga Springs should take about half an hour with light traffic; however, a large number of government workers commute into Albany each day, so be sure to time your drive to avoid the rush. Ideal as a weekend getaway, Saratoga Springs can also work well as a side trip from Lake George, or as a day of civilization before or after a multiday hike through the Adirondack backcountry.

Albany

From names like Ten Broeck to its annual tulip festival, New York's capital city retains much of its early Dutch roots. As the New York State capital since 1797, the city has also preserved much of its 19th- and 20th-century architecture. Walk a few of the city's historical blocks and you'll find many examples of the Italianate, Federal, and Greek Revival styles, in conditions ranging from perfectly restored to borderline run-down.

Albany today contains an appealing mix of architectural masterpieces, art collections, and historic sights. Meanwhile, students from several area colleges support a vibrant sports and nightlife scene. With a population of 100,000, the city is large enough to offer a rich urban experience, but compact enough that you can tour the downtown in a day. Unfortunately, however, many parts of Albany have yet to recover from the economic turmoil of the mid-20th century. As a result, showy state government buildings intermingle with signs of urban misfortune.

DOWNTOWN ALBANY

The modern Empire State Plaza and giant Times Union Center have done much to revitalize downtown Albany since most of its factories shut down in the 1950s; however, the new and restored buildings contrast sharply with the low-income neighborhoods that surround them. City leaders have wooed high-tech companies—making everything from nanotechnology to fuel cells—as a key source of economic growth.

The majority of visitors find themselves in Albany for one of three reasons: a business convention, a school fieldtrip, or a concert or sporting event. Whatever the draw, it's well worth the time to absorb a slice of New York state history while you're in town.

★ Empire State Plaza

The centerpiece of downtown Albany is the 98-acre Empire State Plaza (State St.), where most of the government's 11,000 employees show up for work each day. Ten dazzling skyscrapers surround an open plaza and fountain, including the Corning Tower, which at 42 stories is the state's highest building outside New York City.

In the 1960s, then-governor Nelson A. Rockefeller envisioned an architectural wonder and cultural center that would bring jobs and visitors to downtown Albany again. He commissioned Wallace Harrison, the same architect who built Rockefeller Center, and construction began in 1965. Thirteen years later, the city had a gorgeous new public space. The best view in town is found atop the **Corning Tower Observation Deck** (42nd floor of the Corning Tower, off the Empire Plaza exit in Albany, 518/474-2418, 10am-4pm Mon.-Fri.).

One of the most unusual sights on the plaza is a sculpture-like building called **The Egg** (Empire State Plaza, 518/473-1061, www.theegg.org), a custom-built performing arts center with two theaters and state-of-the-art acoustics.

Albany

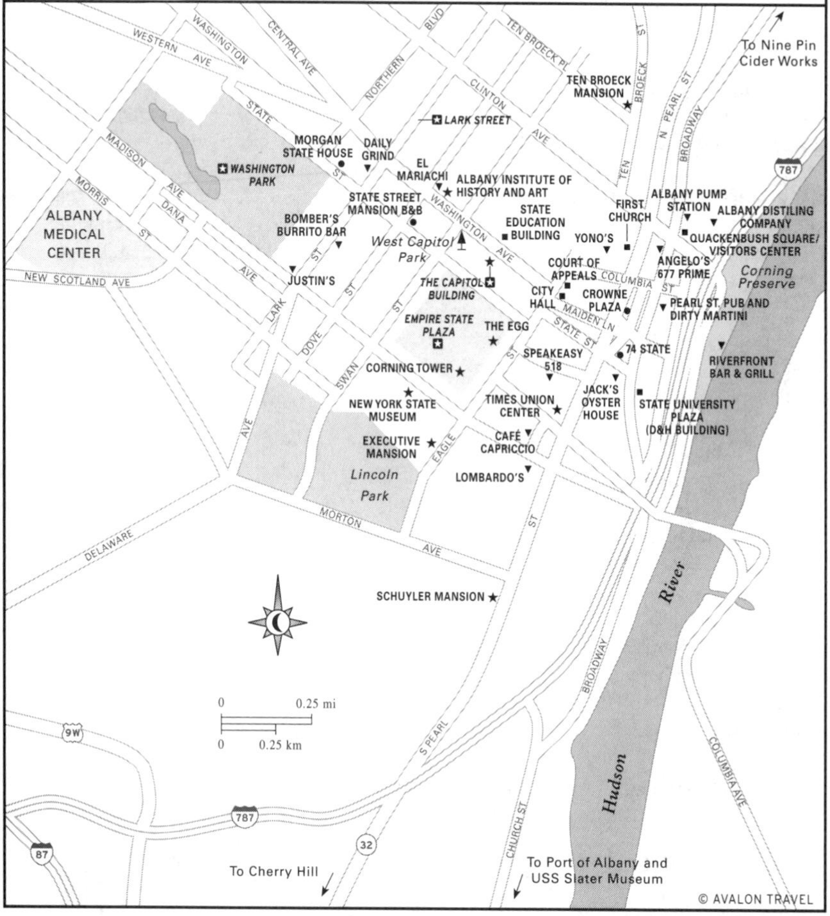

Key to Rockefeller's vision was the incorporation of art into public spaces. (His mother, Abby Aldrich Rockefeller, had been instrumental in the founding of the Museum of Modern Art in New York City.) Accordingly, scattered throughout the plaza, inside and out, are pieces of the impressive **New York State Art Collection** (2978 Corning Tower, 1 Empire State Plaza, 518/474-2418, 8:30am-5pm Mon.-Fri.), featuring the work of New York State artists from the 1960s and 1970s. It is considered one of the most important collections of modern art in the country.

Currently, there are 92 paintings, sculptures, and tapestries displayed on the concourse, in building lobbies, and in outdoor spaces. The collection is especially strong in abstract art. Alexander Caldwell and Mark Rothko are among the best-known artists in the collection. Visitors may view the works anytime government offices are open.

The **Plaza Visitor Center** (518/474-2418, plaza.visitor.center@ogs.ny.gov), located off the main concourse, near The Egg, has maps and information on tours. Additional information booths are located at the north and south ends of the concourse. Take the Empire Plaza exit from I-787. There are several visitor parking lots around the plaza on Madison and Grand Streets. Rates range from $5 to $10 per day, up to $2 per hour (max. $20/day).

New York State Museum

At the south end of the plaza, the **New York State Museum** (Madison Ave., 518/474-5877, www.nysm.nysed.gov, 9:30am-5pm Tues.-Sat., free, donations accepted) began in 1836 as a center for geological and natural history exhibits. Over the years, it has maintained a core focus on geology, biology, anthropology, and history as they relate to the state. Exhibits are organized by regions of the state covering everything from the Adirondack wilderness to the marshland of the Long Island Sound and the A Train to Brooklyn. Particularly moving is the 9/11 exhibit, which includes artifacts recovered from the wreckage of the Twin Towers. The fourth-floor carousel is popular with children. They can ride any of 36 horses, two donkeys, and two deer—all carved around 1895 by Charles Dare of Brooklyn and acquired by the museum in 1975. A Shaker exhibit opened in November 2014.

The Executive Mansion

Governor Cuomo lives in the New York **Executive Mansion** (138 Eagle St., 518/473-7521, www.governor.ny.gov/explore-governors-mansion), one block south of the Empire State Plaza. The home was built in the 1850s and has housed governors and their families since 1875, including Theodore and Franklin Delano Roosevelt. Public rooms contain exquisite artwork and furnishings from the 18th, 19th, and 20th centuries. Guided tours are offered at 10am, 11am, noon, 1pm, and 2pm on Thursdays for groups of 10-30, September through June (reservations required).

★ The Capitol Building

The **Capitol Building** (Washington Ave., 518/474-2418) that towers over State Street hill, adjacent to the north end of the Empire State Plaza, looks more like a European castle than a U.S. state capitol. A stunning set of stairs climbs up to three grand archways, featuring elaborate stone carvings. Construction began by hand in 1867 and took 30 years to complete, by which time Theodore Roosevelt had become governor. The final price tag was

The historic carousel in the New York State Museum is popular with children.

an astronomical $25 million. These days, the building seems to be forever obscured by a wall of scaffolding—signs of ongoing restoration work.

The New York State Assembly conducts its business inside. You can take a guided tour of the building at 10am, noon, 2pm, and 3pm Monday-Friday, excluding holidays. A number of lively inns and restaurants are clustered along State Street, within a short walk for business travelers and midweek lunch-goers.

From the Empire State Plaza, it is a short walk down State Street to Broadway and one of Albany's newest outdoor spaces: The **Hudson River Way** is a pedestrian bridge that crosses over I-787 to **Albany Riverfront Park,** in the Corning Preserve (518/434-2032), where residents come to walk their dogs or read a book on warm afternoons. Along the path are a series of murals depicting Albany's long and colorful history.

Follow Broadway a few blocks farther north to reach the **Albany Heritage Area Visitors Center** (25 Quackenbush Sq., 800/258-3582, www.albany.org, 9am-4pm Mon.-Fri., 10am-3pm Sat., 11am-3pm Sun.), a good place to get an overview of the history and culture of the Capital Region and then enjoy a cold beer at the adjoining microbrewery.

From there, it's a short drive to the handsome **Ten Broeck Mansion** (9 Ten Broeck Pl., 518/436-9826, www.tenbroeckmansion.org, 10am-4pm Thurs.-Fri., 1pm-4pm Sat.-Sun. May-Dec., adults $5, students and seniors $4, children 12 and under $3) where the Albany County Historical Association has set up shop. The Federal-style home was originally built by Abraham Ten Broeck, a distinguished general and statesman who fought at the Battle of Saratoga and later served as mayor of Albany. More than two decades after the wealthy Olcott family had donated the renovated building to the city, museum staff discovered a fully stocked wine cellar in the basement. Many of the surrounding buildings in the once-exclusive Arbor Hill district have been converted into urban apartments.

★ Lark Street and Washington Park

Many of Albany's events, including the popular spring tulip festival, take place in **Washington Park** (www.washingtonpark-conservancy.org), a 90-acre green space in the center of the city that has been public property since the 17th century. Jogging trails circle a small lake and a handful of statues and monuments across the park. A bronze statue

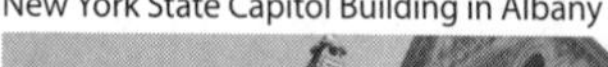

New York State Capitol Building in Albany

of Scottish poet Robert Burns was created by a local sculptor in 1888. The King Fountain was made of rocks from Storm King Mountain in Orange County. Though the park is well loved, it's rarely crowded, and students can always find a quiet place to read. Playgrounds are a draw for kids.

At the east end of the park, bohemian Lark Street is Albany's answer to Manhattan's East Village and San Francisco's Haight-Ashbury. This is the neighborhood of choice for Friday drinks or Sunday brunch. Several blocks of funky shops and trendy eateries between State and Madison Streets attract the city's hippest residents. You'll find everything from vintage video games to boutique clothing and jewelry designers and espresso art.

The historic Center Square neighborhood, bound by Lark, State, Swan, and Jay Streets, connects the Lark Street district to the Empire State Plaza. Stroll through its quiet streets to see rows of brick, brownstone, and clapboard houses more than 100 years old.

Albany Institute of History and Art

For a lasting impression of Hudson River Valley history and culture, save a few hours to visit one of the oldest museums in the United States. Outdating the Smithsonian, the Metropolitan Museum of Art, and the Louvre, the **Albany Institute of History and Art** (125 Washington Ave., 518/463-4478, www.albanyinstitute.org, 10am-5pm Wed. and Fri.-Sat., 10am-8pm Thurs., noon-5pm Sun., adults $10, seniors and students $8, children 6-12 $6, under 6 free, free admission 5pm-8pm Thursdays) was established in 1791. The museum has increasingly broadened its focus over the years to include Hudson River School paintings, artifacts from colonial times, and 19th-century American sculpture. You can easily spend a couple of hours here and still want to return for more.

Schuyler Mansion

Major General Philip Schuyler's home (32 Catherine St., 518/434-0834, www.nysparks.com, 11am-5pm Wed.-Sun. mid-May-Oct., adults $5, seniors and students $4, children 12 and under free) was an important base of operations during the Revolutionary War and is now a New York State Historic Site. Tours begin on the hour and the last tour begins at 4pm.

USS *Slater*

The only restored World War II destroyer

inside the USS *Slater* museum

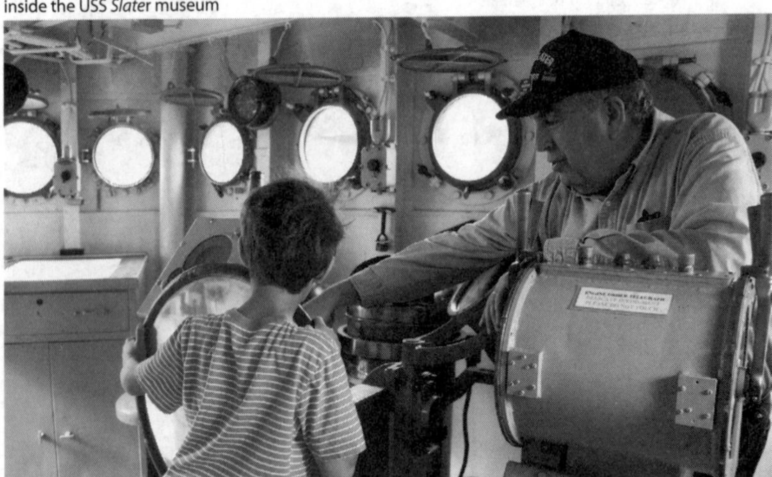

escort, once part of a fleet of more than 500 ships, now rests on the Hudson River at the Port of Albany, as a monument, memorial, and museum dedicated to all the destroyer escorts and their crews. The Allied forces used destroyer escorts to protect convoys of supply ships that were essential to the war effort. The USS *Slater* DE766 is a cannon class destroyer that was built in less than one month and commissioned in May 1944. It served in both the Atlantic and Pacific theaters.

After the war, the ship was transferred to Greece as part of the Military Defense Assistance Program. The ship was active in Greece until 1991, and in 1993, the Destroyer Escort Sailors Association raised enough funding to bring the USS Slater back to the United States. Restoration has been ongoing for nearly two decades, entirely funded by volunteers. A group of veterans visits each fall and stays on board for a week to chip, repaint, and polish various parts of the vessel. Their work is highly detailed—cabins, bunks, and even the refrigeration room look just as they did in the 1940s, thanks to many donated artifacts.

In spring, summer, and fall, the ship is open for **guided tours** (141 Broadway, Albany, 518/431-1943, www.ussslater.org, 10am-4pm Wed.-Sun. Apr.-Nov., adults $8, seniors $7, children 6-14 $6, under 6 free). In winter, it moves one mile south to Rensselaer. The one-hour tour covers several levels of the ship, including the galley, captain's cabin, officer's cabins, and the communications center. Visitors are led up and down ladders and through the narrow hallways of the lower decks. Kids may be invited to try on a helmet and sit in the cannon seats. One of the most interesting aspects of the tour is the retelling of stories shared by previous visitors who served in the military during World War II. The USS Slater does not receive taxpayer funding. Donations are greatly appreciated.

ALBANY COUNTY

Historic Cherry Hill

South of downtown Albany, **Historic Cherry Hill** (523½ S. Pearl St., 518/434-4791, www.historiccherryhill.org, guided tours at 1pm, 2pm, and 3pm Wed. and 2pm and 3pm Sat., adults $5, seniors and college students $4, children 12-18 $2) was once the center of a working farm that belonged to the Van Rensselaer family. A hodgepodge of collections inside the 1787 Colonial-style home document the lives of four generations of the family, ending with Catherine Bogart Putnam Rankin, the great-granddaughter of Philip and Maria Van Rensselaer. On display are ceramics, silver, textiles, books, and photographs.

The home is also known as the site of a famous murder in 1827. Author Louis C. Jones chronicled the story in a book called *Murder at Cherry Hill* and also referred to the murder in a better-known book of ghost stories, *Things That Go Bump in the Night*. From I-787, take Exit 2.

Watervliet Shaker Historic District

In the shadow of the Albany Airport stands an intriguing slice of history, the **Watervliet Shaker Historic District** and the site of the first American Shaker settlement (875 Watervliet Shaker Rd., 518/456-7890, www.shakerheritage.org, 9:30am-4pm Tues.-Sat. Feb.-Oct., 10am-4pm Mon.-Sat. Nov.-mid-Dec.). The first group of Shakers arrived here in 1776 with the founder of the movement, Ann Lee, and built a log cabin as the first communal dwelling. Over the years, the community grew to 350 people, and the last members left the site in 1938.

Visitors can explore several buildings, beginning with a museum in the 1848 Shaker Meeting House. Outside are an herb garden, barnyard, and network of trails around a nature preserve. Lee and other early members are buried in the Shaker Cemetery on the property. Guided tours are offered at 11:30am and 1:30pm Saturdays June-October. This is a convenient place to let young kids run around before or after a long flight to or from Albany.

Albany Pine Bush Preserve

A dry and sandy 3,200-acre preserve just outside of Albany is a geological wonder because it looks like it belongs on the coast, with pitch pines and scrub oak dotting the landscape. This is prime habitat for the endangered Karner blue butterfly, which feeds on blue lupine growing in the dry clearings of the rare pine barrens ecosystem. Visit the **Albany Pine Bush Discovery Center** (195 New Karner Rd., Albany, 518/456-0655, www.albanypinebush.org) to get acquainted with the wildlife and trails in the preserve. Keep an eye out for creatures large and small: Fishers, white-tailed deer, cottontail rabbits, and red and gray foxes all call this area home. Plan your visit in late May, when the lupine is in full bloom, to increase your chances of seeing the Karner blue butterfly.

John Boyd Thacher State Park

West of Albany, **John Boyd Thacher State Park** (1 Hailes Cave Rd., Voorheesville, 518/872-1237, www.nysparks.com, 8am-dusk daily, admission $6) celebrated its 100th anniversary in 2014. It encompasses the Helderberg Escarpment, a six-mile-long limestone cliff that contains billion-year-old fossils and rock formations. Even amateur geologists will be able to spot the distinct change in rock formations as they climb and descend the staircases of the Indian Ladder, an 80-foot cliff on top of the escarpment. The hike leads one back to the time when the area surrounding Albany was covered by a warm tropical sea. For an informative geology lesson, call to sign up for a **guided tour** (518/872-0800) with the park interpreter.

Besides the geological features, the park offers panoramic views of the Adirondack and Berkshire Mountains and of Vermont's Green Mountains. Residents fought hard to keep this park open when budget cuts swept the state. Twelve miles of trails accommodate hiking, mountain biking, cross-country skiing, snowshoeing, and snowmobiling. Also on the premises are an Olympic-size swimming pool, basketball and volleyball courts, playgrounds, ball fields, and picnic areas.

Rensselaerville

In the southwest corner of Albany County lies the 200-year-old hamlet of Rensselaerville (not to be confused with the Rensselaer County city of Rensselaer), named for the Dutch patroon who ran the local manor. Due to its remote location, the site was settled relatively late by colonial standards—in the 1780s—by Revolutionary War veterans from Long Island and New England. A number of handsome 19th-century buildings have been preserved along Main Street, including the original gristmill. **The Grist Mill Museum** (Main St., Rensselaerville, 10am-3pm Wed. and noon-2pm Sat. Memorial Day-Labor Day) is part of the local historical society. Today, they house a dozen antiques shops and restaurants. There is also a 2,000-acre preserve with 10 miles of trails for hiking and exploring the Catskill Creek. To get to Rensselaerville, take I-90 to Exit/Route 85 West and follow Route 85 for 12 miles. If you arrive hungry for dinner, try the **Palmer House Café** (1462 Main St., Rensselaerville, 518/797-3449, www.palmerhousecafe.com, 5pm-9:30pm Thurs.-Sun., $15-25) for dependable American cuisine and a full bar that serves pub fare.

Five Rivers Environmental Education Center

Ten miles of trails meander across fields and streams at this New York State Department of Environmental Conservation park. The **visitors center** (56 Game Farm Rd., Delmar, 518/475-0291, www.dec.ny.gov/education/1835.html) has nature-themed exhibits, maps, and guides. A variety of outdoor education programs are held throughout the year. Wildlife includes the eastern bluebird, pileated woodpecker, wood duck, snapping turtle, and great horned owl.

SPORTS AND RECREATION

Winter Sports

Hockey and figure skating are popular

winter activities in the Albany area. Empire State Plaza and Albany County Hockey Training Facility have rinks with public skate sessions. Nordic skiers will find trails at John Boyd Thacher State Park and at the 400-acre **Five Rivers Environmental Education Center** (56 Game Farm Rd., Delmar, 518/475-0291, www.dec.ny.gov/education/1835.html). And for downhill skiers, Windham and Hunter Mountains are a half hour away in the Upper Hudson River Valley.

The **Empire State Plaza Ice Rink** (279 Madison Ave., Albany, 877/659-4377, www.winter.empirestateplaza.org, 11am-8pm daily, Dec.-Mar., $4 adults, $3 children) offers views of the State Capitol during winter skating excursions. The rink provides rentals and also has a skate lounge with lockers and music, as well as an on-site café. Note that some form of collateral, such as a driver's license, is required for rentals. The rink often hosts special events, such as meet-and-greets with Olympic skaters and special skate clinics.

Hiking

Four short hiking trails loop through John Boyd Thacher State Park, ranging 0.9-2.5 miles in length. The park also marks the northern terminus for the 326-mile Long Path, named for a line in a famous Walt Whitman poem, "Song of the Open Road":

> Afoot and light-hearted I take to the open road, Healthy, free, the world before me, The long brown path before me leading wherever I choose.

The Long Path begins at the George Washington Bridge and meanders across the Hudson River Valley, eventually entering the park from the west.

For more hiking opportunities near Albany, try the Albany Pine Bush Preserve or Five Rivers Environmental Education Center.

Backpackers should continue north to the Adirondack Park, for overnight hikes in the backcountry.

Cycling

The 41-mile-long Mohawk-Hudson Bikeway connects Albany, Schenectady, and Troy along the Hudson and Mohawk Rivers. Call 518/372-5656 or 800/962-8007 for a free map. The **Mohawk-Hudson Cycling Club** (www.mohawkhudsoncyclingclub.org) organizes road and mountain biking trips within an 80-mile radius of the Albany-Schenectady-Troy area, including a September Century Weekend that begins in Saratoga Spa State Park and Mountain Bike Festival at **Grafton Lakes State Park** (100 Grafton Lakes State Park Way, Grafton, 518/279-1155, www.nysparks.com) outside of Troy.

In addition, several hundred cyclists participate each summer in the **Cycling the Erie Canal Tour** (518/434-1583, www.ptny.org/canaltour, $675), an eight-day ride from Buffalo to Albany covering roughly 50 miles a day. The fee includes camping, meals, entertainment, and riding support. In its 16th year in 2014, the event is sponsored by Parks & Trails New York, a local nonprofit.

Albany can also be the starting point for a multiday bike tour of the Hudson River Valley. Order a guide with step-by-step directions and detailed maps from **Parks & Trails New York** (www.ptny.org).

Stop by the **Downtube Bicycle Works** (466 Madison Ave., Albany, 518/434-1711, www.downtubebicycleworks.com, 11am-7pm Mon.-Fri., 10am-5pm Sat., 11am-4pm Sun.) in a convenient downtown location, for gear and information. **The Broadway Bicycle Company** (1205 Broadway, Albany, 518/451-9400, www.broadwaybicycleco.com, 11am-7pm Mon.-Sat.) hosts monthly rides and sells Specialized bikes. It's a good choice for gear, advice, or repairs.

Mountain bikers can find lengthy trail systems at John Boyd Thacher State Park, Grafton Lakes State Park, and Albany Pine Bush Preserve.

Golf

Capital Hills at Albany (65 O'Neil Rd., 518/438-2208, www.caphills.com, $29), designed in 1929, maintains a challenging public course (18 holes) with tough closing holes and considerable elevation change. Rent a cart unless you're looking for a cardio workout. Ten miles north of Albany, **Mill Road Acres Golf Course** (30 Mill Rd., Latham, 518/785-4653, www.millroadacres.com, weekdays 9 holes $15, 18 holes $22, weekends 9 holes $18, 18 holes $27) has a well-maintained nine-hole course.

You can mix and match the four nine-hole courses at the **Town of Colonie Golf Course** (418 Consaul Rd., Schenectady, 518/374-4181, www.colonie.org/parks/golf, 9 holes $22, 18 holes $30). The Red/White course combination has water hazards on six holes.

Swimming and Boating

Dutch Apple Cruises (Madison and Broadway, Albany, 518/463-0220, www.dutchapplecruises.com) operates several cruises per week from Snow Dock in the Port of Albany, right next to the USS Slater museum.

ACCOMMODATIONS

Albany's many business hotels are clustered downtown and near the airport. Unique properties are more difficult but not impossible to come by. Look near Washington Park and the Empire State Plaza.

Under $100

In 1997, Rensselaerville residents Steve and Marlene Omlor restored an 1806 home to create the **Catalpa House** (Main St., Rensselaerville, 518/768-1806, www.thecatalpahouse.com, $85-130), named for a giant catalpa tree that stands on the front lawn. The inn has six country-style rooms, two of which have private baths. The reasonable rates include breakfast and afternoon tea.

$100-150

In the shadow of the state capitol buildings, the **★ State Street Mansion Bed & Breakfast** (281 State St., Albany, 518/462-6780 or 800/673-5750, www.statestreetmansion.com, $125-150) is a three-story brownstone B&B with 12 amply furnished rooms and off-street parking. Smaller doubles with private bath run $125 per night, while larger rooms with two queens go for $150 per night. Flat-screen TVs with cable, wireless Internet, and continental breakfast included.

Two heated pools and a day spa are among the amenities at **The Desmond** (660 Albany Shaker Rd., 518/869-8100 or 800/448-3500, www.desmondhotelsalbany.com, $139-189), primarily a business hotel and conference center with basic rooms in a complex of brick buildings. There are two restaurants on-site: Scrimshaw serves steak au poivre, veal Oscar, and cedar-plank salmon in an 80-seat dining room, while Simpson's is a casual venue for all-American fare. Weekend packages include rooms and meals at discounted rates. Take Exit I-87 to Exit 4.

$150-200

One block from the state capitol and the Times Union Center, the **Hilton Albany** (40 Lodge St., 518/462-6611, www.hiltonalbany.com, $160-260) underwent a $16 million renovation in 2013 when it took property over from Crowne Plaza Hotels & Resorts. The facility includes 384 modern rooms on 15 floors, plus a health club and business center. High-speed Internet is a plus at the eight-story **Albany Marriott** (189 Wolf Rd., 518/458-8444 or 800/443-8952, www.marriott.com, $130-210), a 350-room establishment located four miles from downtown.

Among the most posh in Albany accommodations is the four-room **★ Morgan State House** (393 State St., 518/427-6063 or 888/427-6063, www.statehouse.com, $135-225), where feather beds, robes, and down comforters make for a cozy night's stay. A 12-foot ceiling with skylights makes room No. 4B one of the best in the house.

The **74 State** (74 State St., 518/434-7410, www.74state.com, $155-279) is a boutique hotel with a great downtown location. Some of its 74 rooms have city views; others have just a very small window. Ask ahead of time if daylight matters to you. The service is attentive, though the building itself could use some freshening up.

At the **Hilton Garden Inn-Albany Airport** (800 Albany Shaker Rd., 518/464-6666, $100-120) adjacent to the Albany Airport, the night staff has a tradition of buying breakfast for the last visitor to arrive for the night. A small pantry in the lobby has a variety of healthy snack foods for sale, since restaurants are hard to find at off hours. Rooms come with microwave ovens for simple meal preparation. This property completed a multimillion-dollar renovation in 20111, giving rooms and commons areas a modern look and feel. Rooms with one king bed or two full-size beds are basic but pleasant enough for a one-night stay, and you can't get any closer to the airport. The hotel has an inviting lobby, swimming pool, free Wi-Fi, and high-definition TVs. Accessible rooms have modified bathrooms to accommodate wheelchairs.

At the intersection of Wolf Road and the airport access road, **Hotel Indigo** (254 Old Wolf Rd., Latham, 518/869-9100, www.hotelindigo.com, $145-185) is a dressed-up motel, with contemporary decor and a small café on-site. The suites have small kitchenettes that work well for families. Guest rooms have parquet floors and brightly colored linens. Hotel amenities include a sauna, fitness room, and Internet.

FOOD

There are hundreds of restaurants to choose from in the Albany metropolitan area. A steady stream of politicians and financial executives support a diverse and upscale restaurant scene downtown.

Surf and Turf

One of the oldest and most traditional establishments is ★ **Jack's Oyster House** (42 State St., 518/465-8854, www.jacksoysterhouse.com, 11:30am-10pm daily, $22-40), a turn-of-the-20th-century tavern with a dark wood interior that creates a formal but not stuffy atmosphere. During the busy lunch hour, waiters dressed in snappy uniforms whisk about the dining room carrying trays of fresh oysters from the raw bar. Steaks pair well with the restaurant's private-label red wine from Silverado Vineyards in California.

Inside the Hampton Inn & Suites, **Yono's Restaurant** (25 Chapel St., 518/436-7747, www.yonos.com, dinner Mon.-Sat., $21-36) feels a bit old-fashioned with its ornate dining room, round tables, live piano music, and formal service. But the food is first-rate, representing a who's who of Hudson River Valley farms. Flavors hint of Indonesian and Continental cuisine: hand-rolled vegetable lumpia, satay four ways, pan-seared Hudson River Valley foie gras, lobster curry tamarind soup.

Chef Yono also oversees the more casual **dp: An American Brasserie** (518/436-3737, www.dpbrasserie.com, lunch and dinner Mon.-Fri., dinner only Sat., $10-26), with a menu of small plates, steak frites, salad entrées, and burgers. A Pimm's cocktail at the casual bar hit the spot on a summer evening.

★ **Angelo's 677 Prime** (677 Broadway at Clinton Ave., 518/427-7463, www.677prime.com, lunch 11:30am-2pm Mon.-Fri., dinner 5:30pm-10pm Mon.-Sat., bar menu available 2pm-10pm Mon.-Fri., dinner $26-58) is an excellent steakhouse and wine bar centrally located in Albany's theater district. Chopped or wedge salads, caviar, and a full raw bar complement a menu of Kobe beef, steak *au poivre*, and a 40-ounce porterhouse for two. You can also start with French onion soup or lobster bisque, and order the potato of your choice. Live music plays Wednesday-Saturday 6:30pm-10pm.

Taverns and Pubs

Justin's (301 Lark St., Albany, 518/472-0662, www.justinsalbany.com, 4pm-midnight Mon.-Fri., 10:30am-midnight Sat.-Sun., $16-27), is an eclectic basement restaurant with a small street-side patio that is packed at almost any time of day on the weekend. The bar stays open until 4am daily. The corned-beef hash is deserving of its reputation. Wicker furniture,

Outdoor Dining in Albany and Saratoga Springs

ALBANY

- **Justin's:** Sit under a green awning in a small sidewalk seating area in front of the restaurant and watch the action on Lark Street. Try the Norwegian frittata of salmon, spinach and gouda cheese. Weekend brunch is served 10:30am-3pm Saturday and Sunday. (301 Lark St., 518/472-0662, www.justinsalbany.com)
- **Lark Street Wine Bar & Bistro:** Sip a glass of prosecco on the patio and order from a mostly gluten-free menu. Chef and owner Kevin Everleth is a CIA graduate with a passion for French cuisine. (200 Lark St., 518/463-2881, www.winebaronlark.com)
- **McGeary's:** Order Irish pub fare and choose from 26 beers on tap. Outdoor dining is offered in a small front patio in Clinton Square, near the intersection of North Pearl and Clinton Streets. (4 Clinton Sq., 518/463-1455, www.mcgearyspub.com)
- **Nicole's Restaurant:** For a little romance, head to the quiet courtyard surrounded by flowers at this Quackenbush Square eatery. A husband-wife team prepares Italian fare with a sophisticated twist. (556 Delaware Ave., 518/436-4952, www.nicolescatering.com)

SARATOGA SPRINGS

- **Stadium Café:** This place packs in the sports fans on big game days. But you can relax with a beer at one of a few sidewalk tables under the shade of a wide awning. (389 Broadway, 518/226-4437)
- **Uncommon Grounds:** Cool off with a smoothie or iced coffee at a sidewalk table in front of this café and enjoy the people-watching along Broadway. (402 Broadway, 518/581-0656, www.uncommongrounds.com)
- **Wheatfields:** Choose a sidewalk table in the fenced area along Broadway and enjoy a three-course bistro-style dinner on a warm summer evening after a day at the tracks. (440 Broadway, Saratoga Springs, 518/587-0534, www.wheatfields.com)
- **Chianti Il Ristorante:** This Italian eatery serves a three-course "early seating" menu Monday-Saturday for $19. Some of the restaurant's produce is grown on a newly purchased property called DZ Farm. Order a bottle of red and enjoy the outdoor patio setting. (18 Division St., 518/580-0025, www.chiantiristorante.com)

dim lighting, and dark paint won't detract from the experience of eating the *ropa vieja* sandwich made of braised Cuban brisket.

There are at least two river-based restaurants in the Capital Region: The **RiverFront Bar & Grill** (Corning Preserve, 518/426-4738, www.riverfrontbarge.com, open seasonally, call for hours, $9-18) in Albany and the **Rusty Anchor** (1 Selke Dr., Watervliet, 518/273-2920, 11:30am-2am Mon.-Fri., noon-2am Sat.-Sun., $8-12) in Watervliet both run on floating barges and are modeled on the successful Gully's restaurant at the Newburgh Landing in the Mid-Hudson River Valley.

Next door to the visitors center, ★ **C. H. Evans Brewing Company at the Albany Pump Station** (19 Quackenbush Sq., Albany, 518/447-9000, www.evansale.com, 11:30am-10pm Mon.-Thurs., 11:30am-11pm Fri.-Sat., noon-8pm Sun., $14-24) occupies the 1874 pump station, which once drew water from the Hudson River to the tune of seven billion gallons a year. The owner comes from a family with a long history of brewing in the area. The original Evans family brewery was located in Hudson. The modern-day microbrewery and restaurant serves award-winning brews including the Quackenbush Blonde, Evans Whit, and the Kick-Ass Brown. Beer influences the menu as well, appearing in the pale-ale battered red onion rings and beer-battered fish-and-chips. Other notable dishes include the grass-fed beef smoked chili and harvest medley salad.

Pinto & Hobbs Tavern (142 Washington Ave., Albany, 528/512-5800, 11:30am-close Mon.-Fri., 5pm-close Sat.-Sun., $11-30) operates a full bar and serves sandwiches and Italian-style entrées, as well as tavern classics including wings and burgers. Wednesday is karaoke night.

Italian

More than 100 Italian restaurants are scattered across the Albany area, but a few of them manage to rise above the rest: Locals choose ★ **Lombardo's Restaurant** (121 Madison Ave., 518/462-9180, www.lombardosofalbany.com, 11am-2pm and 4pm-11pm Mon.-Fri., 3pm-11pm Sat., $15-29) for delicious and reasonably priced Italian fare. For northern Italian convenient to downtown, grab a table at **Café Capriccio** (49 Grand St., 518/465-0439, www.cafecapriccio.com, 5pm-9pm Sun.-Thurs., 5pm-10pm Fri.-Sat., $20-35).

After a day of shopping, supersized plates of pasta and giant bottles of chianti define the southern Italian experience at **Buca di Beppo** (44 Wolff Rd., Colonie, 518/459-2822 www.bucadibeppo.com, 11am-10pm Mon.-Thurs., 11am-11pm Fri.-Sat., 11am-9pm Sun., $15-25), outside of Albany.

International

El Mariachi (289 Hamilton St., 518/432-7580, and 144 Washington Ave., 518/465-2568, 11:30am-10pm Mon.-Thurs., 11:30am-11pm Fri., 1pm-11pm Sat.) serves authentic Mexican fare in two downtown Albany locations. The full tequila bar and homemade sangria are a plus. Local students prefer the cheap eats and Ms. Pac-Man game at ★ **Bombers Burrito Bar** (258 Lark St., 518/463-9636, www.bombersburritobar.com, 11am-2am Sun.-Wed., 11am-3am Thurs.-Sat., $8-10).

The Cheese Traveler (540 Delaware Ave., Albany, 518/443-0440, www.thecheesetraveler.com, 11am-7pm Tues.-Fri., 10am-5pm Sat.-Sun., $7-9) is owned by cheesemonger Eric Paul, who opened this cheese, meat, and specialty food shop in 2011. Eric personally takes customers through the process of selecting just the right cheeses, while also providing background info and insight. The sandwich menu is small but impressive, featuring choices like the Sweet and Savory, which consists of pawlet cheese, smoked duck breast, and berry preserves on fresh ciabatta.

The focal point of the **New World Bistro Bar** (300 Delaware Ave., Albany, 518/694-0520, www.newworldbistrobar.com, 4pm-9:30pm Mon.-Thurs., 4pm-11pm Fri.-Sat., 11am-9:30pm Sun., mains $15-26), an 80-seat gastro pub in Albany's Delaware Avenue neighborhood, is an art deco mahogany bar from the 1939 World's Fair. Menus here rotate seasonally to allow for organic, locally sourced ingredients. Classics such as burgers and flatbreads join innovative dishes including asparagus, goat cheese, and green chili cannelloni and meatloaf stuffed with smoked gouda and wrapped in bacon. Vegan and gluten-free menus are also available. Reservations are highly recommended.

Nightclub Restaurants

Restaurants that turn into nightclubs are a growing trend in Albany. Some patrons like the high-energy atmosphere; others feel rushed and overwhelmed when the DJ starts to spin.

The **Pearl St. Pub and Dirty Martini Lounge** (1 Steuben Pl. on South Pearl St., 518/694-3100, www.thepearlstreetpub.com, lunch 11am-4pm Mon.-Fri., dinner 5pm-9pm Mon.-Wed., 5pm-10pm Thurs.-Sat., lunch $8-12, dinner $14-19) hosts karaoke, trivia, and other special events throughout the week. The comfort food menu features salads, burgers, sandwiches, sirloin steak, fillet of sole, lasagna, and pizzas.

Cafés and Quick Bites

With 50 years of experience, **Bob and Ron's Fish Fry** (1007 Central Ave., 518/482-5112, www.bobandronfishfry.com, 11am-8pm Mon.-Thurs., 11am-9pm Fri., noon-8pm Sat., $7-17) does seafood right. Impatient locals will stand in line forever for a basket of fish-and-chips. Meanwhile, **Paesan's** (289 Ontario St., 518/435-0312, www.paesanspizza.com, 11am-1am Sun.-Thurs., 11am-2am Fri.-Sat., $7-11) has mastered the art of the thin-crust pizza. Most weekdays, a host of vendors congregate on the lawn behind the capitol building serving lunch to go. A slice of pizza or a couple of tacos are among the best deals around.

In business since 1976, **The Daily Grind** (204 Lark St., 518/427-0464 or 888/876-3222, www.dailygrind.com, 10am-6pm Mon.-Sat., 9:30am-4:30pm Sun.) is a European-style coffee bar and café that roasts its own beans.

At **Caffe Vero** (260 Lark St., no tel., www.caffeverocoffee.com, 7am-8pm Mon.-Thurs., 7am-9pm Fri., 8am-9pm Sat., 8:30am-7pm Sun.), your latte comes with a signature heart or leaf drawn into the foam.

Culinary Events

Twice a year since 2004, the Downtown Albany Business Improvement District has organized Restaurant Week, inviting thousands of restaurant-goers to enjoy a three-course meal at participating eateries across the city. Prices were $20.14 per person in 2014, to match the year. Some of the city's most upscale establishments participate, including Marché, Jack's Oyster House, the Mansion Hill Inn, and Pearl St. Pub. Search the "things to do" section of www.downtownalbany.org for information.

If you're visiting in August, check the calendar for the **Empire State Plaza Food Festival,** a one-day event including a farmers market, more than 50 food vendors, and live music (www.albany.com/event/esp-food-festival-36224).

The Egg was designed by Harrison & Abramovitz.

ENTERTAINMENT AND EVENTS

Performing Arts

The twin theaters inside **The Egg** (Empire State Plaza, 518/473-1061 or 518/473-1845 for box office, www.theegg.org) showcase theater, dance, music, and comedy. Recent performances at The Egg have included George Thorogood & The Destroyers, Keb' Mo', Béla Fleck & The Flecktones, Ray Manzarek and Robby Krieger of The Doors, Golden Dragon Chinese Acrobats, Hot Tuna, and Steven Wright.

Spectrum 8 Theatres (290 Delaware Ave., 518/449-8995, www.spectrum8.com, adults $10, seniors $8, children 13 and under $7.50) is the place to catch an indie film along with some of the best movie snacks around.

Founded in 1931, the **Albany Symphony Orchestra** (19 Clinton Ave., 518/465-4755, www.albanysymphony.com) plays at the Palace Theatre near Quackenbush Square. Its programs often emphasize contemporary or overlooked American works.

Steamer No. 10 (500 Western Ave., Albany, 518/438-5503, www.steamer10theatre.org) is a nonprofit theater that produces and presents shows for children and families, as well as tours schools and theaters throughout the Northeast. In addition to its professional cast, there is a children's theater that holds family-friendly productions, special acting classes, and children's workshops, as well as Shakespeare in the Park each July-August in Lincoln Park.

The Rolling Stones once played at the **Palace Theatre** (19 Clinton Ave., 518/465-3334, www.palacealbany.com), a restored 1933 theater that has hosted the likes of Chris Tucker, Stone Temple Pilots, and the Moscow Ballet in recent seasons.

Bars and Nightlife

Albany boasts a colorful nightlife scene, with many bars and clubs along Pearl and Lark Streets. The free alternative weekly *Metroland* (www.metroland.net) covers Capital Region happenings in exhaustive detail. Copies are available at many bars, restaurants, and convenience stores, and on many street corners.

Steps away from the Times Union Center, the martini bar at **Pearl St. Pub** (1 Steuben Pl. on South Pearl St., 518/694-3100, www.thepearlstreetpub.com) is open until 4am Monday through Saturday.

Choose from among 30 wines by the glass and 160 bottles at **The Ginger Man** (234 Western Ave., 518/427-5963, www.albanygingerman.com, 11:30am-11pm Mon.-Thurs., 11:30am-11:30pm Fri., 4:30pm-11:30pm Sat.), a wine bar near Washington Park. **Justin's Café** (301 Lark St., 518/472-0662, www.justinsalbany.com, 10:30am-midnight Fri.-Sun.) draws a steady late-night crowd as well.

Speakeasy 518 (42 Howard St., Albany, 518/449-2332, www.speakeasy518.com, 5pm-close Mon.-Fri., 8pm-close Sat.) is an upscale bar in true 1920s style, complete with oil lamps on each table, brick walls, a roaring fire, and a menu of Prohibition-era-inspired drinks. Cell phones are not welcome, and reservations are highly recommended.

Nine Pin Cider Works (929 Broadway, Albany, 518/449-9999, www.ninepincider.com) is new on the scene since 2014, producing hard ciders made entirely from apples grown in the Capital District and throughout the Hudson River Valley. The tasting room (4pm-9pm Thurs.-Fri., 1pm-9pm Sat.) is an opportunity to try a glass of cider or purchase merchandise. Tours are also available by appointment.

Albany Distilling Company (78 Montgomery St., Albany, 518/621-7191, www.albanydistilling.com, tours and tastings 4pm-8pm Tues. and noon-8pm Sat.) is a small operation in downtown Albany, producing one batch of spirits at a time. Spirits include the Ironweed whiskey and Quackenbush Still House rum labels. This is the first licensed distillery in Albany since Prohibition.

Festivals

For almost 60 years, Albany residents have celebrated their Dutch heritage with the annual **Albany Tulip Festival** (Washington Park, 518/434-2032, www.albanyevents.org), which coincides each year with Mother's Day in May. Sample an array of foods and live music while you admire the massive display of flowers. Lark Street has a festival for just about every season. One Saturday each September, the street closes to traffic to host **LarkFEST,** with music, food, and entertainment. **Art on Lark** takes place in June, with hundreds of artists exhibiting or performing their works. And **Winter WonderLARK** is a December event, complete with ice sculptures, holiday shopping, and runners sprinting the length of the street in their Speedos. Details for all of these events are at www.larkstreet.org.

Spectator Sports

Before visiting Albany, check the **Times Union Center** (formerly the Pepsi Arena, 51 S. Pearl St., Albany, 518/487-2000, www.timesunioncenter-albany.com) website for upcoming events. You might be able to catch a monster truck show, the latest mega-concert, or an NBA game. The arena is the home to the AHL (American Hockey League) Albany Devils, Albany Firebirds (arena football), and the Siena Saints college basketball team.

SHOPPING

Albany-area shopping malls draw consumers from hours away for a healthy dose of retail therapy. With anchor stores including Macy's, Burlington Coat Factory, H&M, Home Depot, PetSmart, JCPenney, and Walmart, the **Crossgates Mall** (1 Crossgates Mall Rd., Albany, 518/869-9565, www.shopcrossgates.com, 10am-9:30pm Mon.-Sat., 11am-6pm Sun.), in Guilderland, a suburb of Albany, bills itself as the largest mall in New York State. For a funkier selection of clothing and locally made crafts, head to the shops on Lark Street in downtown Albany. Among the many boutiques and antiques shops is **Elissa Halloran Designs** (229 Lark St., 518/432-7090, www.ehdesigns.com, 11am-6pm Tues.-Wed., 11am-7pm Thurs.-Fri., noon-6pm Sat.), which carries women's apparel and handmade jewelry. Lark Street also has a fun retro video game store, **Pastime Legends Video Games** (292 Lark St., 518/512-5353, www.pastimelegends.com, noon-9pm Tues.-Sat., noon-6pm Sun.).

Bookstores

The Book House of Stuyvesant Plaza (1475 Western Ave. and Fuller Rd., 518/489-4761, www.bhny.com, 10am-9pm Mon.-Fri., 10am-6pm Sat., noon-5pm Sun.) is a reliable independent bookstore featuring local authors in Albany's Stuyvesant Plaza strip mall.

Farm Stands

After checking out the Helderberg Escarpment, pay a visit in spring, summer, or early fall to **Indian Ladder Farms** (342 Altamont Voorheesville Rd., Altamont, 518/765-2956, www.indianladderfarms.com, store 9am-5pm daily year-round) to pick your own apples, raspberries, and blueberries. You can also pick your own strawberries in season at **Altamont Orchards** (6654 Dunnsville Rd., Altamont, 518/861-6515, www.altamontorchards.com, store 9am-6pm Mon.-Fri., 9am-4:30pm Sat.-Sun. year-round). **Ryan's Farmers Market** (114 Railroad Ave., Albany, 518/459-5775, www.ryansproduce.com, 8am-6pm Mon.-Fri., 7am-6pm Sat.) is an indoor farmers market that stays open year-round.

INFORMATION AND SERVICES

The **Albany Visitors Center** (25 Quackenbush Sq., 518/434-1217 or 800/258-3582, www.albany.org, 9am-4pm Mon.-Fri., 10am-3pm Sat., 11am-3pm Sun.) has a wealth of information on local attractions.

GETTING THERE AND AROUND

As a major transportation hub for the Catskill and Capital regions, Albany is easily reached by air, train, car, or bus. Many residents as far south as Dutchess County prefer to fly in and out of Albany International Airport than fight traffic around the New York City airports.

Bus

Dozens of local bus lines serve the Albany metro area. Check the **Capital District Transportation Authority** website (www.cdta.org, base fare $1.50, unlimited day pass $4) for current routes and schedules.

Train

One of the most pleasant ways to get from New York City to the Capital Region is to board an **Amtrak** (800/USA-RAIL or 800/872-7245, www.amtrak.com) train at Penn Station and follow the Hudson River for two hours north. Be sure to get a seat on the left side to catch the views the whole way up the river. Cabs are readily available from the Rensselaer station (525 East St., Rensselaer).

Car

Albany is a major metropolitan area with heavy traffic during commuting hours. I-87 and I-787 are the main north-south highways. The Albany Airport is Exit 13N on I-87. You can rent a car from all the major chains at the Albany Airport.

Rensselaer County

Look at a Grandma Moses painting and you will have a good idea of the atmosphere of much of eastern Rensselaer County, which contrasts greatly with the formerly industrial towns along the Hudson on the western border of the county. The Taconic, Berkshire, and Green Mountains provide the backdrop for the pastoral setting of the east while the cities of Troy and Rensselaer hug the Hudson.

Members of the Van Rensselaer family were the original patroons of the area around Albany, and their name graces not only the county but also the town and the original engineering school in this country—Rensselaer Polytechnic Institute. This premier institution was founded in a city that once made detachable men's shirt collars—there was an Arrow Factory in town, and by 1925, 9 out of 10 people in the country were wearing collars made in Troy. More notably, it's where the Ferris wheel was created. Indeed, Troy did its part to churn along the Industrial Revolution. That history is best explored at the **RiverSpark Visitor Center** in downtown Troy.

The meatpacking industry produced Troy's arguably best-known resident, Samuel Wilson (Uncle Sam), whose statue pays tribute to him near **Riverfront Park** downtown. He is buried in the nearby historic Oakwood Cemetery in the northern part of Troy. Industry brought great wealth to the area, as witnessed by the elegant homes and the plethora of Tiffany glass found in this community.

The city quickly gives way to quieter small-town settings that dot the rest of the county. Opportunity for outdoor recreation abounds in two state parks, Grafton Lakes and Cherry Plain. Sinuous roads lead to oft-surprising small treasures of communities tucked away in the country. Farmers markets sell honey, maple sugar, and produce and range from small roadside stands to larger, well-developed markets. Troy has a weekly farmers market down on the Hudson.

TROY AND RENSSELAER

Troy

Known as the Collar City, Troy was at the heart of the Industrial Revolution. Stroll along its streets to see some of the finest examples

Train tracks cross the Hudson River south of Albany.

Troy

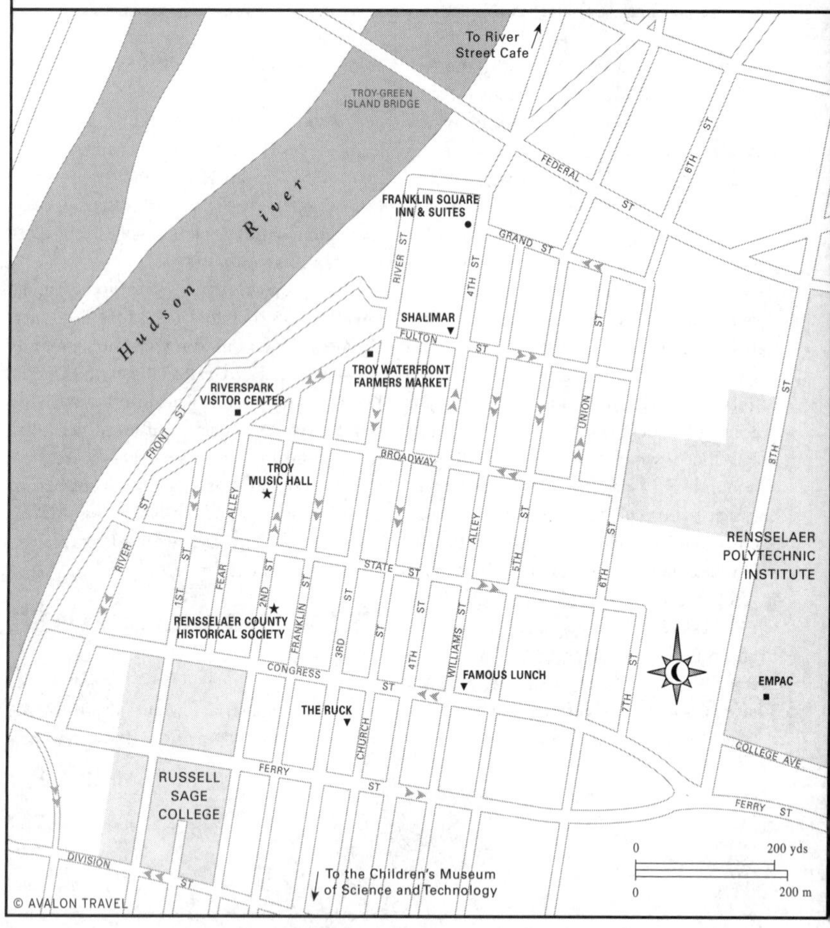

of urban architecture in a concentrated area. The streetscapes appeared in the 1993 movie *The Age of Innocence.*

Known for its superb acoustic properties, the **Troy Savings Bank Music Hall** (30 Second St., 518/273-0038, www.troymusichall.org) reflects beaux arts and French Renaissance influences. George B. Post, who also designed Chickering Hall in New York City, was the architect. The building was completed in 1875.

Just a few steps away, the **Rensselaer County Historical Society** is located in the Joseph B. Carr Building (57 2nd St., 518/272-7232, www.rchsonline.org, noon-5pm Thurs.-Sat. Feb.-Dec. 23, closed major holidays). You can tour the neighboring Federal-style **Hart-Cluett House** on the second Saturday of each month. Guided walking tours of Troy are also offered on Saturdays at 11am, or you can pick up a map from RiverSpark and opt for a self-guided tour.

Antiques shops, restaurants, and other stores line the streets of the downtown area.

The **Troy Waterfront Farmers Market** (49 4th St., Troy, 518/708-4216, www.troymarket.org, 9am-2pm Sat., 6pm-9pm Fri. June-Sep.) is held outdoors in the summer (Broadway St. between 3rd and 4th Streets, 3pm-6pm Wed., and 290 River St., 9am-1pm Sat.) and moves indoors for the winter at the Uncle Sam Atrium (Third St. and Broadway, 9am-1pm Sat., Nov.-Apr.). The market gives visitors the opportunity to select farm-grown foods from more than 80 vendors.

South of downtown is the **Burden Iron Works Museum** (1 E. Industrial Pkwy., 518/274-5267, open when staffed by volunteers, call ahead), which used to cast bells, including the Centennial Bell that hangs in Independence Hall in Philadelphia, but now offers tours of Troy with themes including Tiffany glass and the Iron Works.

The **Children's Museum of Science and Technology** (250 Jordan Rd., 518/235-2120, www.childrensmuseumonline.org, 10am-5pm Mon.-Sat., July-Aug., $5) offers a variety of daily programs including the Lally Digital Dome Planetarium, which features the Molecularium as one of its four daily shows. The Molecularium is the first of its kind in the United States and teaches kids about science at the molecular level. Other shows include an animal show and a Hudson River show.

Rensselaer

Eight miles south of Troy, the smaller community of Rensselaer (pop. 9,392) features the **Crailo State Historic Site** (9½ Riverside Ave., 518/463-8738, www.nysparks.com). Part of the Van Rensselaer patroonship, this farm bears the name of the Van Rensselaer estate in the Netherlands. Now used as a museum, its exhibits focus on the colonial history of New Netherland in the area.

BEYOND TROY

The urban landscape of Troy quickly gives way to small towns and open vistas as you travel toward the eastern parts of the county. The Taconic, Berkshire, and Green Mountains come into view as you pass through towns including Averill Park, Petersburgh, Grafton, and Hoosick Falls.

★ Grafton Lakes State Park

Local residents vote the beach at this pretty **state park** (100 Grafton Lakes State Park Way, off Rte. 2, Grafton, 518/279-1155, www.nysparks.com/parks) the best in the Capital Region, beating out even Lake George in the Adirondacks.

Watch for the tiny sign on Route 2, near Grafton Lakes, for the entrance to the **Grafton Peace Pagoda** (87 Crandall Rd., 518/658-9301, www.graftonpeacepagoda.org, call for information 8am-5pm). Peace pagodas date back 2,000 years and are a symbol of nonviolence. This is one of only a few peace pagodas located in the United States.

Hoosick Falls

Celebrated American folk artist Anna Mary Moses, who became known as Grandma Moses, was first discovered in this present-day town of a few thousand residents near the Vermont border. The town boasts a Grandma Moses-inspired mural on the wall of a building on Main Street, and the artist was buried here in 1961, at the age of 101.

Hoosick Falls is also the gateway to the **Bennington Battlefield** (north side of Rte. 67 between Walloomsac, New York, and the Vermont state line, 518/686-7190, www.nysparks.com), the site of a Revolutionary War encounter.

SPORTS AND RECREATION

Grafton Lakes State Park is known for its network of mountain biking and hiking trails. Visit capitalmtb.org/Resources/Grafton_Lakes_State_Park_Trails for a trail map. Both Grafton Lakes and Cherry Plain State Parks offer swimming holes in the shadows of the mountains to the east, as well as cross-country ski trails in winter.

ACCOMMODATIONS

The options in Rensselaer County are limited, and you will need to book in advance if your trip coincides with a graduation or other important weekend. There are a few bed-and-breakfast inns scattered throughout the region and some interesting motels from which to choose. Downtown Albany accommodations are only a short drive away.

$100-150

Twelve uniquely themed rooms, including a Nautical Room, Adirondack Room, and Rose Garden, welcome guests to the ★ **Gregory House Country Inn** (3016 Rte. 43, Averill Park, 518/674-3774, www.gregoryhouse.com, $115-160). All rooms have private baths, and there is a pool for guests. The on-site La Perla Restaurant offers authentic Italian cuisine.

Hidden off the road, the hilltop setting of the contemporary-style **Berkshire Mountain House** (150 Berkshire Way, Stephentown, 518/733-6923, www.berkshirebb.com, $129-229) allows panoramic views of the nearby mountains. The main house consists of nine individually decorated rooms and one apartment. A separate house can accommodate up to 12 people or be rented as two separate two-bedroom apartments. Guests may walk the trail or take a dip in the pond. The inn is pet-friendly.

In the eastern part of the county, the **Sedgwick Inn** (17971 Rte. 22, Berlin, 518/658-2334, www.sedgwickinn.com, $85-195) offers a small pet-friendly motel on the property with simple rooms decorated in a variety of pleasant, if generic, styles.

Franklin Square Inn & Suites (1 Fourth St., Troy, 518/274-8800 or 866/708-2233, www.franklinsquareinn.com, rooms $108-160, suites $180-280) is a Best Western property with 63 rooms. Centrally located in downtown Troy, the inn is within walking distance of the Hudson River and downtown attractions. Rooms include continental breakfast; complimentary coffee, tea, and juice are available around the clock.

FOOD

Ask the innkeepers in the eastern part of the county what they recommend for dining, and they will suggest eating in Troy. Restaurants are few and far between in the east, but you will find a few local establishments in some of the larger villages.

Known for hot dogs that it ships worldwide, **Famous Lunch** (111 Congress St., Troy, 518/272-9481, www.famouslunch.net, 5am-10pm Mon.-Sat., under $10) is a Troy institution serving breakfast, lunch, and dinner.

For an ethnic food fix, **Shalimar** (407 Fulton St., Troy, 518/273-8744, www.shalimartroyny.com, 11:30am-10pm Mon.-Thurs., 11:30am-11pm Fri., 6pm-11pm Sat., noon-9pm Sun., $8-13) offers a lunch buffet of Indian and Pakistani dishes. The buffet is served 11:30am-2:30pm Monday-Friday ($6.99) and noon-3pm Saturday ($7.99).

Check out the small ★ **River Street Café** (429 River St., Troy, 518/273-2740, www.riverstreetcafetroy.com, dinner from 5:30pm Tues.-Sat., $18-24) for tempting Continental fare at reasonable prices. The café is known as well for its extensive wine list. Reservations recommended.

Carnivores can rejoice in the selection at **Dinosaur Bar-B-Que** (377 River St., Troy, 518/308-0400, www.dinosaurbarbque.com, 11:30am-10pm Mon.-Wed., 11:30am-11pm Thurs., 11:30am-midnight Fri.-Sat., noon-10pm Sun, $11-25.), which serves a variety of chicken, pork, beef, and seafood in sauces like hoisin sesame, Memphis style, and Cajun. Sides are traditional barbecue fare, and 25 varieties of beer are on tap. Vegetarian options are sparse, but there are gluten-free options..

The outdoor patio and live music is the reason for a meal at **Paolo Lombardi's Ristorante** (104 W. Sand Lake Rd., Wyantskill, 518/283-0202, www.paololombardis.com, 4pm-10pm Tues.-Thurs., 4pm-11pm Fri.-Sat., 1pm-9pm Sun., mains $16-30). A selection of traditional Italian dishes fill out the menu, with a few flourishes, including calamari that can be prepared in three different styles: classic, picante, or balsamic; a selection of seasonal risottos; and the catch of the day prepared with lemon butter and herbs.

Since 1998, **The Ruck** (104 3rd St., Troy, 518/273-1872, www.getrucked.com, 4pm-4am Mon.-Tues., 11am-4am Wed.-Fri., noon-4am Sat.-Sun.) has transformed from a dive bar into an establishment known for hearty pub fare and an impressive selection of foreign and domestic craft beers. The "Bitchin' Kitchen Beer Brunch" happens every Saturday, where the special brunch menu is paired with chosen brews. If you order nothing else to eat, try the wings.

At the Gregory House Inn, **La Perla** serves pizza, pasta, veal, beef, chicken, and seafood (3016 Rte. 43, Averill Park, 518/674-3774, www.gregoryhouse.com, 4pm-10pm Mon. and Wed.-Thurs., 4pm-11pm Fri., 3pm-11pm Sat., 2pm-10pm Sun., $14-43).

ENTERTAINMENT AND EVENTS

Nationally known artists perform at the **Troy Savings Bank Music Hall** (30 Second St., 518/273-0038, www.troymusichall.org) throughout the year. **Music at Noon** is a free concert series usually held the second Tuesday of the month from October through May. Check the website for a current schedule of events.

The **Experimental Media and Performing Arts Center** (8th and Congress St., Troy, 518/276-3921, www.empac.rpi.edu) is housed at Rensselaer Polytechnic University. EMPAC is an effort to bridge the arts, sciences, and technology. Four different spaces host artists and researchers who are creating new ways to experience the senses. A full-service café is open daily noon-3pm as well as during all performances, screenings, and events.

INFORMATION AND SERVICES

The **RiverSpark Visitor Center** serves as a tourism office for the county (251 River St., Troy, 518/270-8667, www.riverspark.org, 10am-5pm Tues.-Sat.).

GETTING THERE AND AROUND

Bus

The **Capital District Transportation Authority** (110 Watervliet Ave., Albany, 518/482-8822, www.cdta.org) provides public bus service within Troy and to surrounding cities. The base fare is $1.50; an unlimited day pass is $4. The nearest Greyhound station is in downtown Albany.

Train

The closest rail connection is the Albany/Rensselaer **Amtrak station** (525 E. St., Rensselaer), located approximately eight miles south of Troy and across the river from Albany. Taxis are available at the station.

Car

Rental cars are available at the Albany Airport; it takes approximately 20 minutes to reach Troy from the airport, depending on traffic.

Saratoga County

For the 40-mile stretch from Troy to Fort Edward, the Hudson River becomes an industrial conduit for the Champlain Canal, a shipping channel built in the early 19th century that extends all the way to the Canadian border. A series of locks and dams enables ships to navigate the changing elevation. The most impressive feat of aquatic engineering takes place at Waterford, where the Hudson merges with its largest tributary, the Mohawk River. Managing an elevation difference of 165 feet, the **Waterford Flight of Locks** are the highest in the world.

Route 4 follows the Hudson shoreline northward, passing by a handful of historic sites: On October 17, 1777, British General John Burgoyne surrendered to American General Horatio Gates in a decisive victory that convinced the French to join the American cause and marked the turning point of the Revolutionary War. **Saratoga National Historical Park** (648 Rte. 32, Stillwater, 518/664-9821, www.nps.gov/sara, 7-day pass $5), in the town of Stillwater, commemorates the battles of Saratoga. A nine-mile toll road ($5) open to motorists, cyclists, walkers, joggers, and cross-country skiers winds through the 3,000-acre park and reenacts the battles that took place on surrounding farmlands and woods. The scenery alone is worth a side trip from a Saratoga Springs itinerary. Wildlife is used to having people around, which makes it more likely you'll see an animal or two. Watch for white-tailed deer, red fox, and wild turkeys in the woods and fields, while red-tailed hawks and turkey vultures soar overhead. Park facilities include a visitors center, museum, and bookstore. The Battlefield Visitors Center is open 9am-5pm daily, and the Tour Road is open April 1 to mid-November.

George Washington, Alexander Hamilton, and the Marquis de Lafayette all stayed at the summer residence of General Philip Schuyler, a few miles north in Schuylerville. Visitors can tour the **General Schuyler House** (Rte. 4, Schuylerville, 518/664-9821, adults $3, children $1). The Schuyler House has guided tours 9:30am-4:30pm Wednesday-Sunday, Memorial Day through Labor Day, and is open weekends thereafter through mid-October. Just off Route 4 is the 155-foot-tall **Saratoga Monument** (Rtes. 4 and 32, Victory, 518/664-9821), built in 1877 to honor the historic victory.

Local organizations have renamed Route 4 the **Lakes to Locks Passage** (www.lakestolocks.com) in an attempt to draw more visitors to the area. It's about a 10-mile drive from Schuylerville west into Saratoga Springs.

SARATOGA SPRINGS

History lessons aside, the main reason to visit Saratoga County is to explore the Victorian town of Saratoga Springs. Natural hot springs, world-class horse racing, autumn apple picking, and a vibrant artistic community that revolves around Skidmore College draw an enthusiastic crowd of students, weekenders, and permanent residents.

★ Saratoga Spa State Park

The Iroquois were first to discover the healing powers of Saratoga's natural hot springs, created by a layer of limestone in the ground that produces carbonated mineral water. Like the spa town of Baden-Baden in Germany's Black Forest, Saratoga's legacy as a spa resort dates back to the turn of the 19th century. Envisioning a well-developed destination for rest and relaxation, Gideon Putnam built the first tavern and boarding house and drew the first plans for a town around the hot springs.

In 1930, the state of New York got in on the action and built a Georgian Revival hotel in Putnam's name. In its day, the Gideon Putnam Hotel hosted the likes of entertainers

Saratoga Springs

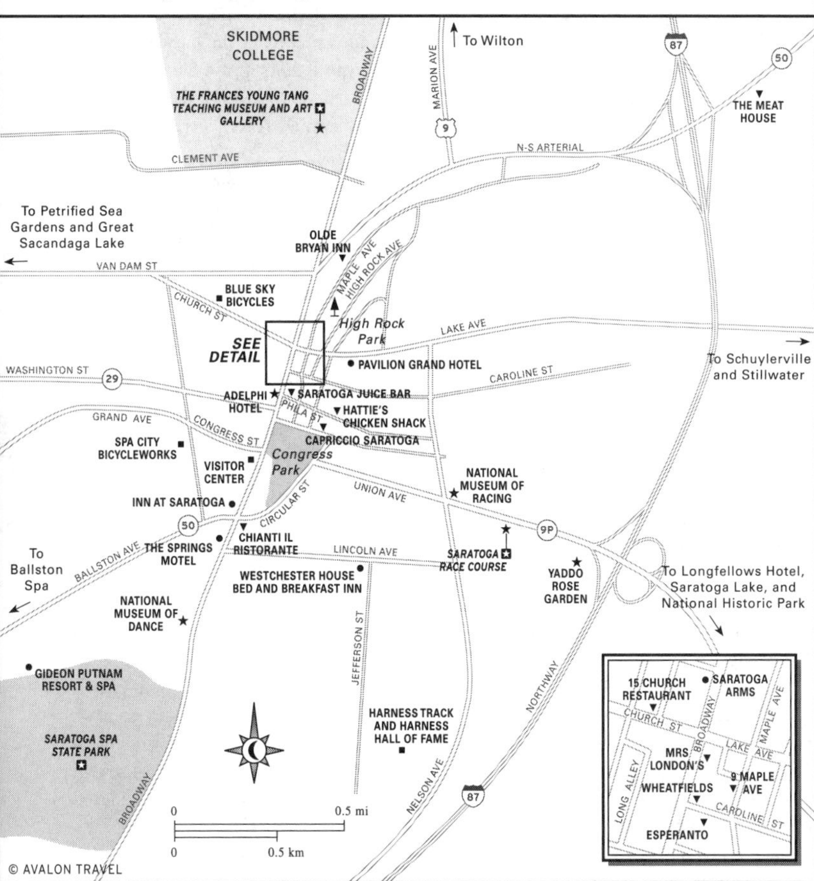

Bob Hope and Fred Astaire, as well as Chief Justice of the U.S. Supreme Court Charles Evans Hughes.

Today, **Saratoga Spa State Park** (19 Roosevelt Dr., 518/584-2535, www.nysparks.com) covers 2,300 acres of tall pines, steaming mineral baths, and tranquil walking paths. Visitors can access the mineral baths through the Gideon Putnam Resort & Spa or the Lincoln Mineral Baths. At a price tag of $1.7 million, the family-oriented Peerless Pool Complex has a zero-depth entry and a waterslide. A second swimming area, the Victoria Pool, is surrounded by brick buildings and arched walkways.

In addition to the great outdoors, the park holds several cultural attractions: There is no better way to spend a summer afternoon than listening to live music at the **Saratoga Performing Arts Center** (108 Avenue of the Pines, 518/584-9330 or 518/587-3330 for box office, www.spac.org). From opera and ballet to pop and rock and roll, this custom-designed amphitheater offers something for everyone. Initially conceived to give the New York Philharmonic a proper summer home,

SPAC opened in 1966 and has hosted the likes of Pink Floyd, Jackson Browne, the London Symphony Orchestra, James Taylor, and the Dave Matthews Band. The New York City Ballet and Philadelphia Orchestra both move to Saratoga for summer performances May-September. The theater holds 5,000 people under an open shelter and has room for 7,000 more on the lawn—measure your chairs before you go, as the height limit of 24 inches is strictly enforced.

SPAC also operates the **National Museum of Dance & Hall of Fame** (99 S. Broadway, 518/584-2225, www.dancemuseum.org, 10am-4:30pm Tues.-Sun., adults $6.50, seniors and students $5, children 12 and under $3), in the old Washington Bath House, built in 1918. The Greek Revival building contains five galleries full of photographs, videos, books, and costumes that document all forms of dance, from ballet to tap.

After a multiyear renovation that cost $5 million, the original Roosevelt Bathhouse, constructed in 1930, is back in business as part of the **Gideon Putnam Resort & Spa** (24 Gideon Putnam Rd., 866/890-1171, www.gideonputnam.com, $199-315). It holds a 13,000-square-foot spa with 42 private spa rooms. From Route 9, turn left onto Avenue of the Pines to reach the park entrance.

★ Saratoga Race Course

At the next exit on I-87 is Saratoga's other main attraction, the **Saratoga Race Course** (267 Union Ave., 718/641-4700, www.nyra.com/saratoga, free parking). Featured in the contemporary book and movie *Seabiscuit,* the racetrack dates back to 1863, making it the oldest continuously operating thoroughbred track in the country. Horse racing became wildly popular in the 1940s and '50s, and the Saratoga Race Course has been a local institution ever since.

Saratoga's population of 27,000 triples during the monthlong summer racing season, from the end of July through Labor Day weekend. Tickets are affordable, and the scene is at once traditional and exciting. Women still don their Sunday best to watch from the grandstand. At the other end of the spectrum, diehard fans barbecue at their cars and watch from the parking lot without buying tickets at all. The hoopla concludes each year with the famous **Travers Stakes,** named for racetrack cofounder William Travers.

Grandstand tickets go on sale at 8am each morning for the day's races. Purchase them at the Union Avenue Gate (limit four per person). You can also rent binoculars at the track for up-close viewing. Take Exit 14/Union Avenue from I-87.

For information before or after the meeting dates, call 718/641-4700 or 516/488-6000. For information during the meeting (late July-Labor Day), call 518/584-6200.

National Museum of Racing

Across from the racetrack, an informative museum demonstrates what traits make the best thoroughbreds and recreates famous scenes on the track. Recent additions to the **National Museum of Racing** (191 Union Ave., www.racingmuseum.org, 518/584-0400, 10am-4pm Mon.-Sat., noon-4pm Sun. May-Dec. 10am-4pm Wed.-Sat., noon-4pm Sun. Jan.-Apr., adults $7, seniors and students $5, children under 5 free) archives include newspaper articles from the mid-19th century. New Jersey-bred Open Mind and Maryland-bred Safely Kept became the newest inductees into the museum's Hall of Fame in 2011.

Beyond the racetrack and museum on Union Avenue is the 400-acre Yaddo estate, an artists' community established in 1900 and housed in an imposing Tudor mansion. Its terraced **Yaddo Rose Garden** (312 Union Ave., Saratoga Springs, 518/584-0746, www.yaddo.org, 8am-dusk daily), modeled after classical Italian designs, has been gradually restored since the founding of the Yaddo Garden Association in 1991.. Docent-led garden tours are offered ($5 per person) on Saturdays and Sundays from late June to early September. During the Saratoga thoroughbred racecourse season (late July through Labor Day), docent-led guided garden tours are also offered on Tuesdays.

Downtown Saratoga Springs

Broadway and Union Avenue both lead to the open lawns of **Congress Park** and the heart of Saratoga Springs. Kids will want to head straight to the park's working carousel or to feed the ducks in the pond. The **Canfield Casino** (Congress Park, 518/584-6920, www.saratogahistory.org, 10am-4pm daily Memorial Day-Labor Day, 10am-4pm Wed.-Sun. the rest of the year, adults $5, seniors and students $4, under 12 free), a major attraction during the spa town's heyday, is now a local history museum.

Along Broadway, between Congress and Van Dam Streets, is a host of tempting options for shopping, entertainment, and dining out. To get oriented, stop by the information booth at the corner of Broadway and Congress. Then continue up Broadway to one of Saratoga Springs's most famous landmarks, the **Adelphi Hotel** (365 Broadway, 518/587-4688, www.adelphihotel.com, $145-350), a four-story Victorian that has stayed in business since the turn of the 20th century. The hotel has been closed since 2012 for top-to-bottom renovations, and is due to reopen in 2015.

★ The Frances Young Tang Teaching Museum and Art Gallery

North Broadway leads to the Skidmore College campus and an innovative museum that hosts programs with titles like "Why Is Contemporary Art So Weird?" **The Frances Young Tang Teaching Museum and Art Gallery** (815 N. Broadway, 518/580-8080, tang.skidmore.edu, noon-5pm Tues.-Sun., open until 9pm Thurs., suggested donation $5 for adults and $3 for children) combines an outstanding permanent collection with provocative lecture topics to engage an audience of students, as well as adults and children in the local community. Exhibits are designed to involve other college departments, from dance to history. Rooftop concerts are a favorite local pastime in summer.

SPORTS AND RECREATION

Winter Sports

When a good nor'easter buries the North Country in snow, Saratoga Spa State Park becomes a winter playland, and the

the historic Adelphi Hotel

cross-country skiing is sublime. You can rent equipment at a ski shop at the golf course and ski 20 kilometers of trails. **Lapland Lake** (139 Lapland Lake Rd., Northville, 518/863-4974, www.laplandlake.com, 10am-4:30pm Mon.-Fri., 9am-4:30pm Sat.-Sun. and holidays, adults $20, juniors $10) has another 38 kilometers of groomed trails for classic and skating-style cross-country. Rentals and lessons are available. For off-site skiing and snowshoeing, try one of the local apple orchards.

Downhill skiers continue farther north to resorts in the Adirondack Park, including **Gore Mountain** (Peaceful Valley Rd., North Creek, 518/251-2411 or 800/342-1234, www.goremountain.com). Adult lift tickets cost $75 per day on weekends. Teens are $59, juniors $40, and kids under 7 ski free.

Hiking

As the gateway to the Adirondack Mountains, the Capital Region affords convenient access to some of the best—and most challenging—hiking and backpacking in the Northeast. The highest peaks in New York State, including 5,344-foot Mount Marcy, are within a 100-mile drive. The Mount Marcy trailhead is located at Adirondack Loj on Heart Lake. Bugs and black bears can be minor or major annoyances, depending on your tolerance. The steep and rocky terrain will challenge even the strongest of hikers: Routes are often longer than they look at first glance, and it's not unusual to encounter thunderstorms, mosquitoes, bears, and flat-out fatigue all in one overnight hike.

Cycling

The **Saratoga Mountain Biking Association** (518/587-0455, www.saratogamtb.org) maintains trails on 538 acres north of Skidmore College. Trails suit riders of all abilities, with single track, steep climbs, and fast descents. If you want to plan a biking tour of the Saratoga area, or need to pick up gear and supplies, head over to **Blue Sky Bicycles** (71 Church St., Sarataoga Springs, 518/583-0600, www.blueskybicycles.com, 10am-6pm Tues.-Fri., 9am-5pm Sat.), where the friendly team will be happy to assist. A 44-mile route takes you from the shop around Saratoga Lake and out to the Saratoga Battlefield and back. Blue Sky does not have rentals, but you can find everything else from spare tubes and CO2 cartridges to bike shorts and tri gear. A good option for a daily or weekly rental is **Spa City Bicycleworks** (79 Beekman St., Saratoga Springs, 518/587-0071, www.spacitybicycleworks.com, 1pm-6pm Wed., 1pm-8pm Thurs.-Fri., 10am-5pm Sat.), located at the start of the Railway Run bike path. They rent cruisers, road bikes, and mountain bikes by the day ($25-40) or week ($125-300) and will even deliver the bike to your hotel. Both shops lead organized rides on the weekends, weather permitting, for cyclists of different abilities. Check their websites for details.

Golf

There are at least a dozen golf courses in the immediate Saratoga area. One of the best is **Saratoga Spa Golf Course** (60 Roosevelt Dr., Saratoga Springs, 518/584-2006, www.saratogaspagolf.com, late May-Oct., weekends $46, weekdays $39), a 27-hole complex with a 7,098-yard championship course. Before your round, you can hit a bucket of balls from the grass tees at the driving range. Private pilots should reserve a tee time at the **Airway Meadows Golf Course** (262 Brownville Rd., Gansevoort, 518/792-4144, www.airwaymeadowsgolf.com, weekends $32, weekdays $28), adjacent to an airstrip and skydiving school.

Slide into a GPS-equipped cart at the **Saratoga National Golf Club** (458 Union Ave., Saratoga Springs, 518/583-4653, www.golfsaratoga.com, summer rates Thurs.-Fri. and Sat.-Sun. before 1pm $150, Mon.-Wed. and Sat.-Sun. after 1pm $130), and you'll forget about the $150 you paid to get away from the crowds. After the round, you can enjoy a meal at Sargo's, which is now managed by one of Albany's top restaurant management companies.

Adirondack Park

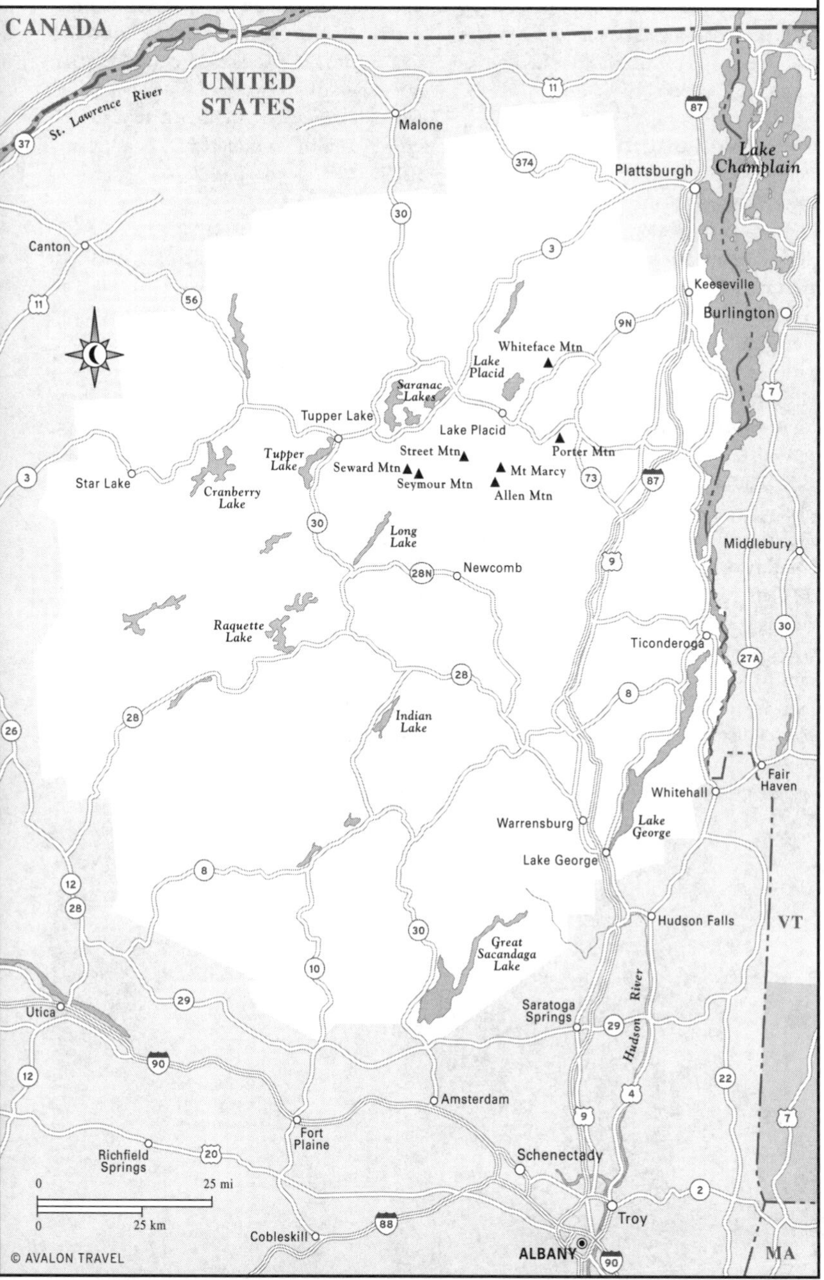
CANADA
UNITED STATES
St. Lawrence River
Malone
Plattsburgh
Lake Champlain
Canton
Keeseville
Burlington
Whiteface Mtn
Lake Placid
Saranac Lakes
Tupper Lake
Lake Placid
Porter Mtn
Tupper Lake
Street Mtn
Seward Mtn
Mt Marcy
Seymour Mtn
Allen Mtn
Star Lake
Cranberry Lake
Long Lake
Newcomb
Middlebury
Raquette Lake
Ticonderoga
Indian Lake
Fair Haven
Whitehall
Warrensburg
Lake George
Lake George
Hudson Falls
VT
Great Sacandaga Lake
Utica
Saratoga Springs
Hudson River
Amsterdam
Fort Plaine
Richfield Springs
Schenectady
Troy
Cobleskill
ALBANY
MA
0 25 mi
0 25 km

Elevation changes are a challenge at the relatively new **Saratoga Lake Golf Club** (35 Grace Moore Rd., Saratoga Springs, 518/581-6616, www.saratogalakegolf.com, Mon.-Fri. $36, weekends $40). Greens were in good condition at last check.

Swimming and Boating

The busiest lake in the Capital Region is **Lake George,** 30 minutes from downtown Saratoga Springs along I-87. Known for its clear water and summer resort scene, the lake measures 32 miles long and three miles across. Several towns have public beaches. Scuba divers can explore underwater shipwrecks with remarkably good freshwater visibility. **Million Dollar Beach** has public parking. An **Antique Classic Boat Show** takes place in August.

In addition to Lake George, several smaller lakes offer ample space for aquatic adventures. You can rent a kayak, canoe, or rowboat from **The Kayak Shak** (Saratoga Outdoor Center, 251 Staffords Bridge Rd., 518/587-9788, www.saratogakayak.com, 9am-7pm, weather permitting, $20 half day, $35 full day for single kayaks) to paddle around **Saratoga Lake.** The larger **Great Sacandaga Lake,** west of Saratoga Springs near Gloversville, is an artificial lake that allows powerboats, personal watercraft, and fishing. Swimming and windsurfing are also popular summer activities. **Moreau Lake State Park** (605 Old Saratoga Rd., Gansevoort, 518/793-0511, www.nysparks.com) has a sandy beach and wooded campsites, though it tends to be crowded in the summertime. Boating and fishing are allowed.

Fishing and Hunting

Anglers cast for largemouth bass, northern pike, and panfish in Saratoga Lake. You can rent a boat and stock up on tackle at **Lake Lonely Boat Livery** (378 Crescent Ave., Saratoga Springs, 518/587-1721, hours vary, call ahead). For more serious sport fishing and charter operations, head to Lake George, where the catch includes lake trout and landlocked salmon, as well as bass.

Spas

The Roosevelt Baths & Spa at the Gideon Putnam Resort & Spa (24 Gideon Putnam Rd., Saratoga Springs, 866/890-1171, www.gideonputnam.com, 9am-7pm) has been a bathhouse since the 1930s. Today, spa-goers continue to soak in the healing mineral waters as part of their wellness routine.

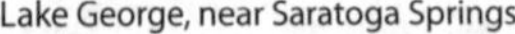

Lake George, near Saratoga Springs

Adirondack Park Stats

- The original forest preserve was established in 1885.
- The park encompasses approximately six million acres.
- It is larger than Yellowstone, the Everglades, Glacier, and Grand Canyon National Parks combined.
- About half of the park is constitutionally protected to remain a "forever wild" forest preserve.
- The remaining half of the park is designated private land, which includes settlements, farms, timberlands, businesses, homes, and camps.
- There are more than 3,000 lakes and 30,000 miles (48,000 km) of streams and rivers inside the park.
- Between seven million and ten million tourists visit the park annually.
- It is the largest area without a city in New York State.

Saratoga Botanicals Organic Spa & Wellness Store (80 Henry St., Saratoga Springs, 518/306-4108, www.saratogabotanicals.com, 9am-8pm Mon.-Fri., 9am-4pm Sat.) sells organic skincare products and offers holistic health services, from facials and massage to nutritional counseling and acupuncture. Check the website for special workshops and talks on topics like DIY face masks and natural remedies for kids.

Inside the new Pavilion Grand Hotel in downtown Saratoga, **All Good Things** (30 Lake Ave., Saratoga Springs, 518/583-2626, www.allgoodthingsnewyork.com) was started by two sisters as a juice bar in Albany and expanded to include spa services in Albany and Saratoga. This is an all-around wellness center, where you can get a facial or massage, or sign up for a yoga class. A one-hour treatment runs $80-100. Enjoy the view from the rooftop deck before or after your session.

ACCOMMODATIONS

Overnight visitors to Saratoga Springs have more than 100 establishments to choose from, including business hotels, smaller inns, motels, and bed-and-breakfasts. Expect much higher rates during the monthlong horse-racing season. Centrally located chains, not covered here, include Hilton Garden Inn, Hampton Inn, Comfort Inn, Residence Inn, and Holiday Inn.

Under $100-150

★ **The Springs Motel** (189 Broadway, Saratoga Springs, 518/584-6336, www.springsmotel.com, $75) has clean and comfortable rooms at a great price. Amenities include free Wi-Fi and flat-screen TVs. You can walk to the racecourse and Saratoga Spa State Park from the motel.

Located on Union Avenue, near Saratoga Lake and across the highway from the racetrack, **Longfellows Hotel** (500 Union Ave., Saratoga Springs, 518/587-0108, www.longfellows.com, $135) is a large conference center that hosts weddings and other special events. Rooms and suites are modern and businesslike.

$150-200

Bob and Stephanie Melvin are your hosts at the **Westchester House Bed and Breakfast Inn** (102 Lincoln Ave., Saratoga Springs, 518/587-7613 or 888/302-1717, www.westchesterhousebandb.com, $145-285, during the horse-racing season $285-490), within a colorful Victorian on a quiet residential street. Rooms are decorated in country-print wallpaper and lacy window coverings. Wireless Internet is provided.

A convenient location and filling breakfast make **The Inn at Saratoga** (231 Broadway, Saratoga Springs, 518/583-1890, www.theinnatsaratoga.com, $150-160) a top pick for many repeat Saratoga visitors. This is the oldest operating hotel in town, and fittingly, the rooms are furnished in an antique motif. Wi-Fi is free, as are the bikes. Guests get free access to the YMCA and Victoria Pool in Saratoga Spa State Park.

Six miles south of Saratoga Springs in the town of Ballston Spa, the **Medberry Inn and Spa** (48 Front St., Ballston Spa, 518/885-7727 or 800/508-1804, www.medberyinnandspa.com, $150-200) has 11 rooms decorated in pastel colors and floral linens. Data ports and whirlpool tubs lend a modern touch to the 200-year-old property. There is a day spa on-site. Note that children under 12 are not encouraged at the inn.

Over $200

Spacious guest rooms and suites cost up to $550 a night at the restored **Gideon Putnam Resort & Spa** (24 Gideon Putnam Rd., Saratoga Springs, 866/890-1171, www.gideonputnam.com, $199-315). You'll be within walking distance of SPAC, but beware that rates go sky-high during the monthlong horse-racing season. The Roosevelt Baths & Spa (9am-7pm) on-site offers a full menu of relaxing body treatments, including a signature mineral water bath.

Centrally located, the ★ **Saratoga Arms** (497 Broadway, Saratoga Springs, 518/584-1775, www.saratogaarms.com, $235-250) has 31 quiet guest rooms with comfortable queen or king beds, luxury linens, fireplaces, and whirlpool tubs as well as a fitness center and spa. Friendly service makes for a most enjoyable stay.

New in summer 2014, the **Pavilion Grand Hotel** (30 Lake Ave., Saratoga Springs, 518/583-2727, www.paviliongrandhotel.com, $220) has 48 suites—studios, one-bedrooms, and two-bedrooms—with kitchens and a long list of modern amenities. There is a juice bar and spa on-site, called **All Good Things** (518/583-2626, www.allgoodthingsnewyork.com), where you can treat yourself to a facial, massage, juice cleanse, or yoga class. A one-hour treatment runs $80-100.

Campgrounds

You can pitch a tent or park an RV under the pine trees at the **Whispering Pines Campsites & RV Park** (550 Sand Hill Rd., Greenfield Center, 518/893-0416, www.saratogacamping.com, tent sites $30-35/day). Services include hot showers, swimming pool, a trout brook, and two ponds.

FOOD

The food scene in Saratoga Springs has blossomed in recent years, as a result of both visitor demand and exposure on The Food Network cable channel. Today, you can find everything from classic French and traditional Italian to international cuisine—and everywhere are chefs who make the most of the farm-fresh ingredients at their fingertips.

Surf and Turf

The **Olde Bryan Inn** (123 Maple Ave., Saratoga Springs, 518/587-2990, www.oldebryaninn.com, 11am-10pm Sun.-Thurs., 11am-11pm Fri.-Sat., $12-30) is a historic affair serving a Continental menu of prime rib, chicken Francaise, and crab-stuffed shrimp.

Fresh seafood is flown in daily to **15 Church Restaurant** (15 Church St., Saratoga Springs, 518/587-1515, www.15churchrestaurant.com, 5pm-9:30pm Mon.-Thurs., 5pm-10pm Fri.-Sat.). Halibut, lobster, scallops, and tuna make regular appearances on the menu. Meat entrées range from a gruyère and bacon burger for $14 to a $45 filet mignon in a cognac mustard cream sauce. Produce is sourced locally when in season. Creative cocktails and tempting desserts round out the dining experience.

Wheatfields (440 Broadway, Saratoga Springs, 518/587-0534, www.wheatfields.com, opens at 11:30am daily, $13-28) serves a special three-course dinner on Thursdays and a late-night menu seven days a week. Favorites here include homemade pasta dishes, steak salad, and the bistro chicken, which can be prepared marsala, Milanese, or parmesan style.

Fried Chicken

Chef Jasper Alexander, a graduate of the Culinary Institute of America, became a local legend when he triumphed over Food Network host Bobby Flay in a surprise fried chicken cooking contest. The celebrated "Throwdown with Bobby Flay" took place in 2007, and ★ **Hattie's** (45 Phila St., Saratoga Springs, 518/584-4790, www.hattiesrestaurant.com, 5pm-10pm daily, $13-22) has continued serving its legendary fare ever since. The "chicken shack" has moved to Wilton Plaza (3057 Rt. 50, 518/226-0000) and the main location on Phila Street has gone upscale, with courtyard seating in summer.

Italian

A father/son duo with 30 years of restaurant success in Albany has expanded to Saratoga Springs with ★ **Capriccio Saratoga** (26 Henry St., Saratoga Springs, 518/587-9463, www.capricciosaratoga.com, opens at 5pm daily, $14-30). This is a cozy trattoria specializing in Neapolitan-style pizzas and everything about the cuisine from Naples. Owner Jim Rua has led many food-themed trips to Italy over the years and immersed himself in the culture and cuisine of the country. His experience shows in the way food is prepared in the restaurant: Pizza sauce is made from San Marzano tomatoes, and pies are baked in a wood-fired over that gets up to 1000°F.

Mio Posto (68 Putnam St., Saratoga Springs, 518/542-7581, www.miopostosaratoga.com, 5pm-9pm Tues.-Sun., $19-34) is a small American/Italian eatery where founding Chef Danny Petrosino started buying local before it became the latest food trend. Noteworthy starters include grilled baby octopus with potato-olive salad and bada-bing shrimp served in a garlic butter cream sauce. His grilled lamb chops are prepared with an apricot demi, spaetzle, and spinach. The Bolognese sauce is ever popular. Petrosino has since moved to Maestro's at the Van Dam, but the restaurant continues to uphold the locavore tradition.

Chianti Il Ristorante (18 Division St., Saratoga Springs, 518/580-0025, www.chiantiristorante.com, $10-26) serves a full menu of Italian specialties, from pasta to risotto to filet mignon and whole sea bass. You can also take a cooking class here.

Cafés and Quick Bites

Don't leave Saratoga without sampling a pastry at ★ **Mrs. London's** (464 Broadway, Saratoga Springs, 518/581-1652, www.mrslondons.com, 7am-6pm Tues.-Thurs. and Sun., 7am-9pm Fri.-Sat., $7-12). Savory options include grilled panini on ciabatta, and a rotating menu of soups and sandwiches. Delicate meringues are a perfect sweet fix after the meal.

Vegetarians and visitors with a case of late-night munchies won't go hungry at **Esperanto** (6½ Caroline St., Saratoga Springs, 518/587-4236, www.go2esperanto.com, 11:30am-2am Tues.-Wed., 11:30am-3am Thurs., 11:30am-4am Fri.-Sat., 11am-midnight Sun.-Mon.). It has a tempting selection of quick eats, including burritos, pizza, and soups, as well as a number of international cuisines, such as Thai, Mexican, and Middle Eastern.

Greenhouse (33 Railroad Pl., Saratoga Springs, 518/450-1036, www.eatgreenhouse.com) serves up a healthy menu of salads. Customers begin by choosing a green and may add four toppings that range from meats and cheeses to nuts and other vegetables. Salads are tossed with one of several homemade dressings. Soups, wraps, and a variety of cookies, chips, and pretzels are also available.

Uncommon Grounds (402 Broadway, Saratoga Springs, 518/581-0656, www.uncommongrounds.com, 6:30am-11pm Mon.-Thurs., 6:30am-midnight Fri., 7am-midnight Sat., 7am-11pm Sun.) serves espresso drinks, smoothies, sandwiches, pastries, and other coffeehouse fare. Comfy chairs and board games are a good way to pass the time on a rainy day; enjoy the sidewalk tables in nicer weather.

The Meat House (Wilton Plaza, 3057 Rte. 50, Saratoga Springs, 518/583-4027, www.themeathouse.com, daily 9am-7pm) has revived the concept of the neighborhood butcher, with premium cuts of meat, a deli counter, fresh produce, freshly baked bread, cheeses from local dairies, and prepared meals too.

The **Saratoga Juice Bar** (382 Broadway, Saratoga Springs, 518/583-1108, www.saratogajuicebar.com, open daily) generated a lot of excitement when it opened on Broadway, bringing the juicing craze to town. Whether you are looking for a health remedy, a preventive treatment, or just a refreshing cold drink, you'll find it on the menu here. A number of cold-pressed juice blends are prepared ahead of time; others can be custom-made on the spot. Key ingredients include spinach, kale, beets, carrots, and ginger.

ENTERTAINMENT AND EVENTS

Performing Arts

The story goes that the **Saratoga Performing Arts Center** (108 Avenue of the Pines, Saratoga Springs, 518/584-9330 or 518/587-3330 for box office, www.spac.org) was originally built to keep the New York Philharmonic from moving to Vermont for its summer home. While the Philharmonic never came to Saratoga Springs, the new venue did become one of the largest producers of first-rate music, dance, and opera performances in the state. Recent concerts have included everything from Stevie Nicks to Toby Keith to Blink 182. A night of ballet or opera here is simply unforgettable. For opera aficionados, **Opera Saratoga** (480 Broadway, Ste. LL16, Saratoga Springs, 518/584-6018, www.operasaratoga.org), formerly Lake George Opera, stages performances at the Spa Little Theater in Saratoga Spa State Park.

The local visitors center produces a series of free concerts in Congress Park during the summer months.

Bars and Nightlife

Between its racetrack spectators and student population, Saratoga Springs has earned a reputation as a party town: Jazz bars, dance clubs, and Irish pubs, as well as coffeehouses and wine bars, offer venues for spirited

freshly baked loaves at Mrs. London's

entertainment. Several of the late-night establishments are on Caroline Street.

Located in a 19th-century brick building on Broadway, **The Wine Bar** (417 Broadway, Saratoga Springs, 518/584-8777, www.thewinebarofsaratoga.com, 4pm-close Mon.-Sat., small plates $4-10, wine flights $12-20) has earned recognition from *Wine Spectator* for its wine list and praise from patrons for a menu of small plates that pair nicely with the pours.

Druthers Brewing Company (381 Broadway, Saratoga Springs, 518/306-5275, www.druthersbrewing.com, open daily from 11:30am) brews its own craft beers, including an unusual apple beer that uses apple cider from nearby Indian Ladder Farms. Also on tap are the Druthers Golden Ale, Against the Grain Weizen wheat beer, Triple Wit, and more. Lunch and dinner fare includes lamb meatballs, mac 'n cheese, shepherd's pie, and osso buco (mains $15-24).

One block off Broadway, jazz aficionados settle in at the beautiful wooden bar of **9 Maple Avenue** (9 Maple Ave., Saratoga Springs, 518/583-2582, www.9mapleave.com, opens at 4pm daily) for a night of live music, well-made cocktails, and a large selection of single malts. **The Parting Glass** (40-42 Lake Ave., Saratoga Springs, 518/583-1916, www.partingglasspub.com) plays live Irish music. **Saratoga Gaming & Harness Raceway** (Crescent Ave., Saratoga Springs, 518/584-2110 or 800/727-2990, www.saratogacasino.com) has 1,300 video gaming machines.

Festivals

Each September since 2001, SPAC has hosted the popular **Saratoga Wine & Food Festival** (Saratoga Performing Arts Center, 108 Avenue of the Pines, Saratoga Springs, 518/584-9330, ext. 3021, www.spac.org), drawing food and wine enthusiasts from across New England and the mid-Atlantic states.

SHOPPING

Storefronts crowd both sides of Broadway in Saratoga Springs, offering a mix of boutique jewelry and apparel, high-end retail chains, and straight-up kitsch. Some seasonal boutiques set up shops for summer months only. **Silverado Jewelry Gallery** (446 Broadway, Saratoga Springs, 518/584-1044, www.silveradonewyork.com, 10am-6pm Mon.-Sat., 11am-5pm Sun.) sells unique silver and semiprecious jewelry from a number of New York City artists. At the corner of Broadway and Phila, you can browse the selection of sundresses, hats, and handbags at **Lifestyles** (436 Broadway, Saratoga Springs, 518/584-4665, www.lifestylesofsaratoga.com, 10am-6pm daily, until 8pm Thurs.-Fri.). **Symmetry Gallery** (348 Broadway, Saratoga Springs, 518/584-5090, www.symmetrygallery.com, 11am-6pm Mon.-Sat., Sun. by appointment), also on Broadway, features art glass works by local artists. And, as the name implies, the **Pink Paddock** (380 Broadway, Saratoga Springs, 518/587-4344, Mon.-Wed. and Fri.-Sat. 10am-6pm, Thurs. 10am-8pm, Sun. 11am-5pm) sells a unique collection of pink apparel, as well as other shades. You'll find everything from seersucker pants and argyle sweaters to ribbon headbands, flip-flops, and flirty summer dresses.

The friendly staff at **Saratoga Trunk** (493 Broadway, Saratoga Springs, 518/584-3543, www.saratogatrunk.com, 10am-6pm Mon.-Sat.) will help you find a beautiful dress for a special occasion or a designer hat for opening day at the racetrack.

Hat sational (510 Broadway, Saratoga Springs, 518/587-1022, www.hatsational.com, 10am-6pm daily) is another place to look for his and hers hats for race day.

Farm Stands

The **Saratoga Farmers Market** (High Rock Ave., Saratoga Springs, 800/806-3276, www.saratogafarmersmarket.org, 9am-1pm Sat. and 3pm-6pm Wed. May-Oct., 9am-1pm Sat. Nov.-Apr.) is a summer tradition, with 50 local vendors set up under a permanent pavilion. If you're planning a whole meal, pick up some fresh-baked bread, organic beef, and smoked salmon while you're there.

Putnam Market (435 Broadway, Saratoga Springs, 518/587-3663, www.putnammarket.com, 9am-7pm Mon.-Sat., 10am-5pm Sun.) supplies the gourmands in town with an impressive display of cheeses and pâtés. Order sandwiches, desserts, and chocolates or pick up fresh fish to cook yourself. The adjoining wine store (Putnam Wines) offers free tastings every day and stays open on Sundays.

Visit **Bowman Orchards** (141 Sugar Hill Rd. Rexford, 518/371-2042, www.bowmanorchards.com), **Charlton Orchards** (140 Charlton Rd., Ballston Lake, 518/381-3601, www.charltonorchard.com), or **Stetkar Orchards** (Fitch Rd., Saratoga Springs, 518/584-6839) for an afternoon of apple-picking and cider-sipping.

Bookstores

Lyrical Ballad Bookstore (7 Phila St., Saratoga Springs, 518/584-8779, www.lyricalballadbooks.com, 10am-6pm Mon.-Sat., 11am-6pm Sun.) displays some of its fine old books and prints in a former bank vault.

Northshire Bookstore (424 Broadway, Saratoga Springs, 518/682-4200, www.northshire.com, 10am-9pm Sun.-Wed., 10am-10pm Thurs.-Sat.) is an offshoot of an independent bookseller based in Manchester, Vermont. Browse the collection of new titles, or check the calendar for upcoming author events.

INFORMATION AND SERVICES

In Saratoga Springs the **Saratoga County Chamber of Commerce** (28 Clinton St., Saratoga Springs, 518/584-3255, www.saratoga.org, 9am-5pm daily) operates an information center near Congress Park late June through Labor Day. Daily guided walking tours are offered in July and August.

GETTING THERE AND AROUND

Bus

The **Saratoga Springs Summer Trolley** (518/482-8822, www.cdta.org, base fare $1.50, day pass $4) stops daily at Congress Park, National Museum of Dance, Roosevelt Baths & Spa, Saratoga Race Course, SPAC, and other points of interest. Trolleys leave SPAC every 40 minutes, with the North Loop operating 11am-7:40pm and the South Loop 10am-7:20pm. The **Capital District Transportation Authority** (110 Watervliet Ave., Albany, 518/482-8822, www.cdta.org) provides public bus service within Saratoga Springs and to surrounding cities. The base fare is $1; an unlimited day pass is $3.

Train

Saratoga Springs has a modern **rail station** (26 Station Ln. at West Ave., Saratoga Springs, 518/587-8354) with Enterprise and Thrifty car rentals on-site.

Car

The Capital Region is a major metropolitan area with heavy traffic during commuting hours. I-87 and I-787 are the main north-south highways. The Albany Airport is Exit 13N on I-87; Saratoga Springs is Exit 14. You can rent a car from the Albany Airport or from several independent companies in the Saratoga area.

Background

The Landscape

Abundant natural resources in the Hudson River Valley played a critical role in the development of trade and commerce in colonial America. The lush display of trees, bushes, and wildflowers astounded Henry Hudson when he first sailed up the river. Native American and European settlers found ample water, arable land, and lumber, fish, and game to support their growing communities.

Nearly half the land in the Hudson River Valley has been developed for urban, residential, and agricultural use, and the rest remains second- and third-growth forest. Elevation in the region ranges from 150 feet in the lowlands to 4,000 feet in the mountains. Lowlands consist of fertile farmland, rolling hills, marshes, and swamps. Mountainous areas feature sheer cliffs, escarpments, and rocky lookout points. In addition, the Catskill region is known for its red clay soil.

GEOLOGY

Dramatic rock formations in the Hudson River Valley tell a story of mountain-building, erosion, and glacial movement that began a billion years ago. The oldest exposed bedrock in the region is found in the Hudson Highlands of Orange and Putnam Counties. Limestone and shale marine sediments remind us that the valley was once the edge of a shallow, tropical sea, much like the Red Sea, complete with pink sand and delicate coral formations.

The Taconic Mountains were formed next in an event known as an orogeny, followed by the Acadian Mountains, which stretched as high as the Himalayas. Runoffs from the mountain range deposited sandstone and shale to create the Devonian Catskill Delta, which forms the Catskill and Shawangunk Mountains of today. Farther south, molten rock carved the sheer cliffs of the Palisades.

In recent geologic history, 40,000 years ago, glaciers carved the fjord we now call the Hudson River. When the ice melted, it formed glacial Lake Albany and a submarine canyon that extends 500 miles offshore from Manhattan.

GEOGRAPHY

The Hudson River Valley is bound by New York City and New Jersey to the south, New England to the east, the Adirondack Mountains to the north, and the Appalachian Plateau and Mohawk Valley to the west. At the center of the valley is the river itself, 315 miles long, 3.5 miles across at its widest point, and 216 feet at its deepest. The river originates from Lake Tear of the Clouds in the Adirondack Mountains and becomes navigable at Troy, above Albany. Dozens of tributaries feed the Hudson, draining the Catskill Mountains to the west and the Taconic Range to the east. The largest rivers and creeks include the Croton, Wallkill, Rondout, Esopus, and Catskill.

A second major river, the Delaware, traverses the western part of the region and empties into the Atlantic to the south.

CLIMATE

The Hudson River Valley enjoys a temperate, continental climate. Four distinct seasons range from the muggy days of summer to the crisp, clear-blue days of fall and below-freezing temperatures in winter. The first frost comes in late September, ending a growing season that lasts 160-180 days. According to U.S. Department of Agriculture Forest Service data, average rainfall is about 40 inches, while

Previous: bridge over the Hudson River; the historic Saugerties Lighthouse, Ulster County.

Average Temperature by Month

Month	High	Low
January	34	15
February	38	16
March	47	26
April	59	36
May	70	46
June	78	55
July	84	60
August	82	59
September	74	50
October	62	38
November	51	30
December	39	21

snowfall measures 165 inches at the mountaintops and 40-60 inches on the valley floor. Extreme weather events include ice storms and blizzards in winter and thunderstorms and the occasional hurricane in summer and fall. The fall foliage season lasts mid-September through late October, with the peak typically around Columbus Day weekend.

ENVIRONMENTAL ISSUES

The Hudson River absorbed a barrage of industrial waste, raw sewage, and agricultural runoff during the late 19th and early 20th centuries. The river was thought to be on the verge of recovery by the 1970s, when scientists tested striped bass for polychlorinated biphenyls (PCBs) and found alarming levels of contamination. The discovery shut down all commercial fisheries along the river, and in 1977, General Electric (GE) was ordered to stop dumping PCBs into the river. But the Hudson was unable to heal itself. The Environmental Protection Agency finally agreed in 2002 to conduct a massive dredging effort to clean up the river, but GE continued to fight the decision for years. By August 2007, GE had begun construction of processing and transportation facilities that will store sediment dredged from the river. The first phase of dredging began in 2009, and in 2011, the second and much larger phase of dredging began near Fort Edward, 50 miles north of Albany. Visit www.hudsondredging.com for the latest project updates from GE and the EPA.

By many accounts, the Hudson River is cleaner now than it has been in a generation. American shad are considered safe to eat again, people are swimming in its waters again, and the river continues to support an astonishing diversity of life. However, PCBs and the efforts to rid the river of them continue to pose a challenge to the community.

A number of influential environmental organizations have stepped in to accelerate the recovery efforts. The **Hudson River Estuary Program of the New York State Department of Environmental Conservation** (www.dec.ny.gov/lands/4920.html) seeks to protect the local watershed for Hudson River Valley residents. The **Beacon Institute for Rivers and Estuaries** (199 Main St., Beacon, 845/838-1600, www.thebeaconinstitute.org) studies and protects rivers, estuaries, and watersheds in the area.

Modeled after the Dutch vessels that sailed the Hudson in the late 18th century, a sloop called *Clearwater* was conceived in the 1960s as a call to action to clean up the river before it was too late. In a unique classroom setting, *Clearwater* volunteers educate local residents about the importance of environmental awareness and conservation. Since 1966, the watchdog organization has battled GE on the dumping of PCBs into the river, prosecuted Clean Water Act offenders, and pioneered the model of encouraging environmental advocacy through a hands-on sailing experience.

Plants and Animals

The constant mixing of saltwater and freshwater as far north as Albany creates a rich supply of nutrients that in turn support a remarkably diverse set of interdependent plants and animals.

TREES

Sixty percent of the entire Hudson River Valley is covered in second- or third-growth forest. Towering red and white oaks and a variety of northern hardwoods—white and yellow birch, sugar maple, hickory, basswood, and ash—make up the majority of the deciduous forest. Acorns and beechnuts provide a key source of food for wildlife populations. Common conifers include blue spruce, hemlock, white pine, and yellow pine. The sand plains around Albany support the growth of pitch pine-scrub oak forests.

FLOWERS

Across the Hudson River Valley, bright yellow forsythia mark the arrival of spring, adding the first splash of color to the barren winter landscape each May. Cultivated daffodils and tulips are close behind, and more than 100 different kinds of wildflowers bloom by midsummer, including goldenrod, buttercups, and daisies, as well as jack-in-the-pulpit, sarsaparilla, and winterberry.

MAMMALS

A variety of critters big and small make their home in wooded valleys, fields, and mountainous areas. Among them are the black bear, gray squirrel, coyote, raccoon, river otter, and bobcat. In addition, many of the Hudson River Valley's suburbs are overrun with white-tailed deer that munch on everything in sight, from geraniums to apple blossoms.

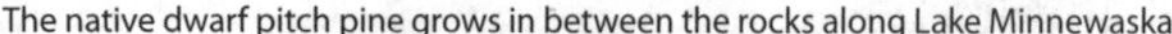
The native dwarf pitch pine grows in between the rocks along Lake Minnewaska.

SEALIFE

The Hudson River once held a large number of saltwater creatures, including oysters, mussels, crabs, and turtles. Most of the shellfish are gone today—blue crabs are an exception—but the river still supports more than 150 types of fish, such as bass, shad, and sturgeon, many of which are prized catches for determined anglers. At the water's edge, muskrats, snapping turtles, and ospreys feed on cattails and other marsh plants.

BIRDS

Ornithologists flock to the Hudson River Valley's wilderness areas to view more than 100 types of nesting birds, migrating raptors, and waterfowl. Among the more unusual species are the red-eyed vireo, found in woodland areas; American redstart, which arrives to nest in late spring to early summer; gray and yellow Canada warbler, found at lower levels of the forest; and Western wood-pewee, which prefers the dense upper canopy. Wild turkeys, grouse, and pheasant are abundant in wooded areas as well. The noisy pileated woodpecker likes a moist habitat where it can feed on carpenter ants. Observing one in action is a treat. Mallard ducks paddle calm, sheltered waters across the valley, while Canada geese enjoy spending the winter near local golf courses. And the American bald eagle has made a comeback along the Delaware River, with sightings as far east as Greenwood Lake.

REPTILES AND AMPHIBIANS

The Hudson River Valley has its share of snakes, frogs, salamanders, and turtles. The friendly garter snake, water snake, and white striped milk snake are common. The only two poisonous snakes are the copperhead, found south of Kingston, and the timber rattlesnake, which lives in parts of the Catskills and along the river valley.

Come March, spring peepers fill the evening air with a familiar song. One of the most common amphibians in the region, peepers live anywhere that standing water is found. Other types of frogs and toads live at the water's edge, including wood frogs, bullfrogs, green frogs, and two dark-spotted frogs, the northern leopard and the pickerel.

Motorists often encounter feisty snapping turtles crossing back roads to lay their eggs. Painted turtles are another common species. Less common are the box turtle, wood turtle, the yellow-spotted Blanding's turtle in the

White-tailed deer look for food at the end of a hard winter.

lower Hudson River Valley, and the map turtle in the Hudson River. A dozen kinds of salamander also inhabit area rivers and ponds. The mudpuppy is found in the Hudson, while the hellbender lives in the southern part of the region.

INSECTS

Mosquitoes and mayflies are a nuisance in wet and wooded areas May through July, while fireflies light up the forest on hot summer nights. Deer ticks, found in fields and woods, can spread Lyme disease.

History

EARLY INHABITANTS

Anthropologists believe that the Hudson River Valley's earliest inhabitants settled the region as many as 10,000 years ago. By the 17th century, three main Native American nations lived along the river: the Mahicans (Algonquin) claimed the east bank of the river, from Long Island Sound to Albany, as well as the west bank from Albany to Catskill; the Mohawks (Iroquois) lived in the Catskill area; and the Lenni Lenapes (Delaware) occupied the west, from the Catskills south to the Potomac. Modern town names like Wappingers, Tappan, Hackensack, and Minisink all refer to Native American tribes.

EUROPEAN EXPLORATION AND SETTLEMENT

Technically speaking, Giovanni Verrazzano was the first European explorer to enter the Hudson River at New York Harbor in 1524. But it was Henry Hudson, commissioned by the Dutch, who made it famous. Hudson sailed the *Half Moon* as far north as Troy in 1609, in search of a northwest passage to the Indies. Hudson did not succeed and turned around when the river became too shallow near Troy, but Dutch settlers returned soon after to settle Fort Orange at present-day Albany.

Despite ongoing conflicts, the Native American and European populations began to trade fur, tobacco, wheat, oysters, beans, corn, pumpkins, and other goods. Dutch settlements grew at Albany, Manhattan, and Kingston.

The Dutch introduced the patroon system of land management, in which an individual was granted proprietary rights to a tract of land in return for bringing 50 new settlers to the colony. When the English took over in the mid-17th century, they introduced a similar approach, the manor system. Robert Livingston, Frederick Philipse, and other historic figures were all benefactors of these preferential land-management practices.

REVOLUTIONARY WAR

Nearly two centuries after the first Europeans arrived, the Hudson River Valley's communities found themselves in the crossfire of the war for independence. Major battles took place at Stony Point, Kingston, White Plains, and Saratoga. Soldiers wheeled cannons along Route 23 between the Hudson and the Berkshires. George Washington established headquarters in Newburgh and other towns along the river, and West Point was fortified to keep the British out.

EARLY INDUSTRY

After the revolution, abundant natural resources created the foundation for industry in the newly independent country: tanneries, bluestone quarries, sawmills, and gristmills opened to support a growing population. Dairy farms and orchards flourished, and the first icehouses appeared along the Hudson.

STEAMBOAT TRAVEL

Inventor Robert Fulton shattered previous Hudson River records on August 14, 1807, when he made the first successful steamboat

Native American Tribes

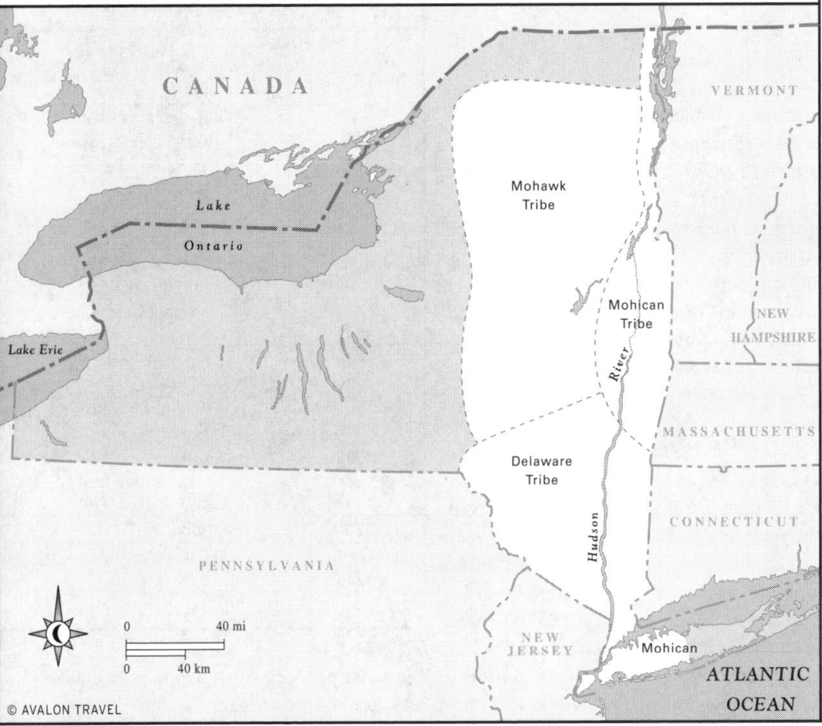

journey from New York to Albany in 32 hours. Backing the venture was Chancellor Robert R. Livingston, who had met Fulton in France a decade earlier.

Engines powered by steam would eventually revolutionize the transport of goods and passengers on the Hudson, spurring a new wave of economic development. Change might have proceeded at a faster clip, had New York State not granted Livingston a 20-year monopoly on steamboat travel between New York City and Albany. Livingston and Fulton were free to seize and impose fines on any competitors. But the sovereign state of New Jersey understandably objected to the arrangement, and the Supreme Court intervened to settle the dispute. In the landmark decision of 1824, *Ogden v. Gibbons,* the court ruled to end the monopoly, setting a precedent for federal control over interstate commerce. In the wake of the decision, between 1819 and 1840, the number of steamboats on the river rose from 8 to more than 100.

RAIL TRAVEL AND RIVERSIDE ESTATES

The advent of the railroad brought a new wave of prosperity to the Hudson River Valley and Catskill Mountain towns. Summer resorts flourished in Greene, Sullivan, and Delaware Counties. Westchester County became a commuter base as early as the 1800s, when rail travel made it possible to reach New York City in just a few hours. In this era of prosperity, families including the Rockefellers, Vanderbilts, Philipses, and Van Cortlandts built or expanded their sprawling country estates along the banks of the Hudson.

INDUSTRIAL REVOLUTION

Factories grew like weeds along the banks of the Hudson during the early 20th century, manufacturing everything from cars to paper to poultry. General Electric began to make appliances in Troy, and IBM settled near Poughkeepsie. As the industrial economy transformed into the information economy and jobs moved overseas, most of these factories shut down. Today's many abandoned plants in Beacon, Newburgh, Poughkeepsie, and other river cities testify to the volume of industry that once thrived across the valley. By the 1960s, the Hudson had earned designation as an industrial river—a body of water polluted beyond repair.

RECESSION AND REVIVAL

Modern auto, rail, and jet travel changed the region forever, sending would-be visitors to ever more exotic destinations in the same amount of time it once took to reach the Catskills from New York City. Farmers, manufacturers, and vacation resorts alike struggled to compete on the international stage, and most towns along the Hudson River fell into a deep and prolonged recession.

The economic boom of the late 1990s triggered a long overdue recovery for many area towns. Weekenders bought second homes, supporting riverfront restaurants and festivals from Newburgh to Kingston. To meet the needs of increasingly sophisticated palates, local farmers began to experiment with boutique crops, such as heirloom vegetables, shiitake mushrooms, organic meat, and microgreens. Winemakers planted French hybrid grapes to produce award-winning labels. Together, these factors set the stage for the intriguing region visitors can experience today.

Revolutionary War Timeline

1774	New York "Tea Party"
1775	Americans capture Fort Ticonderoga and Crown Point
1776	British invade New York City
1777	Saratoga Campaign—the turning point
1778	Fortress West Point begun
1779	Battle of Stony Point
1780	Benedict Arnold and John André treason
1781	Siege of New York City and Battle of Yorktown
1783	British evacuate New York City

Government and Economy

ORGANIZATION AND POLITICAL PARTIES

New York State consists of 64 counties, 11 of which are covered in this handbook. Four of the 11 counties were established when the first New York General Assembly convened in 1683, with the rest to follow by the early 19th century. Several Hudson River Valley cities, including Fishkill, Poughkeepsie, and Kingston, hosted the early state government, before it eventually settled in Albany.

Hudson River Valley communities have representation in 10 of the state senate's 62 districts, and the majority of today's senators are members of the Republican Party. Eight districts, covering Westchester County, Rockland County, Dutchess County, Rensselear County, and the city of Albany, currently have

Architecture 101

Tour the Hudson River Valley's grand estates, and experience an architectural history that spans 400 years, from the earliest Dutch and English influences to the revivalist movements of the 19th and 20th centuries. Here are a few examples of the styles that have been preserved in modern times.

DUTCH COLONIAL

- late 19th century to the 1930s
- Symmetrical two-sided roof with two slanted sides (gambrel) and curved roof edges
- Example: Eleanor Roosevelt's Val-Kill Cottage

FEDERAL

- 1780-1830
- Low-pitched roof, semicircle over the front door, and large windows with usually six panes per window
- Example: Clermont

GREEK REVIVAL

- late 18th and early 19th centuries
- Greek detailing applied to American homes
- Example: 1911 Roxbury Arts Center

NEOCLASSICAL/CLASSICAL REVIVAL

- late 1800s to the early 1900s
- Symmetry and differences in hierarchy; grand entrances and staircases
- Example: Mills Mansion (also called Staatsburg)

Democratic representatives. The New York State Assembly is the lower house of the state legislature. It is made up of 150 districts, with one representative from each.

AGRICULTURE

Some 4,000 farms cover nearly 20 percent of all land in the Hudson River Valley, producing everything from beef, poultry, milk, and cheese to apples, sweet corn, organic produce, wine, hay, and flowers. Most of the area's longtime farmers are struggling to make ends meet in the globalized economy. They face a host of challenges, from achieving profitability and resisting development pressure to updating infrastructure and raising public awareness and support for an endangered way of life.

The locavore movement, which continues to gain momentum across the nation, stands to benefit responsible growers in the Hudson River Valley. Community-supported agriculture and "agritourism" activities such as farm tours, tasting rooms, and educational programs, promise a more sustainable future for farmer and community alike.

INDUSTRY

The larger cities and towns along the Hudson River reached their peak at the height of the

New York's Notable Governors

- **George Clinton** (first: 1777-1798) is remembered as the Father of New York.
- **DeWitt Clinton** (sixth) served two nonconsecutive terms in 1817-1822 and 1825-1828, during which he led the construction of the Erie Canal.
- **Martin Van Buren** (ninth: January-March 1829) was known as Old Kinderhook. His tenure as governor is the second shortest on record for the state.
- **Theodore Roosevelt** (33rd: 1899-1901) was elected in 1899 after returning from the Spanish-American War. He served for two years before becoming vice president to William McKinley.
- **Franklin Delano Roosevelt** (44th: 1928-1932) mobilized New York State's government to aid the economy during the Great Depression.
- **W. Averell Harriman** (48th: 1955-1959) was famous for his diplomacy skills. Prior to becoming New York's 48th governor, he served as ambassador to Moscow and England.
- **Nelson A. Rockefeller** (49th: 1959-1973) was elected governor of New York four times. He grew the State University of New York into the largest provider of public higher education in the country and also improved and expanded the New York State Parks system.

Industrial Revolution, when area factories made everything from automotive parts to ball bearings to men's shirt collars. In the 1980s and 1990s, globalization sent most of those jobs overseas, shutting the old factories down.

Today, employment in the manufacturing sector continues to decline overall. (It has dropped 15.3 percent since 2002, affecting 10,700 workers.) There are some exceptions, however, such as Elna Magnetics, whose workforce has increased by 50 percent since it moved from Woodstock to Saugerties in 2009. In the meantime, employment in a variety of service industries is on the rise. And new jobs are appearing in real estate; educational services; arts, entertainment, and recreation; and health care and social assistance industries. The largest employers (excluding agriculture) in the area are in the government, health care, retail, and food and accommodations sectors.

Despite the cutbacks of the early 1990s, IBM remains the largest private employer in the region, with offices and plants from Somers to Hawthorne and Poughkeepsie to East Fishkill. CH Energy Group, Vassar Brothers Hospital, Vassar College, Saint Francis Hospital, Marist College, the State of New York, and Texaco are some of the other top employers. Tourism (leisure and hospitality) accounts for about 9 percent of employment in the region.

Unemployment in the Hudson River Valley measured 7.1 percent in 2011.

DISTRIBUTION OF WEALTH

Per capita income varies widely across the valley. In Westchester ($48,385), Rockland ($35,214), and Putnam ($40,762) Counties, it is well above the state and national averages. But Dutchess County at $33,037 and Saratoga County at $34,125 measure just slightly above the state level of $32,104 in 2008-2012. The rest of the counties in the region fall below the state average with Delaware County the lowest at $22,695.

Property values fell significantly throughout the region during the economic crisis that began in.2009. More than 80 percent of residents in the region drive or carpool to work. As the Hudson River Valley becomes its own economic center, distinct from New York City, it is encountering the associated challenges of providing affordable housing and managing traffic congestion.

Making Maple Syrup

Sap buckets hang on a maple tree in the Catskills.

A handful of Hudson River Valley farmers continue to produce real maple syrup the old-fashioned way. They drill holes in hard maple trees, collect the sap that drips out, and boil excess water away in a wood-fired evaporator. The end result is Grade A maple syrup that turns a quick breakfast into a gourmet feast.

Once an off-season income supplement for dairy farms, maple sugarhouses today draw late-season skiers and other visitors for a lesson in culinary science. The process begins in late February or early March, when temperatures climb into the 40s during the day and return to the low 20s at night. For four to six weeks, the fluctuating temperatures move tree sap from roots to leaves and back again, allowing the farmer to catch some of the flow without harming the tree. The most authentic sugarhouses hang aluminum buckets on each trunk to collect the sap, although larger operations have upgraded to plastic pipes in order to speed up the process.

Straight out of the tree, sap runs clear, with just a hint of sweetness. Back in the sugarhouse, the farmer boils the frothy liquid in the long flutes of a steel evaporator, staying up all night long when necessary to finish the day's harvest. An instrument called a hydrometer measures the specific gravity of the liquid and tells the boiler when the sap has officially reached the distinctive amber color and thickness we associate with the real stuff. It's a precise and labor-intensive operation—for every 40 gallons of raw sap, a sugarhouse will produce approximately 1 gallon of syrup.

SUGARHOUSES IN THE HUDSON RIVER VALLEY

Delaware County

- Catskill Mountain Maple, 65 Charlie Wood Rd., DeLancey, 607/746-6215, www.catskillmountainmaple.com
- Shaver-Hill Maple Farm, Shaver Rd., Harpersfield, 607/652-6792, www.shaverhillfarm.com

Greene County

- Maple Glen Farm, Scribner Hollow Rd., East Jewett, 518/589-5319
- Maple Hill Farms, 107 C Crapser Rd., Cobleskill, 518/234-4858 or 866/291-8100, www.maplehillfarms.biz

Sullivan County

- Andersen's Maple Farm, 534 Andersen Rd., Long Eddy, 845/887-4238
- Muthig Farm, 1036 Muthig Rd., Parksville, 845/292-7838

Ulster County

- Lyonsville Sugarhouse & Farm, 591 County Rd. 2/Krumville Rd., Kripplebush, 845/687-2518
- Mountain Dew Maple Products, 351 Samsonville Rd., Kerhonkson, 845/626-3466

TOURISM

Tourism is a growing part of the overall Hudson River Valley economy, as new historical sights, museums, farms, and cultural attractions draw visitors from New York City, the greater Tri-State Area, and beyond. West Point alone draws more than three million visitors a year and is one of the top three tourist destinations in New York State.

The People

DEMOGRAPHICS

Historically, Hudson River Valley immigrants were German, Dutch, or Irish. Today, more than two million area residents represent a mix of many nations from Central America to Asia. They are commuters to New York City, farmers, small-business owners, artists, students, second-home owners, and blue-collar workers. The majority of counties in the region exceed the national average in percentage of high school and college graduates within the population.

The migration of creative types from New York City continues, with Beacon, High Falls, and Millerton some of the most popular destinations.

ETHNIC GROUPS

All major socioeconomic groups are represented in the Hudson River Valley, and the ethnic makeup has become increasingly diverse as new immigrants arrive in New York City and gradually make their way north in search of jobs and homes. Black, Hispanic, and Asian minorities live throughout the region, representing the highest percentages of total population in Westchester and Rockland Counties.

Although they played a pivotal historical role in the development of the Hudson River Valley, Native American tribes unfortunately have little presence in modern-day communities. In Ulster and Sullivan Counties, several tribes have been in negotiations with government officials to open casinos that some argue could revive struggling local economies, as well as benefit the tribes; however, a strong contingent opposes this kind of development on the grounds that it would encourage the spread of gambling without generating the kind of economic momentum that's promised.

As immigrant communities take hold and expand in more remote areas, they are introducing international foods and traditions that were once limited to urban areas like New York City. The result for residents and visitors alike is an increasingly diverse mix of options for culture, dining, and entertainment throughout the region.

Essentials

Transportation

AIR

The Hudson River Valley is easily accessible from several international airports, including **John F. Kennedy** (JFK; Van Wyck Expressway, 718/244-4444), **LaGuardia** (LGA; Grand Central Pkwy., 718/533-3400), and **Newark** (EWR; I-95 and I-78, 973/961-6000) in the New York City area, as well as upstate airports **Albany** (ALB; 737 Albany-Shaker Rd., Albany, 518/242-2200, www.albanyairport.com), **Stewart** (SWF; 1180 First St., New Windsor, 845/564-7200), and **Westchester** (HPN; 240 Airport Rd., White Plains, 914/995-4860, airport.westchestergov.com). Numerous county and private airstrips provide local shuttle service.

Stewart and Albany offer convenient access to many Hudson River Valley attractions; however, the busier JFK and Newark airports often have better rates and flight time choices for travelers coming from afar.

Stewart Airport has just one terminal with four rental car agencies and one limousine service inside. Taxis are also available. The only food option outside the terminal is a Quizno's sandwich chain. There is a Hudson's that has books and snacks. There is an ATM near baggage claim.

Newark is closest to destinations in Orange and Rockland Counties, while JFK and LaGuardia serve Westchester and Putnam Counties best. Newark also has the best public transportation to and from New York City. Its AirTrain service connects to NJ Transit and Amtrak, which offer frequent express trains out of Penn Station. Rail service to JFK is a trickier proposition that requires a long subway ride to Queens and then an AirTrain connection to the terminals. Information about all three New York City airports and Stewart, as well as AirTrain services at Newark and JFK, is available at the Port Authority of New York and New Jersey website: www.panynj.gov/airports.

Car services are often the best option for getting to and from Stewart and Albany airports, and listings are available on the airport websites; cabs, rental cars, and shuttle services are also readily available to most destinations.

TRAIN

Metro-North (800/638-7646, www.mta.info/mnr) and **NJ Transit** (973/275-5555 or 800/772-2287, www.njtransit.com) run commuter lines out of New York City's Grand Central and Penn Stations, reaching Poughkeepsie and Wassaic in the north, Port Jervis in the west, and Connecticut in the east. Metro-North offers discount rail fare and admission to popular destinations (www.mta.info/mnr) including Boscobel, Clearwater, Dia:Beacon, and Kykuit.

Amtrak (800/872-7245, www.amtrak.com) offers service beyond the commuter zone, following the eastern bank of the Hudson all the way to Albany and Saratoga Springs. Taxis are readily available at most major stations.

BUS

Greyhound (800/229-9424, www.greyhound.com) buses stop in major cities and towns throughout the valley, including Albany, New Paltz, Newburgh, Poughkeepsie, Saratoga Springs, and White Plains. **Shortline Bus** (800/631-8405, www.coachusa.com) and **Adirondack Trailways** (800/776-7548, www.trailwaysny.com) offer regional connections and package trips.

Public transportation gets less reliable the farther you travel into the countryside, but

---

Previous: the Bear Mountain Bridge over the Hudson River; *RipVan Winkle Flyer* on the Delaware & Ulster Railroad.

most counties run some sort of local bus system to connect major town centers and some rural areas.

BOAT

Several companies run daytime and evening cruises along the river. Major ports include Newburgh, Kingston, and Hudson. The Hudson River Sloop ***Clearwater,*** based in Poughkeepsie, produces environmental education programs and riverfront festivals. **NY Waterway** (800/53-FERRY or 800/533-3779, www.nywaterway.com) runs commuter ferries as well as sightseeing tours to and from Manhattan. Some packages include admission to popular destinations.

CAR

Traveling by car affords the opportunity to meander along scenic back roads, across one-lane bridges, and down bumpy dirt roads; however, drivers should be aware that along with the rural scenery comes some inevitable run-ins with traffic congestion. And once you leave the highway, few roads are straight and flat; hills and curves are part of any Hudson River Valley road trip.

Two major interstates traverse the Hudson River Valley: I-84 connects Pennsylvania to Connecticut through southern Dutchess County. And I-87, the New York State Thruway, runs from New York City to Albany and then on to Buffalo.

Toll Roads

The New York State Thruway (I-87) holds the record as the longest toll highway in the United States. It costs $6.50 to drive the length of the Hudson River Valley northbound, from the New York City line to the downtown Albany exit (141 miles). The return trip costs $11.50, due to one-way bridge fees. Exits are often 15 miles or more apart, so watch carefully for signs to avoid missing your turn. Occasional rest areas have gas, restrooms, and fast food, including Starbucks. Many rental cars are equipped with an E-ZPass transponder that will bill the tolls to your account—a big time saver during busy travel times.

The following five Hudson River crossings have a $1.50 toll in the eastbound direction:

- Bear Mountain Bridge (Westchester and Orange)
- Newburgh-Beacon Bridge (I-84)
- Mid-Hudson Bridge (southern Dutchess and Ulster)
- Kingston-Rhinecliff Bridge (northern Dutchess and Ulster)
- Rip Van Winkle Bridge (Columbia and Greene)

There is a $5 toll to cross the Tappan Zee Bridge between Westchester and Rockland Counties, and an $8 toll for the George Washington Bridge. All bridges and toll roads in New York State are equipped with the E-ZPass (www.ezpassny.com) automatic transponder system, which is compatible with most systems in the Northeast. If you want to use an E-ZPass in a rental car, you must first call E-ZPass to have the license plate registered on your account. Some agencies, including Avis, rent cars with E-ZPass installed. Cash-only lanes are clearly marked at most toll plazas.

Highway Information

The best sources of real-time traffic updates for the Lower Hudson Valley and New York metropolitan area are AM 880 radio "on the eights" (1:08, 1:18, 1:28, etc.) and AM 1010 "on the ones" (1:01, 1:11, 1:21, etc.). **Radio Catskill** is a hydropowered community radio station serving the Catskills, the Upper Delaware, and Mid-Hudson regions (FM 90.5 and FM 94.5, www.wjffradio.org). In Albany, tune to **WAMC Northeast Public Radio** (FM 90.3 in Albany and FM 90.9 in Kingston, www.wamc.org).

Consult www.nycroads.com/crossings/hudson-river for bridge conditions. Also online is the New York State Travel Information Gateway at www.511ny.org, with information by region.

The Taconic State Parkway

The scenic Taconic State Parkway runs north-south from the Sprain Brook Parkway, which comes out of New York City, to I-90 near the Massachusetts state line and offers convenient access to many of the Hudson River Valley's inland towns. Unlike the six-lane interstates that run parallel to it, the Taconic has just two lanes in each direction with a wide, green median in between. It crosses some of the prettiest woodlands, marshes, and fields of Westchester, Dutchess, and Columbia Counties, making it a popular route for motorists.

Several risks make the route one of the more dangerous in the state. When driving the Taconic for the first time, take these factors into consideration:

- **Narrow lanes:** The Taconic's narrow lanes are unforgiving, particularly on icy or wet roads. There are drains every few hundred feet on both sides and no emergency breakdown lanes. If you must stop for any reason, pull all the way onto the grass, as far as possible away from traffic.
- **Cross traffic:** Except for a few of the busiest intersections, the Taconic does not have on- and off-ramps. After one too many accidents, the state closed most of the hazardous crossroads in Dutchess County, but many in Columbia County remain open. Watch for cars braking suddenly in the left lane to turn, or for cars accelerating slowly in the right lane.
- **Deer:** The Hudson River Valley supports a healthy population of white-tailed deer, and many of them feed on the shrubs and bushes that line both sides of the Taconic. Watch for eyes at night, and remember that a deer caught in the glare of oncoming headlights will often freeze in its tracks. When you see one, others are likely feeding nearby.
- **Speed traps:** The speed limit on the Taconic is 55 miles per hour, and New York State troopers are serious about enforcing it. Although traffic moves much faster during rush hour, troopers frequently lurk in the median to catch drivers who exceed the limit by as little as five miles per hour. Bulls Head Road near Rhinebeck and the town of Fishkill are known hot spots.

U.S. Route 9 and Route 9W on the east and west sides of the Hudson River are slower north-south routes through the valley.

Driving Guidelines

The maximum speed limit on New York State highways is 65 miles per hour, and limits are often lower through congested areas or on older highways. Seatbelts are required at all times, and it is illegal to talk on a cell phone while driving, unless you have a hands-free connection. Speed limits in construction zones are strictly enforced. Speed traps are common along major roads and highways. Right turns on red are permissible outside of New York City, unless otherwise marked.

Rental Cars

Rental agencies are easy to come by in the Lower Hudson Valley, but more difficult as you venture north, until you reach Albany. Major brands cluster around the airports, and most sizable towns have at least one independent rental service.

Car rentals are generally much less expensive in the Hudson River Valley than they are at the New York City airports. If you are traveling from these airports to the Mid-Hudson region or farther and plan to stay more than a couple of days, try this cost-saving strategy: Arrange a one-way rental at the higher airport rate, then return the car the next day and reserve a new vehicle at the lower upstate rate for the remainder of your trip.

BICYCLE

Mountain bikes and hybrids are easier to find as rentals than road bikes, but a few shops in the area cater to the cycling community. For example, The **Bicycle Depot** (on Main Street in New Paltz, www.bicycledepot.com)

rents aluminum road bikes in good condition. Cycling enthusiasts Ken Roberts and Sharon Marsh Roberts have posted a wealth of useful information, including maps, online at www.roberts-1.com/bikehudson. You can travel with bikes on Shortline Bus and Metro-North.

Sports and Recreation

Excellent outdoor recreation is one of the top reasons people come to the Hudson River Valley. You can escape the crowds in summer or winter on the expansive network of trails in the Catskills or in one of the region's many state parks. Approximately 100,000 acres of wilderness are preserved in more than a dozen state parks, including Bear Mountain, Harriman, Minnewaska, and Saratoga Spa. Catskill Park encompasses another 900 square miles of "forever wild" state land. And the expansive Taconic State Park encompasses 5,000 acres at the base of the Taconic Range, near the Massachusetts and Connecticut state lines. Hiking, boating, and fishing rank among the most popular activities.

State Parks

All told, the Hudson River Valley, Catskills, and Capital-Saratoga regions encompass more than 40 state parks and 20 designated state historic sites. The state plays an active role in preserving the Catskill Park: It runs the Belleayre ski resort, maintains a network of 33 trails, stocks rivers and creeks with fish, and operates a number of campgrounds. See individual chapters for specific park profiles. Or contact the New York State Office of Parks, Recreation and Historic Preservation at Empire State Plaza in downtown Albany (518/474-0456, nysparks.state.ny.us). The New York State Historic Preservation Office is located at the Peebles Island Resource Center in Waterford (518/237-8643). For camping reservation, call Reserve America (800/456-2267, www.reserveamerica.com).

Hiking

Most state parks maintain their own trail systems and camping facilities, and some 200 miles of trails traverse the Catskill Forest Preserve. High above the Hudson River Valley are **Kaaterskill Falls** and the **Escarpment Trail,** a magical wilderness setting where the Hudson River School of painters found inspiration and the Catskill Mountain House entertained prominent guests. **Slide Mountain** in Ulster County is the highest peak in the Catskills and offers a challenging day hike.

In Minnewaska State Park, part of the Shawangunk Ridge, hikers may see two rare species: the dwarf pitch pine and peregrine falcon. Taconic State Park has Bash Bish Falls, as well as miles of trails that invite exploration.

Camping in all of these areas is unrestricted below 3,500 feet, although backpackers are encouraged to camp in designated areas to diminish the impact on the forest.

Cycling

Cyclists enjoy endless miles of rolling hills on quiet country roads, and several counties have converted long stretches of abandoned train tracks into paths for walking, jogging, or biking. **Piermont** and **New Paltz** are popular cycling towns, and many local clubs plan group rides on summer weekends. You might tour one county at a time, or attempt the 180-mile multiday ride from New York City to Albany. Include as many bridge crossings as possible, and allow time to take in some of the sights along the way. Several companies offer guided bike tours of the area; an amateur bike race is another way to discover many of the back roads.

Saratoga Springs-based **Escapades Bike Tours** (877/880-2453, www.escapadesbike-tours.com) organizes a six-day fall-foliage tour in October for cyclists of all levels ($1,795).

Average daily mileage is 25-45, depending on individual preferences and abilities.

The **Great Hudson Valley Pedal** (www.ptny.org), sponsored by Parks & Trails New York, takes place in August. Participants ride from Albany to New York City in a fully supported six-day, 200-mile tour.

The **Tour of the Catskills** (www.touroftheCatskills.com) is a challenging multiday cycling event held in early August. Hundreds of amateur and professional cyclists compete in a Friday time trial and two stages Saturday and Sunday. The route follows some of the most scenic country roads through Greene and Ulster Counties. The town of Windham is a good place to watch the action.

Swimming and Boating

The Hudson and its tributaries support all manner of water sports. Boats are available for rent at marinas on both shores—the **Village of Catskill** is a good place to launch. Tubing on the **Esopus** in Ulster County is especially popular in summer. Sailing school is an option out of Kingston. **Greenwood Lake** in Orange County, **Lake Taghkanic** in Columbia County, and several lakes near Saratoga Springs have beaches for swimming and facilities for boats.

Kayakers can paddle lakes, ponds, creeks, and of course the Hudson River in Dutchess County. **The River Connection** (9 W. Market St., Hyde Park, 845/229-0595 or 845/242-4731, www.the-river-connection.com), offers water sports instruction, as well as equipment sales and rentals. Certified instructors lead trips from various launch points along the river, including Norrie Point (Staatsburg), Tivoli, Croton Point, and Poughkeepsie ($100 pp). Experienced paddlers may join the guided day trips from Athens to Saugerties, Saugerties to Norrie Point, and Cold Spring to Annsville Creek, which make up the annual Great Hudson River Paddle (ages 16 and up only, $100 pp).

Fishing

Anglers can fish the tidal Hudson River, freshwater creeks and streams, or reservoirs. Guided tours are available in many locations, including the Willowemoc Creek and Beaver Kill river near **Roscoe (Trout Town USA)** and the **Pepacton Reservoir.** Popular catches include American shad, striped bass, perch, herring, and sturgeon in the Hudson; and wild trout and bass in lakes, streams, creeks, and ponds throughout the region. The **Catskill Fly Fishing Center and Museum** in Sullivan County pays tribute to the fathers of the sport in a series of informative exhibits. Bass tournaments draw large crowds to the river near the town of Catskill in summer.

Winter Sports

New Yorkers flock to **Windham, Hunter,** and **Belleayre Mountains** for downhill skiing and snowboarding. Runs are relatively short at all three resorts; **Belleayre** (Belleayre Ski Center, Rte. 28, Highmount, 845/254-5600 or 800/942-6904, www.belleayre.com) caters to beginners, while **Windham** (Rte. 23, Windham, 800/754-9463, www.windhammountain.com) and **Hunter** (Rte. 23A, Hunter, 800/367-7669, www.huntermtn.com) have more terrain for experienced skiers and boarders. Resorts with snowmaking equipment open in late November or early December, as soon as temperatures dip below freezing. Spring conditions typically last through the end of March.

For more of a wilderness experience, many state parks—especially **Harriman, Minnewaska,** and **Saratoga Spa**—maintain trails for Nordic skiing, snowshoeing, tubing, and tobogganing.

Accommodations and Food

ACCOMMODATIONS

Hudson River Valley accommodations range from budget motels to modest inns to luxury resorts. In most counties, there is an appealing option for just about every type of trip and budget.

Resorts

Scattered throughout the region—mostly in the Catskill Mountains—are a handful of full-service resorts that offer golf, spa treatments, and other activities on-site. Prices are often given per person per week and include meals. The **Mohonk Mountain House** (1000 Mountain Rest Rd., New Paltz, 855/883-3798, www.mohonk.com) near New Paltz, and the **Emerson Resort and Spa** (5340 Rte. 28, Mt. Tremper, 877/688-2828 or 845/688-2828, www.emersonresort.com) near Woodstock are a couple of examples. Most of the area's ski resorts have a variety of slopeside and nearby rooms and condos for rent.

Hotels and Motels

You can find everything from major chains to boutique hotels along the Hudson River. Some of the most charming properties are housed in historical homes that have been restored and converted for guest use. Many of the top establishments also run award-winning restaurants, staffed by graduates of the prestigious **Culinary Institute of America** in Hyde Park (1946 Campus Dr., 845/451-1588 or 845/452-9600, www.ciachef.edu). Belvedere Mansion and the Beekman Arms, both located in Rhinebeck (Dutchess County), and the Inn at Lake Joseph in Forestburgh (Sullivan County) are a few examples.

Bed-and-Breakfast Inns

By far the most popular places to stay in the Hudson River Valley are bed-and-breakfast inns, which range from a few rooms in a private home to rooms with private entries in a converted barn or carriage house. With these types of accommodations, you may have the opportunity (or obligation, depending on how you see it) to socialize with the owners over breakfast. Another bonus: Innkeepers often hire CIA graduates to prepare gourmet country-style breakfasts. Some B&Bs are centrally located in the valley's most popular towns; others are more remote. Quality varies widely too, so it pays to do your homework before you book.

Efficiency Cabins

Many motels and campgrounds also provide rustic one-room cabins with kitchenettes. These are often heated by wood-burning stoves or fireplaces. Expect a cozy atmosphere but very basic amenities in this type of lodging.

Camping

From dozens of state parks to the Catskills and Shawangunks, outdoors enthusiasts can choose from hundreds of appealing places to pitch a tent. For car camping, Yogi Bear's Jellystone Camp-Resort has several locations in the Mid-Hudson region. Some parks, such as Taconic State Park, also rent cabins for year-round activities. Backpackers can camp anywhere below 3,500 feet elevation in the Catskills, but rangers ask that you choose designated camping areas out of consideration for the forest.

Other Options

Simple guesthouses—a room or two in someone's home—are another possibility, as are vacation rental homes. Yoga institutes and alternative lifestyle centers like the Omega Institute in Rhinebeck offer yet more choices in accommodations. Another interesting option is the rustic two-room **Saugerties Lighthouse** (168 Lighthouse

Dr. off Mynderse St., 845/247-0656, www.saugertieslighthouse.com).

FOOD

Whether you intend to plan a trip around the valley's good eats or you simply want to know where to get sustenance while you're on the go, it will be extremely difficult to go hungry in this part of New York State. Gourmet restaurants are scattered all over the area, while numerous taverns, pubs, delis, and diners reflect their individual locations and communities. Many of the best places to eat are not centrally located in the valley's towns and villages, but either a few miles away on a scenic country back road or hidden in a commercial plaza. Either way, it's often worth the drive to seek out a memorable culinary experience.

In summer, you can get your fill roaming from one roadside farm stand to the next, with an occasional pause to pick your own fruit and vegetables. During summer, ice cream stands pop up in every town, and the hardest decision will be whether to choose homemade or soft-serve. If all of this fails to please, fast-food chains are everywhere, too.

Travel Tips

STUDENTS

Students will find a range of programs at the Hudson River Valley's many colleges and universities. The **State University of New York** (www.suny.edu) has campuses in Albany, New Paltz, and Purchase. Private institutions include **Vassar College** (www.vassar.edu), **Marist College** (www.marist.edu), **Bard College** (www.bard.edu), **Skidmore College** (www.skidmore.edu), and the **Culinary Institute of America** (www.ciachef.edu). Job seekers should consult local newspapers and county websites for current listings.

FEMALE TRAVELERS

Women traveling alone should feel safe throughout the Hudson River Valley, but be aware of surroundings when exploring urban areas like Albany, Newburgh, and Poughkeepsie. Get detailed directions for places you want to visit in these areas so you don't wander too far off-course, and leave

the vegetable stand at Hahn Farm Market

valuables behind. In general, take the same precautions you would in any midsize U.S. city.

GAY AND LESBIAN TRAVELERS

In 2004, the town of New Paltz brought same-sex marriage to the national spotlight. A year later, the New Paltz Pride March and Festival brought together a group of volunteers who soon after formed the **Hudson Valley LGBTQ Community Center** (300 Wall St., Kingston, 845/331-5300, www.lgbtqcenter.org). Some 800 members have joined the organization since it was founded. Among other awareness- and community-building initiatives, the center sponsors an annual Come Out & Find Out conference, covering hot-button topics facing the lesbian, gay, bisexual, transgender, and queer/questioning community of the Mid-Hudson Valley.

While many of the Hudson River Valley's towns are diverse in their makeup and progressive in their way of thinking, gay and lesbian travelers are still likely to encounter a quietly conservative attitude in some rural areas. For accommodations, New Paltz, Woodstock, Rhinebeck, and Hyde Park all have a number of inns that are especially welcoming to gay couples—specifically, **Cromwell Manor Historic Inn in Cornwall** (174 Angola Rd., 845/534-7136, www.cromwellmanor.com), **Ecce B&B in Barryville** (19 Silverfish Rd., 845/557-8562, www.eccebedandbreakfast.com), **Journey Inn B&B** in Hyde Park (1 Sherwood Pl., 845/229-8972, www.journeyinn.com), and **Morgan State House** in Albany (393 State St., 518/427-6063 or 888/427-6063, www.statehouse.com).

The Day to Be Gay in the Catskills Festival draws a crowd of residents and visitors with music and entertainment (www.galacatskills.org). The website for Out in the Catskills (www.outinthecatskills.com) provides a list of gay-friendly establishments in Sullivan County.

New York City-based ***Go Magazine*** (www.gomag.com) occasionally features lesbian-friendly destinations in the Hudson River Valley.

TRAVELERS WITH DISABILITIES

With a few exceptions, travelers with disabilities will find most major attractions in the region easily accessible. The exceptions are some of the outdoor garden tours, which may not be wheelchair-friendly. Travel plazas along the New York State Thruway are fully accessible, and people with disabilities can purchase full-service fuel at self-serve rates.

FAMILIES TRAVELING WITH CHILDREN

Families will find many kid-friendly establishments across the Hudson River Valley, including historic museums, interpretive nature trails, and water parks. Restaurants often have special menus for children, and many historic sights and attractions offer reduced admission fees for families. Students also often receive preferential rates. A few of the region's luxury inns do not allow young children. Check before making reservations.

SENIORS

Senior citizens enjoy reduced admission fees at most attractions throughout the region; however, some walking tours of historic homes and gardens, such as the Rockefeller Estate, may be dangerous for travelers with limited balance or mobility. If you're concerned, call ahead for details.

PETS

Pets are welcome at many, but not all, outdoor spaces throughout the Hudson River Valley. Inquire at inns and hotels before bringing your dog along. Restaurants do not allow pets inside, but many don't mind if your pooch curls up at your feet outside.

FISHING AND HUNTING

Trout fishing on lakes and streams is permitted April 1-October 15. You can fish for crappie, whitefish, shad, and perch year-round. Certain rivers and counties have additional restrictions. Trout fishing on New York City reservoirs is open year-round with size limitations. A free New York City Public Access permit is required to fish on the reservoirs. The application can be downloaded and printed from the Department of Environmental Protection at www.nyc.gov/html/dep/pdf/recreation/accesspermit.pdf.

A wide variety of game is available for hunting in designated seasons within the Hudson River Valley. Deer, turkey, bear, ducks, and upland game are popular species. You'll know you're in a hunting town when you see signs advertising Hunter Breakfasts.

New York State is divided into four hunting zones: Northern, Southern, Westchester, and Suffolk. Seasons are divided into regular (for rifles), archery, and special firearms. Hunting season dates and regulations vary from year to year.

Before hunting or fishing, make sure you have the correct license, tag, and federal stamps. Licenses are available in many sporting goods stores. Contact the **New York State Department of Environmental Conservation** (518/402-8845, www.dec.ny.gov) for the latest information.

HEALTH AND SAFETY

The Hudson River Valley has a severe problem with ticks and Lyme disease. Wear long sleeves and pants when hiking in grassy or wooded areas, and always check for ticks when you return and call your doctor immediately if you discover you've been bitten. Poison ivy is another nuisance that can cause minor skin irritation and itching.

Hypothermia is a concern for hikers, paddlers, and cyclists who may be subject to rapid temperature changes. Bring layers and plenty of fluids for any outdoor adventure.

Campers need to take precautions against black bears, who often visit campsites in search of food. Don't cook near your tent, and bring rope or a bear canister to store your food out of reach.

Deer are a perennial hazard when driving roads at night; take it slow and watch for their eyes.

Dial 911 for emergencies, or 0 for the operator. Area hospitals are open around the clock to treat injuries and illnesses. Bring proof of medical coverage.

Crime in New York State has dropped steadily over the past few years, and Hudson River Valley communities are known to be among the safest in the United States. Crime rates in the largest towns and cities measure average or better across the valley. Albany and Newburgh are the exceptions, with the highest crime rates in the region. Take the same precautions you would at home.

Information and Services

Businesses in New York are generally open 9am-5pm Monday-Friday. Banks close earlier, around 3pm, although some are open on Saturday mornings as well, and ATMs are accessible 24/7. Shops in tourist destinations stay open on Saturday and part or all of Sunday, and some grocery stores are open 24 hours. (Price Chopper is often open 24 hours, and ShopRite stores are generally open 6am-1am.)

Most stores, hotels, and restaurants accept credit cards for payment, but there are exceptions, so be sure to ask before you attempt to pay with plastic. The state sales tax is 4 percent, but when you add local county taxes, the markup usually exceeds 8 percent.

MAPS AND TOURIST INFORMATION

Jimapco publishes one of the best atlases to the region. The spiral-bound *Hudson Valley Street Atlas* covers Greene, Columbia, Ulster, Dutchess, Sullivan, Orange, and Putnam Counties, with detailed maps of the largest cities (Kingston, Poughkeepsie, Newburgh, Middletown, Monticello, Catskill) and the tiniest hamlets (Maplecrest, Freehold, Ancram).

The fifth edition is available at www.jimapco.com for $26.95. Hagstrom (www.hagstrommap.com) publishes a laminated foldout map to the Hudson River Valley and Catskills for $8.95. Individual county maps from both companies are available in convenience stores throughout the region. Cyclists can print detailed route maps for scenic road rides on the website of cycling enthusiasts Ken Roberts and Sharon Marsh Roberts (www.roberts-1.com/bikehudson).

COMMUNICATIONS AND MEDIA

Post offices, found in even the most rural towns, are generally open 8:30am-5pm Monday-Friday and 8:30am-noon Saturday.

Public libraries across the region offer Internet access free or for a nominal charge. In addition, Internet cafés and wireless hotspots have been making their way up the valley to Barnes & Noble, Starbucks, and a growing number of independent locations.

Telephone Area Codes

There are four main area codes in the Hudson River Valley.

- 518: Albany, Saratoga, Greene, Columbia
- 607: Parts of Delaware
- 845: Rockland, Putnam, Orange, Sullivan, Dutchess, Ulster, and parts of Delaware
- 914: Westchester

Local Media

The ***New York Times*** (www.nytimes.com) features regular coverage of upstate towns and issues. The ***Poughkeepsie Journal*** (www.poughkeepsiejournal.com) is a respected regional paper owned by a national publisher. Many other towns have low-circulation newspapers, and several regional magazines contain useful information for travelers: ***Hudson Valley Magazine*** (Suburban Publishing, www.hvmag.com), ***Westchester Magazine*** (Today Media, www.westchestermagazine.com), and ***Kaatskill Life*** (The Delaware County Times, www.kaatslife.com). ***Chronogram*** is a free, large-format print magazine focused on art and culture in the valley. Look for copies in tourism offices, hotel lobbies, and visitors centers. ***The Hudson River Valley Review,*** published by the Hudson River Valley Institute at Marist College (3399 North Rd., Poughkeepsie, 845/575-3052, www.hudsonrivervalley.org/review), prints scholarly research and literature connected with the region.

Most local television networks are based in New York City or Albany. Albany radio station WAMC 90.3 is an NPR-member station, as is WNYC 93.9 out of New York City.

Resources

Suggested Reading

CULINARY

Greenberg, Jan. *Hudson Valley Harvest: A Food Lover's Guide to Farms, Restaurants and Open-Air Markets.* Woodstock, VT: Countryman Press, 2003. This fascinating overview of the region's microterroirs covers everything from heirloom beans to shiitake mushrooms. Chapters are organized by type of food.

Manikowski, John. *Wild Fish & Game Cookbook.* New York: Artisan, 1997. Not only is Manikowski an accomplished outdoorsman and writer, but he also illustrated his own book.

New York State Farm Fresh Guide Metro Region. New York State Department of Agriculture and Markets. This free guide to what to expect when and where is available through the New York State Department of Agriculture and Markets (718/722-2830).

The Valley Table. The Valley Table, Inc. This quarterly print publication maintains an informative website (www.valleytable.com) of local culinary news and events.

Zagat. *Zagat Westchester County/Hudson Valley Restaurants 2012-2013.* New York: Zagat Survey, 2013. Comprehensive restaurant listings with extensive coverage of Westchester County and select coverage across the valley. This guide does not cover Albany or Saratoga Springs.

FICTION

Adams, Arthur G., ed. *The Hudson River in Literature: An Anthology.* New York: Fordham University Press, 1980. This anthology, which includes the writings of James Fenimore Cooper and William Cullen Bryant, provides a good overview of writers who wrote about and were influenced by the Hudson River Valley.

Cooper, James Fenimore. *The Last of the Mohicans.* New York: Bantam Classics, 1982. The second Leatherstocking Tale and the most popular of Cooper's novels, this adventure of the French and Indian War in the Lake George region takes place in 1757.

Cooper, James Fenimore. *The Leatherstocking Tales.* New York: Library of America, 1985. The five books that make up Cooper's Tales are set in the Hudson River Valley.

George, Jean Craighead. *My Side of the Mountain.* New York: Puffin Books, 1988. Many young readers have fallen in love with this story about a boy who runs away from home to the Catskills.

Goodman, Allegra. *Kaaterskill Falls.* New York: Delta, 1999. This book, about three Jewish families who spend summers in the Catskills, was contemporary novelist Allegra Goodman's first.

Irving, Washington. "The Legend of Sleepy Hollow." Rockville, MD: Wildside Press,

2004. Washington Irving lived in Sleepy Hollow and found inspiration for his writing in local residents and villages.

Irving, Washington. "Rip Van Winkle." Hensonville, NY: Black Dome Press Corp, 2003. Irving's classic tale of a very sleepy man takes place in the Catskills.

HISTORY

Benjamin, Vernon. The History of the Hudson River Valley: from Wilderness to the Civil War. New York: The Overlook Press, 2014.

Chernow, Ron. *Titan: The Life of John D. Rockefeller, Sr.* New York: Vintage Books, 2004. This biography has sections on Kykuit and the Pocantico Hills and gives a good overview of the economy and culture that defined the Hudson River Valley in the 19th century.

Diamant, Lincoln. *Chaining the Hudson: The Fight for the River in the American Revolution.* New York: Fordham University Press, 2004. This book provides a historical account of defending the river at West Point.

Evers, Alf. *The Catskills: From Wilderness to Woodstock.* Woodstock, NY: Overlook Press, 1982. This book serves as the definitive history of the Catskills.

Hall, Bruce Edward. *Diamond Street: The Story of the Little Town with the Big Red Light District.* Hensonville, NY: Black Dome Press, 1994. Hudson's red light district is researched and explained.

Lewis, Tom. *The Hudson: A History.* New Haven, CT: Yale University Press, 2007. A professor at Skidmore College tells the story of the Hudson River, from early explorers to modern times.

Rinaldi, Thomas E., and Robert J. Yasinac. *Hudson Valley Ruins: Forgotten Landmarks of an American Landscape.* Hanover, NH: University Press of New England, 2006. The authors portray lesser-known historic sites and abandoned buildings across the Hudson Valley in photos and text.

Ruttenber, E. M. *Indian Tribes of Hudson's River to 1700* and *Indian Tribes of Hudson's River 1700-1850.* Saugerties, NY: Hope Farm Press, 1992. These two titles present a thorough history of the Native Americans who first inhabited the valley.

Van Zandt, Roland. *The Catskill Mountain House: America's Grandest Hotel.* Hensonville, NY: Black Dome Press, 1991. Roland Van Zandt offers an in-depth look at one of the most famous hotels in the nation's history.

MEMOIR

Jorrín, Sylvia. *Sylvia's Farm: The Journal of an Improbable Shepherd.* New York: Bloomsbury Publishing, 2004. A Delaware County farmer reflects on her experience of learning to raise sheep in the Catskills.

Mullen, Jim. *It Takes a Village Idiot.* New York: Simon & Schuster, 2001. A humorous account of an urbanite's adjustment to country life.

NATURE

Boyle, Robert H. *The Hudson River: A Natural and Unnatural History.* New York: W. W. Norton & Company, 1979. This is required reading for anyone who takes an environmental interest in the Hudson River.

Burroughs, John. *In the Catskills.* Charleston, SC: BiblioBazaar, 2007. One of America's first conservationists and a contemporary of Walt Whitman and John Muir, Burroughs writes about Slide Mountain and his hometown of Roxbury in a collection of eight essays.

Cole, Thomas. *Thomas Cole's Poetry: The Collected Poems of America's Foremost Painter of the Hudson River School*. York, PA: George Shumway Publisher, 1972. Cole was a poet as well as a painter. More than 100 of his poems and a chronology of his life are included in this edition.

Klinkenborg, Verlyn. *The Rural Life*. New York: Back Bay Books, 2002. This memoir of life on a farm takes place largely in Columbia County.

Titus, Robert. *The Catskills: A Geological Guide*. Fleischmanns, NY: Purple Mountain Press, 1998. This must-read for armchair geologists contains basic explanations and recommended field trips.

Titus, Robert. The Hudson Valley in the Ice Age: A Geological History & Tour. Fleischmanns, NY: Purple Mountain Press, 2012. The latest title from the valley's foremost geological expert.

TRAIL GUIDES

Green, Stella, and H. Neil Zimmerman. *50 Hikes in the Lower Hudson Valley: Hikes and Walks from Westchester County to Albany*. Woodstock, VT: Countryman Press, 2008. Hikes on both sides of the Lower Hudson are detailed, authored by the past vice president and president of the New York-New Jersey Trail Conference.

Henry, Edward G. *Catskill Trails: A Ranger's Guide to the High Peaks*. Hensonville, NY: Black Dome Press, 2000. This pair of trail guides is an essential resource for hikers. Book 1 covers the Northern Catskills, and Book 2 covers the Southern Catskills.

Kick, Peter. *Catskill Mountain Guide (Hiking Guide Series)*. Boston, MA: Appalachian Mountain Club Books, 2002. A guide to more than 90 trails and a pullout map by a local outdoorsman.

Kick, Peter. *25 Mountain Bike Tours in the Hudson Valley: A Backcountry Guide (25 Bicycle Tours)*. Woodstock, VT: Countryman Press, 2006. An updated edition on rail trails, bikeways, and shops.

Parks and Trails New York. Cycling the Hudson Valley. Albany: Parks and Trails New York, 2012.

TRAVEL ESSAYS

Carmer, Carl. *The Hudson*. New York: Farrar and Rinehart, 1939. In the early 20th century, Carl Carmer wrote a guide to the region, filled with personal anecdotes and observations.

James, Henry. *The American Scene*. Reprinted in *Henry James: Collected Travel Writings*. New York: Library of America, 1993. This book, first published at the turn of the 20th century, captures Henry James's reflections on his return to upstate New York.

Lossing, Benson J. *The Hudson: From the Wilderness to the Sea*. Hensonville, NY: Nabu Press, 2010. Lossing presents a 19th-century perspective of the region in a travel narrative format.

Lourie, Peter. *River of Mountains: A Canoe Journey down the Hudson*. Syracuse, NY: Syracuse University Press, 1998. This contemporary travel narrative follows a paddler from the Adirondacks to New York Harbor.

Van Zandt, Roland. *Chronicles of the Hudson: Three Centuries of Travel and Adventure*. Hensonville, NY: Black Dome Press, 1992. This book captures an interesting cross-section of travel writing related to the Hudson River.

Internet Resources

Most New York State counties maintain a tourism website with information on attractions, activities, lodging, and dining out. In addition, most establishments maintain at least a basic website with general information. Here are some of the unique sites that cover broader issues and trends in the region.

Black Dome Press
www.blackdomepress.com
This publisher has a large online catalog of regional fiction and nonfiction titles.

Chronogram
www.chronogram.com
Online version of the free, monthly print publication dedicated to supporting the arts in the Hudson Valley.

Clearwater
www.clearwater.org
This organization gathers information about the ongoing cleanup of the Hudson River.

Historic Hudson Valley
www.hudsonvalley.org
This organization publishes information about visiting several National Historic Landmarks in the area, including Kykuit, Philipsburg Manor, and Montgomery Place.

Hudson River Bridges and Tunnels
www.nycroads.com/crossings/hudson-river
Check here for current traffic conditions before you drive the next leg of your trip.

The Hudson River Valley Institute
www.hudsonrivervalley.net
This Marist College organization is dedicated to scholarly research and writing about the Hudson River Valley National Heritage Area.

Hudson Valley Magazine
www.hvmag.com
This regional print publication has timely information for residents and visitors and articles about local food, business, and culture.

Hudson Valley Tourism
www.travelhudsonvalley.org
A promotional agency, connected with the I Love New York state tourism office, representing the counties in the region with a detailed calendar of events.

I Love NY
www.iloveny.com
The central New York State tourism site contains trip ideas, event information, and more.

Index

A

B

C

D

E

F

G

H

IJ

K

L

M

N

O

P

QR

S

T

U

VWXYZ

List of Maps

Acknowledgements

This edition of *Moon Hudson Valley & the Catskills* was written while cycling around Saratoga Lake in the rain, drinking raw milk at Shunpike Dairy, relaxing in the spa at the Kaatskill Mountain Club, spotting a fisher as large as a bear on a run through the woods, slipping down the slides at the Zoom Flume, picking more apples than we could carry at Fix Brothers Fruit Farm, sipping tea on a rainy day in Millerton, strolling the carriage trails around Lake Minnewaska, and catching the Black Francis concert at Club Helsinki.

Special thanks to my fearless travel companions and local scouts: Jill Ippolito, Mavis Morris, Dominique Maack, Sue and George Goth, Jenn Nisi, and Paul Itoi. Several organizations contributed professional photos to this edition, including Lyndhurst, Historic Hudson Valley, Bethel Woods Center for the Arts, Orange County Tourism, Putnam County Tourism, and Stone & Thistle Farm.

Finally, the talented team at Avalon Travel, including Erin Raber, Darren Alessi, and Kat Bennett, worked their magic once again, and I am grateful for their efforts.

Photo Credits

All photos © Nikki Goth Itoi except page title page © Dreamstime.com; page 4 © Dreamstime.com; page 8 © dreamstime.com; page 15 © Dreamstime.com; page 21 (top) © Karen M. Sharman/Historic Hudson Valley, (bottom) © Lee Snider | Dreamstime.com; page 23 © Dreamstime.com; page 31 © Tom Nycz/ Historic Hudson Valley; pages 32, 33 © Mick Hales/Historic Hudson Valley; page 34 © Jaime Martorano/ Historic Hudson Valley; page 50 © Lanny Stock/istock.com; page 53 © Songquan Deng/123rf.com; page 60 (bottom) © Dreamstime.com; page 61 © Dreamstime.com; page 66 © Jerry L. Thompson; page 99 © Dreamstime.com; page 139 © Dreamstime.com; page 146 © Elizabeth Itoi; page 155 (all) © Dreamstime.com; pages 160, 162 Courtesy of Bethel Woods Center for the Arts; page 180 © Andrew Kazmierski/123rf.com; page 181 Courtesy of Stone & Thistle Farm; page 185 (all) © Dreamstime.com; page 228 (botttom) © Dreamstime.com; page 229 © Bratty1206 | Dreamstime.com; page 228 (bottom) © Dreamstime.com; page 229 © Bratty1206 | Dreamstime.com; page 235 © Dreamstime.com; page 244 © Demerzel21 | Dreamstime.com; page 258 © Elizabeth Peters/123rf.com; page 265 (all) © Dreamstime.com; page 277 © Dreamstime.com

MAP SYMBOLS

- Expressway
- Primary Road
- Secondary Road
- Unpaved Road
- Trail
- Ferry
- Railroad
- Pedestrian Walkway
- Stairs

- Highlight
- City/Town
- State Capital
- National Capital
- Point of Interest
- Accommodation
- Restaurant/Bar
- Other Location
- Campground

- Airfield
- Airport
- Mountain
- Unique Natural Feature
- Waterfall
- Park
- Trailhead
- Skiing Area

- Golf Course
- Parking Area
- Archaeological Site
- Church
- Gas Station
- Glacier
- Mangrove
- Reef
- Swamp

CONVERSION TABLES

°C = (°F - 32) / 1.8
°F = (°C x 1.8) + 32
1 inch = 2.54 centimeters (cm)
1 foot = 0.304 meters (m)
1 yard = 0.914 meters
1 mile = 1.6093 kilometers (km)
1 km = 0.6214 miles
1 fathom = 1.8288 m
1 chain = 20.1168 m
1 furlong = 201.168 m
1 acre = 0.4047 hectares
1 sq km = 100 hectares
1 sq mile = 2.59 square km
1 ounce = 28.35 grams
1 pound = 0.4536 kilograms
1 short ton = 0.90718 metric ton
1 short ton = 2,000 pounds
1 long ton = 1.016 metric tons
1 long ton = 2,240 pounds
1 metric ton = 1,000 kilograms
1 quart = 0.94635 liters
1 US gallon = 3.7854 liters
1 Imperial gallon = 4.5459 liters
1 nautical mile = 1.852 km

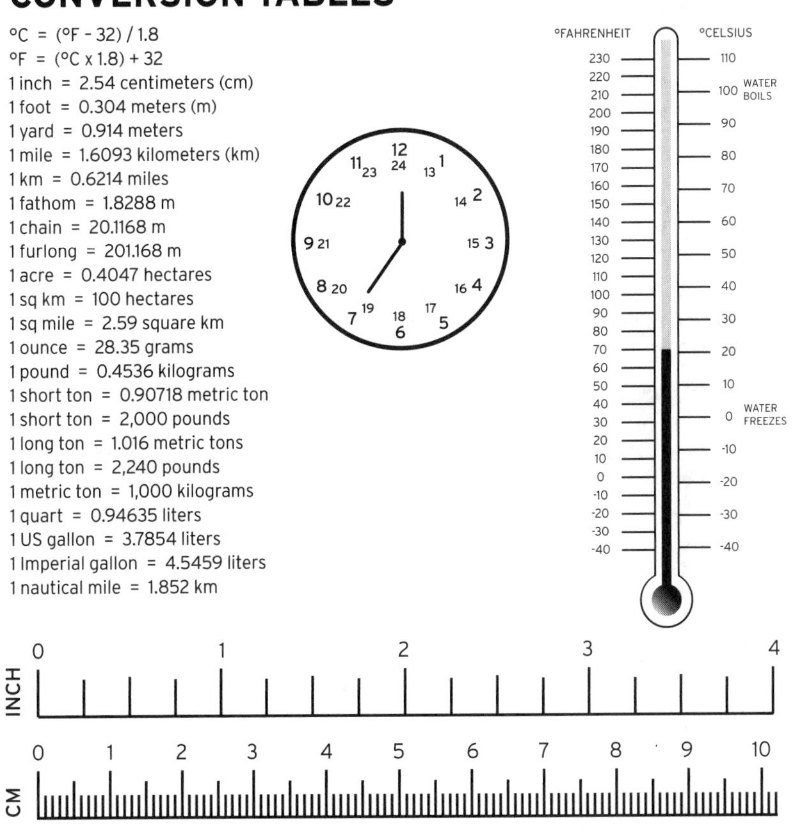

MOON HUDSON VALLEY & THE CATSKILLS
Avalon Travel
a member of the Perseus Books Group
1700 Fourth Street
Berkeley, CA 94710, USA
www.moon.com

Editor: Erin Raber
Series Manager: Kathryn Ettinger
Copy Editor: Alissa Cyphers
Graphics Coordinator: Darren Alessi
Production Coordinator: Darren Aessi
Cover Design: Faceout Studios, Charles Brock
Moon Logo: Tim McGrath
Map Editor: Kat Bennett
Cartographers: Brian Shotwell, Stephanie Poulain
Indexer: Greg Jewett

ISBN-13: 978-1-63121-004-4
ISSN: 1554-2327

Printing History
1st Edition — 2005
4th Edition — June 2015
5 4 3 2 1

Front cover photo: Bear Mountain with Hudson River and bridge in autumn © Songquan Deng /Alamy

Printed in Canada by Friesens